Transactions Without Borders

A Client and Lawyer's Guide to Overseas Operations

DAVID A. STEIGER

Cover design by Tamara Kowalski/ABA Publishing.

The materials contained herein represent the opinions of the authors and/or the editors, and should not be construed to be the views or opinions of the law firms or companies with whom such persons are in partnership with, associated with, or employed by, nor of the American Bar Association or the General Practice, Solo and Small Firm Division unless adopted pursuant to the bylaws of the Association.

Nothing contained in this book is to be considered as the rendering of legal advice for specific cases, and readers are responsible for obtaining such advice from their own legal counsel. This book is intended for educational and informational purposes only.

© 2014 American Bar Association. All rights reserved.

No part of this publication may be reproduced, stored in a retrieval system, or transmitted in any form or by any means, electronic, mechanical, photocopying, recording, or otherwise, without the prior written permission of the publisher. For permission contact the ABA Copyrights & Contracts Department, copyright@americanbar.org, or complete the online form at http://www.americanbar.org/utility/reprint.html.

Printed in the United States of America.

18 17 16 15 14   5 4 3 2 1

Library of Congress Cataloging-in-Publication Data

Steiger, David A., 1965-
  [Globalized lawyer]
  Transactions without borders: a client and lawyer's guide to overseas operations / David A. Steiger. — Second edition.
     p. cm.
  Includes index.
  Revision of the author's Globalized lawyer.
  ISBN 978-1-62722-583-0 (alk. paper) — ISBN 978-1-62722-584-7 (e-book)
 1. International business enterprises—Law and legislation—United States. 2. Offshore outsourcing—Law and legislation—United States. 3. Contracting out—United States. 4. Offshore outsourcing—Law and legislation. I. Title.
  KF299.I5S745 2014
  346.73'065—dc23   2014002783

Discounts are available for books ordered in bulk. Special consideration is given to state bars, CLE programs, and other bar-related organizations. Inquire at Book Publishing, ABA Publishing, American Bar Association, 321 N. Clark Street, Chicago, Illinois 60654-7598.

www.ShopABA.org

Contents

About the Author xiii

Acknowledgments xv

Introduction xvii

Chapter 1
Twenty-First Century Legal Practice: The Art of Solving International Business Problems in a Client-Led World 1
   Well, How Did We Get Here? 2
   The Global Economy of Tomorrow Means More Than Just
      China and India 6
   Globalization Is Not Just for Multinationals Anymore 8
   Multinationals Have Shown Smaller Firms the Way 10
   Small Firms May Actually Have an Edge 13
   Opportunity Drives Globalization, Too 15
   How Global Competition Flipped
      the Attorney-Client Relationship on Its Head 17
   A Globalized Legal Practice Does Not Assume a Total
      Shift to Cross-Border Work 19
   Your Choice: Master Cross-Border Issues
      or Watch Your Clients/Customers Migrate 20

Chapter 2
Who Should Be Doing What: The Most Effective Uses of In-House and Outside Counsel 23
   What Are the Capabilities of Your In-House Staff? 23
      Outside Counsel as Strategic Consultant 25

Outside Counsel as Issue Specialist	28
Outside Counsel as Coordinator of Other Disciplines	29
Outside Counsel as Due Diligence Nexus	30
Outside Counsel as Risk Manager	31
Outside Counsel as Drafter and Negotiator	32
Intersection with Other Disciplines	32
Cultural Experts	33
Tax and Other Issue Specialists	33
Applicable Product/Service Technicians	35
Foreign Counsel	36
Intersection with Vendors/Vendors' Counsel	37
Intersection with U.S. and Foreign Regulators	39

Chapter 3
The Counseling Function   43

Overview	44
Core versus Noncore: Evaluating Risks Inherent in Transactions Based on the Relationship-to-Client Business Model	50
Use of Technology versus Wage Arbitrage	52
The Case for Cost-Benefit Analysis	52
Rightsizing the Client's Global Vision	55
Identifying Key Parameters Related to Targeted Transactions	56
Amount of Oversight Needed	57
Transitional Time Frame	57
Necessary Facilities and Infrastructure	57
The Bottom Line: Cost Savings Needed to Justify Costs and Risks	58

Chapter 4
Due Diligence Issues: An Overview   61

Managing a Complete Due Diligence Investigation	61
Strategic Considerations: Shacking Up versus Tying the Knot	61

Operational Considerations	64
Legal Structure	66
Retaining and Managing Consultants	70
Strategic Concerns Surrounding Intellectual Property: A Preview	73
The Impact of Regulatory Concerns on Due Diligence	74
The Importance of Defined Scope and Objectives as a Part of Due Diligence	75

Chapter 5
Due Diligence: Evaluating Offshore Destinations — 77

Overview: Where in the World Do You Want to Do Business?	77
Purely Exogenous versus Semi-Exogenous Factors	78
Prevailing Labor Costs	78
Socio- and Geopolitical Risks	79
Physical and Time Zone Displacement	87
Ecosystem and Trade Options	89
Business Environment	89
Communications	91
Culture	91
Infrastructure	94
Prevalence of Distinctive Competencies	95
Leg Work	95
The Big Chessboard	97

Chapter 6
Due Diligence: Examining Vendor Partners — 99

Beginning the Selection Process: Establishing Criteria	101
The Process: Going It Alone versus Using a Third-Party Selection Consultant	103
Gold Key Matching Service	104
Competitive Selection	104
Financial Considerations	108
Leadership	109

History and Reputation	110
Technical Competence and Quality Control	111
Capacity for Growth	113
Comparable Strategic Direction	114
Comparable Business Ethics	115
Strength and Capabilities of Key Suppliers to Vendors	116
Available Infrastructure	117
Governmental and Regulatory Issues	118
Turnover of Key Personnel	121
Danger of Cooption: Knowledge Transfer, Trade Secrets, and Relationships	121
Pricing	122
Personal Relationships and Intuition	123
The Decision	124

Chapter 7
The Foreign Corrupt Practices Act and Other Cross-Border Compliance Issues — 127

Overview and History of the FCPA	128
How the FCPA Works	131
Enforcement of FCPA	139
FCPA Defenses	149
Fines and Penalties	153
FCPA Opinion Procedure	155
Criticism and Potential Reform of the FCPA	158
FCPA Resource Guide	160
U.K. Bribery Act	160
Yet Another Layer: Local Anticorruption Laws	166
Building Effective Compliance Programs	168
Additional Coming Challenges from Whistleblowers?	179
Preparing for Post-Closing Anticorruption Compliance Needs	180
A Few More Thoughts on International Compliance Issues	185
OFAC Basics and Where You Fit In	185

Regulations on Blocked Persons and Specially Designated Nationals	187
Current Sanctions Programs	188
Licensure	189
Penalties	189
Designing and Monitoring Appropriate OFAC Compliance	189
Contemplating the Bigger Compliance Picture	192

Chapter 8
International Intellectual Property: Issues and Its Essential Value in Twenty-First Century Business

	193
Types of IP: The Four Traditional Categories and Beyond	195
TRIPS and Attempts to Create International IP Protection	197
Enforcement: Limitations on the International IP Paradigm	198
Protecting Your IP Rights	199
Forming the IP Security Steering Committee	199
Mapping Out the IP Inventory	200
Formulation and Implementation of a Security Plan	202
Contracting for Ownership of IP	204
Dealing with Contract Breach	210
Confidentiality and Conflicts with IPR and Licensing Provisions	211
Staffing	212
Protecting IP from Infringement by Third Parties	213
Trade Secrets	217
Patents	221
Trademark	224
Copyright	227
Unfair Competition	233
A Word About Economic Espionage by Foreign Governments	234

Chapter 9
Cross-Border Labor Law
and Global Mobility Issues — 239
The Challenges of "International Labor Law" — 240
Labor Law and M&A Scenarios — 243
Due Diligence in the Labor Context — 253
Understanding the Target and the Local Environment—
  General Considerations — 258
Issues Affecting the Deal — 261
  Purchase Agreement Drafting and
    Employment Issues — 261
  Permanent Establishment — 263
  Labor Organization Issues — 265
  Labor Compliance Issues — 269
    Dealing with Conflicts Between U.S. and Local and
      Foreign Law — 269
    Employee Monitoring and Data Privacy — 270
    HR Policies — 275
  Payroll and Benefits Compliance — 276
  Employment Agreements — 277
Dispute Avoidance — 279
Human Rights Issues — 282
  Code of Conduct — 282
  Workplace Bullying — 284
  Alien Tort Claims Act Litigation — 287
Global Mobility — 291
  General Considerations — 291
  Expatriate Policy — 292
  Immigration Issues — 297

Chapter 10
Negotiations — 305
Assembling Your Negotiating Team, or the Noah's
  Ark Principle: Every Specialist That You Need, None
  That You Don't — 305

        In-House Team   308
        Outside Legal Team   309
        Financial Team   310
        Cultural Team   311
      Pre-Negotiation Preparation   313
        Understanding the Effects of Cross-Cultural Issues   315
        Ability to Commit   318
        Choosing Location, Timing, and Language   318
        The Agenda: Who Proposes and Who Responds?   319
      Six Tips for Negotiating the Cross-Border Deal   321
        Tip 1: Monitor Information Exchange   321
        Tip 2: Engage in Creative Give and Take
          to Save Deals and Build Relationships   323
        Tip 3: Know When to Pause and Regroup   324
        Tip 4: Factor in the Unanticipated   324
        Tip 5: Know When to Come to Agreement on the
          Issues—or Not   325
        Tip 6: Avoid Doing Too Good a Job: Is the Deal Fair to
          Both Sides?   326
      Getting More Specific: Some Current Key Issues   328
        Benchmarking   328
        Service-Level Agreements—Terms and Penalties   329
        Exit Strategy   330
        Indemnification for Compliance with New or Changed
          Regulations   331
        Structuring a Joint Venture   331
        Intellectual Property Issues   332
        Sarbanes-Oxley/U.S. Regulatory Issues   333

Chapter 11
Reducing the Agreement to Writing   337
  Start with Clarity   337
  Cultural and Language Issues: Ensuring a Meeting of the
    Minds   339
  Use of Local Counsel   340

Overview of Key Provisions	340
Choice of Law Issues	342
Scope of Services	343
Monitoring and Audits	345
Criteria for Selection and Training of Workforce	346
Process Management	346
Labor and Tax Law	347
Dispute Resolution	347
Exit Provisions	349
Dealing with Last-Minute Changes or Attempts to Renegotiate	350

Chapter 12
Implementation and Dispute Resolution — 353

Converting Paper Oversight into Practical Oversight	354
Managing from a Distance versus Expatriate Placement	359
Transition	362
Management of Issues Based in Culture	362
Strategies for Addressing Vendor Knowledge Deficits	364
Use of Inspections and Audits	366
"Scope Creep": Relationship versus the Deal	366
Working the Relationship: Resolving Everyday Disputes	368
International Arbitration: Using the Contractual Dispute Mechanism	371
Preparing for Arbitration: Clear Identification of Desired Results	375
Choosing the Arbitration Forum and Arbitrators	376
Venue	377
Choice of Law	377
Negotiating Through the Dead Spaces	379
Traditional Litigation and Enforcement of Judgments	379

Epilogue: A Look Ahead — 383

Increased Overseas Political Risk for U.S.-Based Businesses	383

Chinese and Asian Companies: Coming to a Location Near You?	390
China and Greater Southeast Asia's Place in the World of the Future	392
Whither India?	395
Africa Rising	399
A Few Thoughts on the Middle East	404
Latin America: Growing Pains from Emerging Market to Strategic Market	408
U.S. Backlash: Always Looming	410
Takeaways	413

Appendix A
U.S. Purchase Order Terms and Conditions — 415

Appendix B
Checklist for Preparation of International Distributor and Sales Representative Agreements — 423

Appendix C
Motivating the Distributor, Sales Rep, or Licensee; Performance Levels; and Other Standards and Termination for Nonperformance — 437

Appendix D
Checklist for International Expansion — 443

Appendix E
Letter of Intent for a Joint Venture — 449

Appendix F
Basic Outline of Initial Terms and Conditions to Be Addressed for the Proposed Joint Venture — 457

Appendix G
Detailed Outline of Initial Terms and Conditions to Be Addressed for the Proposed Joint Venture   463

Appendix H
FCPA Illustrative Red Flags List   471

Appendix I
FCPA Compliance Program Checklist   473

Index   477

About the Author

David A. Steiger is an attorney, author, and lecturer who has taught on aspects of the global economy and various legal topics for fifteen years.

Steiger was born in Gary, Indiana. His father, Norman, whose formal education ended in the eighth grade to allow him to work on the family farm, rose from the position of deckhand to ship Captain and ultimately Ocean Pilot. His mother, Mary Ann, was a housewife and former ballroom dance instructor. ("The most expensive dance lessons I ever had," remarked Norman, on how he met his future wife). Norman passed away after a two-year bout with cancer in 1983 but not before giving his teenaged son a coffee mug embossed with the word "Lawyer" on it—a statement of faith that remains a most treasured possession.

Attending Indiana University at Bloomington, Steiger received a bachelor's degree in political science in 1987 and a Juris Doctor in 1990. After passing the Illinois Bar, he began his professional career as a litigation associate with a Chicago-based law firm. By early 1999, Steiger left private practice to manage complex products liability litigation for the American subsidiary of a global insurance conglomerate.

Pursuing a long-held ambition to teach, Steiger then joined the Adjunct Faculty of DePaul University's School for New Learning. The success of his debut course, "Global Capitalism," led to an opportunity to moderate a series of panel discussions on issues in globalization, featuring current and retired Ambassadors to the United Nations. Steiger followed this up by designing and teaching courses to cohorts of native students at the International Bank of Asia in Hong Kong and St. Gabriel's College in Bangkok, Thailand.

Recognizing that the increasing number of small and medium sized businesses being pulled into the global economy had few resources to guide them, Steiger set out in 2005 to create one for them. Over the next three years, he logged tens of thousands of miles to visit outsourcing centers in India, met with in-house legal staff in Singapore and developed guanxi with Chinese-based business insiders, while pulling together an impressive roster of experts in order to offer a truly global perspective on doing business overseas. In 2008, ABA Publishing released "The Globalized Lawyer: Secrets to Managing Outsourcing, Joint Ventures and other Cross-Border Transactions," in which Steiger explained in clear, understandable terms critical methods and cautions related to the negotiation and implementation of cross-border transactions.

Now, with the publication of his second book, *Transactions Without Borders: A Client and Lawyers' Guide to Overseas Operations*, Steiger expands his easily accessible explanation of international transactional topics into such critically important areas as anti-corruption compliance, intellectual property and data protection and labor and immigration issues. Targeting an audience of not only transactional attorneys but also the client executives who oversee their work product, this book will prove a useful guide to anyone involved in the planning, negotiation and implementation of an international business operation. In particular, the book is written with an eye towards educating and empowering transactional clients in a world in which the balance of power in their relationship with attorneys is already decidedly shifting in their favor.

A sought-after speaker, Steiger has addressed a variety of audiences, ranging from students at Pepperdine and Notre Dame Schools of Law to annual meetings of the California State and Michigan Bar Associations, and from a local chapter of the American Society of Mechanical Engineers to the International Roundtable at the University of Chicago's Graham School of Business. He has also contributed to the *Chicago Tribune* and the nationally syndicated Chicago Public Radio program Worldview.

Still affiliated with the law department of an insurance company with global operations, Steiger lives and works in Chicago, where he continues to pull for the local sports clubs (Let's Go, Hawks!) when he is not wandering through California wine country.

Acknowledgments

As I complete my second book, I am reminded once again how humbling an experience publishing a professional text like this one really is. This is because reflecting upon how many people have helped me in a variety of ways over the past several years, I recognize this book wouldn't have to come to be without the input and support of literally hundreds of people. I owe them all a debt of gratitude—and even though there may not be enough room on this page for a specific mention of each and every person who has assisted and encouraged me, they should all know from my heart how much I appreciate their unique contribution.

This book would not have been completed and published without the patience and consistent advocacy of my editor, Rick Paszkiet. I thank Rick and so many others at the ABA who have helped transform a raw manuscript into a completed volume and otherwise assisted in marketing and preparing it for distribution, including Marisa L'Heureux, Tamara Kowalski, Nick Panos, Amanda Wilander, and Kelly Keane.

A number of former students and colleagues assisted me by providing background material, research, and editing. Having been so generous with their time, I would like to shine an appreciative spotlight on Fran Lee, Lisa Wiet, Mollie Sitkowski, Katherine O'Connor, Jamie Virostko, and Amber Coisman.

Special recognition is also due to David Hickey for his assistance in putting together the book's Advisory Board and facilitating contributor introductions and for his miscellaneous bursts of creative brainstorming. So many within my professional and personal circles have helped expand my network around the globe, especially Brent Caslin, Steven Spronz, Harvey Cohen, Andrew Weil, Allison Walton, and Linda Weaver.

I am extremely appreciative of those who supported and facilitated my writing even while I maintained full-time law department duties. In particular,

I would like to express my gratitude to Brian Frankl, Mike Warnick, and Jerry Alpine for their understanding and flexibility.

For his assistance with development for the book's companion website and the book's cover design, I am indebted to Bill Baykan. I am also most grateful for Cheryl McPhilimy's advice and assistance on a number of fronts.

Last but not least, I want to acknowledge all the kindness, patience, and support of L.B.M. since this project began. You are so generous in so many things: for every labor of love, you will always have my deepest thanks.

Introduction

Whether you are an old hand at cross-border transactions or have spent the last several hours staring at a map of the world asking how you ever got talked into managing one, welcome. This book was designed to help you either way.

Transactions Without Borders is a book designed for more than just an audience of lawyers and legal scholars. This is an age where the legal profession is finally being forced to think and act like a business, in terms of efficiency, client-oriented service models, cost-containment, and overall doing more with less. Executives and business managers who have to work with and manage inside and outside counsel will nonetheless readily agree that many of the lawyers they work with are still struggling a bit with these concepts. While MBA programs rarely if ever teach business students how to manage attorneys in order to get the maximum benefit out of the attorney-client relationship, the current economic climate calls for this skill in spades. This book will help businesspeople involved in international operations understand the role their attorneys and other supporting personnel play throughout the process of a transaction in a way that will assist them in getting the most from their legal spend.

Of course, attorneys themselves will also learn a lot from this text. This is true whether we are talking about a small firm lawyer with little previous international experience or an attorney who already jets around the globe on behalf of multiple multinational clients. Based on hundreds of hours of one-on-one interviews with the author, this text incorporates the experience and practical observations of dozens of transactional counsel, consultants, and executive experts on cross-border deals from around the world. It is fair to say that virtually any reader will pick up useful insights into a host of topics involved in overseas operations.

This book is organized in a logical, easy-to-follow format. Chapter 1 argues that in a globalizing world in which clients have felt compelled to remake the attorney-client relationship to the client's benefit, more and more attorneys are being challenged to develop a global practice, because that is what clients increasingly need and demand. Chapters 2 and 3 explore the appropriate roles of outside counsel and other professionals in various contexts. Chapters 4, 5, and 6 review the critical due diligence process, including investigation and evaluation of both international venues and potential business partners.

The next three chapters address specific issues that are routinely recognized as mission-critical to overseas transactions. Chapter 7 undertakes a thorough examination of compliance issues, through the prism of the Foreign Corrupt Practices Act (FCPA), the U.K. Bribery Act, and related topics. Chapter 8 examines international intellectual property concerns, and Chapter 9 provides a detailed overview of cross-border labor and employee mobility matters.

The next three chapters focus on dealmaking and its aftermath. Chapter 10 deals with issues relating to the negotiation of a cross-border business transaction, while Chapter 11 reviews questions related to reducing agreements to writing. Chapter 12 addresses both common problems surrounding implementation of transactions and resolving disputes that arise.

Finally, the new Epilogue takes the reader on a look ahead to consider what current trends can tell us about where the global economy is heading in the years to come and suggests some dangers and opportunities in international operations that flow from these trends.

Let's begin by understanding how globalization has helped to transform the relationship between attorney and client and what this sea change means for lawyers and the businesses they represent in an increasingly competitive world.

Chapter 1

Twenty-First Century Legal Practice: The Art of Solving International Business Problems in a Client-Led World

Lawyers and nonlawyers alike have come to see that the business of law is in a remarkable, perhaps historic state of flux today. What most purchasers of legal services understand—but unfortunately fewer attorneys have yet taken to heart—is that the upheaval going on is a reflection of the fact that the twentieth-century model of legal practice has been judged to serve lawyers much better than their clients. And clients who are facing an unprecedented scope of legal and business challenges have in the last decade collectively concluded they can no longer accept their counsel's halting half steps toward adjustment to a changing and challenging world. Instead, businesses have shed their historically passive role in the attorney-client relationship and fundamentally redefined the provision of legal services in a way that allows them to extract maximum value at minimum cost. To put it bluntly, lawyers better get used to the idea that they are now subject to the same rules of procurement as any other vendor. In a globalizing world, that means more and more attorneys are being challenged to develop a global practice, because that is what clients increasingly need and will demand.

Well, How Did We Get Here?

At the dawn of the new millennium, the American legal profession was divided, as it had seemingly always been, into two parts: in-house and outside counsel who largely specialized in international transactions or cross-border litigation, and everyone else. Many lawyers in this second group were so focused on the day-to-day business of running their practices that the seismic shifts in the way their clients' business was being conducted was largely lost on them. Sure, they understood that manufactured goods were being imported from China in record numbers, or that if they called an information technology (IT) help desk or a customer service line, they were just as likely to be talking to someone in India as someone in Indiana. They just did not see how their clients' national, regional, or local footprint—and hence their own practice—was affected by any of that.

These lawyers would perhaps have told you that their clients were companies that never had any overseas presence. They might have been doing all of the legal work of a third-generation family business, a small or medium-sized manufacturing concern, or a closely held company providing services to a discrete set of communities. Their clients might have sought state or federal tax advice, management of their litigation, or help with much dreaded Sarbanes-Oxley compliance issues. The one thing these attorneys were confident of, though, was that their clients would never be global and simply would not want or need legal advice touching on international issues. So, they concluded, adapting a legal practice like theirs to the needs of the global economy was wholly unnecessary.

As it happened, however, even a decade ago, the businesspeople and in-house legal staff with whom these attorneys interacted were already becoming aware of the coalescence of a global marketplace that was reaching into virtually every industry. This market was engaging not just Fortune 1000 leviathans with long-established cross-border presences, but small and medium-sized product and service suppliers as well. Globalization had already moved far beyond the production of electronics, steel, and source code, and even beyond the provision of back office services. In fact, it had already spread to sophisticated research and development functions, financial analysis, processing of insurance claims, and preparation of architectural drawings, among other things. This sea change could be explained in starkly simple terms: millions of people in the developing world were learning the skills necessary to compete with Western businesses, head to head.

Howard Mills, a tax director with Deloitte, observed that it was the expansion of information technology that made outsourcing possible within the service industry: "Before we had net meetings and instant access through e-mail, outsourcing wouldn't have worked in the service industry—or at least not as effectively." As a white paper released by former Senator Joseph Lieberman's office put it,

> global availability of cost effective, high speed digital internet connections, combined with net based and other communications tools such as email, instant messaging, faxes, videoconferences, and cellular phones have empowered foreign workers to provide services that do not necessarily require direct physical contact.[1]

In an op-ed piece I penned for the *Chicago Tribune* in September 2003, I argued that given the generally positive reception that IT and business process outsourcing (BPO) had garnered, it was only a matter of time before outsourcing would move into higher-value services, including professional services.[2] In fact, as communications and information technology continued to grow in sophistication, outsourcing vendors were able to do precisely that. Ramesh K. V., at the time a partner with the Indian law firm of Kochhar and Co. in Mumbai, witnessed vendors with only simple BPO work such as basic accounting evolve into providers of more complex services to the pharmaceutical industry. Western clients recognized that Indian vendors often had PhDs working for them, allowing for greater risk tolerance, if not blind leaps of faith. "The thought of western companies," Ramesh observed, "[was] that if I can outsource the lower end of the work successfully, why not

---

1. OFFICE OF SENATOR JOSEPH I. LIEBERMAN, OFFSHORE OUTSOURCING AND AMERICA'S COMPETITIVE EDGE: LOSING OUT IN THE HIGH TECHNOLOGY R&D AND SERVICES SECTORS 15 (May 11, 2004) [hereinafter LIEBERMAN, OFFSHORE OUTSOURCING].
2. David A. Steiger, *Your Job Next? The Bottom Line Doesn't Recognize National Boundaries*, CHI. TRIB. (Sept. 30, 2003), http://articles.chicagotribune.com/2003-09-28/news/0309280091 _1_developing-country-services-supply-chains-attorneys-and-health-professionals.

outsource more complicated work as well?" Vendors who once advertised only cost savings could offer added value by building economies of scale.

In a 2005 interview, Vikas Bhalla, now Executive Vice President and Head of Outsourcing for EXL Services, a United States–based outsourcing and transformation company with operations in India, was looking beyond price-sensitive call center and collections work that was already becoming commoditized. Actual handling of business processes, such as accounts payable work, insurance claims, and end-to-end customer operations—all of which require vendors to gain an understanding of what has gone wrong in the consumer's experience and how to fix it—became the new goal.

Indeed, both a 2005 Financial Services Roundtable study of the Information Policy Institute and a Deloitte research study's findings on financial services offshoring confirmed Bhalla and Ramesh's experiences on the ground. The results of the Roundtable's analysis found that the types of services offered included more sophisticated business functions such as equity research and credit risk analysis.[3] A contemporaneous roundtable survey involving Indian BPOs with U.S. financial services clients found insurance claims processing and underwriting then being done by more than 75 percent of respondents; accounting by roughly 70 percent of Indian BPOs surveyed; and billing and transaction payment processing by nearly 60 percent of surveyed BPOs.[4] More complex processes, such as human resources management and tax processing, were already reported by 18 percent of Indian BPOs surveyed.[5] Indeed, within a few years of my September 2003 prediction, knowledge process outsourcing (KPO) was already being discussed in connection with a host of sectors, including pharmaceuticals, biotechnology, technology, legal services, intellectual property, research and design, and development of automotive and aerospace industries.[6]

---

3. INFORMATION POLICY INSTITUTE, HOW SAFE AND SECURE IS IT? AN ASSESSMENT OF DATA PRIVACY AND SECURITY IN BUSINESS PROCESS OUTSOURCING FIRMS IN INDIA, FINANCIAL SERVICES ROUNDTABLE 11 (2005).
4. *Id.*
5. *Id.*
6. Kusum Makhija, *The Knowledge Processors*, FIN. EXPRESS (Aug. 2, 2005), http://www.financialexpress.com/news/the-knowledge-processors/138916/0.

As a result of these developments, during the 2007–2008 period, KPO was growing at approximately a 40 percent annual clip worldwide.[7] While the Great Recession, among other factors, caused growth in the sector to drop to just 5 percent in 2008–2009, the following year saw a return to double-digit expansion.[8] NASSCOM reported that as of 2010, India's Global Knowledge Services Outsourcing industry had grown to a value of $2.9 billion, more than double the assessment assigned to it in 2006.[9] Looking forward, the worldwide Knowledge Services Industry market is expected to grow to $7.9 billion by fiscal 2015, with small and medium enterprises (SME's)[10] participating in the leveraging of the sector.[11]

This is not at all surprising. When one considers that two of the primary forces driving globalization involve increasing competition from—and a shift in world gross domestic product (GDP) growth to—the developing world, it logically follows that neither the West's continued sluggish growth nor its sovereign debt and political challenges are likely to turn the tide. If anything, the current challenges facing businesses based in the United States and elsewhere in the developed world only heighten competitive pressures across a wide spectrum and further encourage movement toward deeper integration with global markets.

At this point, the evidence for continuing integration is hiding in plain sight. According to an April 2012 article in the *Wall Street Journal*, an analysis of 35 large multinational companies indicated that between 2009 and 2011, nearly 75 percent of the jobs they added were overseas positions.[12] The *Journal* notes that during this same period, 60 percent of the subject companies' revenue growth came from outside U.S. borders, and the increase in foreign-based positions was attributed to the pursuit of

---

7. *KPO Industry Growth Impacted by the Great Recession*, EVALUESERVE 4 (Aug. 2010).
8. *Id.*
9. *Indian Knowledge Services Outsourcing Industry: Creating Global Business Impact*, NASSCOM 4 (Aug. 2011).
10. There are many ways to define an SME by size. For the purposes of this text, I employ the definition of 250 employees or less, put forward by Claude Marcotte and Jorge Liosi in their article *Small and Medium-Sized Enterprises Involved in Technology Transfer to China: What Do Their Partners Learn*, 23 INT'L SMALL BUS. J. (Feb. 2005).
11. NASSCOM, *supra* note 9, at 7.
12. Scott Thurm, *U.S. Firms Add Jobs, but Mostly Overseas*, WALL ST. J. (April 27, 2012), http://online.wsj.com/news/articles/SB10001424052702303990604577367881972648906.

sales there.[13] Additionally, the International Trade Association reported that in 2013, a record $2.3 trillion in exports supported approximately 11.3 million U.S. jobs.[14]

To the extent these companies and many others not surveyed follow this strategy, they are only acknowledging economic reality. The International Monetary Fund's *January 2014 World Economic Outlook Update* projects that the economic output of developed countries including the United States will grow by 2.2 percent in 2014 and by 2.3 percent in 2015, compared to projections of 5.1 percent growth in 2014 and 5.4 percent growth in 2015 in emerging and developing countries.[15] It is reasonable for companies to seek to expand where economic circumstances permit growth. Many businesses that are not yet themselves expanding operations across borders are beginning to incorporate greater amounts of outsourced functions based overseas, such as cloud computing. As they do, the next steps of global integration begin to come within reach for them as well—and a larger business world will be opening to them.

The Global Economy of Tomorrow Means More Than Just China and India

Much of the business world's attention to the competitive tsunami that continues to wash in is still largely focused on the twin giants of China and India. It is easy to understand why—both have exhibited phenomenal rates of economic growth for a decade or more. China has become the world's factory and India the developing world's most sophisticated services provider. Together, the two nations comprise a still largely untapped market of staggering proportions, representing over one-third of the world's total

---

13. *Id.*
14. INTERNATIONAL TRADE UPDATE, Record Year of Exports and Jobs Supported by Global Business (March 2014), http://trade.gov/publications/ita-newsletter/.
15. *World Economic Outlook Update, January 2014: Is the Tide Rising?*, INT'L MONETARY FUND (January 21, 2014), http://www.imf.org/external/pubs/ft/weo/2014/update/01/pdf/0114.pdf.

population, according to the U.S. Census Bureau.[16] While both nations are likely to remain key components in the global economy in the decades to come however, a myopic focus on China and India ignores the opportunities that abound elsewhere. New York University economics and business professor Michael Spencer, for example, observes the following:

> The World Bank estimates that over the next 5 to 10 years, China will export something like 85–100 million jobs to earlier-stage developing countries, and that they will be replaced by higher-value-added activities. This is the opportunity of the century for the earlier stage developing countries, because for a long time they've been saying, rightly or wrongly, that they can't compete with China. Well, China is moving on just like Korea did before, and now is their chance.[17]

As the more established economies of China and India see demand for skilled workers translate into increased hourly wages, lower margin industries that require cheaper labor inputs will naturally migrate to those nations that can provide them. Surprisingly to some, this may focus global attention on heretofore marginalized regions such as sub-Saharan Africa and Latin America.

The business pages have begun to provide some surprising headlines supporting the reality of changes in these parts of the world. A former Chinese Vice Minister of Commerce has been quoted in *The Chinese Daily* as opining that Africa would eventually surpass both the United States and the European Union as China's largest trading partner.[18] Moreover, economic growth is being driven less and less by commodities, and while huge challenges remain in many African nations, *The Economist* has noted that in recent years governance "has made huge strides."[19]

Meanwhile unemployment in Latin America, at 6.5 percent, is down by almost half from a decade ago, despite youthful demographics in which

---

16. Rich Exner, *36 Percent of World"s Population Lives in China and India: Sunday's Numbers*, Cleve. Plain Dealer (July 3, 2011), http://www.cleveland.com/datacentral/index.ssf/2011/07/36_percent_of_worlds_population.html.
17. World Economic Forum, *The Continued Quest for Economic Growth*, *in* Global Agenda Outlook 2013 11 (2013).
18. *Id.*
19. *Id.*

just 10 percent of the population is aged 60 or above.[20] Moreover, this region, which was scurrilous for its public finance woes from the 1970s through the 1990s, has in the past several years achieved an average public sector debt below 35 percent of GDP. Compare that to Italy, Belgium, and Greece, which recorded public sector debt of over 100 percent.[21] Although Argentina, Venezuela, and Jamaica still exhibit a variety of political and economic issues, as a whole, a growing middle class, improved labor markets, and pro-growth fiscal policies are attributed to the region by experts such as Asieh Mansour, head of Latin American research for global real estate services company CBRE.[22]

While there are no guarantees in projecting future economic performance, the point of citing recent past developments is to demonstrate that trends as this book goes to press point to a broadening of the global economy and new opportunities that will likely only further attract Western-based companies into establishing a greater international presence.

Globalization Is Not Just for Multinationals Anymore

Another casualty of further global marketplace integration is the conventional wisdom that that only mega-corporate leviathans can truly profit from it. The reality is that even "SMEs" are discovering that going global is a necessary step in their competitive strategy.[23] The Commerce Department reports that of nearly 6,000 American companies that were able to export for the first time or increase their exports to new markets in 2011, roughly half were SME's.[24] This is a strong indication that SME's are continuing to follow larger business concerns to overseas markets.

---

20. Joel Kotkin, *U.S. Late to the Party on Latin America, Africa*, NEWGEOGRAPHY.COM (Feb. 18, 2013), http://www.newgeography.com/content/003500-us-late-party-latin-america-africa.
21. Gideon Long, *Latin America Is Enjoying the Good Times—At Last*, BBC NEWS (Jan. 22, 2013), http://www.bbc.co.uk/news/business-21146858.
22. Mimi Whitefield, *Bright Spots in Latin America Despite Global Economic Uncertainty*, MIAMI HERALD, 4 (Feb. 3, 2013), *available at* http://www.miamiherald.com/2013/02/03/3215384/bright-spots-in-latin-america.html.
23. LIEBERMAN, OFFSHORE OUTSOURCING, *supra* note 1, at 20.
24. U.S. Dep't of Commerce, *supra* note 14.

Kumkum Dalal, president of Global Reach Consulting, Inc. of Naperville, Illinois, pointed out several years ago that twenty-first century manufacturers have their choice of suppliers from around the world. Many Tier I companies that provide finished components to original equipment manufacturers (for automobiles—think GM, Ford, and Toyota) and Tier II companies (the Tier I companies' part suppliers) frequently have truly global operations, and so competition can now come from many more places. As a result, there is a sort of domino effect where smaller and smaller players are being affected by globally competitive forces. Howard Mills of Deloitte has seen the same thing: "Western automakers are telling their suppliers, 'Hey we've got a facility here in China and we want you there. If you want to do business with us, you're going to open a facility in Beijing.'"

For the increasingly fewer number of companies and industries where this phenomenon has not yet taken hold, many are outsourcing just to get a competitive edge, or to get assistance in areas where they lack expertise. In Asia, mid-tier financial institutions have been "using outsourcing as a strategy to level the playing field against their technically richer first-tier competitors."[25]

Numerous brokers can easily be located online to assist in offshoring techniques.[26] A 2006 *Chicago Tribune* article gives an example that illustrates that small business has accepted these developments for some time. It gives the real-world example of Lori Booker, who handled her company's human resources (HR) issues herself for a decade, but then decided about ten years ago to sign up with a professional employer organization (PEO) that is now her HR operation.[27] Besides saving her time and energy, Booker said of the PEO, "they keep me from making mistakes that could hurt the agency" by keeping track of changes in employment-related laws and regulations.[28] The article points out that there are a growing number of companies available to do virtually any kind of work for another business

---

25. Mark Hollands, *Deal or No Deal*, 3 THE OUTSOURCING INSTITUTE (Winter 2005), http://www.outsourcing.com/content.asp?page=01b/other/oe/q405/dornod.html&nonav=false.
26. LIEBERMAN, OFFSHORE OUTSOURCING, *supra* note 1, at 20.
27. Joyce Rosenberg, *Outsourcing of Some Tasks Can Help Bring in More Profit*, CHI. TRIB. (Feb. 6, 2006).
28. *Id.*

and that "outsourcing continues to expand as a necessary part of doing business for a growing number of small businesses."[29]

Multinationals Have Shown Smaller Firms the Way

Loring Knoblauch, retired chief executive officer (CEO) of Underwriters' Laboratories, was one of the pioneers of outsourcing. In 1982, he was part of team for Honeywell that was involved in the first wave of setting up *maliquadoros* (factories located immediately across the border in Mexico). Knoblauch was chosen by Honeywell's CEO to take part in the project as part of a team of five or six professionals because he was a generalist. He will forthrightly say that he and many others were a little dubious about the project because they had the impression then that the Mexican people were "nice, but sleepy, not too hard working, and not at all reliable." Still, Knoblauch believed the project could be successful because of the huge wage differential between Mexico and the United States.

After the first plant was set up in Chihuahua, Knoblauch was stunned. The plant hired 150 employees. There was not a single turnover in the first 18 months. Moreover, he found the Mexican employees did their jobs better than their American counterparts because of their work ethic—they were very careful in everything they did because their jobs were of critical importance to them. To top it off, Knoblauch quickly found that the Mexican workers could do the most complicated jobs that Honeywell had, and do them with excellent quality.

From 1986 to 1992, while Knoblauch was running Honeywell's $2 billion Asia Pacific business, he set up a manufacturing joint venture in Pune, India. Even in 1986, the Tata Group had high-tech process control, and the Pune plant, while a joint venture, produced some of the best quality products in the world. Knoblauch has since heard a litany of reasons why you cannot manufacture in India or China—and believes that none of them hold water. To the contrary, he is of the opinion that everyone *must* do it.

---

29. *Id.*

As CEO of Underwriters Laboratories from 2001 to 2005, Knoblauch had the opportunity to meet a number of CEOs of lighting manufacturing companies. The lighting industry has relatively low profit margins and so is particularly predisposed to outsourcing. Still, Knoblauch was surprised when he met a lighting company CEO who had shut down every single one of the eight factories he had in the United States and switched all of his production over to China. (Knoblauch doesn't recommend moving 100 percent of a company's manufacturing to a single country; generally he recommends maintaining multiple sites. Transportation and logistics are often a factor.) The man did not want to move the production and the jobs that went with it, but he said he was forced to do it. He cited several other manufacturers who said they would stay in the United States no matter what. They did and were forced to close.

Many people who think they do not need to be global will say that they are much more capital intensive than labor intensive, and that wages and benefits are just not that big a piece of their operations, perhaps 10 percent. But Knoblauch says that a time will come when the difference between success and failure for virtually every business *is* the labor component, even if it is only 10 percent of costs. Service companies may continue to be local or regional, but they will still be increasingly vulnerable to outside competition. Successful companies will adopt a proactive, not a defensive, strategy. Because of all these factors, the number of companies that now need to be global, whether they know it or not, is much higher than it used to be.

Knoblauch's experience is not unique. Many of the world's best-known and most successful companies, such as Bank of America, Dell, AMEX, Citibank, IBM, Accenture, EDS, Oracle, PG, Delta Air Lines, Prudential, and DaimlerChrysler, have literally thousands of employees in nations as varied as India, the Philippines, China, Russia, Ireland, Israel, Canada, Poland, and Malaysia.[30] Having grown familiar with their offshore partners, corporations have for some time now been handing over more complex work such as integrated circuit design, engineering, prototyping, testing, consulting, statistical analysis, aerospace design, and nanotechnology research.[31] As

---

30. LIEBERMAN, OFFSHORE OUTSOURCING, *supra* note 1, at 19.
31. *Id.*

of 2004, IT multinationals had already established some 223 research and development (R&D) centers in China.[32]

Years ago, Knoblauch pointed out that General Electric (GE) had constructed a 500,000-square-foot R&D facility in Bangalore, which handled a full 25 percent of GE's global product development. (GE had facilities in China, India, Europe, and Connecticut that shared the work.) Knoblauch was quick to highlight that GE did not come to India to do R&D work for low cost—it came because it wanted access to talented, educated people. GE had noticed that in its Connecticut facility, 35 percent of the PhDs on staff were of Indian descent. Someone got the idea to "just go to the source." The rising numbers of international mergers and acquisitions—as well as collaborations such as the International Space Station, Antarctic Field Research, and the Human Genome Project—have facilitated collaborative R&D efforts.[33] Indeed, as the number of U.S.–born science and engineering graduates continues to decline, American companies will have a difficult time meeting their skill needs short of tapping developing world talent.[34]

As Professor Daniel Trefler of the University of Toronto suggests, the more multinationals utilize service providers from China, the more likely it will be that other companies that follow them can find a good match for their needs.[35] Taking advantage of the vendors' broader experience, the later-comers will require relatively little customization and, logically, less start-up costs.[36] Moreover, Trefler argues that as multinationals necessarily delegate control over knowledge to their Chinese service providers, it will give the Chinese incentive to do more "incremental innovation," which in turn will make them even more experienced, requiring even less customization, and so forth.[37] Trefler's argument easily translates to providers located outside of China.

---

32. *Id.*
33. *Id.*
34. *Id.* at 17.
35. Daniel Trefler, *Offshoring: Threats and Opportunities* 25 (July 22, 2005) (prepared for the Brookings Trade Forum 2005, *The Offshoring of Services: Issues and Implications*, May 12–13, 2005, Washington, D.C.).
36. *Id.*
37. *Id.*

Small Firms May Actually Have an Edge

Some studies have shown that SMEs actually have advantages over multinationals in ways that allow them to be even more competitive in the global environment. First, "as niche producers with a smaller range of technologies to offer," SMEs may provide firms in developing countries with simpler ways to learn.[38] Second, "the competitive advantage of smaller U.S. firms, derived mostly from their technological leadership, allowed them to adapt and evolve with changes in the international economy, particularly in the industrializing parts of the world."[39]

Small and medium-sized firms may distinguish themselves by highly specialized technological and human assets, or "tacit knowledge."[40] Only a fraction of knowledge and skills acquired by employees through practical experience is captured in written instructions and documents.[41] However, tacit knowledge may present opportunities:

> Foreign partners located in developing countries are often looking for this type of complementary knowledge in order to understand and use effectively blueprints and related documents. In fact, one of the major complaints from Chinese partners involved in technology transfer agreements was that not enough tacit knowledge was provided by firms from industrialized countries.[42]

Additionally, the flexibility and capacity to react quickly to change inherent in SMEs give them an edge in managing foreign operations over the often more bureaucratic management structures of large companies.[43]

The Organization for Economic Cooperation and Development (OECD) argues that in a more fundamental way than bigger, global competitors, SMEs need to network with and seek out outside sources of "information, knowledge, know-how, and technologies in order to build their own

---

38. Marcotte & Jorge Liosi, *supra* note 10, at 28.
39. *Id.*
40. *Id.* at 40.
41. *Id.* at 31.
42. *Id.* at 32.
43. *Id.*

innovative capability and to reach their markets."[44] To survive in an increasingly dynamic global marketplace, SMEs must focus on innovation as the "core of their business strategy."[45]

Networks and collaboration have many potential benefits. As the OECD points out, collaboration agreements allow for companies to share the increasingly higher costs associated with innovation.[46] Moreover, many technological developments today require a complex combination of scientific and commercial knowledge over different fields of expertise.[47] Also, collaboration assists in the continuous learning that companies today must pursue in order to adjust to rapid market and technological changes. Collaboration enhances such learning about new and prospective technologies.[48]

This is not just the stuff of ivory towers and white papers. Ask experienced practitioners on the ground. Richard Wageman, a Canadian-born lawyer who is now a partner and Intellectual Property and Technology Group Head–Asia in the Beijing office of DLA Piper, has observed that medium-sized companies are starting to come to China not only for sourcing but also to establish a business entity in the country. This used to be a prohibitively expensive investment for smaller companies—generally at least $200,000, not including "soft costs" such as international travel, legal fees, and housing. In the past few years, changes in Chinese law have allowed foreign businesses to avoid the cost and uncertainty of joint ventures with local businesses by use of wholly foreign-owned entities (WFOE's).[49] The WFOE gives foreigners the ability to directly engage in profit-making activities, while maintaining complete operational control of their businesses and paying taxes on profits only and not expenses.[50] (The Chinese government does impose minimum capital requirements on WFOE's and still requires

---

44. OECD, Networks, Partnerships, Clusters, and Intellectual Property Rights: Opportunities and Challenges for Innovative SMEs in a Global Economy, Organization for Economic Cooperation and Development 4 (2004), http://www.oecd.org/cfe/smes/31919244.pdf.
45. Id. at 8.
46. Id. at 13.
47. Id.
48. Id.
49. Small Business Handbook for China Businesses, AmCham China, http://www.amchamchina.org/smallbusinesshandbook#anchor4 (last visited May 5, 2013).
50. Id.

a local partner for some sectors such as education, telecoms, nuclear, automobiles, and insurance, among others.[51])

Likewise, Ramesh K. V. used to see big companies outsourcing to India. Accenture, Dell, and Convergis would run BPO operations of 3,000 to 5,000 people. In recent years, however, many small enterprises are involved. Some vendors servicing smaller Wall Street brokerages might dedicate as few as 20 people. The vendors are setting up very transparent processes. As Ramesh puts it, "there is now a definite way of going about it."

Millions of graduates are coming out of Indian universities with the requisite training to perform outsourced tasks. Training companies in India are offering English language and cultural courses to help call center and BPO employees acclimate themselves to Western consumer expectations, with the government providing tax incentives. As noted above, this phenomenon is happening not just in these two well-publicized locations. Mills has been involved in deals in Mexico, the Netherlands, the United Kingdom, Japan, Singapore, Thailand, and Canada. He says small or medium-sized companies that ten years ago would not have thought of going international are finding that they have to globalize in some way because of the competitive pressure. And they are struggling with fundamental questions: Do I go over myself? Do I form a joint venture? Do I come up with some other entity? How should I do this? How can I do this? What makes sense?

Opportunity Drives Globalization, Too

Businesses today do not even have to actively plan to venture into the globalized world to find themselves a part of it. Harvey Cohen, a partner with the Cincinnati, Ohio, office of Dinsmore & Shohl, has observed that in the past, the U.S. Midwest market did not feature endless numbers of companies going abroad. Now, however, even smaller companies find themselves going international, oftentimes because someone from abroad comes to them.

Indeed, sometimes companies do not so much decide to go global as stumble into a new world of opportunities. In the early 1980s, Michel Feldman,

---

51. *Id.*

who is now a partner at Seyfarth Shaw, LLP, was the CEO of a company that manufactured radio antennas. One day, out of personal curiosity, he started reviewing the comment cards returned by new customers to see who was buying the company's product and to see if he could identify any trends.

Feldman did identify a trend, and one that stunned him: a significant number of the company's customers lived in Europe. This was surprising, since the company had no official distribution network in Europe. So how, Feldman wondered, were so many of his company's products ending up there? After some investigation, he discovered that a New York distributor was loading up containers with his antennas and shipping them to Europe. They had identified a market opportunity that his company had missed. Feldman eventually set up a distribution network in Europe and became a market share leader there.

Feldman's experience preceded the advent of globalization by about a decade and the explosive growth of the Internet by nearly two. Today, faced with flat demand in their home markets and ever more aggressive calls for cost cutting from management and markets, many businesses are actively cultivating overseas sales and instituting sourcing arrangements across borders for strategic reasons. For Feldman, who now serves as a director of a New York Stock Exchange-listed pharmaceutical company, this trend manifested in the form of a joint venture negotiated with an Indian pharmaceutical manufacturer in 2003. The Indian company manufactures various generic drugs, and the American venture partner obtains Food and Drug Administration approval and maintains sole U.S. marketing rights. The pharmaceutical company now has several of its own facilities in India, as well as one in China.

How Global Competition Flipped the Attorney-Client Relationship on Its Head

From the 1980s—if not earlier—on, American businesses have been under significant pressure to cut costs through downsizing and other efficiencies.[52] Through the 1980s and 1990s however, legal departments largely managed to exempt themselves from the deafening mantra of *do more with less* that virtually every business area was confronting head on. They did this largely by pleading that the variety, complexity, and sheer unpredictability of legal challenges facing a business made the law department budget a breed apart and not amenable to the same kinds of controls with which other areas were forced to reckon.

This line of argument began to lose currency as the new millennium dawned for several reasons: the success of IT outsourcing demonstrating ways in which the supply chain model could be adopted to high concept services—including legal or quasi-legal functions; the demands of cost cutting growing to the point that law departments could not practically be counted as exempt; and increasing sophistication of metrics, just to name a few. Increasingly, C-level executives questioned why the legal budget was not susceptible to better measurement and cost containment.

Eventually, businesses began to demand that their general counsel hold to finite budgets, budgets which then began to decrease year after year, much as had been happening in other departments across the board. At the same time, the business climate was growing more complicated, offering greater legal challenges than before. Still, business executives, weaned on decades of *do more with less*, were unmoved by the plaintive cries of legal staff; they would have to find a way to address additional responsibilities with the same or even less available legal spend. Additional pressures brought on by the onslaught of the 2008 recession only added an exclamation point to a story that had already largely been written.

It is through the prism of these unprecedented challenges faced by in-house legal staff that the changes to the attorney-client relationship must

---

52. Henry Hornstein, *Downsizing Isn't What It's Cracked Up to Be*, Ivey Bus. J. (May/June 2009), http://www.iveybusinessjournal.com/topics/strategy/downsizing-isn%E2%80%99t-what-it%E2%80%99s-cracked-up-to-be.

be viewed and understood. The great majority of in-house attorneys served as outside counsel at some point in their careers, and particularly in connection with their trusted "go-to" firms, there is no benefit in punishing or abusing the people who are handling their companies' most sensitive issues. By necessity of the circumstances, however, clients came to realize that because they held the purse strings, they had a great deal more power in the attorney-client relationship than they had ever exercised. And now they really needed to use it to make the partnerships with their legal service providers more accountable to the clients' cost cutting needs and goals.

The value proposition was no longer just the province of the *subject matter* of legal services provided—it would from now on also extend to *how the service was delivered*: rates, staffing, efficiency in bringing matters to conclusion, and close examination of noncore services that had traditionally served as profit centers for law firms.

Given the assertiveness on the part of clients on the cost cutting/efficiency side of the ledger, it is not that difficult to imagine that clients who are also facing unprecedented challenges internationally will likewise insist that their trusted legal advisors be able to step up and assist with these new challenges, even if the clients had not needed such service before.

Having one counsel speak to both domestic and international concerns makes fundamental sense from the perspectives of both efficiency and strategic consistency, but it also speaks to the "x factor" that has not changed in the attorney-client relationship—trust and the human element of the professional relationship. In-house counsel and company executives seek comfort in knowing that their most intractable problems are under the watchful eyes of those professionals who have demonstrated the ability and responsiveness necessary to successfully address them. What this suggests for those counsel who haven't yet seen the need to expand to a globalized practice is that they need to be more flexible in anticipating their clients' needs, because there is little question that the twenty-first century will most assuredly be "the century of the client."

A Globalized Legal Practice Does Not Assume a Total Shift to Cross-Border Work

The global marketplace is still evolving, and there is no doubt that there will be plenty of firms that will retain a national, regional, or even local focus. Still, as demonstrated above, the ongoing changes in both the general business and legal business models will make it increasingly necessary for counsel by and large (whether they are with larger firms in metropolitan areas or not) to be able to give competent advice on international topics to their business clients, including small and medium-sized concerns. For some counsel, that will be mostly an exercise in issue spotting and development of a network of professionals who can be retained to give specific advice on given international issues. For others, depending on whether their clients join the growing ranks of businesses whose strategy adopts some sort of international presence, a more thorough understanding of the issues and a more complete network of international professionals and consultants may be in order.

The fact is that these days, international work often leads to more domestic work. Harvey Cohen of Dinsmore notes that even though he is based in Cincinnati, he does work for companies outside the Midwest region. Cohen is convinced that if you are not working in one of the larger cities such as New York or Chicago, the current market forces will compel you to consider doing work outside of your home geographic region.

As globalization has progressed, many cities have lost their global headquarters. However, in return they tend to acquire facilities and massive foreign investments from German, French, and British companies, among others. These new entities' concerns are now domestic American issues. This work, though domestic, comes to Cohen through the international work he does and through international organizations. Like Western companies in China, these newcomers to the United States start small and see how things go. They start with a few employees through an independent network and eventually set up distribution and then assembly operations. They find they need to have a U.S. office. European stalwarts such as Henkel, Siemens, and Bayer have been in the United States for years. Now privately owned $50–$100 million companies and independent divisions of larger companies need to have people here.

Your Choice: Master Cross-Border Issues or Watch Your Clients/Customers Migrate

As discussed above, many attorneys' most important clients—even clients who would never have dreamed of having global operations or partnerships before—either may be preparing to develop them now or soon will be. Many companies have already concluded that over the long term, it will be necessary to leverage the low-cost, high-quality labor available overseas to help maintain a competitive business model. Although the media hoopla over offshore outsourcing has largely subsided, the interest in pursuing effective cost savings through an offshore sourcing strategy has not. If clients are even considering such a move, getting the proper due diligence and legal advice throughout the process will be critical to their success.

The global economy also presents unparalleled opportunities for many clients. Perhaps they are niche producers of equipment needed to create state-of-the-art manufacturing facilities. Odds are that they could multiply their sales many times by selling their products to a quickly growing and relatively untapped overseas market in Southeast Asia or Latin America. But after some investigation, management determines that they would need to create a joint venture with a local company that has the distribution network and political connections needed to effectively sell the product there. When key clients ask for advice in putting together such a joint venture, what will their lawyers say to them?

Their lawyers can, of course, continue to provide the same limited service they have delivered in years and decades past, and let the clients seek out international advice from law firms with expertise in global transactions. As it happens, though, those same firms often also offer tax advice, litigation management, or any number of other services that encompass existing counsel's specialties, and those firms can integrate these services together with cross-border advice into a coherent overall strategy. If a client's current outside counsel cannot, or will not, offer international services as well, why would the client not move all its business to someone who can service all its needs? Perhaps a given firm won't lose all its best clients this way, but just how many of them *can* a firm afford to lose today? And how many potential clients can it afford to go elsewhere?

One of the best statements of the principles discussed here comes from Seyfarth Shaw Chairman J. Stephen Poor:

> In order to meet business demands, corporate counsel are increasingly looking for firms that deliver greater value. Looking out on a landscape that includes a wider variety of choices than ever before—regional firms, national firms, global firms, virtual firms, legal outsourcing providers and contract firms, among others—their purchasing decisions continue to evolve.
>
> If the recent recession teaches anything for the legal industry, it is this: The changing demands of our clients require the legal services profession to find different paths to deliver value to those who buy our services. Lawyers today should be asking themselves nontraditional questions: how to apply resources more effectively, to shorten cycle time and lower the cost of their work product and other deliverables, while raising the level of service. In the end, your client will reward you by giving you more work across more areas, and your relationship will deepen.[53]

Indeed, Mr. Poor's last statement is the takeaway. If a given law firm—even one that has a long-standing relationship with a client—is not capable of providing services that include cross-border advice that many businesses find they need today, another one will. That competitor may be the one that receives "more work across more areas." Outside counsel need to understand that they are now faced with much the same choice as their clients: master cross-border issues or watch customers migrate.

Businesspeople are largely already on board with the changes that flow from this simple concept, while some lawyers struggle to accept the new

---

53. J. Stephen Poor, *Re-Engineering the Business of Law*, N.Y. Times (May 7, 2012), http://dealbook.nytimes.com/2012/05/07/re-engineering-the-business-of-law.

reality. Loring Knoblauch, former CEO of Underwriters Laboratories and a law school graduate himself, has wisely stated that it is lawyers who are most disadvantaged by globalization. He simply observes that lawyers are trained from the start to look backwards by the principles of precedent and *stare decisis*, whereas the global economy requires forward thinking. This makes it most difficult for lawyers in particular to cope with the rapid change the world is experiencing. Clients today need attorneys who can adapt—quickly—to the new world that is developing all around them. Lawyers can take advantage of a whole world of opportunity—or be left behind, trying to provide stale answers to yesterday's problems. So, for lawyers reading this who might still be on the fence: what's it going to be?

Chapter 2

Who Should Be Doing What: The Most Effective Uses of In-House and Outside Counsel

What Are the Capabilities of Your In-House Staff?

"You can divide the world into two groups," says Loring Knoblauch, retired chief executive officer (CEO) of Underwriters' Laboratories (UL), "the GEs of the world who build in-house capabilities, and medium-sized (and smaller) businesses that don't have the necessary background or internal resources to do that." May Tan, formerly an in-house counsel with Hewlett-Packard's (HP's) Asia Pacific office in Singapore, agrees. "HP doesn't need to use outside counsel that often," she says. "They have a large in-house legal staff." Their drafting of contracts, transactional work, and intellectual property issues are each dealt with by individual departments within the in-house legal team.

A medium-sized company is likely to have a general counsel on staff, and perhaps a small team of lawyers and nonlawyer staff supporting him or her. You may be fortunate enough that at least someone on staff has some cross-border experience. A smaller business, of course, may have no permanent in-house legal staff at all, choosing instead to use trusted outside counsel as "quasi-general counsel" when the circumstances warrant it. Whatever the case, it is the size and experience of your in-house staff that will guide you in the planning, diligence, negotiation, and implementation of a cross-border transaction.

If you have in-house legal personnel, says Karen Klein, formerly general counsel of popular travel websites Kayak.com and Orbitz.com, their job consists primarily of two things: issue spotting for management and managing outside counsel. Outside counsel's job is to advise. Klein recommends staging an initial "all-hands" meeting with the nonattorney business people who will be involved in the transaction and then dividing up the work.

Tan strikes a similar note. In previous companies she worked for, such as information technology (IT) firm Computer Sciences Corporation, they farmed out work to outside counsel for things that they did not have experience to do. Still, when they engaged external counsel, they managed the kind of advice they were seeking and paying for. Logically, if you do not have dedicated in-house counsel to handle these tasks, trusted outside counsel can function as the manager of, and liaison between, outside issue specialists and company management.

How much work should stay in-house? Donald Chenevert Jr., in-house counsel for heavy equipment giant Caterpillar, recalls that in his experience, a combination of in-house counsel and outside counsel is generally used. There is no "one-size-fits-all" approach on how to divide up tasks, Chenevert says. In-house managers generally do initial internal research. Their proposals go up through the ranks of management to upper-level management. Then you might start to work with outside personnel.

If, for instance, you are interested in purchasing a local company to gain access to a new market, you might ask outside consultants to identify potential target companies and narrow down the prospects to the desired profile. Still, it is the in-house legal staff that typically begins to explore the legal, strategic investment, and taxation issues. At a later stage, outside counsel will work on issues such as confidentiality and other specific agreements.

Chenevert finds that the internal business manager—not in-house counsel—is typically responsible for accounting, return on investment (ROI), and personnel issues. The lawyers provide the legal and conceptual framework and help assemble the team that is responsible for collection and assessment of data about the potential target. The end product of this phase is a selective volume of information that allows you to go back to the target during the diligence phase and ask about those areas where more information is needed.

In considering how to divide up the work, it is helpful to think about some of the various roles that outside counsel can potentially play in cross-border transactions.

Outside Counsel as Strategic Consultant

Charles Hallab, a partner at Baker & McKenzie, observes that many of his clients are not fully prepared for the complexities of international business, and that the level of experience can vary dramatically from client to client. He notes that some clients require "handholding" right from the start, although in such cases it creates a deference that can allow Hallab to offer truly open and comprehensive advice.

On the other hand, Hallab relates, "some clients are savvier than we are." In those cases, Hallab adjusts his representation and seeks to provide a sounding board and analysis that complements the client. Each client comes in with his or her own personality and capabilities. The challenge for the lawyer is to "recognize and adopt an approach that best suits the individual client. What's right for BP is not right for Starbucks or for the start-up down the street." Hallab says he never purports to offer purely "business advice" to clients; it is in the lawyer's purview and responsibility to see to it that there is proper communication among the relevant parties.

Howard Mills, of Deloitte, tells of representing a company in Latin America that happened to use the law firm Baker & McKenzie. Mills was on a conference call, and his Mexican specialist had a difference of opinion with the Baker lawyers in Mexico on a particular tax issue. Naturally, the client was confused. What did the client do? They brought the general partner from Baker who went through and grilled both sides. It wasn't that the partner had more technical knowledge than the other two guys on the phone. But he was a "good overall quarterback"—that is, someone with a business sense who could see the "big picture" and with whom the client had a trusted relationship. "You could just see how he posed the right questions to both sides," Mills says, and ultimately the Baker partner got to the right answer.

Mills recalls that both sides had to rethink their positions, but he was very impressed by the way the Baker partner handled himself. The partner presented himself as a domestic corporate lawyer who did some international work, but he would not portray himself as a Mexican specialist per se. The decision maker knew this partner was not a specialist on this issue but trusted his business judgment. You do not have to be the expert on China or India or even international transactions to have that role, Mills says. He sums it up this way:

> I always tell my people, the sign of a really good professional is not knowing what you do know—it's knowing what you *don't* know. And it's knowing how to get answers—how to get a network together so that you can serve that client. I've even seen that with clients with other law firms that are big. [Those firms] don't necessarily have offices in all the jurisdictions where my clients are, but they do have contacts.

Mills has seen plenty of clients use big firms for a transaction because they believed they needed the expertise. They moved to the big firm from a competitor, perhaps a small or midsized firm. For example, a client decides to go international and looks for additional expertise, so they come to Deloitte. But conversely, some of Mills' best business relationships involve getting a referral and working with the accountant who knows the company inside and out, and Deloitte just brings some technical value to the table. "It takes a long time to develop a relationship," Mills notes. "You don't get to be a trusted business advisor overnight. You've got to sweat it out with the client and be there when the chips are up and the chips are down . . . and it's very helpful when you've got somebody who has got that relationship and you're working with them."

Mills compares it to the role of a medical internist. An internist does not have to be a cardiologist or a surgeon. "But when I go to my internist," says Mills, "I want him or her to tell me what it is that those guys are all doing and what has to get done, and to help me make the final decision."

In his article "Expect the Unexpected," Jay Horton argues that in outsourcing transactions "what's needed is an approach for evaluating the strategic risks, anticipating key moments of change, and identifying trade-offs between short-run or narrower needs and longer-term or broader goals."[1]

Conventional business planning "tends to extrapolate past trends and to conceal risk," says Horton, leading business leaders to "underestimate uncertainty." Horton therefore advocates scenario planning, which he describes as "the art of thinking the unthinkable: 'What could bite us?'"[2] Exploring how strategies and decisions pan out over a series of hypothetical futures can "provide a framework for making sound decisions in the face of unexpected developments."[3] Anticipating the worst-case scenario and planning contingencies for it is one of the principal strengths of lawyers—an essential element of the consulting function.

Understanding the ways in which long-term outsourcing arrangements can best manage uncertainty is crucial to success, Horton concludes. The challenge is to stimulate "out-of-the-box" thinking that exposes "entrenched and outmoded viewpoints."[4] The strategic "out-of-the-box thinking" that a good outside lawyer can provide, particularly where in-house legal and/or nonattorney stakeholders are trapped in a fog of groupthink, may prove to be the difference between success or failure for a given transaction.

What kind of qualities should one look for in such outside counsel? Michel Feldman of Seyfarth relates that from his perspective, you want someone who knows that "asking the right questions is key." Feldman recalls a time when he went to a prospective client's office with several of his partners. One partner initially tried to emphasize his skills as a litigator. Feldman, though, took the opportunity to ask some probing questions. It quickly became apparent that the client was highly adverse to litigation. The client was looking for someone who could provide counsel and advice on how to *avoid* litigation. If Feldman had not asked the right questions, he would not have grasped the bigger picture, and the client may have found different representation.

---

1. Jay Horton, *Expect the Unexpected*, 3 THE OUTSOURCING INSTITUTE (2005), http://www.outsourcing.com/content.asp?page=01b/other/oe/q405/expecttheunexp.html&nonav=false.
2. Id.
3. Id.
4. Id.

Moreover, Feldman believes that outside counsel needs to have both general industry knowledge and an understanding of the specific business risk factors in order to know what questions to ask. To gain this, Feldman suggests pulling the 10-K report the client files with the Securities and Exchange Commission (assuming they are public) and those of their competitors. If they are private, zero in on specific knowledge of the client's company. This allows you to ask management intelligent questions. Knoblauch of UL also believes that an expert at cross-border transactions has to be able to figure out different strategies. For this, lawyers are needed who have experience working in the business world (Feldman, for example, was a general counsel and remains a corporate board member).

Outside Counsel as Issue Specialist

Tan, formerly of HP, notes that even in smaller companies, in-house attorneys normally have some sort of previous law firm experience and are capable of providing general advice to management. They only farm out work they cannot do internally, such as matters of specific expertise or ones that require knowledge of various countries' laws. Tan was once asked to set up a subsidiary in Thailand and Indonesia. She had no difficulty in doing so with only the assistance of a local law firm. Still, that assistance can be crucial, since it is necessary to know if any local laws will affect a transaction. For instance, local privacy laws might have important effects on the outcome of an intellectual property deal.

To the extent that a larger company would utilize outside counsel, Tan believes that the scope of work you might offer depends on a variety of other factors. These include the type of business unit or units involved in the transaction, whether in-house counsel is available in the relevant location, and who the "delivery people" are within the management side of the company. For example, smaller companies are less likely to have in-house counsel already stationed in the target location. These firms might need to rely on outside counsel on a greater number of issues.

Working for a large firm, Feldman has the advantage of having access to a law librarian who can collect the information he needs to educate himself about various issues important to a given client. But Feldman notes that today much information is easily gathered from the Internet. Press releases, industry trade magazines, speeches given by the new CEO, Dun & Bradstreet, and Hoover's are all excellent sources of information about your client, their potential business partners, and their competitors. This competitive intelligence can also be used to learn more about the other side's lawyers, as well.

Harvey Cohen of Dinsmore & Shohl relates the example of outside counsel being asked to what extent a client would need to have "tail insurance" for a deal, to protect against an exposure to a long-term risk. In this capacity, outside counsel can generally tell you what is typical in the market. According to Cohen, counsel develops a baseline—"this is what we see in deals we have done." However, applications may vary from sector to sector, and that's where consulting with the client's in-house team comes in.

Outside Counsel as Coordinator of Other Disciplines

As stated earlier, Mills finds the most helpful lawyers are the "quarterbacks." They do not have to have every answer, but they know how to speak English well, are familiar with the customs, and know where the clients are coming from in their thinking. Quarterbacks also understand the other side's thinking and can help to mold it. For instance, a quarterback might say, "Putting up a building here in this location isn't going to work," and then explain why the local customs will prevent it from succeeding as designed. But in many instances, rather than doing the explaining, Mills says, the quarterback sends the issue to a set of contacts who, in turn, can connect a client with people in the local country who can cast the difficulties into a clearer perspective.

Mills' work on a cross-border transactional team could last from cradle to grave, or counsel might just call when they need specific advice about a tax issue. The extent to which outside counsel, in-house counsel, or even Mills himself coordinates the team ultimately depends on the client. The client may say to Mills, "We're going overseas and we want help. We want you involved in the whole thing; help us find the contacts overseas, help us get this set up, and help us to line up our contacts on the other side." Sometimes a law firm Mills works with will call and say, "We want to move this segment of business or do this transaction—can you help us figure out how it's going to be taxed and how to structure it?"

Again, it is the client's decision about who coordinates. Often the in-house legal staff themselves fills this role. Tan acknowledges that she has *never* given outside counsel a leading role. By contrast, Klein, former general counsel of Kayak.com, notes that sometimes the choice of person to coordinate efforts may be driven by other factors. For instance, Europeans typically look to accountants instead of lawyers for tax advice. Whether privilege will attach to the accountants' advice is an open question, since European in-house counsel communications are not always deemed to be privileged. This illustrates the point that even when dividing up the work between internal and external sources, a big-picture mentality is essential.

Outside Counsel as Due Diligence Nexus

As the following chapters demonstrate, the due diligence process in a cross-border transaction can be so involved and time consuming that smaller companies might be inclined to have outside counsel manage and coordinate it. A company with more internal resources might want to consider other options, however. In the case of a company such as Caterpillar, the internal business manager actually manages the due diligence process. Chenevert notes that, depending on the circumstances, the company may approach a target directly or may have third parties (i.e., consultants) initiate contact with a target company's management to determine their interest in being acquired. Once that interest is demonstrated, he typically engages more consultants and a local outside counsel to work on the due diligence phase. In addition to being managed by internal resources, counsel is supplemented by internal subject matter experts in such areas as human resources (HR) and engineering. They evaluate, for instance, the skills of the existing employees or the quality of the target company's existing facilities (e.g., location and condition of buildings, quality and age of machinery, etc.).

Outside counsel might be expected to argue that they should be in control of the process. Not necessarily so. Cohen believes that it is best if clients do *not* turn over the due diligence process to outside lawyers. They should leave it primarily to their employees or independent contractors. That is not to say the outside lawyer has no role. The outside lawyer adds value by promoting communication among the internal team members. Also, the in-house team should *selectively* assign specific diligence issues to lawyers and accountants. Allen Bargfrede, formerly a member of Orbitz.com's in-house legal department, follows this philosophy. In an Indian development project with which he was involved, he used local outside counsel to run employee checks. He found that this was not only efficient but also more effective—they knew where to look for the relevant information. Ramesh K. V., formerly of Kochhar and Co, advises his foreign clients primarily on type of entity, employment issues, and regulatory approval.

If you assign the entire diligence process to outside counsel, Cohen says, it is generally inefficient and "a boondoggle for outside counsel." Most companies ask their own finance, benefits, and HR people to review the key contracts, and they generally know what they are looking for. What is the chain of control? Are the contracts, as drafted, signable or not?

Outside Counsel as Risk Manager

Cross-border transactions by their nature carry more, and different, risks than do domestic transactions. As Samir Gandhi, a partner with Sidley Austin's New York office, succinctly puts it, "it's more complicated than you think." International outsourcing, for instance, involves cultural, financial, political, technological, and managerial risks and complexities that have to be recognized and accounted for in the client's overall strategy. Inevitably, Gandhi points out, these numerous and interconnecting practical risks involve legal risks that arise in the context of creating, negotiating, implementing, and enforcing an outsourcing contract, or any other cross-border transaction. So this aspect of international deal making suggests some use of outside counsel as well.

As with other aspects already discussed, the extent to which outside counsel is used in the risk-management role varies with the circumstances. Gandhi notes that the legal risks follow the particular nature of the business operations involved. From that it seems reasonable to conclude that here, too, internal staff involvement and, if practical, overall control of the risk management process may be advisable. That way, the client's own people will, if properly advised, be in the best position to fully assess the risks associated with their industry.

Outside Counsel as Drafter and Negotiator

Practitioners such as Bargfrede reason that whether to involve outside counsel directly in negotiations depends on in-house counsel's experience level. Outside counsel can always be used as a resource, Bargfrede notes. Cohen speaks in a similar vein. Each transaction is different. Is the in-house person too busy to take the lead? Is there a junior staff member involved whom they want to train?

In any event, Cohen says, outside counsel must make sure to include the in-house person. It is about more than the fact that the internal people are already familiar with particular issues that are unique to their company. They can also talk to their colleagues and get a quicker turnaround than outside counsel can because in many instances they work in the same building as the decision makers. If they need a critical approval, they can walk into the executive offices, go to the right person, and insist, "I need approval on this—now." Even mid-level executives often do not understand that their inaction is what is holding up an entire transaction, Cohen observes.

From the client's perspective, how much outside counsel should get involved in negotiations is also about the training and background of outside counsel. Knoblauch tells of a young lawyer from Detroit who had never worked outside of the United States. He was very bright but unfamiliar with the overseas environment, to begin with. Still, this lawyer had good negotiating skills—an ability that Knoblauch found could transcend national and cultural boundaries. Ironically, in Knoblauch's opinion, the worst training for international lawyers is at a law firm; a trained mediator, on the other hand, can do well in the international arena.

Intersection with Other Disciplines

Once it has been determined how much outside counsel will manage a given transaction, depending on the complexity of the project, in-house staff may require the additional input of a number of consulting experts, as well. Some examples include cultural experts, tax and other issue specialists, product and service technicians, and foreign counsel.

Cultural Experts

Mills, of Deloitte, suggests that the first thing to consider doing if you are new to business in a given locale is to spend time there taking applicable cross-cultural classes and perhaps finding a mentor familiar with the area. "I think that's one of the mistakes my clients will make," Mills observes. "They try to go into another jurisdiction and just assume that doing business in Mexico is the same as doing business in Detroit. And it's not."

Depending on their level of sophistication, a client might ask Mills for a recommendation of professionals from various disciplines they could use in India, or for someone from Deloitte's India office to participate in the meetings with them. Mills may even proactively suggest such consultation because having worked in India, he can advise about some of the cultural issues of which a client may need to be aware. The advice may be as simple as "have a driver; don't drive yourself." If you have ever seen New Delhi traffic, day or night, you know why Mills says this. When it comes to cultural issues, it is wise to glean the many little things that members of your team have picked up from the transactions they have worked on in the past.

Tax and Other Issue Specialists

Consulting houses such as Deloitte have the capacity to provide focused services limited to specific subspecialties, or virtual "one-stop shopping" over a range of services necessary to support a cross-border transaction. The extent to which these houses become involved, and when, once again is determined by the size and experience of in-house staff and outside counsel, the nature of the transaction, and the budget associated with it. Mills notes that Deloitte has traditional audit and business advisory services. Their corporate finance group helps to "identify venture candidates, help on diligence issues, business modeling, and evaluations . . . kind of like the investment banker advisor side of the business." Meanwhile, their consulting group is "good at systems and computer implementation, logistics, and risk management." The consulting group's background tends to be in engineering or computing, not accounting.

Worldwide, Deloitte has affiliate offices in most countries. "So," Mills relates, if I've got a client who wants to relocate to Mexico for example, I can assist them in setting up in Mexico. There is an office in Mexico where somebody there, a local, would be able to assist them with the Mexican rules. I don't do the Mexican stuff here in the U.S. as much as I coordinate and help bring the locals together, so that they are getting the service in Mexico and we would deal with the U.S. consequences. When there is going to be a cross-border transaction, you actually need a team—someone on both sides—to put together what's going to happen under Mexican law, what's going to happen under U.S. rules, and make sure the client is getting the results they are trying to get.

Whether the lawyers involved bring consultants on board (or vice versa) also depends on the client and what they are doing. Sometimes the client will come directly to the consultant. At other times a U.S.-based Deloitte professional will put the client in touch with their local office in the target country, conduct calls and meetings, and "actually recommend a law firm and other professionals that can help (the client) out." On still other occasions, a U.S. law firm will call Mills, saying, "Hey, I've got a client that wants to go to India and I don't have any contacts there. Can you assist us?" Now and then, even other accounting firms will pick up the phone and say, "I've got a client that's going to Europe, and we don't have any particular expertise. Would you be able to help us and work with us on the client and work on the international part with us?"

Depending on what steps have been taken in a given transaction, the consultants can often assist with the big picture view early on (to the extent the lawyers have not yet had a chance to) by talking the client through some of the initial issues. What is your business plan? What are you trying to accomplish? What is your time frame? Is it realistic? How much do you intend to invest? If the client is ready to move forward, Mills will start putting together an appropriate Deloitte team that will help the client implement that plan.

Even for worldwide consulting houses, Mills notes, "it's getting harder and harder to be everything to everybody." The answer, says Mills, is to set up a network, be it formal or informal, "with folks that you feel comfortable referring things back and forth to, and that you can work with." For example, accountants in smaller to midsized practices will call Mills and ask for help on a project in India, and they are comfortable because they know they will still be the quarterback—that Mills will not take their clients.

There is a lesson in this for the firm that is looking to become global. "It's really difficult for a 50–75 person firm to [independently] develop enough expertise for even one of the jurisdictions," Mills notes. He concludes,

> they can get good at the domestic business issues and then they need that network to help them bridge some of the overall issues that are out there that are going to be so technical and so specific that, unless they are doing enough volume . . . that is probably not worth their time.

The lesson, then? As you have done all your professional life, when you are faced with a new jurisdiction you have never dealt with before, or an issue with which you are unfamiliar, find trusted professionals to add to your network. Rely on them to help close the gap in your own experience. And always be willing to listen and learn.

Applicable Product/Service Technicians

Whether you are dealing with manufacturing, IT or service functions, sales, or corporate acquisitions, identifying key in-house people who early on can tell you exactly what is needed is a crucial step in any transaction. It is essential to involve them throughout all stages of planning, negotiation, and implementation. Cohen sums it up thusly:

> Exhibits and schedules [to the main agreement] are where the *whole game* is. And this is where your relationship with the client's technical people is so important. What you need typically is an in-house person who is detail oriented that can "ride herd" on the technical people so you get the right attachment [laying out specifications or technical requirements] when you need it. If you don't include everything, that is when you get involved in a lot of change orders. [Initially] you need to diagram operational flow. Do you need a server here or not?

One additional point is worth considering here. It is important not only to identify these key people, but also it is crucial that they "buy-in" to the transaction. Their indifference, let alone their active opposition, can cause delays, cost overruns, and implementation issues—at a minimum. One way to promote successful transactions is to avoid sabotage from within.

Foreign Counsel

Another division of labor that needs to be determined early on is what work will be done by domestic outside counsel versus foreign-based counsel. There are different ways to approach the problem. Cohen sees the domestic outside client counsel's role as filtering what foreign counsel is being asked to do. "A strategy that often works," Cohen says, "is to structure the deal exactly as if it were taking place in the client's home country." If an American company wants to do something in Belgium,

> you start by drafting everything as if it were taking place in the U.S. Then, you send it to a Belgian law firm and tell them to "Belgianize" it. What you find is that the foreign lawyer gets "knee deep" into the negotiations, but that's OK. You let them pick up the ball and run with it. This is why the choice of foreign counsel in these deals is *crucial*.

You start with a medium-length agreement and try to force the terms to stay as much as possible within your parameters. "For example," Cohen relates,

> I was involved in a JV [joint venture] between a German company and a U.S. company in Mexico. We pulled out language from venture agreements both in Mexico and New Zealand. Then we handed it off and said, "Make it work."

That's not to say, however, that you should simply copy boilerplate domestic-contract language and paste it into a new offshore-outsourcing agreement without giving thought to the changes that are necessary.[5]

---

5. Darren Skinner, *Boilerplate Blunders: A Reminder That "Standard" Contractual Provisions Should Be Used with Care*, THE COMMERCIAL LAW CONNECTION (Winter 2005), http://www.arnoldporter.com/publications.cfm?action=view&id=305.

Another point worth noting is that the explosive growth in international transactional work in hot markets means that demand sometimes outstrips supply for qualified lawyers there. Richard Wageman, of DLA Piper, notes that as China opens up various business sectors, a developing mergers and acquisitions practice has been created there. As a result, there is an increasing demand for the limited supply of experienced professionals in the legal field in China. With laws expanding rapidly in areas such as product quality, property rights, stock, and security exchange, there is now a need on the part of privately held and state-owned companies for legal services.

Dr. David Liu, retired CEO of insurance broker Aon China (and formerly chief advisor of Greater China with Swiss insurer Zurich), agrees. He notes that Aon's representative office in China and other large multinational firms have no problems whatever in finding legal representation in China. Aon, for instance, has used Sidley Austin. But in Liu's experience, small and medium enterprises in many instances "have had no place to go."

Still, Liu points out, big-name legal or consulting firms can have their limitations. They may know how to do business in China in general, but you really need them to know the specific industry in which you do business. Many large firms may lack staff in the country that have expertise in the areas your clients need. It is important to be certain that, regardless of the size or reputation of the law or consulting firm you use in a foreign location, the team members you rely on have their bona fides in the fields in which you are engaged.

Intersection with Vendors/Vendors' Counsel

In many transactions involving the developing world, there was—and often still is—little interaction between the lawyers on both sides. Wageman observes that Chinese companies, for instance, have not previously used lawyers extensively—and if they have, the lawyers are not brought in until the end of a transaction to prepare and review documentation. In one weekend in 2004, Wageman recounts, he was involved in negotiating two separate joint ventures, and neither of the Chinese parties brought a lawyer to the negotiations. In many developing countries, notes Hallab, of Baker

& McKenzie, "lawyers are bureaucrats . . . so bringing attorneys into diligence or negotiations might confuse [the clients] more than offend them."

Newer Chinese companies, however, are using lawyers in a more proactive way, either as a function of growing sophistication in international transactions or simply as a matter of saving "face" if they know the foreign party will have its legal counsel actively involved in the transaction. If a Western company brings their lawyers to negotiations, Wageman has noticed, the Chinese companies want to have lawyers present as well. Even in that case, however, the Chinese party's lawyers take a "back seat" in the meetings. Chinese executives do most of the talking, while the Chinese lawyers in some cases sit quietly taking notes and only become involved in the discussions if asked to do so by their client.

Because of the cultural sensitivity involving use of lawyers in the early phases of negotiations, Wageman encourages his Western clients to consult with him in advance of negotiations, but not to directly involve lawyers during initial phases. Simply put, in business transactions in China, there historically has been a suspicion of lawyers. Involving lawyers at the negotiating table early in the process may stifle discussion. Even today it is typical for Western clients in China to have only their business representatives in initial meetings with their Chinese counterparts.

The more effective practice, Wageman finds, is to consult with the business people on the initial negotiations and then let them draft a term sheet document that is then sent back and forth between the parties. The terms of a tentative agreement are then brought to the lawyers so that a memorandum of understanding can be prepared. Law firms in China prefer simple agreements, so some "head butting" over provisions can occur at this stage.

Ramesh K. V., formerly of Kochhar, notes that in this regard India is similar to China; lawyers are often not brought in until the last moment. In India as in China, this is slowly changing, as interactions with Westerners become more commonplace. Many Indian vendors now have large in-house legal teams. Still, whether as in-house or outside counsel, you may have little or no interaction with the other side until late in the game, and you will need to carefully prepare in-house business staff to take into account this fact.

Mills, of Deloitte, agrees:

> I do see that the business guys want to work with the [opposing side's] business guys before they bring the lawyers and other professionals to the foreground and a lot of times we'll have a lot of discussions behind the scenes. The business guys are on the forefront. They don't want the lawyers out there negotiating. Maybe the other side doesn't have lawyers yet or is doing the same type of thing behind the scenes. But until there is a business deal it doesn't make sense for lawyers and accountant[s] to be up on the forefront dealing with the "nitty-gritty" issues. You have to get the big picture nailed down and then negotiate from there. I think most of my clients would tell you that is their strategy.

But as with most issues related to international transactions, there is rarely a single, simple "right" answer. "I've got some clients," Mills notes, "who get the professionals . . . in up front and really do a good job," an approach he believes is the best thing from a client's perspective. Even so, "it's a judgment call on their part on when the right time [to bring in the professionals] is." Timing is a decision best approached on a case-by-case basis, using the cultural sensitivity that you, your network, and your transactional team have cultivated.

Intersection with U.S. and Foreign Regulators

Recognizing that any government official not only can potentially delay or even block a transaction but also can exercise police powers, it makes sense to carefully consider who should be doing the talking. Cohen tells his clients that in the United States, the outside U.S. lawyer should be the force behind the call to the Customs office, for instance. But oftentimes regulators have a dual role of enforcement and, for example, promotion of trade. So, according to Cohen, having an executive as an interface in the client company may well increase your chances of a successful outcome with U.S. regulators. Overseas, Cohen says bluntly, "I have foreign counsel deal with foreign regulators." Given the need for intricate knowledge of both local laws and local business and regulatory customs, that approach seems to be based on solid ground.

Chenevert, of Caterpillar, has outside counsel deal with foreign officials, too, but notes that he will also have the lead internal people meet with the higher-level governmental representatives. It is important to meet with them, Chenevert reasons, and to be the "human face" of the company to these critical decision makers. Each level of leaders tends to have a cadre of lieutenants who are in charge of implementing policy. "You need all of these people to be working in the same direction, not gumming up the works," Chenevert wryly observes. Sending the message down the chain of bureaucracy that your project is both important and approved by senior officials makes this approach very useful in the appropriate circumstances.

You may find a welcome, if unexpected, ally in dealing with trade barriers experienced in foreign countries—the U.S. Department of Commerce.[6] A white paper released by the office of former Senator Joseph Lieberman notes that the Trade Compliance Center (TCC) under the Department of Commerce

> is required to help U.S. exporters by making sure America's trade agreements work for U.S. businesses, particularly small–medium enterprises. The TCC responds to trade complaints by assembling experts from ITA [(International Trade Administration)] and other agencies to help solve compliance problems. TCC has a website (www.export.gov/tcc) with texts of over 300 trade agreements the United States is party to, exporter guides explaining the major WTO and bilateral trade agreements, and a hotline to report trade complaints online.[7]

That being said, senior management should not be sent into meetings with foreign officials without careful preparation. Klein, formerly of Kayak.com, emphasizes, "you need to have an FCPA [Foreign Corrupt Practices Act] presentation for businesspeople, because of the potential for criminal

---

6. OFFICE OF SENATOR JOSEPH I. LIEBERMAN, OFFSHORE OUTSOURCING AND AMERICA'S COMPETITIVE EDGE: LOSING OUT IN THE HIGH TECHNOLOGY R&D AND SERVICES SECTORS 32 (May 11, 2004).
7. Id.

liability, and the possibility that violations might harm the company." She notes that not only are common business practices that are encouraged by local officials sometimes outlawed by the FCPA, but under its language, there is potential liability for not keeping accounting records of gifts given or entertainment provided, which could fall under the definition of bribes under the act. The FCPA is, of course, just one example of U.S. law that must be taken into account when interacting with businesses and officials overseas. It is critical to identify the various local laws applicable to the industry and type of transaction with which you are involved as well. If you put together the right team, unnecessary and unpleasant surprises can be avoided.

Chapter 3

The Counseling Function

Outside counsel often say that they are not involved in formulation of a client's internal strategy. Harvey Cohen, of Dinsmore & Shohl, says that in his experience, many clients do not want to pay outside counsel to sit in initial meetings. It is understandable for smaller businesses to do all they can to reduce costs, particularly at the earliest stages of a project when management buy-in may not yet be complete. In many instances, though, this strategy may end up being "penny wise and pound foolish."

What the client is often missing at initial in-house meetings is structure and efficiency, says Cohen. That said, outside counsel should keep in mind that they might not get the opportunity to provide "a voice of reason" until later in the process. Regardless of when they get involved, they should be prepared to question the basis on which decisions were reached and ensure that potential risks have been addressed.

Cohen gives the example of his dealings with a group of international clients who, in Cohen's opinion, had not done their homework. "People tend not to think about governance or co-owning equity in a company," Cohen observed. He emphasizes how important it is to consider things such as which party will have the right to call meetings and which specific events trigger exit provisions. "Exit provisions should be cut and dried, as this will cut off excessive legal fees later." Cohen called to these clients' attention factors that had not been included in their analysis: Which party keeps technology licenses, trade names, and logos? Is a noncompete clause necessary, and if there is none, how would it affect the process of buying out partners? "The lawyer's added value," Cohen concludes, "is telling the client that 'what you want to do doesn't make sense.'" Of course, the lawyer's value is also in helping the client achieve well thought out strategic goals in a way that *does* make sense.

Overview

Assumedly, there is at least one stakeholder, or a small group, at the client company contemplating the feasibility of a cross-border transaction. When working with a closely held company, outside counsel may immediately be dealing with a key decision maker. At a larger, midsized public company, the contact may be several steps away from "go-ahead" authority.

So, where to begin? A logical place to start is to consider the competitive forces, mentioned in Chapter 1, that are driving your clients toward international activity in the first place. IBM Consulting refers to these as "external forces" and "internal drivers."[1] What aspects of the global economy are affecting your client's business today, and what global trends are likely to impact them five or ten years from now? What cost savings and opportunities can be found by moving across borders?

To define "external forces," consider the example of a Tier II auto parts supplier. This supplier is either already under pressure to expand to China and perhaps other locations to which the original equipment manufacturers such as Ford or Toyota and Tier I companies have already migrated, or soon will be. Or consider a family printing business that recognizes how low-cost, high-volume printers in various countries overseas are expanding ever deeper into their local market. If they partner with such a firm, even on only a few jobs, they may be able to go after an entirely new business segment. By contrast, "internal drivers" might be represented by companies that recognize the cost savings, ease of administration, and service upgrades that can result from outsourcing their human resources (HR) functions.[2]

---

1. Eric Lesser & Joanne Stephane, *Preparing for Human Resources Business Transformation Outsourcing*, IBM BUSINESS CONSULTING SERVICES 2 (2005), http://www-935.ibm.com/services/multimedia/ge510-4015-hr-bto.pdf.
2. *Id.* at 3.

In what ways can working with an overseas vendor or business partner increase efficiency and profitability?

Once you have identified these forces and drivers, consider your client's strategic plan, which should in most instances project forward seven to ten years.[3] Does your client's strategic plan take these forces and drivers into account? More to the point, if you are dealing with a smaller, privately held, entrepreneurial company, do they even *have* an up-to-date strategic plan? If not, now would be a good time for the client to come up with one. What is the company's profile in terms of products or services offered, markets served, supply chain, distribution network, and labor allocation?[4] Given observable trends, such as new and potential competitors, opening of new markets, requirements of existing customers, and so on, what changes in the way the client does business are suggested?

Since counsel rarely possesses in-depth knowledge of the industry and of the client's unique circumstances, this step is generally taken by the client, perhaps with some assistance. Vikas Bhalla notes that a company like EXL uses six sigma black belts and consultants to help clients create a long-term strategic plan.

In any event, counsel's job is to see to it that the client thinks through the ultimate goals now—at the beginning—and thereby avoids entering into a transaction that never made sense for the client's business in the first place. For lack of a better analogy, counsel should think of themselves as the faithful, dispassionate best friend who goes along to the car dealer to make sure the potential purchaser does not buy the first thing he or she sees.

"Some joint ventures are doomed from the day the client calls," states Charles Hallab, of Baker & McKenzie. The lawyer's job is to act in the best interests of the client, Hallab says, and "business issues sometimes outweigh legal ones." In the end, Hallab relates, "joint ventures are like restaurants—their success rate is not 100 percent. For them to succeed requires ongoing business and legal attention."

A strategic plan is by its nature a general document. Depending on whether the relevant forces and drivers suggest that outsourcing, entry

---

3. Warren S. Reid, *Outsourcing: The 20 Steps to Success* 3 (1996), http://www.wsrcg.com/Articles/OutSourcing.pdf.
4. *Id.*

into a new market via local distributors, or acquisition of a state-owned company should be considered, a strategic sourcing/sales/acquisition plan that identifies with *specificity* the company's long-term needs in those areas must be developed.[5] Using sourcing as an example, Bhalla, of EXL, says that, particularly with smaller companies that have decentralized platforms and operations, you need to carefully map the organization. This allows the client to break down their operations into processes. At that point, you can meaningfully determine your needs, current capabilities, and alternatives, and evaluate the risks and benefits of outsourcing that particular process or function.

Through a strategic sourcing plan, your client can examine future needs in terms of factors such as capability, performance, costs, and user satisfaction.[6] It can then review the current sourcing model and determine the extent to which alternatives (either onshore or offshore) meet those needs more effectively and cost efficiently, taking into account foreseeable trends such as budget constraints, changing needs, management commitment or resistance to change, lack of tools and human resources, and so forth.[7] A technical analysis should be undertaken to determine the extent of current infrastructure, its scalability, and what improvements are needed to update particular processes.[8] All stakeholders need to provide input so that a complete list of requirements and their relative importance can be created.[9]

It is important to emphasize that, to be of real use, a strategic support plan (for sourcing, sales, etc.) must allow the client to fully understand its cost structure and perform educated estimates of future costs to create and support the projects identified. According to technology consultant Warren S. Reid, this includes estimates of manpower and equipment to build, maintain, operate, control, and, where desired, expand such projects.[10] This, in turn, requires estimates of

---

5. *Id.* at 2.
6. *Id.*
7. *Id.*
8. Andrew Anderson, *Methodology Removes Guesswork: A Structured Approach to Selecting Outsourcing Partners Reduces Risk and Improves ROI*, 40 Comm. News (Aug. 2003), http://www.thefreelibrary.com/Methodology+removes+guesswork%3A+a+structured+appro ach+to+selecting...-a0106646798.
9. *Id.*
10. Reid, *supra* note 3.

all relevant capital; operating and supervisory costs; cost of living increases in salaries, benefits, service contracts, etc.; "cost of money"; interest; residual value of equipment and facilities; cost of transition, including personnel; cost of changes in direction and level of resources; cost of contract modification, etc.[11]

For most small and medium-sized businesses, it is especially helpful to use outside experts for this task.[12]

The construction of alternate fact scenarios as described in the previous chapter will allow you to identify those factors and forces that are most important and uncertain.[13] Once all of the alternate scenarios are compiled, the organization can determine what it should do under each set of circumstances, what elements of a proposed project work consistently well, what elements could be very risky under a given fact pattern, and whether any negative outcome would affect the company's survival.[14]

The end result of the strategic process is the establishment of a formal set of evaluation criteria[15] that will serve as a foundation for decision making on which transactions to pursue and what their scope should be. In *no* way can this be a "once and done" process. As discussed in later chapters, the state of perpetual change that the global economy mandates means that the strategic planning process never ends. It must be constantly questioned and updated based on the information gained in each succeeding step the client takes. Again, counsel must resist any tendency for the client to "just do it" without carefully thinking through how choices will impact the operation—on all relevant levels. Or as Lee Nelson, formerly of Hewlett-Packard and Palm, puts it, "being a good in-house counsel means being able to say 'no' within the politics of being in-house."

Of course, an in-house counsel's role is not to be the perpetual naysayer—just ask business people how much they dislike lawyers like that. Their job is to point out legal and practical problems the client cannot see or foresee

---

11. *Id.*
12. *Id.*
13. Jay Horton, *Expect the Unexpected*, 3 The Outsourcing Institute (2005), http://www.outsourcing.com/content.asp?page=01b/other/oe/q405/expecttheunexp.html&nonav=false.
14. *Id.*
15. Lesser & Stephane, *supra* note 1, at 3.

and then provide a solution that allows the businesspeople to achieve their goals in a way that avoids the pitfalls.

Armed with the strategic preparation the client has done, counsel and client can consider the next major issue in planning an international transaction: what is the best legal structure to achieve the formulated needs and goals? Taking sourcing again as an example, a number of alternatives are available, each with its own strengths and weaknesses: a standard third-party supplier outsourcing contract, establishment of a direct foreign subsidiary, setting up a joint venture with an offshore partner, or perhaps a "BOOT" (build, own, operate, and transfer) arrangement. As discussed in Chapters 4–6, any number of factors can affect the choice of structure, including local regulations, tax law, the particular industry involved, and so on. Bhalla, of EXL, recounts that when information technology first boomed in India, those companies that did not have experience with actual offshore operations became involved in outsourcing or some sort of hybrid between outsourcing and overseas presence. Bhalla notes that this continues today; companies that do not have the experience and scale tend to outsource before setting up offshore operations.

At this point in the process, a feasibility study can be conducted, with the goal of obtaining full management and stakeholder buy-in. IBM cites Paul Adler, professor of management at the University of Southern California, and other outsourcing practitioners regarding various factors that organizations should consider when outsourcing HR functions. A number of these criteria apply in determining the feasibility of most international transactions:

- Dependency: Are there specific assets that require dedicated facilities, equipment, capacity, training, or investments?
- Spillover: Is there confidential information or sources of advantage that could be leaked to competitors?
- Trust: Is there a positive relationship between the two organizations involved that could reduce transaction costs associated with contracting and monitoring?
- Competence: Can the transaction lead to improved results?

- Commitment/Flexibility: Are the components of the subject transaction stable enough so that changes in capacity/technology are not required on a frequent basis?
- Physical Presence: Does the process require regular assistance from a local onsite presence (i.e., cannot be provided remotely)?[16]

The list of parties who must fully buy in to the transaction may be longer than you think. May Tan, formerly of Hewlett-Packard, relates that in a smaller company, you have more centralized control, so it's easier to process a legal review. The larger the company, however, the more specialized its management is likely to be. And in more specialized settings, Tan notes, in order to get anything done, approval is needed from a number of different departments.

Naturally, the frontline decision makers have to be on board. That is to say, the head of the department or departments directly responsible for the processes outsourced, the product lines sold, and the entities purchased and all other persons who have a direct say in those decisions—such as the chief financial officer and/or the manager of procurement—must be brought on board.[17]

In addition to the usual suspects, however, it is important to identify other key personnel who, while not part of the formal decision-making process, have the power to influence the ultimate success or failure of the project. This includes the leaders of the business units directly affected by the transaction and the employees under them who are most likely to be directly affected by the changes being initiated.[18] Failure to identify these personnel and to obtain their support and cooperation at the outset could cause delays, miscommunication, and, at worst, a failed transaction.

Finally, the chief executive officer (CEO), board of directors, and any other parties responsible for final approval of the decision must also be brought on board, at least once a feasibility study has been completed. The more significant the transaction, the sooner the top leadership need to become directly involved. For instance, if a significant number of processes are being

---

16. *Id.* at 4–5.
17. *Id.* at 7.
18. *Id.*

outsourced, if the transaction will impact a large number of jobs throughout the organization, or if the arrangement will require communication with important external stakeholders such as industry analysts and financial markets, senior management naturally need to be intimately involved. As one executive doing business in China observes, the job of in-house staff is to make management comfortable with all aspects of a transaction. That means constant sensitivity to both time and budget constraints.

While in-house personnel can generally be counted on to seek out and obtain approvals and buy-in from the necessary players, outside counsel can assist by anticipating what information and reporting will be needed at each stage, and seeing to it that the client contact has everything necessary at each step of the process. Having gone over the counseling function in general terms, we now turn to some discussion of several key issues in detail.

Core versus Noncore: Evaluating Risks Inherent in Transactions Based on the Relationship-to-Client Business Model

Conventional wisdom in the outsourcing business provides two very big don'ts: don't outsource problems (fix them first) and don't outsource your core competencies. But just what is a "core competency?" Think of the key services or products that differentiate your client from their competition.[19] The closer the process comes to the center of your client's business and strategy, so the theory goes, the less advisable it is to outsource.[20] Stephanie Moore, an analyst at Forrester Research, says that many businesses do not want outsourcing vendors to "own too much of their competitive differentiation—their crown jewels, if you will."[21] For instance, Bob Denis, chief information officer at Trimble Navigation, once observed that Japanese automakers who built plants in the United States in the 1980s "recognized

---

19. *Id.*
20. Dr. Leslie P. Wilcocks, *Myth Understanding*, 3 THE OUTSOURCING INSTITUTE (Winter 2005), http://www.outsourcing.com/content.asp?page=01b/other/oe/q405/mythunderst.html&nonav=false.
21. Mike Ricciuti & Mike Yamamoto, *Companies Determined to Retain "Secret Sauce,"* CNET (May 5, 2004), http://news.cnet.com/2009-1022_3-5198605.html.

that you need to partner, but they're not going to build their transmissions here, because that's the 'secret of their sauce.'"[22]

The experience of the Schwinn bicycle company provides a cautionary tale about how much outsourcing is too much. In 1981, Schwinn sent equipment and engineering talent to Taiwan and thereafter outsourced millions of bicycles from its supplier, Giant.[23] Only six years later, Giant introduced the world's first mass-produced carbon-fiber bicycle frame, going on to sell products under its own brand in more than 50 countries.[24] In the meantime, Schwinn filed for Chapter 11 bankruptcy protection twice, in 1993 and 2001.[25] Professor Shih-Fen S. Chen suggests that rather than "delegating the dirty work of managing factories to subcontractors," it is essential to "deploy foot soldiers to set up production around the globe, as Japanese and German manufacturers have been doing all along."[26]

Similarly, Bhalla, of EXL, advises that if a client is dealing with a core competency, the client should not seek to outsource it, but rather should seek to improve it. There are exceptions to every rule, of course. The fund management and insurance sectors have, for some time, outsourced activities that could be considered core functions. For instance, many insurers and fund managers now outsource investment management to external parties or related group entities. Some underwriters have given insurance brokers the authority to accept certain risks on their behalf and to process claims.[27] The point is, no matter which industry you are in, you need to carefully consider how crucial the subject of any given transaction actually is to your continued existence. The more crucial it is, the more you need to consider maintaining direct control over the subject of the transaction.

For noncore processes, it is still necessary to decide if outsourcing makes sense under the circumstances. For example, are you dealing with a process that is using paper rather than an electronic system? What kind of

---

22. Id.
23. Shih-Fen S. Chen, *IBS Professor Laments American Firms' "Suicidal" Outsourcing*, Providence J. (Dec. 19, 2004), http://www.vindy.com/news/2004/dec/24/how-he-sees-it-us-firms-committing-suicide-by/.
24. Id.
25. Id.
26. Id.
27. Basel Committee on Banking Supervision, *Outsourcing in Financial Services*, The Joint Forum, 6 (Feb. 2005), https://www.bis.org/publ/joint12.pdf.

investment is necessary to convert the process to an electronic format in order to work practically with that process offshore?

Use of Technology versus Wage Arbitrage

When deciding whether to set up operations overseas, it is important to keep in mind that there are potentially at least two ways to save on labor costs. One is to utilize low-cost human labor; the other is to replace human labor with a technological solution. In situations where there are various options to evaluate, Don Chenevert, of Caterpillar, notes that a lot of assessment is generally done at the planning stages. For instance, Caterpillar does some of its design work in India, using younger (and less expensive) engineers than in the United States. A U.S.-based engineer might have the same productivity levels as several Indian engineers who do not have the depth of experience that the engineers from the United States do. But because of the wage differential, notes Chenevert, "you can throw a lot more minds at a problem."

In other situations where the goal is cost savings, the use of applied technology can sometimes effectively substitute for even low-wage workers. For example, call center workers in countries such as India and the Philippines have already been replaced by increasingly sophisticated voice-automation technology that generates responses to inquiries concerning account balances, payment locations, rate plans, and so on.[28]

The Case for Cost-Benefit Analysis

Kumkum Dalal, president of Global Reach Consulting, Inc. of Naperville, Illinois, advises her small business clients that multinational corporations (MNCs) take a very methodical approach to their international operations, which may have application in the small and medium enterprise (SME) context. MNCs carefully set up a process and re-evaluate its effectiveness once

---

28. Paul McDougall, *Automation Takes Toll on Offshore Workers*, INFO. WEEK (Jan. 26, 2004), http://www.informationweek.com/automation-takes-toll-on-offshore-workers/d/d-id/1022794?.

it is in place. The people who work in these companies are accustomed to working with others in remote locations and perhaps with facilities abroad and immigrants in the United States. Consequently, working as part of an international team within an efficient and effective framework becomes second nature. By contrast, Dalal has observed that small companies too often embark on projects without sufficient preplanning and due diligence. No calculated effort is made in the first place to put processes together, or later to see if the processes work as intended. Small businesses would do well to adopt a systematic method, Dalal concludes, anticipating possible problem areas prior to beginning on a project, putting in a timeline that allows for modifications along the way, and being willing to carefully revisit and strengthen existing processes.

Bhalla agrees, noting that larger organizations tend to have already dealt with many issues. Smaller companies with decentralized operations have to redesign, reengineer, and consolidate before they can function effectively. Assuming that you have mapped the organization and broken down operations into processes, you can assess the risks and benefits of outsourcing a given function. One thing is clear: a process as complicated as offshoring should not be considered "a quick-fix, cost-cutting initiative, nor a one-size-fits-all solution."[29]

Feasibility, risks, and benefits are all linked in a continuum, Bhalla reasons. Legal, technical, and skill-level factors have to be considered in deciding how to proceed. For example, Bhalla relates that in 2001, a bank did a study on core versus noncore processes. It determined that in year one, it would outsource "green channel" processes that could be outsourced with low risk and with high benefits as a result. In year two, it would outsource noncore functions that required effort up front. In year three, it would seek to improve core processes.

The more critical the business process, the more data sensitivity involved in the transaction; and the more inexperienced the customer, the greater the need (and cost) of implementing security and compliance processes. Costs

---

29. Ken Shiu, *Outsourcing: Are You Sure or Offshore? Identifying Legal Risks in Offshoring*, NSW Soc'y for Computers & L. (June 2004), https://www.nswscl.org.au/index.php?option=com_content&view=article&id=130:outsourcing-are-you-sure-or-offshore-identifying-legal-risks-in-offshoring&catid=28:june-2004-issue&Itemid=31.

associated with these processes may affect the offshoring business case[30] and must be anticipated to the fullest extent possible from the beginning. This suggests that those companies with little or no experience in cross-border business would be wise to take smaller bites of the apple to start. That is, they should begin with "smaller pilot projects or projects with lower operational or intellectual property risk," to weigh deficiencies in controls, deal with any cultural issues, install all the necessary processes, and allocate adequate resources for monitoring performance.[31]

This is particularly important because some studies suggest that SMEs generally are not as effective as are multinationals in teaching foreign partners the necessary technological skills that accompany their operations. As noted above, knowledge bases in smaller companies are often "tacit"—that is, they are stored in the minds and memories of employees rather than committed to written manuals, blueprints, or drawings, partly because of lack of personnel to codify the technology and partly because many of the skills in SMEs are acquired through personal experience.[32] Because of this, SMEs must often send their limited pool of technical experts abroad to aid in technology transfer, but because of the high cost to the organization of doing so, they cannot devote as many employees or as much funding to aiding the transfer process as can larger companies.[33] This frequently results in "difficulties alleviating the concerns and addressing the assimilation deficiencies of foreign affiliates and/or alliance partners."[34] The relevant literature also suggests that owners of SMEs, who themselves initiate and manage international projects, often lack the time to collect sufficient information about the complexities of international technology transfer.[35]

---

30. *Id.*
31. *Id.*
32. Claude Marcotte & Jorge Liosi, *Small and Medium-Sized Enterprises Involved in Technology Transfer to China: What Do Their Partners Learn*, 23 INT'L SMALL BUS. J. 30 (Feb. 2005).
33. *Id.* at 31.
34. *Id.*, citing L. Eden, E. Levitas, & R. Martinez, R. (1997). *The Production, Transfer and Spillover of Technology: Comparing Large and Small Multinationals as Technology Producers*, SMALL BUSINESS ECONOMICS 9(1): 53–66, at 63.
35. *Id.* at 31.

Rightsizing the Client's Global Vision

One corporate general manager with experience in starting a business in China observes that senior management, or "CXOs," of companies often have no global vision. While they have a vague idea that making some international move might be profitable or even essential to the survival of their business, they still have a national, or even local, way of thinking about their business. Worse yet, instead of seeing the world as it has become, they carry stereotypes based on the past. As counsel for such companies, you must assist the client's senior management to see and understand the opportunities (and threats) as they really exist today.

Circa 2008, this general manager gave the example of businesspeople who pictured bicycles filling the main streets of Shanghai, as countless documentaries of years gone by always showed. Anyone who visited China in that time period, however, would have seen for themselves the millions of cars on the roads and many new superhighways (complete with signs in English). But by then, the reality was so much farther away than that: Shanghai also had maglev trains that traveled from Pudong International Airport to downtown at an average speed of 268 miles per hour.[36]

The "old school" way of looking at China is to view it as a "cheap place to make cheap goods" where strikes and political unrest are for all practical purposes unknown. The new reality is that Chinese private sector wages rose 14 percent in 2012 alone,[37] large-scale work stoppages are on the rise,[38] and demonstrations against pollution[39] and corruption[40] are being regularly reported. Moreover, Chinese firms have for several years been coming to the United Kingdom and the United States to do business. Early examples

---

36. *Shanghai Maglev Train*, WIKIPEDIA, http://en.wikipedia.org/wiki/Shanghai_Maglev_Train.
37. Tom Orlik, *Rising Wages Pose Dilemma for China*, WALL ST. J. (May 17, 2013), http://online.wsj.com/article/SB10001424127887324767004578488233119290670.html.
38. Vivian Ni, *Foreign Investors Should Be Aware of Labor Strike Tactics in China*, CHINA BRIEFING (Nov. 29, 2011), http://www.china-briefing.com/news/2011/11/29/watch-out-for-china%E2%80%99s-flaring-labor-unrest.html.
39. Monica Tan, *New Dawn for Chinese Activism*, SBS NEWS BLOG (May 23, 2013), http://www.sbs.com.au/news/article/1769886/Blog-New-dawn-for-Chinese-activism.
40. Tang Min, *"Strolling" Protests Escalate in Chongqing*, EPOCH TIMES (June 12, 2012), http://www.theepochtimes.com/n2/china-news/strolling-protests-escalate-in-chongqing-251013.html.

included Nanjing Auto and Shanghai Auto buying Britain's MG Rover automaker and Lenovo acquiring IBM's PC operations. The takeaway here is that senior management must be brought up to speed (and kept up to speed) on developments around the world so that they can properly analyze the risks and potential rewards of a given international transaction.

Identifying Key Parameters Related to Targeted Transactions

It is critical during the early phases of exploring potential transactions to fully consider secondary and even tertiary consequences of moving forward. IBM's HR outsourcing site lists parameters worth taking into account:

- Has the complexity of global operations made it more difficult to manage the number of programs and the associated regulations?
- Does the organization have the capacity and capability to integrate recent acquisitions or provide the targeted services for newly created businesses?
- Has the company identified any synergies that could be developed by outsourcing multiple processes?
- What level of involvement is required from the various functional departments participating in the outsourcing decision process?
- Has the company identified the appropriate organizations and individuals to be involved in vendor selection and have their roles and responsibilities been clarified?
- Does the company have a sense for who needs to be involved in leading the outsourcing effort and how and when these individuals will be released from their current responsibilities?
- Has the organization developed a communication strategy that addresses issues and concerns prior to the formal start of the outsourcing arrangement?
- Has the company developed a strategy for formulating a business case for outsourcing, including a plan for collecting the necessary data?[41]

---

41. Lesser & Stephane, *supra* note 1, at 12.

These factors suggest several other considerations: How much oversight will be needed to see the project to a successful conclusion? What type of transitional time frame is both reasonable and cost-effective? What infrastructure will be required, both in the short term and beyond? Finally, is the initiative justifiable by a simple cost-benefit analysis?

Amount of Oversight Needed
Naturally, the degree of oversight needed depends on many factors, including the location of the target operation, the experience of the workforce, the complexity and unique aspects of the targeted function, and so on. That being said, Richard Wageman of DLA Piper cautions that very few foreign companies can run their own operations in China without having experienced Chinese management assistance. They find out quickly that they need a local connection that works with foreign and local players to navigate the mazes of bureaucracy and regulation.

Bhalla points to the consultative or partnership approach that his company, EXL, takes with clients. They assess the client's organization and create a road map, including identification of the investments that are needed. Doing this work up front can lessen the problems associated with oversight later.

Transitional Time Frame
Dalal insists that it is crucial to phase implementation of projects. Moreover, while it might seem simplistic, any processes put in place during the first phases must be carefully evaluated and debugged to ensure they actually work before beginning the next phase. Enough time to perform this analysis and diligence must be built into the project time frame.

Necessary Facilities and Infrastructure
One of the many challenges in working overseas, particularly in managing foreign facilities, is making them compatible with your needs from an infrastructure standpoint. As Chenevert observes, "the purchase of interests in foreign companies has been a bit of an education for our own people." In Caterpillar's U.S. operations, he explains, the plants are kept so clean that you can eat off of the floor, and the work areas are clearly delineated with

bright yellow paint lines. But in many less developed places in Asia where Caterpillar has looked at acquiring operations, some plants are open-air sheds with dirt floors. Chenevert is quick to point out that Caterpillar has found the same thing—open sheds with employees wearing dirty t-shirts—in other U.S. plants they have bought. If operations are not to your or your clients' taste, money and time will need to be allocated for upgrades in many cases.

The Bottom Line: Cost Savings Needed to Justify Costs and Risks

As Bhalla and virtually any other vendor will attest, the CEO and other chief officers all have to buy in to a project for it to go forward, and they are always going to be looking for a very quick return on investment. Still, as Samir Gandhi, a partner with Sidley, points out, you would be wise not to overestimate cost savings. While labor that might cost $8 per hour in the United States might only cost $1 per hour in India, there are other factors to consider in the overall cost of production. Is the market timing right to outsource this process? Gandhi presents a major company's help desk outsourcing project as an example where offshoring a process was premature: the project underestimated the value to end consumers of having someone come to their desks and physically assist them with their computer issues. Another consideration is the productivity of the low-cost source versus the domestic source. Still another is the quality of the output. Cheaper production with less quality does not always translate into effective cost savings. Gandhi asks the fundamental question: What is the "all in" cost? Will it require you to build a brand new plant or service center?

Companies moving call centers offshore have had to fight the perception that customer service suffers as a result and have had to deal with very real challenges, such as shortcomings in infrastructure and cultural differences.[42] It is worth considering that, given the high level of education of, for example, the Indian outsourcing workforce, moving work offshore might ultimately present an opportunity for *improved* customer service. Can implementation of the project include sufficient training and contingency

---

42. Alex Blyth, *Foreign Exchanges*, MKTG. WK., 43–44 (Feb. 13, 2003).

planning to guarantee a baseline of service? If not, is any quantum of cost savings enough to outweigh the disruption caused?

Cohen argues that, ultimately, when it comes to the counseling function, good lawyers have the ability to work on details *and* still keep sight of the bigger picture. I would add that it is the job of both outside and staff counsel to assist management in understanding how various details and issues affect the big picture. But once you have considered both the details and the bigger picture, and determined that savings and opportunities outweigh identifiable costs and risks, you are prepared to begin due diligence.

Chapter 4

Due Diligence Issues: An Overview

Managing a Complete Due Diligence Investigation

A general manager for a large manufacturer starting a business in China once told me that relationships must be in place before even starting what ordinarily is understood as "due diligence." There are a number of steps involved. Unless you want to court frustration and delay, you must first identify and obtain all the necessary internal approvals before proceeding. To obtain those approvals, it is necessary to conduct comprehensive technical and commercial feasibility studies. In both realms, a key question is "what type of foreign entity is suitable to do business with us?"

Strategic Considerations: Shacking Up versus Tying the Knot

Many companies that lack international experience are often too quick to fully commit to joint operations with a foreign business entity they barely know. Before jumping into a joint venture with a company halfway around the world, a company should first consider a licensing arrangement or perhaps a strategic partnership. A strategic partnership in business is much like "living together" is in a personal relationship—it gives the parties an opportunity to get to know each other before entering into a deeper commitment. The point is that if there is reticence on the part of senior management to go forward with a given international foray, starting with a more limited strategic partnership might provide an opportunity to sufficiently demonstrate the real-world benefits of the relationship to the extent that you can ultimately consummate a joint venture.

It is important to make sure that products, strategic vision, and legal issues are squared. It is also possible that a key member of management will change during the course of the project. One example of this would be where a new chief executive officer comes on board with a number of questions about an ongoing venture in an offshore location. Be prepared to address the various concerns of new stakeholders throughout the process and to defend the strategic rationale for continuing forward. As David L. Margulius rightly puts it, "the offshoring landscape is littered with the spectacular failures of companies that missed or lost sight of the big picture."[1] Do not let changes in senior management, which have become so frequent in recent years, cause you or your client to lose big-picture focus.

Even in relatively smaller companies, there is value in setting up a management steering committee that can take practical and philosophical ownership of an international project. This steering committee should include representatives of key operational groups to help ensure and maintain buy-in from them, the absence of which could likely create severe problems during implementation.[2] The committee's membership should also include personnel necessary to consider how internal needs, market conditions, distribution, and so on are likely to evolve over time, so the project as negotiated and implemented is not obsolete before the ink on the contract is dry.[3]

So just how should the steering committee strategize? Jay Horton lays out a pragmatic framework. Horton suggests that the key is to get the committee to agree and concentrate on a single "focal question" at the outset.[4] That question will vary depending on the company or the industry. As Horton suggests, the issues may be "How can we augment and leverage our

---

1. David L. Margulius, *Offshore Partnerships Demand a Wide Range of Expertise*, INFO WORLD, 35 (Aug. 25, 2005), *available at* http://www.infoworld.com/d/developer-world/offshore-partnerships-demand-wide-range-expertise-519.
2. Warren S. Reid, *Outsourcing: The 20 Steps to Success* 1 (1996), http://www.wsrcg.com/Articles/OutSourcing.pdf.
3. *Id.* at 2.
4. Jay Horton, *Expect the Unexpected*, 3 THE OUTSOURCING INSTITUTE (2005), http://www.outsourcing.com/content.asp?page=01b/other/oe/q405/expecttheunexp.html&nonav=false.

critical capabilities through our partners?" or "What are the priorities for [the project]: access to new resources, markets and technologies; or cost advantages from scale and scope economies?"[5]

Next, Horton suggests that you identify "driving forces" or the "causes of causes"—that is, what market or business forces are really pushing you to consider making the change (e.g., shareholder expectations or the ability to cut costs while still improving service), and the most uncertain forces (e.g., supplier ability to deliver as promised or maintain conformity with legal requirements).[6]

At this point, the committee should rank the key factors and driving forces on their importance to the overall success of the project and consider the amount of uncertainty surrounding them.[7] From a technical standpoint, it is necessary to examine infrastructure and processes currently in place, what changes current processes and existing infrastructure will support, and what enhancements will be needed to support improvements. As discussed later in this chapter, the committee can also seek advice and input during the discovery process from outside technology experts, and even from potential vendors, in order to develop key features for potential solution providers to address or to prepare a request for proposals. This allows you to construct divergent scenarios that avoid the dangers of "groupthink" and watered-down consensus. Is there a "win-win" solution under all likely scenarios? Is there a solution that has fantastic upside under some scenarios but great risks under others—risks that may be too great to take?[8]

Dean Davison points out that "a common oversight for IT organizations is a contingency plan—what happens if the vendor, all best intentions and contracts aside, simply fails to deliver."[9] Davison concludes that organizations should assess the implications of vendor failure (and, by extrapolation, any business partner failure) and shift its strategy (e.g., from a single vendor to multiple vendors) as appropriate.[10]

---

5. Id.
6. Id.
7. Id.
8. Id.
9. Dean Davison, *Top 10 Risks of Offshore Outsourcing*, META GROUP (Feb. 16, 2004), http://searchcio.techtarget.com/originalContent/0,289142,sid19_gci950602,00.html.
10. Id.

Horton's method of scenario building allows the committee to identify both risks and opportunities that might otherwise be ignored. It exposes those parts of the proposed project that require more research and analysis, and creates an atmosphere in which structured, yet innovative, thinking can occur and a company can have meaningful discussions with its lawyers, consultants, vendors, and overseas partners about its needs and concerns as it goes forward.[11]

The steering committee's work is not of the "one and done" variety. As new information is gathered and conditions change, the committee needs to re-evaluate its initial decision and make necessary adaptations to both the overall strategic framework generally and the implementation of the given project in particular.[12] Newly identified risks and the strategy for containing them must be factored in regularly.

Operational Considerations

Howard Mills, a tax director with Deloitte, insists that before moving into the diligence phase, the first phase is business. Unless a company is locating in a foreign country solely for a tax benefit, it is going there because it makes sense businesswise to be in a new market. Mills points out that, ultimately, it is the client organization that needs to make sure the business model works. "The tax tail and legal tail," Mills says dryly, "shouldn't wag the dog." If you have quantitatively determined that you will save 75 percent by moving a process overseas, the next step is to ask, "Now how am I going to implement?"

The answer to that question, says Vikas Bhalla, of EXL, begins with "baselining," or looking at implicated operations in detail. What are your current systems capable of delivering? If it is clear that the current systems and infrastructure you are dealing with cannot support the cost structure or level of service to which you aspire, it is necessary to first fix the processes before proceeding any further.[13]

---

11. Horton, *supra* note 4.
12. Reid, *supra* note 2, at 2.
13. Margulius, *supra* note 1.

The committee needs to identify critical staff, including personnel to train and help manage vendors and the new business partner's employees, intellectual property requirements, and other resources that must be made available to the overseas operation for the relationship to be successful.[14] Additionally, it is important to determine how to phase in new methods and players in such a way as to avoid undue business interruption,[15] and ensure that robust lines of communication—both in terms of technology (videoconferencing) and detailed communication protocols—adequate to the development and implementation of the project can be maintained.[16]

The first step is to understand the nature of the operational risks involved and to assess the probability of various risk types impacting the outsourced project or process.[17] The committee must address the four basic types of operational risk: "people, process, technology, and non-predictive events."[18] There are "people risks" throughout the course of any project of course, some of which we will deal with later in this chapter and others in subsequent chapters. At this point, it is important to remember there is always a very real risk due to perceived and actual loss of jobs at the firm's home locations.[19] Additionally, if employees with critical roles feel threatened by the changes happening around them, they are often well placed to wreak havoc in the later implementation of the project. So, addressing and calming the fears and misunderstandings of your own employees should begin early and be revisited often to ensure maximum buy-in.

Likewise, each of the other factors presents numerous risks. For instance, the lack of an effective knowledge management process can make vendors unduly dependent on certain key people, whose departure could cause delays and performance issues.[20] Information technology (IT) failures and encroachments can severely impact operations and create significant potential liabilities, given the unprecedented reach and speed of the Internet.[21]

---

14. Reid, *supra* note 2, at 1–2.
15. *Id.* at 2.
16. N. Raja Venkateswar, *Mitigating Operational Risk in Outsourcing*, INFO. MGMT. (May 2005), http://www.dmreview.com/specialreports/20050524/1028024-1.html.
17. *Id.*
18. *Id.*
19. *Id.*
20. *Id.*
21. *Id.*

"Nonpredictive risks" include both threats to a company's reputation and all-important brand identity, and the consequential damages incurred by stakeholders and shareholders.[22] After all is said and done, however, you may end up with net lower-risk probabilities by offshoring a process, due to the creation of better processes at the vendor site and improvements due to value-additions from vendors.[23]

Legal Structure

Many companies enter into their first overseas experience with a preconceived notion of how the transaction should be structured, based on how they organize themselves domestically or perhaps on what their direct competitors have done in a given market. Of course, the effects and consequences of the legal structure chosen are numerous and far reaching. Obtaining expert advice in this area is critical, since all the benefits of correctly doing everything else in the process can be erased by just one bad judgment call.

Mills has expertise in crafting structures that fit a client's business model and also works with a host of other requirements and concerns the client is unlikely to have thought about. Naturally, this includes an inquiry into the U.S. tax consequences of setting up a joint venture rather than a subsidiary or a branch or whatever other form of structure might be applicable.

Foreign tax consequences and capital repatriation must also be accounted for. Michel Feldman, of Seyfarth Shaw, notes that in some cases if you use a foreign subsidiary, you can take profits in lower tax countries. Deferral mechanisms can be made available. Of course, some nations have currency controls in place that may restrict some repatriation of profits earned there.[24] Developing countries have offered tax incentives to promote foreign

---

22. Id.
23. Id.
24. Ken Shiu, *Outsourcing: Are You Sure or Offshore? Identifying Legal Risks in Offshoring*, NSW Soc'y for Computers & L. (June 2004), https://www.nswscl.org.au/index.php?option=com_content&view=article&id=130:outsourcing-are-you-sure-or-offshore-identifying-legal-risks-in-offshoring&catid=28:june-2004-issue&Itemid=31.

investment in certain industries; India for instance has done so to promote its domestic IT industry.[25]

Finance and currency arbitrage can also be harnessed for the benefit of international business projects. One transaction Loring Knoblauch (of Underwriters' Laboratories) managed in Japan required payment of $60 million in eight yearly installments. He was able to borrow the money in Japan at the time at a rate of 1.5 percent. Don Chenevert, of Caterpillar, explains that currency fluctuations can be a significant enough factor in transactions that his company maintains an internal group that manages the hedging of its fluctuations. Of course, as Chenevert observes, the importance of currency issues to a given transaction depends in part on the scale of the transaction—is it three hundred thousand dollars or three hundred million?

But the analysis goes beyond simply crunching numbers. Mills asks clients point blank "What is the long-term goal?" and a series of other, related questions:

> Are we going to stick to this particular country, or are we going to Europe and then branch out? Do we want the capital permanently or long-term re-invested, or will we look to repatriate capital right away? What is the cost of putting additional capital in? How do I deal with debt vs. equity fund-in? What are the ramifications of bringing cash back to the U.S.? What is the cost of doing that? How can I structure it to repatriate more effectively? In the case of a publicly traded company, what are the consequences to the tax provision and the financial statements? What is the impact on EPS (Earnings per Share)?

After detailed consultation with the client company, Mills then works with his audit colleagues to identify additional bookkeeping or accounting issues. One such issue Mills has dealt with in the past is whether to structure an international project as a corporate subsidiary or as a "check-the-box entity," a term of art in which the company elects for U.S. tax purposes to be treated as either a pass-through entity or as a partnership, depending on whether the project is owned by one entity or by two or more.

---

25. *Id.*

Assuming that you prefer the tax treatment afforded to a "check-the-box entity," be careful to employ the kind of foreign structure that will allow you to take advantage of it. Mills has in the past offered an example of clients setting up a company in Canada. If the client used a corporate form called a Nova Scotia Unlimited Liability Company, it could be taxed as either a foreign corporation for U.S. tax purposes or a pass-through–type entity for U.S. tax purposes. Both approaches involve various kinds of planning opportunities and pitfalls. But if the same client set up its Canadian entity as an Ontario corporation, it would not have the opportunity to make a check-the-box selection.

Experts such as Mills can isolate specific planning issues that will assist you in determining which structure to choose to keep certain tax options open. If, for instance, the client anticipates that the venture is going to incur early losses, Mills points out that a "check-the-box," pass-through–type entity may allow the client to deduct those losses in the United States. In that instance, using the "check-the-box" form may reduce outgoing U.S. tax dollars. If, on the other hand, the client is doing business as a more standard corporation and does not check the box, those losses accumulate in the foreign jurisdiction but the client will not gain any immediate benefit from them in the United States. Which choice is more beneficial to the client in the long run has to be analyzed and addressed.

Mills reminds us that tax consequences do not occur in a vacuum. Specific aspects of contract law, commercial code, and statutes regarding capitalization within the operative foreign jurisdiction are all sometimes at odds with what you want to do from a U.S. tax or business perspective. There may not be a "perfect structure." In fact, usually there is not. Instead there are advantages and disadvantages to various scenarios, and the examination of likely scenarios can guide you in determining which is better for the client.

In short, when looking at various structures, take the time to consider all the options. A modified or hybrid structure may best serve your needs, cost savings objectives, and level of risk adversity or risk tolerance. Most businesses focus on the four primary transaction structures: outsourcing, joint ventures, direct foreign subsidiaries, and "BOOT" transactions (where the vendor builds, owns, operates, and then later transfers the operation to the client company).[26] Each has its strengths and weaknesses, which may not ideally match up with your needs.

Take for example the standard third-party vendor outsourcing arrangement. In its most basic form, the client contracts directly with a foreign entity. By doing so, the client company maintains maximum cost savings and a direct connection to the provider of products or services. But such an arrangement may often present the most risks in terms of cross-cultural dissonance, supervision and training issues, accountability, and so on.

An alternate model that has become very popular involves a client company contracting with a well-known service provider, such as IBM, that, in turn, outsources all or part of a project to lower-cost subcontractors.[27] Although cost savings may be diffused, and control is somewhat attenuated, attendant risks of the transaction can be transferred to a trusted partner with sufficient, available assets on which you can obtain recourse in a worst-case scenario.[28] Additionally, intellectual property, knowledge, and control of processes developed can be retained by the client.[29] For some clients, sacrificing a share of the cost savings to lay off risk represents a much better balancing of goals and objectives. The point to remember is that it is important to identify and consider all such alternatives before locking in partner selection and diligence processes.

Again, what is your endgame? Is it just to reduce costs or to develop a physical presence in a new market? Recognize that the deeper your commitment to an overseas market, the more will be expected of you. As author Ken Shiu points out, setting up a direct foreign subsidiary requires compliance with the foreign investment, labor, and tax laws of the offshore location.[30] Depending on the industry you are in, you might add many more areas such as data privacy, environmental, public health and safety, and so forth. Ongoing compliance and management costs have to be accounted for as

---

26. *Id.*
27. *Id.*
28. *Id.*
29. Shalini Agarwal & Sakate Khaitan, *The Case for Offshore Outsourcing in the Legal Sector*, ALMT LEGAL INDIA BRIEF (January 2005) http://almtlegal.com/newsletters-pdf/India%20Brief%20January%202005.pdf.
30. Shiu, *supra* note 24.

well.[31] And it is well recognized that a captive subsidiary will mean more capital investment for the client and is not as appropriate unless you are contemplating a longer-term strategy.[32]

Specific models have unique issues that must also be addressed. Setting up a joint venture company in the offshore territory generally involves leveraging local knowledge and resources of the foreign partner.[33] Shiu notes that under joint venture arrangements, appropriate contractual and governance structures need to be in place to avoid potential conflicts of interest and to address contribution valuation, shareholder exit, dispute resolution, and supervision issues that the model creates.[34] Whatever structure is ultimately chosen, it must be designed in such a way that compliance with U.S. and foreign law and industry standards is unimpeded.

Retaining and Managing Consultants

Consultants are an expensive addition to any project, and so there is naturally a concern about their role in any given transaction. As we will discuss throughout the remainder of this text, however, some issues require expertise beyond that found within a client's own organization, or even within the client's outside counsel. Recognizing what those issues are goes a long way toward answering the next logical questions: What types of consultants are needed, and how can they be used most cost-effectively?

Mills believes that no matter what issues are involved, one of the most important things to look for in consultants is an ability to see the "big picture." He has found that his clients "want their professionals to help and challenge them, and come up with ideas of how their business model can be improved." So each issue, no matter how technical, has to be evaluated as to whether proposed solutions make sense in terms of the overall business model. Mills gives an example of a transaction that promised 75 percent

---

31. *Id.*
32. Agarwal & Khaitan, *supra* note 29.
33. *Id.*
34. Shiu, *supra* note 24.

cost savings, but that as you repatriate, cash incurs 40 percent in extra taxes. Does the overall business proposition still work in light of that?

Small and medium-sized businesses in particular are sensitive to the significant expense that consulting fees represent. Still, Mills cautions that clients

> have to weigh the one-time set-up fee vs. their planning on being there long term and making a significant investment. And the client should budget a percentage of what they are going to invest and say it is just part of the investment to get the professionals involved.

In a cross-cultural context, assume that your consulting team will include, at a minimum, two sets of professionals: one versed in the subject matter from a U.S. perspective and one familiar with the situation on the ground in the anticipated foreign location. Mills adds that in more complicated transactions involving multiple jurisdictions, more sets of professionals may be needed.

It is not necessary to look beyond the issue of investing in appropriate professional support to understand why so many international transactions fail to live up to client expectations. Mills sums it up succinctly:

> If the client wants to succeed they have to do their homework up front and part of that homework is going to require an investment up front in time and money. They're going to need to get the right people involved to get some education, and education costs money. Most of the foreign business executives that you talk to at the bigger companies will tell you that when you're going into a country for the first time, that you've got to spend time and money to get up to speed and get a couple of your own people on the ground to make it work.

That education is often going to be a continuing process throughout the project. Early on, an expert team should be formed of those outside consultants from critical fields who can assist through the negotiation and implementation of the project.[35] This will generally include people with

---

35. Reid, *supra* note 2, at 2.

experience facilitating across cultures to guarantee smooth administration and those with knowledge of local politics and regulations to ensure the contract takes into account the quirks of the foreign domicile.[36] In addition to having the benefit of the experts' subject matter knowledge, the expert team also gives you the benefit of independent, critical thinking. Keep in mind that in many instances where you are trying to improve a product or service, the decisions of your in-house people may be affected by their own perceived or real deficiencies.[37]

It is also reasonable to expect that your in-house team might differ in its views of a project's scope or objectives. The independent subject matter experts can be of assistance in helping to drive the various parties toward a unified and defined scope and objectives set.

When considering the overall viability and profitability of an overseas operation, trying to cut corners in the diligence and risk management arenas is—in a word—inadvisable. While it may be that, as CSO Online succinctly put it, "It ain't cheap," diligence is part of the cost of doing business:

> For business process outsourcing, which can involve highly sensitive data, risk management measures can eat up 15 percent to 19 percent of the cost savings of going offshore, according to researchers at Tower Group. For software development, which involves less access to sensitive data, due diligence and risk management eat up 6 percent to 10 percent of the savings. Yet even then, the overall savings are there.[38]

Charles Hallab, of Baker & McKenzie, has a simple maxim that underscores this point: "The more you invest, the more sophisticated the diligence needs to be." Hallab adds that the more sophisticated the diligence needs to be, the more comfortable clients should be with lawyers being involved "early and heavily."

---

36. *Ib.* at 4.
37. *Id.* at 2.
38. Christopher Koch, *Don't Export Security When Outsourcing*, IT WORLD CANADA (June 23 2005), http://www.itworldcanada.com/article/dont-export-security-when-outsourcing/13009.

Strategic Concerns Surrounding Intellectual Property: A Preview

In a knowledge-based economy, virtually any company in any industry has to be concerned about protecting intellectual property (IP). As Peter J. Gerken points out,

> approximately 60 to 80 percent of companies' assets today are intangible. They include brands, technology, and know-how, as well as the legally protected assets, defined as intellectual property. Essential for attracting investment, particularly for small- and medium-size businesses, IP allows companies to charge premium prices and increase their market share. It gives companies of all sizes freedom to operate in patented areas.[39]

For small and medium enterprises in particular, IP assets are necessary to attract investment.[40]

IP touches not just a company's legal department but its finance, research and development, and other departments as well.[41] One of the most common IP issues in business today is infringement liability litigation, much of which is uninsured.[42] Gerken points out that both parties in an IP suit face extensive legal costs, and adverse verdicts can cause extensive money damages or the loss of a counted-on property right that may have been used as collateral in financing, for example.[43] Insurance products may be available to address some risks in this area, including IP enforcement coverage and protection from lost profit due to patent invalidity, injunctions, or defective title.[44] Cross-licensing agreements may be negotiated with competitors to cut off potential infringement suits.[45] Otherwise, companies need to

---

39. Peter J. Gerken, *Gray Matters: Protecting and Increasing the Value of Intellectual Property*, MARSH & MCLENNAN COMPANIES, http://www.mmc.com/knowledgecenter/viewpoint/archive/spring03Gerken.php (last visited Feb. 14, 2014).
40. *Id.*
41. *Id.*
42. *Id.*
43. *Id.*
44. *Id.*
45. *Id.*

budget and plan for litigation expense in this area as part of their strategic planning.[46] The complex issues raised in this critical area are dealt with in detail in Chapter 8.

The Impact of Regulatory Concerns on Due Diligence

Chenevert relies on outside counsel for advice on issues presented by international trade regimes, such as World Trade Organization (WTO) regulations, the Agreement on Trade-Related Aspects of Intellectual Property (TRIPS), and various bilateral and multilateral agreements between nations. What he has seen regarding WTO issues is that since national governments sign off on bilateral or multilateral trade agreements, they are responsible for implementing them. Unfortunately, some governments have not funded implementation or have not yet issued the necessary regulations. Since for issues such as IP, implementation of various regulations is critical, he has worked through local embassies to ensure there is actually a rule with which to comply. Still, Chenevert warns, you often have to move forward knowing that unanswered regulatory questions exist.

Regulatory issues can also arise because of conflicting positions taken by different national agencies. Karen Klein, formerly of Orbitz and Kayak.com, gives the example of travel agents caught in a potential bind between a U.S. Department of Transportation request for travelers' data and European Union (EU) privacy laws. There is an exception in the EU privacy policy for requests by foreign governments, but the point is that part of your diligence process should be to identify potential regulatory traps and, if necessary, work with the relevant agencies to craft a mutually acceptable solution—before any legal unpleasantness results.

---

46. *Id.*

The Importance of Defined Scope and Objectives as a Part of Due Diligence

In many of the hottest developing markets, having a defined scope for your new business is not optional. Attorney Richard Wageman, of DLA Piper, points out that in China for instance, when establishing a legal business entity, the governmental authorities have required the business entity—that is, the foreign-invested enterprise—to have a defined business scope. Moreover, your ability to operate within that scope will depend in part on the level of foreign investment involved in your venture.

The definition of scope and objectives comes from the strategizing discussed earlier in this chapter. If the steering committee to this point has done its job, you should know, for instance, whether you will try to build a business from the ground up in the foreign location or acquire an existing organization, the amount you can afford to invest, and the scope of processes you will be outsourcing. Is it a routinized process? Is it a core process that requires independent judgment?

One approach to consider in the outsourcing decision is an impact assessment. That is, have the steering committee identify all the activities inside and outside of the firm that the process in question affects and then estimate "the impact on efficiency, effectiveness and productivity of those activities if they did not have access to the process" to be outsourced.[47] Have other companies outsourced a similar process, or have their results demonstrated benefits to keeping it in-house?[48]

If the decision is to outsource, the client must have given some definite thought to its level of risk tolerance or risk aversion. That is because, as it starts to develop a request for proposal, the client will have to strike a balance between the amount of control it gets to keep over the vendor and the amount of innovation it might like to receive from the work of its vendor.[49] Skipping over all the strategy and analysis at this point in the process will require ad hoc decision making on key issues without sufficient

---

47. Exervio Management Consulting, *Do You Really Want to Outsource that Process?*, 3 (May 2004), http://www.slideshare.net/Shelly38/do-you-really-want-to-outsource-that-process.
48. *Id.*
49. *Id.* at 4.

input from all relevant players at moments of higher stress. That is not a recipe for success. The analysis and planning may seem overly structured and time consuming, but whether or not you do this work on the front end is probably the best predictor for whether the transaction as a whole will succeed. Consider it a huge, expensive math problem. Be prepared to show your work!

We will next consider the process of selecting an overseas destination for your transaction.

Chapter 5

Due Diligence: Evaluating Offshore Destinations

Overview: Where in the World Do You Want to Do Business?

Based on the attention they have received in the media in recent years, it is easy to get the impression that China and India are the only places where U.S. businesses are investing overseas. To be fair, as both of these mammoth economies have deregulated key market sectors and relaxed foreign investment caps, they have seen a flood of new businesses set up within their boundaries. But as mentioned earlier in this text, they are not the only game in town. As Harvey Cohen, of Dinsmore & Shohl, observes, a lot of foreign investment continues to go to Europe, Mexico, and Canada.

As a matter of fact, virtually every country in the world beckons investors to come to their environs. Depending on the industry and your need for quick repatriation for capital, infrastructure requirements, and so on, there are likely to be dozens of potential locations for a new subsidiary, joint venture, or distribution network. The question is: How do you choose the right location? This chapter will assist you with this crucial decision.

Purely Exogenous versus Semi-Exogenous Factors

Many authorities have arrived at various factors for determining which venues to choose and which to avoid, and, if nothing else, they serve as a good starting point for an examination. Indian outsourcing mainstay NeoGroup (formerly known as Neo IT) has offered a straightforward approach to classifying and analyzing the risks faced within various overseas business destinations for their clients. They classify the key factors as either purely exogenous—that is, pervasive factors that generally cannot be mitigated—or semi-exogenous—that is, factors that can be at least partly offset through individual strategy, investments, hiring decisions, and employee development practices.[1]

The purely exogenous factors identified by NeoGroup are prevailing labor costs, socio- and geopolitical risks, physical and time zone displacement, ecosystem and trade options, and business environment. The semi-exogenous factors are communications, culture, infrastructure, and prevalence of distinctive competencies.[2]

Prevailing Labor Costs

Clearly, cost savings and the wage arbitrage that makes them possible are an important, if not paramount, concern for many companies doing business across borders.[3] It is worth noting however that even if costs are the sole or primary driver, it is still necessary to be looking beyond the prevailing hourly wage in a given country or region. That is to say, it is not a given that if wages in China are 50 cents per hour while in Vietnam they are 40 cents per hour, you should always choose Vietnam. That is because the gross wages in a given country do not in themselves tell what the true net labor cost really will be.

Take, for example, productivity of the workforce. If as in the previous example, wages are 50 cents per hour and 40 cents per hour in China and Vietnam, respectively, and it takes a given Vietnamese workforce 50 percent longer to turn out the same amount of goods or services as a given Chinese

---

1. NEOIT, NO. 7, MAPPING OFFSHORE MARKETS, OFFSHORE INSIGHTS, 2 (April 2003).
2. Id.
3. Id.

workforce, then the small hourly wage advantage that Vietnam provides is clearly not going to save money in the long run. This is just one example. Organizations must guard against inflated expectations about how much they can save on labor costs in low-wage destinations. Dean Davison notes that after considering "hidden costs and differences in operating models, most IT organizations save only 15–25 percent during the first year."[4] These savings increase over time as the client company better adapts to the offshore model.[5]

A number of the other factors we will discuss have some effect on what the true net labor cost to your organization actually is. As you calculate the effect of each factor, an individual company's risk adversity or risk tolerance may influence your perception of its impact on your operations. It is important to remember though, that no matter how risk tolerant you are, you should build in some sort of price differential to take identified risks into account.

Socio- and Geopolitical Risks

This category includes risks such as "border unrest, religious strife, unstable political processes, government policies (taxes, duties, and regulatory hurdles), international relations, war, and probability of terrorist-related incidents."[6] You can buy political risk insurance coverage, notes Jed Hepworth, of Cargill, but just understand that it generally has a lot of restrictions on it. And don't forget bilateral investment treaties in your structuring decisions; you can invest via a company that enjoys "BIT" protection and add a layer of protection against expropriation or discriminatory treatment without buying an individual policy.

Lesley Lahm, a lawyer with more than 20 years of experience in both the private and public sectors in Asia, will tell you from experience that overseas, you have to go in with eyes wide open and have a strong understanding of the local situation. "It is critical that one has a strong understanding of the

---
4. Dean Davison, *Top 10 Risks of Offshore Outsourcing*, META GROUP (Feb. 16, 2004), http://searchcio.techtarget.com/originalContent/0,289142,sid19_gci950602,00.html.
5. *Id.*
6. N. Raja Venkateswar, *Mitigating Operational Risk in Outsourcing*, INFO. MGMT. (May 2005), http://www.dmreview.com/specialreports/20050524/1028024-1.html.

potential risks involved in entering a foreign market where the rules of the game can be vastly different from what one is used to."

How well do you know the current political situation, not just in the countries that you are considering but also within the specific provinces or states and communities in which your operations will be? And how up-to-date is your information? Particularly in developing nations, the ground can shift dramatically in a relatively short time. Are you relying on dated data? As Keith Nelsen, General Counsel at Best Buy, says, "you simply cannot do enough pre-due diligence—not just legal and structural, but commercial and cultural."

"Due diligence has been refined to a science in the U.S.," notes Baker & McKenzie's Charles Hallab, "and the rest of the world is slowly adopting." One of the great challenges in the international transactional context, says Hallab, is "how do you get information on the ground?"

It is critical that you get updated information from someone who is on the ground in the subject location in order to get an accurate view of these types of risks. Lesley Lahm stresses a strong country risk assessment based on going to people who already do business in the subject location: "Institutions and individuals who are familiar with your way of doing business." Naturally, Hallab points to the ability of his firm, Baker & McKenzie, to survey a given locale's political risk. Baker currently has over 70 offices in 46 different countries around the world.[7] In those countries where it does not have an office, Baker maintains close correspondence with firms in proximate jurisdictions.

Lahm warns of the dangers of approaching a random local firm for such an assignment: "While local law firms can provide invaluable advice, it is important to familiarize yourself with any political connections they may have. You need to understand the regulatory situation you are working under too."

Ed Bathelt, of Komatsu America, agrees that selecting overseas local counsel is a challenge. In the United States, he explains, you develop resources that tell you who works well in a given jurisdiction—websites, various

---

7. *Firm Facts*, BAKER & MCKENZIE, http://www.bakermckenzie.com/firmfacts/ (last visited Feb. 14, 2014).

chambers of commerce, etc. But in unfamiliar places, such as Ecuador, who do you have to tell you who is good? Bathelt continues:

> In a multinational business concern, there are so many countries in which you have to hire people for specific purposes. You often don't get to meet everyone in their offices. You make choices with references from others.

In the end, Bathelt concludes, "it's a learning process."

What kinds of sources can help with preparing the country risk assessment? Lesley Lahm points to the International Monetary Fund, Transparency International reports, and think tanks. For smaller businesses that are budget conscious, she states that hiring an expensive consulting firm may not necessarily be needed. Organizations such as the International Finance Corporation, Asian Development Bank, and World Bank put a lot of information online. Another good idea is to maintain consistent contact with the in-country U.S. Embassy Commercial Services Division and the U.S. Chamber of Commerce to stay abreast of any potential or developing political risks.[8] Additionally, for example, every year the U.S. Chamber of Commerce in Beijing produces a white paper with current, updated information about doing business in China, on an industry-by-industry basis.

Jed Hepworth of Cargill adds a number of things to think about in terms of political risk:

> Is there a degree of predictability in the judicial system? What kind of investor protection laws do they have? Is there an ability to repatriate profits? Does the location feature security of ownership over property? What kind of facilities do you want to locate in the country, and are you a recognized brand?

One general counsel, who spoke on condition of anonymity, has explained that medium-sized and small businesses generally have less to worry about in terms of political risk. Globally recognized companies with "branded

---

8. Antoinette Forth, *Offshore, On Strategy*, 114 U.S. BANKER 56 (May 2005).

consumers" such as Proctor and Gamble and Nestle have more of chance of being targeted by governments in political risk terms than a low-profile company that local politicians and local protesters haven't heard about. That said, when a government goes looking for companies to blame for corruption or shortages or quality problems, a foreign company is an easy target, as recent experience in China suggests. And, warns the anonymous general counsel mentioned above, "being smaller and low profile doesn't mean that you won't get leaned on for bribes—it can tempt local officials to pressure a company they see as relatively powerless."

Dr. David Liu, formerly of Aon and Zurich Greater China, warns that it is essential to do your research if you are going to do business in China. His points however, are just as valid for many developing nations whose legal systems are struggling to conform to global business standards. In China, Liu explains, any action is legal, illegal, or alegal. The alegal or grey area constitutes the zone of "do it at your own risk." "If you are in that grey area," Liu cautions, "check what you are doing very carefully." With that caveat, you should endeavor to move without delay, because, as the Chinese say, "if timing is correct, do it quickly—for tomorrow there is a law against it."

Keith Nelsen asks, "If you are looking at new geography, what's the picture in terms of the destination's willingness to allow FDI [foreign direct investment]?" Rules are different, Nelsen notes. Sometimes local capital rules end up dictating structure. You may need to find a local partner. Specifically, Nelsen asks you to consider what type of business you want to have and what type of structure fits best. Lesley Lahm warns in connection with working with indigenous businesses, "JV [joint venture] structures can be dangerous but are often required in order for foreign businesses to operate in-country. If there is a falling out among the parties, one should assume the local partner will have the upper hand in terms of attempting to resolve any disputes."

One question to consider is do you need to be based in a particular country at all to do business there? One alternative to going straight to a number of countries in Southeast Asia, advises attorney Rod Jacob, is to consider a base of operations in Guam. Guam is the best venue for doing business with Japan and the Philippines in Jacob's view. First, the territory is still part of the United States. That means it has all the stability of the U.S. system. The courts follow the U.S. Federal Rules and Codes, and the Federal District Court can confirm an award in arbitration, allowing enforcement in a number of foreign countries (e.g., a Philippine company operating in Vietnam). Moreover, Jacob argues, Guam works out to be a far less expensive base of Pacific Rim operations than alternatives such as Hong Kong, Singapore, or Tokyo. Guam has daily nonstop flights to Japan and the Philippines and daily flights to Seoul. Just as importantly for many pragmatic U.S.-based executives, Jacob concludes, Guam represents "a good place to bring your family for a couple of weeks."

Even if a revolution is not impending, knowing the details of conditions in a given region can be important to avoid negative consequences. Samir Gandhi, of Sidley Austin, offers the example of a Singapore-based company with a subsidiary in India. In recent years, a fair amount of investment to India has traveled through Mauritius, an island nation of just over 1.2 million people, located in the Indian Ocean, east of Madagascar, which has a well-developed financial sector. There are, however, tax issues in India that have arisen from such transactions. In particular, Indian authorities have considered whether there is enough activity in Mauritius to avoid having a "permanent establishment" in India and thus increased tax liability. Advising clients at such a nuanced level is only possible when you have an accurate and up-to-date awareness of the overall situation in a given locale.

The complications of local laws must not be overlooked in the diligence process. As U.S. State Department official Martin Lahm reminds us, "all politics is local." Don Chenevert, of Caterpillar, relates that a number of jurisdictions he has worked in have restricted the amount of foreign ownership within certain industries or business sectors. In some locations, things are changing for the better, however. For those interested in doing business in China, Richard Wageman, of DLA Piper, notes that in most business sectors, the minimum capitalization levels have been substantially reduced. Shrikar Dole, formerly of the Federation of Indian Export Organisations, has noted that there are few structural roadblocks in establishing a distribution network in India today. Retail marketing was restricted until 2006, when 51 percent foreign ownership in retail joint ventures was allowed. It was the same in manufacturing 20 years ago. The permissible foreign stake moved from 20 to 50 percent, then to 75 and eventually 100 percent.

Chenevert emphasizes that it is often necessary to negotiate buy-in from multiple levels of foreign governments. So the political situation needs to be considered not only at the national level but also at the provincial and local levels. McDonald's is finding this out as it deals with provincial differences in China, notes Liu. "They are doing very good business in the provinces, but have to deal with different officials, dialects and customs," Liu concludes.

Dealing with local politics and political players raises particular issues and concerns. Martin Lahm points out that local politics often involve very strong competing interests. As such, he emphasizes that

> operating among them has to be done with recognition that it's not the same as Peoria. Being in business with the wrong people can become a real problem. Many countries including those in Southeast Asia, for example, have the disease of oligarchs. If you partner with party A, and tomorrow A & B are fighting, you can quickly find yourself on the wrong side. Remember: unless you are a member of the family, you are always on the outside.

Hepworth wholeheartedly agrees:

> Know who you are dealing with up front—don't be impatient. It's common for outsiders to favor a guy who graduated from a U.S. university and speaks impeccable English and then fail to look into his family and business connections. It is always important to do your due diligence and have a long-term view. The partner you choose for his political connections is likely to have a corresponding set of political enemies. Being seen as having taken sides by the choice of your partner can make his enemies your enemies. And if you end up in a dispute with a politically powerful partner, that political power can be used against you—and what you originally saw as an advantage can be a big disadvantage. Companies that endure and thrive in countries where they operate as foreign investors never forget that they are guests.

A location can pose regulatory traps for the unwary, as well, warns Clemens Ceipek, Global Product Officer for LexisNexis. Ceipek tells the story of being asked by an Austrian company at which he was employed to liquidate a Hungarian subsidiary, which still had cash in Hungarian bank accounts. He learned that the managing director had left in the early 1990s and, under Hungarian law, the directorship had expired. When Ceipek learned that the new director would personally assume potential liabilities the subsidiary still had on the books—and that the new director might not be allowed to leave Hungary until the liabilities were satisfied—the Austrian parent decided to write off the amount left under account.

Exchange rate fluctuations, local currency inflation rates, applicable interest rates, and other financial issues may affect the foreign exchange rate involved in the operation of the project.[9] Ignoring these factors can convert a cost-savings exercise into regular quarterly losses—and numerous apologies and explanations.

Another very important strategic consideration is whether it is possible—considering a given country's current bilateral relationship with the United States or the overseas destination's own laws—to move data, employees, materials, or goods and services as needed for your operations.[10] Failure to identify any such issue before operations commence could lead to major disruptions and perhaps threaten the viability of the entire venture. (Detailed discussion of issues surrounding this topic follows in Chapter 9.)

According to Karen Klein, formerly of Orbitz and Kayak.com, it is also important to consider the full effect of legal sanctions that apply to doing business with certain nations. For instance, the U.S. government maintains significant political and economic sanctions against the nation of Cuba. A British travel company that is purchased by a U.S. company can no longer write any Cuban travel. Or consider that in the European Union (EU), travel agents may have a duty to investigate the facilities they book for their clients. So, if a U.S. travel agent books a client into a "firetrap" hotel, might the travel agent be liable under EU law? A travel agent has a number of other compliance issues to take into account. The Office of Foreign

---

9. Venkateswar, *supra* note 6.
10. Kevin C. Taylor, *Legal Briefs*, 3 THE OUTSOURCING INSTITUTE (2005), http://www.outsourcing.com/content.asp?page=01b/other/oe/q405/lawyers.html&nonav=false.

Assets Control, as an agency of the U.S. Department of the Treasury, may impose a separate duty to investigate that you are not booking travel for a "known terrorist."

It is necessary to ask whether establishing a relationship in a given locale will cause the client company to be subject to foreign laws and courts.[11] Understanding the full dimensions of your liabilities under the laws of various jurisdictions provides a clearer picture of just what sorts of socio- and geopolitical risks a venture faces. Martin Lahm, of the U.S. State Department, warns that many courts in Southeast Asia for example are, in his view, "problematic." "Judges often look to their own interests or succumb to local pressures, and local lawyers may not watch out for your interests," he opines. His advice? Include an international arbitration clause—not venued in the region—in London or New York to the extent possible, or otherwise Hong Kong or Singapore. And if the deal is China-based, he suggests not arbitrating in Hong Kong. That said, you need to be careful not to paint with too broad a brush, and take the time to carefully examine the courts and applicable law in the subject foreign jurisdiction as well as the range of likely and potential disputes you would have to bring before a judge there before too quickly committing to a default arbitration versus litigation decision.

Any company operating overseas must also develop appropriate contingency plans and exit strategies should a political situation suddenly deteriorate. As part of an organization's need to consider business continuity issues, the steering committee should consider whether its operations could quickly be brought home in an emergency.[12] In Asia, as in many parts of the developing world, volatility is many times hidden just beneath the surface. As Martin Lahm states, a crucial question international businesspeople have to ask when considering a foreign location is, "When it all goes wrong, how do we protect what we've got?" He offers a sobering point of view:

> Always have a set of exit strategies—contingency plans for pulling out. What is your plan B? Things may go well, but you still need to

---
11. *Id.*
12. Basel Committee on Banking Supervision, *Outsourcing in Financial Services*, THE JOINT FORUM, 7 (Feb. 2005), https://www.bis.org/publ/joint12.pdf.

revisit this regularly. If your money, equipment, and technology are physically located in a foreign jurisdiction, you may need to consider them gone if something goes wrong—or even if it doesn't. When a joint venture breaks up, [your former partners] will make the product five miles away. Typically, the time frame is short before competitors discover there is money to be made. This puts a premium on nimbleness.

One way to avoid the downside risks that come from worst-case political risk situations is to adapt a short-term operation such as the manufacture of cheap goods with low technology. "If need be, you can abandon it," Mr. Lahm counsels. In his opinion, selling an experience is an excellent way to enter markets. "That's why fast food and Apple have done so well," he explains.

Still, Mr. Lahm believes that Google went into China with the best business model—selling something that doesn't exist, other than in cyberspace. When Google decided to pull out of China, the withdrawal took place with remarkable speed. "And by doing that," Mr. Lahm muses, "Google loses what? The China search market?" Google actually helped its brand by leaving China, Mr. Lahm reckons.

Your business simply may not have the luxury of choosing to avoid a significant physical investment in a new market. If that is true, however, it only underscores the importance of the diligence that your team must do into the risks discussed above.

Physical and Time Zone Displacement

Common sense says that the farther away your overseas partners are from your home office, the more difficult and expensive it becomes to regularly visit and supervise or monitor operations there. Likewise, if the location is many time zones distant, logistical difficulties in coordinating conference calls or videoconferences may result.

Some companies actually use time zone delays to their advantage, as in the famous "follow the sun" practices developed by the software industry. This allows work to be passed from one part of the globe to the next, with the result that projects get attention 24 hours a day. Moreover, depending on the size and sophistication of your commitment, it may be wise to spread around your operations a little. Dole notes that as the result of currency issues, politics, and overall risk management, many companies already manufacturing in China are seeking to diversify by manufacturing in India. Dole's observation is consistent with "risk portfolio assessment" techniques advocated by Rod Kleinhammer, of Deloitte:

> Such an assessment applies established stock portfolio management concepts to a company's portfolio of outsourcing initiatives in order to reduce overall risk through diversification. The aim is to position IT development or business process activities in different geographies in order to maximize the operational cost savings and manage the risk of project or business interruption.[13]

The endgame is straightforward enough: "Find the highest incremental return offered by geographic and business function choices at the lowest risk of business disruption."[14]

Like investing in stocks, "the company must balance high potential returns with equally high risks should political, regulatory or economic conditions shift." But unlike with stocks, Kleinhammer notes, your failure may cost more than the amount invested—"the future success of the company may be at risk."[15] To avoid this, companies must assess risk and benefit and create a "portfolio" of transaction locations "to match their desired risk-reward profile."[16] How vital is the subject process or activity to the company's success? The more vital, the more one should keep it in a low-risk venue. Others with a less direct impact on the bottom line under this approach can be moved to places with more cost-saving opportunities but also more political risk.[17] The creation of such a portfolio "requires data, analysis, constant monitoring and planning."[18]

---

13. Rod Kleinhammer, Todd Nelsen & A.J. Warner, *Balancing the Risks* (June 1, 2003) www.darwinmag.com, http://www.zoominfo.com/CachedPage/?archive_id=0&page_id=1578438396&page_url=//www.darwinmag.com/read/060103/risk.html&page_last_updated=2006-06-11T07:00:34&firstName=Todd&lastName=Nelsen.
14. *Id.*
15. *Id.*
16. *Id.*
17. *Id.*
18. Venkateswar, *supra* note 6.

For others, the answer to this issue is "nearshoring." This involves choosing an overseas location in the same or a nearby region or time zone as the clients. While in some instances, sacrifices in labor and other costs need to be made to take advantage of a closer overseas base of operations, some companies prefer the greater opportunity for direct control.[19]

Such risk hedging may have less priority in your plans, though, depending on the reasons you are moving overseas and the industry. Howard Mills, of Deloitte, observes that Mexico has gotten a lot of outsourcing just because of its proximity to the United States. "Especially in the goods area," Mills adds, "if you're a manufacturer you don't want to ship goods to India and back—it's much closer to do it in Mexico." In the case of services, Internet connections and phone connections render the distance between Michigan and India or Mexico meaningless. But container costs and the time required to ship goods suggest that Mexico will continue to be an outsourcing player, in Mills' estimation. The analysis and strategy of the steering committee will, as in many areas, help you arrive at the right decision for your client.

Ecosystem and Trade Options

What we are talking about here is market access. The steering committee may have determined that a strategic goal of your company should be to access the Latin American or European market. If true, relatively lower costs or other advantages elsewhere are not likely to be very persuasive.

In locales that have been deemed particularly desirable in recent years, such as China, foreign direct investment and local job creation may well be expected by government officials as a quid pro quo to obtain market access.[20] As NeoGroup rightly points out, laying such groundwork can net you valuable experience in the target location and good business contacts.[21]

Business Environment

This factor includes issues such as "taxes, ease of dispute resolution through the legal system, ease of starting a business, and intellectual property

---

19. NEOIT, *supra* note 1, at 3.
20. *Id.*
21. *Id.*

protection."[22] How favorable are government policies toward competitiveness, and to what extent are local businesses able to perform in an "innovative, profitable and responsible" manner?[23] Are there trade associations, such as NASCOM in India, or direct government support in the target locale in your industry sector?[24] Are tax breaks available for setting up businesses in particular parts of a country or provinces, or in relation to particular industries?

Samir Gandhi of Sidley advises that India has a greater respect for contracts and the rule of law than many other foreign destinations do, because Indian law is based on the English common law. In other developing nations, the legal systems that allow for the enforcement of contracts are lacking, resulting in "hold-up problems" that undermine the offshore venture.[25]

In any event Gandhi warns, "you do have to ask, what kind of licensing will be required?" Although many firms will attempt to enforce written agreements, noncontractual enforcement of intellectual property (IP) rights is important as well and "is heavily influenced by cultural and resource factors which are often at a level below the expectations of many Western countries."[26] As discussed later in detail, in-depth IP due diligence must also be undertaken prior to negotiating an offshore operation.

Additionally, as also discussed more fully in a later chapter, labor laws can add some unexpected twists. For example, under Indian law, Gandhi notes, city women are not allowed to work after hours. You also have to consider whether local labor laws require employers to guarantee a certain number of jobs or affect your ability to fire employees under various circumstances. Germany, for instance, presents a complex regulatory framework in terms of dismissing employees. Mills offers another example:

---

22. *Id.*
23. Venkateswar, *supra* note 6.
24. NeoIT, *supra* note 1, at 3.
25. Daniel Trefler, *Offshoring: Threats and Opportunities* 25 (July 22, 2005) (prepared for the Brookings Trade Forum 2005, *The Offshoring of Services: Issues and Implications*, May 12–13, 2005, Washington, D.C.).
26. Ken Shiu, *Outsourcing: Are You Sure or Offshore? Identifying Legal Risks in Offshoring*, NSW Soc'y for Computers & L. (June 2004), https://www.nswscl.org.au/index.php?option=com_content&view=article&id=130:outsourcing-are-you-sure-or-offshore-identifying-legal-risks-in-offshoring&catid=28:june-2004-issue&Itemid=31.

Say you've got this legal requirement that's going to cost you because of social insurance. Or you aren't planning on having to capitalize for 10 million dollars but that is what you're going to need to do in this particular sector in this particular country. Should we maybe be looking at some other place to do this transaction if we're going to do it at all? In Mexico the cost of closing up a plant is prohibitive. You've got to consider that when you go in . . . it's going to cost you some money to get out. You can't just turn off the spigot and say "I'm done."

Liability standards also must be evaluated, advises Gandhi. The client needs to consider what exposure the parties have under U.S. and foreign law, such as what export control issues are involved and the consequences of contracting with government customers. Moreover, the team members charged with responsibility for risk management must determine whether insurance adequately covers potential loss and whether you should require the vendor to purchase insurance.

Communications

India produces two million English-speaking graduates each year.[27] Still, communication capability is about more than just speaking the same language. It includes "accents, use of colloquialisms, and even body language."[28] In services and other models that require significant amounts of verbal interaction, such as customer contact, employee support, and telemarketing, consideration might be given to a labor pool with natural English skills (i.e., Ireland, Canada, the Philippines, India, and, according to NeoGroup, Bulgaria).[29]

Culture

We often fail to appreciate how much our cultural assumptions color our expectations and drive our reactions until we are forced to interact with those who do not share them. Religious observances, dress, social activities,

---

27. NeoIT, *supra* note 1, at 5.
28. *Id.* at 3.
29. *Id.*

and the appropriate method for answering a question are all affected by the cultural context involved.[30]

Cultural differences can be worked around, but it is fair to say you will have to expect that delays and mistakes will occur as your people and their foreign counterparts learn to work together. This aspect is difficult even for seasoned transactional experts such as Mills, of Deloitte. As Mills explains,

> even with our affiliation and the shared values that we try to instill in all the professionals around the world, it's hard to coordinate and talk the same languages as the guy in the foreign jurisdiction—and get the same deadlines. You know that's probably one of my biggest challenges when I'm working with the folks overseas is getting everyone on the same page and getting used to each other—how we do business.

Complex projects that require a high degree of trust and unscripted interactions that require "empathetic response" or "rapid bonding" benefit most from natural cultural affinity.[31] Gandhi asks,

> are you outsourcing to the right place for this type of product or service? For companies based in France or Italy, rather than sending processes to Brazil, vendors in Eastern Europe might well work out better. By contrast, Korean manufacturers might prefer vendors in India or China.

For U.S.- and U.K.-based firms, the Philippines and Canada are deemed to offer the "closest cultural fit."[32]

Cultural dissonance can cause all-too-real operational problems. Kumkum Dalal, of Global Reach Consulting, observes that U.S. business language tends to be colloquial. As all communication is nuanced by the culture of the speaker, it is important to speak clearly so there is no ambiguity. She has had experiences where Indian nationals she was working with did not

---

30. Dean Davison, *Top 10 Risks of Offshore Outsourcing*, META GROUP (Feb. 16, 2004), http://searchcio.techtarget.com/originalContent/0,289142,sid19_gci950602,00.html.
31. NEOIT, *supra* note 1, at 4.
32. *Id.*

properly understand what the U.S. speaker intended, and suggests that in cross-border exchanges it is better to err on the side of caution and ask for clarification rather than assume understanding.

Still, other factors, such as cost savings and market access, might outweigh ease of cultural interaction in your unique calculations. An increase of the value in a given foreign nation's currency, for instance, means that cost savings there may be more difficult to realize. On the other hand, Pete Foster, a research director at Pierre Audoin Consultants, is one of many who have said that companies may be forced to look at locations other than India for cost savings,[33] as skills and resources become scarcer and costs rise.

If you are going to do business with people from a distinctly different culture, differences need to be managed on both sides of the value chain, and there needs to be a "defined process of knowledge management" on both sides.[34] A clear initial understanding of cultural differences by everyone involved is necessary in order to close the gap between the working groups.[35] Training, possibly incorporating popular culture (TV, movies, sports popular outside of the native culture), and accent neutralization can assist in addressing any "cultural gap."[36]

Practical effects of cultural disconnects in overseas operations are put into context by Ed Bathelt, General Counsel of Komatsu America. Say you need to set something up in a country you haven't worked in previously, such as Peru—how do you know whom to hire? Then, how do you vet people the first time you are there? Bathelt emphasizes the need to establish infrastructure and support—and that takes time:

> Set up and turnaround time can be slower in some countries than in the United States. Local counsel are at times not yet as connected with immediate access and can have a different approach to the relationship than U.S. attorneys are used to. There can be a mismatch in expectations.

---

33. Mike Yamamoto, *Will India Price Itself Out of Offshore Market?*, CNET (March 29, 2004), http://www.news.com/2100-1022-5180589.html.
34. Venkateswar, *supra* note 6.
35. *Id.*
36. NEOIT, *supra* note 1, at 4.

Similarly Jeffrey Paulsen, former General Counsel at Brunswick Bowling and Billiards Corp., points out that when doing business overseas, Americans have to remember while on the airplane heading to another country of the need to change their mindset. U.S. business culture is contract driven, and our court system is geared to that. Going to China? "You have to think Chinese." Paulsen proposes the following:

> You have to adopt the mind set that I can't pound the table and win every point for my client. In Asia, it's about the relationship: a lot of food, eating and drinking. The contracting parties can barely communicate, but still are all there together. Getting to know each other on a personal level is all about establishing trust and a win-win mentality. Without that, a JV or other business venture is destined to fail. You have to learn what battles to fight and which ones not to. How to tell the difference? Ask . . . what is this overall business relationship about? What are the chances you will actually end up litigating over this point you are fighting to win?

Infrastructure

What infrastructure will be necessary for the contemplated operations? Generally, reliable telecommunications bandwidth and electric power will be on virtually any company's list,[37] although these things are often not guaranteed in even the hot markets of the developing world. Still, many countries are moving quickly to address shortcomings in these areas. In the Philippines for example, the long U.S. military presence has resulted in a solid telecommunications network.[38]

Many companies take the wise precautions of acquiring generators and satellite or microwave communication networks to bridge the gap between local resources and actual day-to-day needs.[39] Costs of such equipment and their maintenance should be factored in as various locations for your overseas ventures are considered.

---

37. *Id.*
38. *Id.* at 7.
39. *Id.* at 4.

Prevalence of Distinctive Competencies

Each locality's labor pool will have developed different skill sets. As Neo-Group notes, the skill sets that exist in a given place are heavily influenced by the educational infrastructure available and the training of already-existing industries.[40] So, for example, in Russia and parts of the former Warsaw Pact nations, an education system that historically placed greater emphasis on basic mathematics and science, coupled with significant military and aerospace employment, has created large numbers of computer programmers with an ability to produce technical software.[41]

From the perspective of Chenevert, a two-step process is involved in this analysis. First, it is important to consider the demographics of the existing labor force, including the more and less experienced workers. Second, the broader pool of workers in the surrounding area could be hired and trained to be adequately skilled. "Once a target is acquired," Chenevert observes, "it is generally easier to assess the labor pool."

Again, if you have a vested strategic interest in a given location, there are ways of addressing a local labor pool that lacks the particular skills that you seek—at a cost, of course. In-house training or partnerships with local universities are two possible solutions.[42] Keep in mind, however, that another major consideration is the availability of local managers who can lead local workers to create world-class output.

Leg Work

While all of the above factors need to be carefully analyzed, this work cannot be done in a vacuum. You must be prepared to travel to the location or locations you are considering and see them for yourself. You need to get acclimated to the culture and people there. After all, if this location is going to be a critical part of your strategic direction on an ongoing basis, you need to understand it as well as your home base of operations.

---

40. *Id.*
41. *Id.*
42. *Id.* at 4.

Wageman observes that for many Western companies who are very new to China, a good way to build business is to engage in a two-step process. The first trip to China is often purely for information-gathering purposes, or as Wageman puts it, "Investing in China 101." Wageman notes that in the past, Western companies did not conduct extensive due diligence on the ground. Today companies are significantly more careful; they may spend weeks and months gathering information about how the specified business sector operates in China and about the target Chinese commercial or equity partner. The due diligence is then followed by negotiations with the chosen vendor or business partner.

Why is legwork so important? Loring Knoblauch, of Underwriters' Laboratories, has observed that in still-developing countries such as China, the business paradigm changes very rapidly. What was true two years ago, or even nine months ago, may no longer be valid now. This underscores how important it is to have someone on the ground there, and how important it is for the client to spend time there and understand how various business parameters are trending and what that means for the future of the planned operation. Dr. Liu agrees: "At the end of the day, "there are still things in China that are quite opaque. Doing business there still requires a 'leap of faith.'"

Even today, not everyone does due diligence on location, although if they do not, they often have reason to regret it. Wageman tells of a large European company that entered into a joint venture with a well-known Chinese company. Problems surfaced right away, and documents revealed significant deficiencies. Unfortunately, the European company had not consulted a Chinese lawyer, and their in-house counsel knew nothing about China. The joint venture failed, costing the European company over 2 million Euros.

Many people want to save as much as they can on start-up costs. This is particularly understandable in terms of small and medium-sized businesses. One of the best ways to save money is to learn from the mistakes of the businesses that have come down the road before you. Budget sufficient time and money to get some real perspective about the location or locations you are considering. In that way, you can best save yourself the cost of failure, which in the final analysis is the most important cost savings of all.

The Big Chessboard

Mills sums it up well: "You really do have to view the world as a big chessboard." If making a move to a particular locale doesn't make sense for any number of reasons, there is generally another move he can suggest to his client.

Sometimes outsourcing is the right answer; at other times a joint venture allows you to enter the jurisdiction to partner locally. "Now you've got to be careful with that when you start partnering with people," Mills warns. That is where our next chapter picks up.

Chapter 6

Due Diligence: Examining Vendor Partners

The last several chapters have emphasized the need for extensive analysis and planning to enable the client company to develop a clear understanding of its objectives, the deliverables needed to obtain those objectives, and the risks that must be avoided or, at least, taken into account. At this point, contingency planning, executive buy-in, matching of strategic goals to a particular business structure, and selection of a suitable location for the offshore project should be complete. Now you are ready to select a vendor or business partner to help convert this planning into reality. In this chapter we will be discussing this issue in terms of "vendor selection," but the same basic principles apply to "partner selection" as well.

While dealing with the Soviets during the Cold War, President Ronald Reagan popularized the saying "Trust, but verify." In this post-Cold War, global economy, the operative advice when choosing a vendor or business partner now might be "Verify, then trust." As discussed below, a number of factors will allow you to verify that the entity you are considering is capable and shares your values enough to be compatible with your strategic direction. Unlike in personal relationships, in the realm of vendor due diligence, "opposites"—in terms of company values—rarely attract and should be avoided at all costs.

According to the Financial Services Roundtable, the types of risk a firm must examine when considering overseas vendors are similar to those in the domestic arena:

due diligence in the selection of a service provider; validation of controls and recovery capabilities; the definition of contractual, service-level, and insurance agreements; and, the definition of management requirements, oversight, and the ongoing process of verifying that contractual obligations are being met.[1]

Still, you are not dealing with the guy down the block. "Extensive diligence on the outsourcing vendor cannot be overemphasized," says Samir Gandhi, of Sidley Austin. "You must know who you are dealing with." Some questions Gandhi routinely asks include the following:

Can the vendor meet your expectations? Can they dedicate the necessary resources to your project? How economically viable is the vendor? Will they be around 3–5 years from now? What kind of turnover does this vendor have? What kind of training do their people have? Who are the vendor's clients? Who do they no longer work for? Is the vendor working for your competitor? There are "control of technology" issues as well. What business knowledge is lost in the process of implementing this arrangement? How comfortable are you with your technology being placed in the hands of third-party providers? What happens to your technology and know-how if they are no longer around?

Allen Bargfrede, formerly of Orbitz, agrees. He tells of working on one deal with a U.S. shell entity owned by an Indian company. The assets all resided in India. Bargfrede went to outside counsel to obtain a guarantee from the Indian corporation. He concludes that "someone has to go and physically see the vendors' facilities and meet with people. You need to drive to the facility, see that it exists and kick the tires." IBM Consulting Services advocates that such visits provide a view not just to organizational structure and technology utilized but also "a glimpse at the level of professionalism and

---

1. Information Policy Institute, How Safe and Secure Is It? An Assessment of Data Privacy and Security in Business Process Outsourcing Firms in India, Financial Services Roundtable 11 (2005).

service that their internal clients will likely receive and the level of investment the vendor is putting into its own staff and operations."[2]

Sushil Bhasin, formerly of EXL and now Marketing Head at Aon Hewitt, advises that vendors should invite clients to speak to other existing clients. To market themselves, vendors should attend offshoring events and also industry-specific conferences, which allows them to spread the word by networking and speaking at events attended by the chief financial officers and procurement staff that usually start the process.

But after all the factors and hard metrics are taken into account, Kumkum Dalal, among others, still emphasizes that "you need to build a *relationship* with a vendor." From Dalal's point of view, a successful vendor-client relationship "begins with a solid CEO-CEO relationship which then has to trickle down to the team members on both sides that interact daily on a project." Ultimately the vendor-client relationship has to be a win-win for both parties to be successful.

Beginning the Selection Process: Establishing Criteria

The Outsourcing Institute proposes that there are four basic phases to the outsourcing process: assessment, request for proposal (RFP), selection, and governance.[3] Some companies secure a vendor first, then independently come up with criteria that they must work by. But it is more effective to come up with the criteria first, so that you can clearly convey the client's needs to the vendor or business partner.

Consider the frustration of a relationship with someone who is demanding but never really communicates what he or she wants or how her or she can be satisfied—only dissatisfaction. If you are unclear about your needs and criteria, it can be equally frustrating for a vendor or partner dealing with you in a business context. Figure out what you want and learn how

---

2. Eric Lesser & Joanne Stephane, *Preparing for Human Resources Business Transformation Outsourcing*, IBM BUSINESS CONSULTING SERVICES, 8 (2005), http://www-935.ibm.com/services/multimedia/ge510-4015-hr-bto.pdf.
3. *8th Annual Outsourcing Index: Money Matters*, 3 THE OUTSOURCING INSTITUTE (2005), http://outsourcing.com/content.asp?page=01b/other/oe/q405/moneymatters.html&nonav=false.

to communicate it—clearly. If you do, your relationship with your overseas vendors and partners will stand a chance for success.

Your evaluation criteria should focus on the most critical needs of the business, as prioritized by the steering committee. A *vendor evaluation team* should be established, which should include personnel from the areas that will be dealing with, and will be affected by, the vendor's operations.[4] The vendor evaluation team, by virtue of its members' "hands-on" knowledge, can flesh out and add critical detail to the selection criteria.

The next challenge is to determine how to compare the relative qualifications of vendors, one to the other. A scoring model, weighted again according to the priority of factors, allows the members of the vendor evaluation team to most effectively compare notes with each other as they consider the relative merits of each candidate.[5]

When the evaluation team has narrowed the candidates down by this process to a "short list," the finalists can be invited to give an in-person presentation and demonstration of their products and services, which will also be judged by the scoring model.[6] Some companies develop a standard questionnaire that they submit to vendors under consideration. The questionnaires may seek to glean information about the vendors' areas of expertise, their approach to contract development, and how they address changes in project scope, among other things.[7]

Face-to-face meetings with vendor candidates are helpful on multiple levels. Understanding the vendor's managerial style and gaining familiarity with their key personnel begins the process of building trust that is the key to a successful partnership.[8]

---

4. Andrew Anderson, *Methodology Removes Guesswork: A Structured Approach to Selecting Outsourcing Partners Reduces Risk and Improves ROI*, 40 COMMUNICATIONS NEWS (Aug. 2003), http://www.thefreelibrary.com/Methodology+removes+guesswork%3A+a+structured+approach+to+selecting...-a0106646798.
5. *Id.*
6. *Id.*
7. Lesser & Stephane, *supra* note 2, at 8.
8. *Id.*

The Process: Going It Alone versus Using a Third-Party Selection Consultant

According to a study cited by IBM Consulting Services, 53 percent of companies who outsourced a component of human resources used consulting help during the decision-making process.[9] Such consultants assisted with the process in numerous ways, including

- determining requirements,
- developing bid process and evaluation criteria,
- developing the request for proposal,
- determining which vendors will receive the request for proposal,
- evaluating submissions and determining the short list of potential candidates,
- conducting screening interviews and site visits,
- assisting in the due diligence process,
- developing service level agreements, and
- assisting with contract development and negotiation[10]

There are pros and cons to involving such consultants. They often utilize a proven methodology, use their experience to eliminate inadequate or mismatched candidate vendors, and offer an independent viewpoint, free from the internal biases and distractions that often plague internal senior management.[11] But there are costs associated with using consultants, and the third party may reduce early direct interaction between client and vendor, thus increasing the time it takes to build trust and communication between the two.[12] The vendor selection committee should determine whether the particular strengths, experience, and resources of the committee suggest selection by internal means only or with the assistance of a reputable third party. It is true that the use of a consultant may require similar diligence as for the vendor or partner being considered. The difference typically is that

---

9. *Id.* at 9.
10. *Id.*
11. *Id.* at 10.
12. *Id.*

the consultant is more easily evaluated and oftentimes has offices located in the client's home country.

Gold Key Matching Service

An important asset in this process that can be of special assistance to small and medium-sized businesses is the Gold Key Matching Service, operated by the U.S. Commercial Service of the Commerce Department. In an effort to assist U.S. businesses in exporting products and services, Commercial Service experts on the ground in 145 U.S. embassies and consulates around the world can arrange meetings with pre-screened business partners, professional associations, and government contacts.[13] The Gold Key program offers

- customized market and industry briefings,
- market research,
- post-meeting debriefing with trade specialists and assistance in developing appropriate follow-up strategies, and
- help with travel, accommodations, interpreter services, and clerical support.[14]

For smaller companies with limited travel budgets, Gold Key offers videoconferencing services.[15]

For those companies with limited resources, leveraging the expertise and resources of the U.S. federal government may be an important tool in bringing your international operation to fruition.

Competitive Selection

Competitive bidding through an RFP process can produce cost savings—but not always. When badly managed, such a process can add significant

---
13. http://export.gov/salesandmarketing/eg_main_018195.asp.
14. Id.
15. Id.

delays and costs to a project.[16] In many instances, poor management of the selection process revolves around the failure to treat potential vendors or partners with respect or to share information necessary for the vendor/partner to provide carefully thought-out proposals. Should you choose to develop an RFP, it should require candidates to provide complete answers so that they can be compared with those from competing vendors.[17]

The bottom line is that the more you "hide the ball" from your vendors out of mistrust or in an effort to gain leverage from them, the more likely it is you will create delays and change orders because of the unnecessary learning curve you will have created. Once you have exercised proper diligence in choosing a candidate to work with, it is important to trust them enough to allow the relationship to work for you.

However, before you can trust, you must verify. Vikas Bhalla, of EXL, suggests that one way his company helps to bridge the trust gap is by first entering into a consulting relationship with a client. Bhalla notes that many companies are used to opening up their operations to consultants within their facilities. Using business process outsourcing (BPO) as an example, the vendor acting as consultant can first do the documentation and process mapping to demonstrate expertise. This leads to building a comfort level with the client. EXL strives to offer the same identification of opportunities to save costs, investigation, and analysis as the Big Four consulting offices do. EXL can compete with them based on the deeper understanding gained from having developed and implemented BPO solutions.

Whether you choose a traditional RFP process or an alternate method of selection, your client's company will face risks common to most businesses operating overseas, as well as a number of more particular risks arising out of its own unique characteristics. This not only includes the specific industry involved, the client company's current size, and the number and strength of its competitors, but also the type of process at the heart of the subject transaction, and the business model being used (outsourcing, joint venture, subsidiary, etc.). As has been demonstrated in previous chapters, many of

---

16. Dominic Conlon, *Nearshore/Offshore Outsourcing, Part II: Implementation*, A&L GOODBODY (April 12, 2005), http://www.worldservicesgroup.com/publicationspf.asp?id=1171.
17. Warren S. Reid, *Outsourcing: The 20 Steps to Success*, 4 (1996), http://www.wsrcg.com/Articles/OutSourcing.pdf.

the risks a company faces in international business are not very different from those it faces at home. Make no mistake, however: there are a host of specific risks introduced by an offshore environment,[18] and failing to take into account any one of them at the diligence stage will lead to difficulties at best, utter catastrophe at worst.

As an example, a recent Financial Services Roundtable report cited a recent analysis by the Federal Deposit Insurance Corporation (FDIC) that, apart from the location risk discussed earlier, identified five principal areas of risk for U.S. financial firms working with offshore vendors:

- Reputation Risk—risks to earnings or capital arising from negative public opinion, for example, in the event of a security breach
- Operations/Transactional Risk—risks associated with service or product delivery
- Compliance Risk—risks associated with liability for legal noncompliance
- Strategic Risk—risks associated with adverse business decisions and inadequate management
- Credit Risk—risks associated with the financial condition of the third-party provider.[19]

The Federal Financial Institutions Examination Council adds "liquidity risks," defined as "problems of investment processes and repayment assumptions" (i.e., capital repatriation and foreign exchange issues); "transactional risks" relating to operating costs (stemming from contract drafting, implementation, enforcement, and dispute resolution); and "geographic risks" relating to the likelihood of potential disasters.[20]

Taking reputation risk as an example, Michael Mensik, of Baker & McKenzie, notes that security breaches were not on the "radar" as recently as 2006. In January 2007, however, the hacking of credit cards and other transactions in the computer network of TJX, parent company of the TJ

---

18. INFORMATION POLICY INSTITUTE, HOW SAFE AND SECURE IS IT? AN ASSESSMENT OF DATA PRIVACY AND SECURITY IN BUSINESS PROCESS OUTSOURCING FIRMS IN INDIA, FINANCIAL SERVICES ROUNDTABLE 11 (2005).
19. Id.
20. Id.

Maxx discount chain, which compromised over 45 million credit card accounts, received a lot of publicity.[21] The resulting class action brought by the Massachusetts Bankers Association, representing over 200 Massachusetts banks,[22] and $118 million charge in to TJX in the second quarter of 2007[23] highlighted the nondelegable legal and reputation risk that security breaches by a vendor represent today. Since then, of course, a massive data breach of Target Corporation's operations during the 2013 holiday season has left the company contemplating $1.4 billion in costs before even taking into account the downward pressure on sales that the bad publicity may have caused.[24]

This reveals a heated debate that is emerging in the international transactional community—who should bear the cost of the hidden costs of compliance? Mensik boils the issue down to the question, "What is the scope of indemnity that should be negotiated from the vendor?" To answer this question, Mensik adds, "it is incumbent on customers to do their homework."

This is a part of the risk allocation that must be hammered out during the negotiation process. Larger companies take risk allocation more seriously, Mensik reflects, simply because in general, the bigger the client involved, the bigger the risks. Certainly different companies will have differing levels of risk tolerance. Mensik gives simple but wise advice to small and medium-sized businesses on this subject:

> Use your common sense. Keep it simple. Don't spend a lot of time on a fancy tax structure. Come up with a range of issues. Prioritize them, focus on the top 3–6 issues and have awareness of what further issues to look for as the business increases. Be practical, and focus on what's really important—now, and down the road.

---

21. Jaikumar Vijayan, *Banks File Class Action Suit against TJX*, COMPUTERWORLD, 1 (April 25, 2007), http://www.networkworld.com/news/2007/042507-massachusetts-banks-file-class-action.html?nwwpkg=breaches.
22. *Id.*
23. Sharon Gaudin, *TJ Maxx Breach Costs Soar by Factor of 10*, INFO. WEEK (Aug. 15, 2007), http://www.informationweek.com/tj-maxx-security-breach-costs-soar-to-10-times-earlier-estimate/d/d-id/1058172?.
24. Spencer Jakab, *Target's Valuation Largely Hits the Mark,* WALL STREET JOURNAL (February 26, 2014) at C1.

In addition to identifying and considering industry-specific risks, you must also consider broader risks that have more general application. The following sections are general factors to consider when choosing a vendor. These factors are not meant to be exclusive in any way; as mentioned previously, the selection committee is best equipped to produce a complete list of factors relevant to a transaction.

Financial Considerations

Undoubtedly, examining a vendor's financial health is at the heart of due diligence, if for no other reason than to have a reasonable basis for believing the vendor will continue to survive.[25] A vendor's finances will also help determine its quality of support, as well as the vendor's overall approach to service. For example, can the vendor afford to hire qualified personnel?[26]

A thorough examination of available resources—including Internet searches, financial statements, regulatory reporting, corporate organization, and strategic plans—may reveal interesting and occasionally eye-opening information.[27] Performance bond, insurance, and litigation history will highlight what mistakes the vendor has made and whether it has learned from those mistakes.[28] Its credit score, too, may be of interest.[29]

Harvey Cohen, of Dinsmore & Shohl, argues that in his experience, only doing background checks on a vendor "on the sly" is generally less effective than asking the vendor where it banks and what loans it has up front. "Asked directly," Cohen states, because "they will reveal to you things you might never find otherwise." It is still important to do the checks, Cohen warns, because the truth rarely comes out the same as what you have been told. In China, for instance, ownership may have changed hands enough times that the current management of a company may not even know who owns what anymore.

---

25. Reid, *supra* note 17, at 6.
26. *Id.*
27. *Id.*
28. *Id.* at 7.
29. Lesser & Stephane, *supra* note 2, at 8.

When thinking of acquiring ownership in a foreign target, Don Chenevert, of Caterpillar, warns that you may very well be offered a "bottom feeder." In China, for instance, a state-owned enterprise put up for sale to foreign investors might well have the oldest factories, the least productivity, and the most remote location in a far-flung corner of an isolated province with inadequate infrastructure serving it. In many developing countries an important step is to develop accurate financial information about a target company or a potential vendor that will allow you to verify their actual worth and viability. As Chenevert says, "identifying the owners of a target company and its assets is no mean feat in a Communist state."

Leadership

As in U.S.-based businesses, human resource policies are the key to the success or failure of any offshore vendor. The overall qualities of new hires, how well-managed employees are, their training, and their attrition rate are just a few of the factors to consider.[30] Leadership is also demonstrated by clear communication internally and with the client.[31]

Clients are sometimes watchful for signs that the vendor is a potential takeover candidate, since a change of leadership during the course of a project at a minimum is distracting and at worst can seriously hamper the vendor's efforts to meet agreed-upon goals.[32]

Leadership can be most critical at the beginning of the project, when coordination and decision-making processes are uncertain and slow. Lack of authority in the chain of command can leave the vendor little ability to cope with the unexpected.[33] As Howard Mills, of Deloitte, observes,

> as hard as it is with turnover in the states, if you lose key people abroad all of sudden you can take an entity that was working out

---

30. N. Raja Venkateswar, *Mitigating Operational Risk in Outsourcing*, INFO. MGMT. (May 2005), http://www.dmreview.com/specialreports/20050524/1028024-1.html.
31. *Id.*
32. Lesser & Stephane, *supra* note 2, at 8.
33. Venkateswar, *supra* note 30.

wonderfully and it just falls apart. You need to have a contingency plan and a backup plan. What happens if your key manager gets hit by a bus? One person makes a huge difference a lot of times.

History and Reputation

Common sense tells us that how long a vendor has been in business, the quality of its staff, the strength of its client base, and its commitment to the requisite industries must be examined closely.[34] Investigating each potential vendor's background often involves speaking to as many comparable customers in the same industry as possible.[35] While others may be reticent to directly admit that they selected the wrong partner, asking for lessons learned at various points in the process will allow you to gauge the vendor's overall effectiveness and learn from someone else's mistakes.[36]

The offshore vendors that work with consultant Dalal are recommended by someone else she knows. Word-of-mouth referrals from a trusted source are hardly a secret; this is often the way domestic businesses form new partnerships or other new relationships. This approach requires that you determine who knows the "lay of the land" for a given type of vendor. Select a firm that is of a high caliber in its industry; that firm will be able to look ahead and anticipate requirement changes.

Bhasin, formerly of EXL, likewise acknowledges that many people are talking with consultants such as NeoIT or Price Waterhouse, using them as intermediaries with the vendors. Once the clients decide to outsource, they come to India, hire a consultant, and choose vendors themselves by way of an RFP. They float a few companies to their consultant or go to the National Association of Software and Services Companies (NASSCOM), which facilitates business and trade in the information technology (IT) and BPO sectors in India.

Not surprisingly, Shrikar Dole, formerly of FIEO, feels that business owners from the Northern Hemisphere should not try to venture on their

---

34. Reid, *supra* note 17, at 6.
35. *Id.* at 6–7.
36. *Id.* at 7.

own into the Indian market. He notes that there are government-sponsored organizations that allow companies to be exposed to whole databases of vendors. For instance, a foreign enterprise seeking to partner with an Indian engineering firm can choose from over thirty thousand such companies. Some business owners rely on friends or contacts made in India, but those contacts may not be in the same industry, and if the first deal turns out badly, the owners may sour on doing business in India entirely. Using a government-sponsored service enables a client to narrow his or her vendor search from thousands of candidates to a short list of between two and five; this all happens without the foreign client having to leave his or her office. Moreover, when the foreign client arrives in India, the local offices of these organizations will organize meetings with the finalists under consideration. The finalists all come to meet with the client in one place.

Dole tells of a company president who tried on his own to work with an Indian partner and could not get what he wanted. Later, he used the Engineering Export Promotion Council (EEPC India), and now this president has seven sourcing providers based in India.

Any of these approaches—direct referrals from trusted colleagues, consultants, or sponsored organizations—can lead to success. Which one you choose depends, among other things, on the particular location you have chosen, the subject industry, and the level of trust you have in the recommendations you have received.

Technical Competence and Quality Control

Exervio Management Consulting rightly suggests that "the minimum standard for any vendor's performance ought to be [on] par with the customer's current in-house process."[37] Nevertheless, Exervio cites a Dun & Bradstreet survey in which 70 percent of clients felt that providers "didn't understand what they were supposed to do."[38]

---

37. Exervio Management Consulting, *Do You Really Want to Outsource that Process?*, 4 (May 2004), http://www.exervio.com/docs/Do%20You%20Really%20Want%20To%20Outsource%20That%20Process.
38. *Id.*

Clearly, whether you are outsourcing services or partnering with a manufacturer of components or finished goods, the foreign entity must have detailed knowledge of specific methods and experience in the industry.[39] Understanding how the vendor trains and integrates its employees is a good indicator of this.[40] Knowing how much of its revenue (and profits) comes from the activities involved in the subject transaction will also be an indication of its ability to successfully partner with you.[41] The willingness of the vendor to guarantee service levels or other measures of performance and its ability to manage transition risk are also factors worth considering.[42]

As you implement your operation, there is little time for a vendor learning curve. The vendor should have a proven method for providing the desired products or services, but that method should be flexible enough that it can be adapted to your needs as they arise.[43]

Sometimes, Dalal observes, the product or service itself defines who the vendor should be. She gives an example of a project involving a hand-tools supplier and a patented product where a vendor would be producing a nonpatented piece of the tool. She needed a vendor who had the requisite skill to produce at the level of precision and tolerances the client needed.

Another example Dalal offers is that of a Canadian company that operates very high-end restaurants and hotels. The company wanted an Indian vendor to produce interior CAD drawings for it. Could the vendor do it? Yes, but the employees of this Indian vendor had never seen facilities as exotic and luxurious as the client's; without some exposure to similar facilities, they would have no frame of reference with which to work on the project.

The in-house commercial folks at a company like Caterpillar know who the players are in their industry, and they can easily come up with a short list of appropriate manufacturers in a given locale, says Chenevert. If your company does not have knowledge of manufacturers or vendors in a particular place you have targeted, there are numerous avenues to get the necessary information, including trade associations, trusted colleagues in the industry,

---

39. Reid, *supra* note 17, at 6.
40. *Id.*
41. *Id.*
42. Lesser & Stephane, *supra* note 2, at 7.
43. Reid, *supra* note 17, at 6.

and intermediaries like Dalal, just to name a few. Ultimately, the manufacturer or vendor's work product is likely your best measure of its capabilities in this area. You must demand domain expertise and require evidence that the vendor is familiar and complies with industry best practices.[44]

Dalal likes to match small and medium-sized vendors with small and medium-sized enterprise (SME) clients. She observes that "their needs are generally the same." Big outsourcing firms can dictate terms to smaller clients, and vice versa. A large Indian firm might not be that interested in a smaller account. The question is, "Where will the client company get the proper amount of attention?" Dalal points out those smaller companies can be extremely price sensitive, which is generally a good thing for their SME clientele.

Indeed, blind reliance on the larger and better known "usual suspect" firms can lead to missteps if those firms do not have the specialized knowledge to work with the specific business involved or to make changes as necessary.[45] It sometimes makes business sense to locate smaller firms that have the focused expertise to manage particular processes, including attendant legal issues.[46] Of course, the more sensitive the client is to risk and the ability to transfer risk to a vendor, the less likely it will find a smaller vendor a good fit.

Whether big or small, if a vendor can apply and develop best practices garnered from working with many clients, the resulting innovation and process improvement can help clients rise above the competition by lowering costs and enhancing quality.[47]

Capacity for Growth

In a fast-moving global economy, the concept of scalability applies to much more than just IT infrastructure. As Dalal underscores, to anticipate changes

---

44. David L. Margulius, *Offshore Partnerships Demand a Wide Range of Expertise*, INFO WORLD, 35 (Aug. 25, 2005), *available at* http://www.infoworld.com/d/developer-world/offshore-partnerships-demand-wide-range-expertise-519.
45. Venkateswar, *supra* note 30.
46. *Id.*
47. Exervio Management Consulting, *supra* note 37.

and take advantage of growth opportunities, it is essential to work with a vendor who knows the industry and the leading players—or "someone who has the Rolodex and someone who understands what direction the industry is going in." Thus, one author suggests that a vendor "will need to have the commitment to respond adequately to the ever-changing business environment, technology needs, and functional demands of the firms."[48] The service provider must also "maintain flexibility and responsiveness in meeting customer demand."[49] Exervio Management Consulting warns that while some providers represent that "they have the capacity to handle a client's volume . . . when the work gets heavy, their systems crash and their people fail to resolve problems."[50]

Depending on your strategic goals and risk-management profile, you may want to consider the capacity of the vendor to assist you in the future on a regional, or perhaps even a global, basis. Determining the vendor's experience and resources related to working outside its own borders is important if this need is foreseeable.[51] Does the vendor have adequate research and development resources?[52]

Comparable Strategic Direction

The expectations and goals of both parties must be compatible if any relationship between them can be expected to succeed:

> An existing vendor might not be able to scale up the processes if suddenly required by the Client firm due to lack of funds, capability or choice; as it might not be in his best interest. On the other hand it is also possible that vendor might invest significantly in processes, which might not be very critical for a particular firm but significant to others and vice versa.[53]

---

48. Venkateswar, *supra* note 30.
49. *Id.*
50. Exervio Management Consulting, *supra* note 37.
51. Reid, *supra* note 17, at 6.
52. *Id.* at 7.
53. Venkateswar, *supra* note 30.

According to the Outsourcing Institute, many chief information officers choose not to outsource because, among other things, they are worried about providers suddenly changing business strategies and focus.[54] This fear is not necessarily unfounded. Offshore deals involve a calculated loss of management control to outside parties, a loss of control with which executives are often uncomfortable.[55] Aside from technical and industry-specific criteria you review, in-depth study of the vendor's or partner's business plan is crucial.[56]

Comparable Business Ethics

While it is important to avoid the urge to impose United States' means and methods on other cultures in ways that do not make good business sense, you cannot leave your ethical standards behind when doing business overseas. Ethical breaches have a way of leading to noncompliance with legal and regulatory obligations. While discussed below in terms of e-business, the principle has broader application:

> Perhaps the greatest risk of all in the e-business world is the harm to reputation and the catastrophic, unlimited financial consequences that could stem from liability claims by damaged stakeholders (customers, suppliers, shareholders, etc.). As the Internet continues to evolve as a business tool, stakeholder accountability will be the prime motivator and in certain events a possibility for criminal action.[57]

Below are some examples of the harm potentially caused by an unethical business partner or vendor:

- Firm secrets are stolen by a competitor and used against the firms;

---

54. Mark Hollands, *Deal or No Deal*, 3 THE OUTSOURCING INSTITUTE (2005), http://www.outsourcing.com/content.asp?page=01b/other/oe/q405/dornod.html&nonav=false.
55. *Id.*
56. Reid, *supra* note 17, at 3.
57. Venkateswar, *supra* note 30.

- Public display of intimate and sensitive information by a hacker;
- Loss of employee morale when internal hackers gain access to private human resource records;
- Liability claims that result from digital risk exposures inherited from firm acquisitions and outsourcing.[58]

Patricia Gill recalls that while at Motorola, she typically dealt with independent "finders" who, unlike traditional distributors, did not take title to the seller's merchandise. The finder's' value-add was that they knew the ins and outs of dealing with customers. Gill, however, recalls having concerns about exposure to the Foreign Corrupt Practices Act (FCPA) regarding a particular Haitian finder whose ties to a government official called into question the nature of what he was doing.

Finders were required by Motorola to go through an application process for due diligence purposes. They were asked to agree that they did not knowingly give gifts to foreign officials—using language right out of the FCPA. Gill advises that in the end, you need to be able to show U.S. government officials that you did your due diligence; fines and criminal penalties might result otherwise. This is especially true for China, Gill adds.

Strength and Capabilities of Key Suppliers to Vendors

An FDIC study cited by the Financial Services Roundtable argues that outsourcing to offshore vendors who, in turn, "suboutsource" to third-party providers may expose clients to data security and privacy risks because of the lack of direct control of the subcontractors.[59] The Roundtable noted,

> the U.S. firms we interviewed either prohibit the further subcontracting of BPO that involves consumer information to another firm by the vendor or allow it only after they, the client, scrutinize the arrangements.

---

58. Id.
59. INFORMATION POLICY INSTITUTE, HOW SAFE AND SECURE IS IT? AN ASSESSMENT OF DATA PRIVACY AND SECURITY IN BUSINESS PROCESS OUTSOURCING FIRMS IN INDIA, FINANCIAL SERVICES ROUNDTABLE 116 (2005).

One U.S. client required a contract between it and the sub-subcontractor. All interviewees, clients and vendors alike, insist that [third]-party subcontracting does not take place without the express consent of the financial institution and their vendor.[60]

If the vendor is relying in a significant way on various suppliers or partners by way of strategic alliances to help it produce deliverables, your investigation should include these outside entities, as well.[61] Some would argue that having the extra tools and resources to bear in a given situation is to be welcomed. Others, however, contend that contractual responsibility is important. Lalit Arora, formerly of IBM Consulting and now with HCL Axon, notes that some entities that have contracted with IBM have outsourced development to small boutique IT shops. This can lead to finger pointing between the primary vendor and the subcontracting vendor. The client suffers as a result. Arora concludes that it is better for the primary vendor to be contractually responsible.

Available Infrastructure

Chenevert, of Caterpillar, notes that good infrastructure from a manufacturing standpoint includes easy access by road, rail, river, or sea so that you can easily move raw materials and subassemblies in and finished products out. It also includes a dependable supply of electrical power, adequate water supplies, and a well-built and maintained facility. Lesley Lahm, of the Asian Development Bank, asserts that many developing countries present significant gaps in such critical infrastructure: "In India, for example, the power goes out every hour, the roads are bad and there is no refrigerated transport."

    A vendor's shortcomings in this area have to be carefully factored into the total expected cost to determine how much capital will be required to remedy them. Do they have adequate backup resources to ensure business continuity should natural or man-made disaster strike? As the Joint Forum

---

60. *Id.*
61. Reid, *supra* note 17, at 7.

asks, does the candidate vendor share the same continuity services provider as others in the area, such that a major disruption could result in a shortage of such contingency services?[62]

Governmental and Regulatory Issues

In evaluating a vendor, one must consider the corresponding governmental environment within which it operates. This can vary from locale to locale within a given country, or even within a province, as some areas may receive preferential treatment that others do not.

Richard Wageman, of DLA Piper, notes that in China, for instance, every industry has a specific ministry assigned to administer it. All foreign investment is carefully scrutinized. The scope of proposed business activity must be specifically defined, and the business scope will dictate the level of investment required by the Ministry of Commerce. In fact, Ministry of Commerce licensing, Administration of Industry and Commerce (AIC) approval, and, in some situations, additional licensing must be obtained.

An initial step toward doing business in China can be to set up a branch office by way of a representative office to conduct market research and to provide liaison services for the parent offshore company. If a foreign investor sets up a business entity in some business sectors such as real estate, obtaining secondary licensing often becomes an issue. The Chinese government is highly bureaucratic and tends to micromanage. As Wageman points out, there are three levels of property management approvals. Food processors require additional secondary licensing such as a health department hygiene license. Fees for such licenses generally are not high; there is simply an interest by government officials in maintaining good quality and efficiency of services. Utilities, banks and financial service providers, and healthcare organizations, among others, are all subject to government oversight in varying degrees.[63]

---

62. Basel Committee on Banking Supervision, *Outsourcing in Financial Services*, THE JOINT FORUM, 17 (Feb. 2005), https://www.bis.org/publ/joint12.pdf.
63. Dean Davison, *Top 10 Risks of Offshore Outsourcing*, META GROUP (Feb. 16, 2004), http://searchcio.techtarget.com/originalContent/0,289142,sid19_gci950602,00.html.

A client company must ensure that the offshore vendor or business partner adequately complies with all levels of government regulation and is willing to demonstrate sufficient "transparency" of such during audits.[64] The audits disclose the extent to which the vendor has been fined for noncompliance and whether they have access to regulatory and legal specialists on staff or on retainer.[65]

If the focus of your transaction is service-based, such as BPO or knowledge process outsourcing functions, another regulatory concern will be compliance with privacy and data security laws. Interestingly, a study released by the Financial Services Roundtable concludes that, at least with respect to Tier 1 and Tier 2 Indian BPO firms (those employing five hundred or more), "sensitive medical and financial data about American citizens is generally as safe and secure being processed in India as if it were being processed in the U.S."[66] The Roundtable's extensive investigation found that Indian data security practices compared well to those maintained by U.S. financial services institutions, and reported breaches were rare: survey respondents reported only twelve data breaches over three years.[67] It is not entirely clear whether every breach is being reported, but of the personal information breaches cited in the Roundtable survey, approximately 70 percent in the industry were "inside" jobs by employees.[68] As an unidentified BPO executive rightly notes,

> in the United States, tens of billions of dollars worth of fraud and identity theft are perpetrated every year. Yet in India, if even a single dollar is stolen as a result of fraud or ID theft, then it becomes a front page story in every major American daily newspaper.[69]

How can you be reasonably sure that your vendor or partner will not draw you into such a catastrophic public relations firestorm? One way is to determine whether the BPO firm under consideration subscribes to internationally

---

64. *Id.*
65. Lesser & Stephane, *supra* note 2, at 8.
66. INFORMATION POLICY INSTITUTE, *supra* note 18, at 4.
67. *Id.*
68. *Id.* at 23.
69. *Id.* at 5.

accepted security standards, such as BS7799 or ISO17799 certification.[70] CSO Online reminds us that security due diligence

> does not mean reading a provider's customer list and watching a PowerPoint show about its security practices and metrics. Nor does it mean accepting claims that the vendor adheres to international security standards ... Given the dramatic growth and turnover in many offshore companies, customer references age quickly. Worse, customers may not admit to security problems they've experienced offshore because they fear bad publicity if word of the problems reached their own customers and the media. Indeed, very few companies were willing to go on the record ... or discuss their offshore security practices.[71]

Some client companies hire security consultants to investigate the local reputations of the providers and perform employee background checks, since it is often hard to obtain information such as past employment and criminal records.[72] Although they may take 30 to 45 days to complete, background checks can be surprisingly thorough, including interviews with family and neighbors, local police officials, on-site verification of school records, and meetings with professors and school administrators.[73] However, there have been reports of candidates bribing investigators in order to get the relatively well-paying jobs.[74]

Third-party security consultants also sometimes retain local lawyers to review the standard contract offered by the vendor to determine if provisions can be enforced.[75] If a security issue is discovered, given the human-intensive nature of many processes in the developing world, it may take months rather than weeks to properly address it.[76] Your schedule must take such potential delays into account. Karen Klein, formerly of Kayak.com, points

---

70. *Id.*
71. Christopher Koch, *Don't Export Security*, CSO MAG. ONLINE (May 2005), http://www.csoonline.com/read/050105/offshore.html.
72. INFORMATION POLICY INSTITUTE, *supra* note 18, at 23.
73. *Id.*
74. *Id.* at 24
75. Koch, supra note 71.
76. *Id.*

out that another concern in this area is that competitive intelligence (CI) gathering is often outsourced. She advises that you should make sure your CI vendors are privacy policy compliant, as well.

Compliance, though, needs to be tempered by common sense. You cannot expect to achieve cost savings if you insist that a vendor adopt a hyper-customized security policy, warns Mensik, of Baker & McKenzie: "You will save money by standardizing. Read *their* [the vendor's] security policy and change it only at the margins as necessary. For instance, the dual authentication that is required for banks is not needed for others."

Turnover of Key Personnel

While the turnover statistics offshore vendors often quote appear relatively low, the more important statistic to manage is the turnover of key personnel on an account, who may be lured away by competitors in "hotspots" such as India.[77] Dean Davison notes that "common turnover levels are in the 15 percent to 20 percent range, and creating contractual terms around those levels is a reasonable request."[78] It seems these terms include ones that pass the costs of locating and training new replacements on to the vendor.[79]

Danger of Cooption: Knowledge Transfer, Trade Secrets, and Relationships

Knowledge transfer has both positive and negative implications in the vendor's due diligence context—based on whether the transfer is intended or not. For those transfers that are intended and necessary to the overseas operation, the time and expense of properly diffusing operative bodies of know-how is often ignored. Davison observes,

---
77. Davison, *supra* note 63.
78. *Id.*
79. *Id.*

most IT organizations experience a 20 percent decline in productivity during the first year of an agreement, largely due to time spent transferring both technical and business knowledge to the vendor. Many offshore vendors are deploying videoconferencing (avoiding travel) and classroom settings (creating one-to-many transfer) to improve the efficacy of knowledge transfer. In addition, employee turnover often places a burden on the IT organization to provide additional information for new team members.[80]

One potential solution is to employ a phased strategy of implementation to lower risks and limit lost productivity.[81]

In thinking about unintended and unwanted knowledge transfer, the Financial Services Roundtable notes that, in the case of overseas vendors, an additional level of security and monitoring must be put in place.[82] Bargfrede, formerly of Orbitz, determines whether systems are secure in part by asking practical questions such as whether the vendor does background checks on its employees. For which other companies are they doing work? Kayak.com's former general counsel Klein recalls that a few years ago she was working on an e-mail customer support project. She demanded that the work be done on secure floors—all the indemnification clauses in the world cannot protect a company today against bad public relations, she notes. Doing background checks on one out of every five employees is not good enough.

Pricing

When the survey participants from The Outsourcing Institute's 8th Annual Outsourcing Index were asked to name the most important factors in selecting a vendor, the greatest single response was, not surprisingly, "price."[83] Vendors should be asked to clarify pricing details so that you can readily

---

80. *Id.*
81. Venkateswar, *supra* note 30.
82. INFORMATION POLICY INSTITUTE, *supra* note 18, at 11.
83. *8th Annual Outsourcing Index: Money Matters*, *supra* note 3.

understand which services are included in base quotes and which will be the subject of change orders.[84] Accounting for administrative costs and reasonable profit margin ensures that vendor proposals are realistic, increasing the likelihood of a smoothly running relationship over time. The vendor selection committee may also develop savings estimates for the recommended vendor, an anticipated payback schedule, and a proposed implementation plan with suggested milestone dates.[85] Fixed pricing can sometimes be utilized to better predict overall costs. The vendor selection committee, in conjunction with the vendor, would need to determine the details necessary to compute a fixed pricing model.[86]

Personal Relationships and Intuition

In China there is an emphasis on merging business and personal relations, known as *guanxi*.[87] The ability of foreign companies to build strong social, as well as business, relationships has often been identified in academic literature as an important determinant of performance there.[88] This is true in many nations outside the United States.

In some ways this is also true of business in the United States. Whereas in the United States two companies might work together in some capacity before a strong personal bond forms between the employees of both firms, elsewhere the vendor or service provider needs to reach out initially to establish trust on a personal level for a working relationship of any significant duration to occur.

Societal differences do have an impact. It is probably fair to say that building *guanxi*, or its equivalent in other parts of the world, will take a significant investment of time, perhaps years. This is yet another reason to analogize international transactions to a marriage. In the end, you will

---

84. Reid, *supra* note 17, at 4.
85. Anderson, *supra* note 4, at 1.
86. *Fixed Price Model*, SAVITR, http://www.savitr.com/v1/outsourcing/fixedpricemodel.php.
87. Claude Marcotte & Jorge Liosi, *Small and Medium-Sized Enterprises Involved in Technology Transfer to China: What Do Their Partners Learn*, 23 INT'L SMALL BUS. J. (Feb. 2005).
88. *Id.*

get the most out of your vendor relationship if you take the time to build a good social relationship with the principals and key personnel involved.

The Decision

Having carefully taken into account all crucial criteria, it is time to evaluate all proposals against those criteria.[89] It is important to consider different approaches recommended by various potential partners, determine how they differ from your planned methodology, and clarify any ambiguities.[90] Make sure the winning candidate is not missing any "must have" criteria as determined by the selection committee.[91] Whatever decision you make as to the leading candidate, designate a backup vendor, just in case negotiations break down or some other issue arises at the last minute with the winning entity.

While I have tried to provide a method that provides a logical selection process, any activity involving the human element requires some aspect of intuition. As Dalal states, "like many things in business, choosing a vendor is partly based on gut feelings." After all the decision makers have passed on your criteria, evaluated proposals and standard contracts, and perhaps listened to a presentation or three, the ultimate decision should take into account your informed business intuition, as well.

Chenevert also reminds us that while it is important to be aware of the limitations of the people with whom you are doing business, "you should not be too quick to write them off." Whatever decision is made, it should be made with all decision makers looking at the same data, whether personnel, facilities, supply contracts, or other items.

Charles Hallab, of Baker & McKenzie, concludes that the choice of a business partner is a business decision that has to be left up to clients. "You [as counsel] flag risks, issues and concerns for them—and leave it to them to put a price on them," he states. If you have done the other things properly, this should not present a daredevil's leap across a canyon, but a

---
89. Reid, *supra* note 17, at 5.
90. *Id.*
91. *Id.*

calculated leap of faith—and isn't that true of most business transactions? As Klein says, "diligence is a continuing process." You must continue to gather information on your vendor and evaluate throughout the process.

Now, with our vendor or partner candidate in hand, our next chapter considers the critical issue set surrounding various compliance regimes.

Chapter 7

The Foreign Corrupt Practices Act and Other Cross-Border Compliance Issues

As new overseas operations are considered and plans put together to take them from concept to implementation, there are a host of issues that can affect whether they will result in profit or loss, strategic success or underperforming disappointment. Hands down though, the first notice of a governmental investigation that could impose millions of dollars of penalties on the books and years of personal jail time for senior management—perhaps including you—can make for the worst of exceptionally bad days. Perhaps that explains why the Association of Corporate Counsel's Chief Legal Officer (CLO) 2013 Survey shows that for 87 percent of CLOs surveyed in over 1,100 legal departments in 36 countries, "dealing with increasing scrutiny related to compliance and ethics issues is how the majority of their time is spent."[1]

It stands to reason then that as you lay the groundwork for your next cross-border expansion, you must take the necessary steps to protect your bottom line and your personal liberty from the very beginning, no matter the industry to which you belong. Attempting to touch on all the various regulatory regimes that a given business might be subject to is clearly beyond

---

1. Steven T. Taylor, *ACC Survey Explores the Concerns of CLOs and Reveals... Opportunities for Law Firms*, 32 OF COUNSEL (March 2013), http://www.acc.com/aboutacc/newsroom/accinthenews/upload/Of-Counsel-March-2013.pdf.

the scope of this book. Given its broad application across sectors and the potential penalties for violations however, examination of the Foreign Corrupt Practices Act (FCPA) is perhaps the best vehicle to assess regulatory risks and construct the appropriate compliance response.

Overview and History of the FCPA

"The FCPA can be a very difficult minefield for an unsophisticated company," notes Eric O'Neill, formerly with the FBI and now the head of The Georgetown Group, an investigative and risk management company based in Washington, D.C. "The FCPA itself is very straightforward, though," O'Neill quips, "if you violate it, you may get arrested." Even large corporate legal departments find compliance issues such as this to be a significant challenge in an era where every line item is scrutinized. For many companies, associated costs are expensive, and resources and real buy-in from management are often in limited supply.[2]

Still, with recognition that enforcement is much increased in recent years, there has been a noticeable change in the deal making arena, observes Harvey Cohen of Dinsmore Shohl. Years ago, it was not uncommon for Cohen to get pushback from clients or opposing parties abroad at the suggestion that they insert FCPA clauses into contracts and require certifications periodically etc. "I sometimes had to force them in," Cohen recalls. Now? "No one pushes back . . . at this point, it would really be malpractice not to put it in and not best practice for a contracting party to resist." Third-party vendors are slowly adapting as well, relates Arvind Vij, Senior Counsel for JPMorgan (India):

> We see they are now being more professional about these issues, given that they need to compete on the international stage for developed market work and international companies pay attention to these

---

2. *Best Practices in Preventing Fraud and Corruption in a Global Business*, Lex Mundi Publications 2009, http://www.lexmundi.com/images/lexmundi/PDF/BestPractices/BestPractice_FraudCorruption.pdf.

matters when conducting their due diligence, so this is a priority for the vendors.

Prior to enactment of the FCPA, there was nothing in U.S. law that explicitly prohibited the bribing of foreign officials or that mandated disclosure of such activity.[3] In fact, in some countries, commercial bribery was actually tax deductible.[4] This, unfortunately, included the United States.[5]

As often happens, the impetus for change was an unintended consequence of an entirely unrelated phenomenon: investigations into the Nixon Administration's connection to the break-in at Democratic National Committee headquarters at the Watergate hotel in 1972.[6] What began as a probe into illegal corporate contributions to Richard Nixon's reelection campaign expanded when the Securities and Exchange Commission (SEC) determined that hundreds of companies had hidden hundreds of millions of dollars in secret, mislabeled accounts that were used to make many other forms of illicit payments, including bribes to high officials of foreign governments.[7] The SEC's enforcement chief, Stanley Sporkin, sought a law requiring companies to identify bribery payments on their books, reasoning that it would have a deterrent effect on companies making such payments.[8] Congress did Sporkin one better and drafted legislation that made the bribing of foreign officials itself a crime.[9] President Jimmy Carter signed the FCPA into law on December 19, 1977.[10]

The FCPA has had two major amendments. The first, in 1988, saw Congress among other things clarify that the scope of facilitation or so-called "grease" payments (which were exempted from prohibition) would not

---

3. DONALD R. CRUVER, COMPLYING WITH THE FOREIGN CORRUPT PRACTICES ACT: A GUIDE FOR U.S. FIRMS DOING BUSINESS IN THE INTERNATIONAL MARKETPLACE 1–2 (2d ed. 1999).
4. *March 2003 Update on the Implementation of the OECD Recommendation on the Tax Deductibility of Bribes to Foreign Public Officials*, OECD, http://www.oecd.org/document/7/0,2340,en_2649_34551_2514631_1_1_1_37447,00.html.
5. Paul D. Carrington, *Enforcing International Corrupt Practices Law*, 32 MICH. J. INT'L L. 129, 148 (2010).
6. John Gibeaut, *Battling Bribery Abroad*, ABA J. (March 2007), http://www.abajournal.com/magazine/article/battling_bribery_abroad/.
7. *Id.*
8. *Id.*
9. *Id.*
10. CRUVER, *supra* note 3, at 8.

include discretionary acts on the part of officials that amounted to obtaining, retaining, or directing business.[11] Additional amendments enacted in 1998 applied antibribery measures to foreign companies and individuals who act in furtherance of corrupt payments within U.S. territory.[12]

At the beginning of the twenty-first century, the sheer scale of bribery around the world beggared the imagination. For example, the World Bank has calculated that bribes totaling one *trillion* dollars were paid in 2002.[13] By 2010, an Association of Certified Fraud Examiners report divined through survey participants that the typical organization loses 5 percent of its annual revenue to fraud, which if true generally would translate to potential global fraud loss of over $2.9 trillion.[14] Research firm Ipsos found in a survey covering respondents from 36 countries that 42 percent of senior corporate managers and directors were aware of their own companies understating expenses or overstating revenue.[15]

This kind of data represents more than a textbook ethical problem. As argued by Professor Paul Carrington, corruption of higher officials disables effective government, causing failing or weak states to "serve as havens for all sorts of gangsters, pirates, and terrorists."[16] These rogue elements challenge not only the effective conduct of business in the developing world, but, as has been demonstrated repeatedly in recent years, the personal safety of citizens even in the developed world. It's been noted that though corruption often facilitates drug trafficking, money laundering, prostitution, and other criminal activities, it is not necessarily restricted to those enterprises.[17]

---

11. *End of Grease Payments Coming*, FCPA COMPLIANCE AND ETHICS BLOG (Dec. 18, 2009), http://tfoxlaw.wordpress.com/2009/12/18/end-of-grease-payments-coming/.
12. *Foreign Corrupt Practices Act: Overview*, U.S. DEP'T OF JUSTICE, http://www.justice.gov/criminal/fraud/fcpa/ (last visited May 7, 2011).
13. Carrington, *supra* note 5, at 131.
14. *2010 Report to the Nations—Key Findings and Highlights*, ASSOCIATION OF CERTIFIED FRAUD EXAMINERS, http://www.acfe.com/uploadedFiles/ACFE_Website/Content/documents/rttn-2010.pdf.
15. Floyd Norris, *A Troubling Survey on Global Corruption*, N.Y. TIMES (May 17, 2013), http://www.nytimes.com/2013/05/18/business/economy/a-troubling-survey-on-global-corruption.html?ref=business&_r=3&.
16. *Id.*
17. *Best Practices in Preventing Fraud and Corruption in a Global Business*, *supra* note 2.

How the FCPA Works

As noted above, the FCPA statute combines two related requirements in an effort to act against bribery of foreign officials. Specifically, it combines a prohibition of the corrupt payment of (or offer to pay) "anything of value" to a foreign official in order to obtain, retain, or direct business with a requirement for companies designated as "issuers" to keep accurate books and records and maintain effective internal controls.[18]

More explicitly, the elements of a violation of the antibribery portion of the statute are

(a) use of an instrumentality of interstate commerce in furtherance of
(b) a payment, or offer to pay, anything of value
(c) to any foreign official, political party, or political candidate
(d) in such a way as to assist the company in obtaining or retaining business or in directing business to any particular person to secure an improper advantage.[19]

A corrupt intent on the part of the person making or authorizing the payment to induce misuse of the foreign official's authority is a necessary element,[20] although "willful blindness," conscious disregard, or deliberate ignorance of known circumstances can satisfy the requirements of the statute.[21]

The Books, Records and Internal Control section of the statute requires those to whom it applies to keep books, records, and accounts with "reasonable detail to accurately and fairly reflect transactions and dispositions of assets."[22] It also mandates creation of a system of internal accounting

---

18. F. Joseph Warin, Michael S. Diamant, and Jill M. Pfenning, *FCPA Compliance in China and the Gifts and Hospitality Challenge*, VIRGINIA LAW & BUSINESS REVIEW (Spring 2010), 34, 43–46, http://author.acc.com/chapters/wmacca/upload/9_Background-Materials-Virginia-LBR-2010.pdf.
19. *The Foreign Corrupt Practices Act of the United States FCPA Checklist*, http://www.acc.com/chapters/canada/upload/fore-corr-prac-acts.pdf (last visited May 14, 2011).
20. *Foreign Corrupt Practices Act's Antibribery Provisions*, LECTRIC LAW LIBRARY, http://www.lectlaw.com/files/bur21.htm (last visited May 14, 2011).
21. Stephanie L. Connor & R. Christopher Cook, *DOJ Targets Pharmaceutical Industry and Individuals for FCPA Enforcement*, JONES DAY (Nov. 23, 2009), http://www.martindale.com/business-law/article_Jones-Day_849758.htm.
22. Warin, et al., *supra* note 18 at 45–46.

controls to ensure proper authorization by management and recorded accountability for assets that allows for preparation of adequate financial statements and comparison with existing assets to allow for action to be taken on any differences discovered.[23]

Criminal liability for record keeping is enforced by the SEC and would apply where a defendant knowingly circumvented or failed to implement the required internal system of accounting controls or knowingly falsified any book, record, or account.[24]

So, to whom does the FCPA apply? The current list includes

1. "issuers" and individuals who serve as officers, directors, agents, and employees in those companies;
2. "domestic concerns," which includes U.S. citizens, wherever they are located; any business entity organized under the laws of the United States; or any business entity that has a principle place of business in the United States;
3. any foreigner committing an act in furtherance of a foreign bribe while in the United States;
4. U.S. businesses and nationals acting to further unlawful payments made wholly outside the United States; and
5. U.S. citizens, nationals, or residents who act on behalf of a foreign subsidiary, where the subject payment would violate the FCPA.[25]

Exactly who qualifies as an "issuer" is not always entirely clear. Companies who have issued securities or otherwise are required to file reports with the SEC are deemed "issuers" by the terms of the statute; this otherwise straightforward-sounding definition can become confusing when considering non-U.S.–based companies.[26]

That being said, the FCPA is generally held inapplicable to foreign individuals, provided they do not otherwise fall under the "issuer" or "domestic

---

23. Id.
24. *The Foreign Corrupt Practices Act of the United States FCPA Checklist*, supra note 19, at 11.
25. Id. at 3.
26. Mike Koehler, "*Understanding Issuers*," FCPA PROFESSOR (Feb. 22, 2010), http://fcpaprofessor.blogspot.com/2010/02/understanding-issuers.html.

concern" categories.[27] Overall however, the FCPA obviously casts a fairly comprehensive net, one that might catch many of the uninitiated unawares. For instance, management of U.S.-based private companies might correctly conclude that they do not qualify as "issuers" and therefore that the bookkeeping provisions of the statute do not apply to their firm. That is only half the story though: if the entity is organized under U.S. law or if it has a principle place of business in the United States, the antibribery provisions of the act still apply.[28]

Likewise, a company might think that a payment to a foreign official simply to secure a government license or permit needed to do business would not trigger an FCPA violation, since it is not "obtaining or retaining business." Unfortunately, the U.S. government does not agree, having initiated enforcement proceedings for just such conduct, as well as payments seeking special tax and custom treatment or foreign government licenses, permits, and certifications which assisted the payer in generally doing business in a foreign country.[29]

Even novices to international business are likely to understand that large cash payments to foreign officials could land them in legal difficulty. Nevertheless, the statute does not require so blatant an act, but merely an offer to pay "anything of value." Whether a given transaction triggers this provision is determined by the subjective perception of the recipient—and something as simple as discounts, meals and drinks, or transportation can potentially qualify.[30]

Professionals who counsel overseas businesses have to be aware that the Department of Justice (DOJ) has used the far-reaching jurisdictional ambit of the FCPA to pursue foreign entities and individuals with relatively limited contacts with the United States.[31] Even cases in which the jurisdictional

---

27. *The Foreign Corrupt Practices Act of the United States FCPA Checklist*, *supra* note 19, at 3.
28. Jennifer Dawn Taylor, *Ambiguities in the Foreign Corrupt Practices Act: Unnecessary Costs of Fighting Corruption?* LOUISIANA LAW REVIEW (Summer 2001), at 864, http://digitalcommons.law.lsu.edu/cgi/viewcontent.cgi?article=5899&context=lalrev.
29. *FCPA 101*, FCPA Professor (2014), http://www.fcpaprofessor.com/fcpa-101#q8.
30. Michael L. Volkov, *Most Common FCPA Myths*, Worldcompliance.com (2010), http://www.fcpa-worldcompliance.com/pdf/most-common-fcpa-myths.pdf.
31. *Best Practices in Preventing Fraud and Corruption in a Global Business*, *supra* note 2.

nexus was described by outside commentators as "tenuous" have resulted in fines and felony pleas.[32]

In evaluating one's potential liability under the FCPA, it is important to remember that the statute can hold a company liable for violations even when the violations are committed by someone other than the company's own employees. Companies and individuals who qualify as issuers or domestic concerns are charged under the statute with those facts they *should have known* with regards to consultants, joint venturers, teaming partners, distributors, subcontractors, suppliers, and other international business associates.[33]

This can create tremendous problems even for companies who have taken what would otherwise be the necessary steps as to their domestic operations. In *SEC v. IBM Corporation*,[34] the books and records of one of IBM's foreign subsidiaries were alleged to have been improper. There was no evidence that any employee of the parent company had knowledge of the improper bookkeeping, nor was it alleged that the parent had failed to set up adequate internal controls. The SEC pursued the parent for the subsidiary's violations regardless.[35] Criminal liability for book and record keeping of another entity does not apply, however, if the issuer owns 50 percent or less of the subject business.[36]

Paul Peterson, a forensic accountant and FCPA expert currently based in China at Grant Thornton, calculated that 85 percent of all FCPA enforcement actions used the books and records and internal controls provision against multinational companies. Since evidence of a bribe is often difficult to find, the Feds go after the accounting of suspect transactions. It's a similar concept to how Al Capone was brought down; it wasn't from bootlegging alcohol, prostitution, or gambling but for tax evasion.

---

32. *Restoring Balance: Proposed Amendments to the Foreign Corrupt Practices Act*, U.S. CHAMBER INSTITUTE FOR LEGAL REFORM, 4 (Oct. 2010), http://www.millerchevalier.com/portalresource/RestoringBalance.
33. *The Foreign Corrupt Practices Act of the United States FCPA Checklist*, *supra* note 19, at 6.
34. 00-Civ-3040 (D.D.C. Dec. 21, 2000).
35. *The Foreign Corrupt Practices Act of the United States FCPA Checklist*, *supra* note 19, at 15.
36. *Id.* at 11.

Because third parties' actions can potentially create criminal liability for your company, practitioners emphasize the overarching importance of diligence in this area. Kathryn Woodward, former Compliance Director at Sara Lee Corporation, asks the threshold question: "Do you know who these people are?" As you take time to find out who they are, Jed Hepworth, of Cargill, recommends "When you are choosing a distributor, you want someone who shares your values."

Yet another trap for the unwary is raised by attorney Cohen. The FCPA applies to transactions with foreign officials, so many people let their guard down when they are dealing with what they believe to be a "private company." But, Cohen warns, if you are in a developing nation such as Nigeria or China, "don't be so sure." Many companies in such locales may in fact be state-owned enterprises, and the DOJ has consistently argued that their employees fall under the definition of a foreign official as employees of an "instrumentality of a foreign government."[37]

This position was tested in a recent California Central District court case, *United States v. Noriega et al.*[38] The court found persuasive a DOJ argument that the 1998 amendments to the FCPA sought to bring the statute in line with U.S. obligations to the Organisation for Economic Cooperation and Development (OECD) Convention, which defines foreign officials to include those exercising public functions for any entity over which a government may "directly or indirectly exercise a dominant influence."[39] Most recently, the 11th Circuit in *U.S. v. Esquenazi*[40] weighed in on the definition of instrumentality under the FCPA. Per the website secaction.com:

> the Court defined the term instrumentality "as an entity controlled by the government of a foreign country that performs a function the controlling government treats as its own . . . what constitutes control and what constitutes a function the government treats as its own are fact-bound questions . . . To decide if the government 'controls' an

---

37. Dulce J. Foster, *Who Is a Foreign Official? Recent FCPA Litigation Sheds New Light*, FREDRIKSON & BYRON, P.A. (May 12, 2011), http://www.fredlaw.com/news__media/2011/05/12/219/who_is_a_foreign_official_recent_fcpa_litigation_sheds_new_light.
38. 10-1031 (C.D. Ca. 2010).
39. Foster, *supra* note 37.
40. No. 11-15331 (11th Cir. Opinion filed May 16, 2014).

entity, courts and juries should look to the foreign government's formal designation of that entity; whether the government has a majority interest in the entity; the extent to which the entity's profits, if any, go directly into the governmental fisc, and, by the same token, the extent to which the government funds the entity if it fails to break even; and the length of time these indicia have existed." These factors were informed by the OECD Convention commentary.[41]

On May 10, 2011, Lindsey Manufacturing became the first corporate defendant in history to be convicted on FCPA charges rather than settling with the government.[42] Could there be a better example of the overriding importance of knowing exactly with whom you are doing?

Various lists of "red flags" for both the anticorruption and records and bookkeeping parts of the FCPA have been collected to assist executives and counsel in spotting and addressing potential issues proactively. Although it is not all-inclusive, what follows is a list of some FCPA red flags for corrupt business practices:

- Third Party refuses to certify compliance with antibribery or FCPA requirements
- Third Party refuses to complete agent/consultant/third party questionnaire regarding relationship with or interests involving foreign government officials
- Third Party does not appear to be qualified to perform the duties for which it is engaged to assist your company
- Third Party is related to a government official
- Country has a reputation for corruption and bribery
- The industry has a history of FCPA and anticorruption problems
- Breakup of a company or association with one or more foreign companies is unexplained or inadequately explained

---

41. Thomas O. Gorman, *FCPA: The First Circuit Court Decision Defining Instrumentality*, Dorsey & Whitney LLP (May 18, 2014), http://www.secactions.com/fcpa-the-first-circuit-court-decision-defining-instrumentality.
42. Foster, *supra* note 37.

- Requests for commissions to be paid in a third party country, to a third party, or in cash or untraceable funds
- Heavy reliance by party on political or government contacts as opposed to knowledgeable staff and investment of time to promote the Company's interests
- Refusal or inability to develop or implement a market strategy
- A desire to keep third party representation secret
- Relationship problems with other foreign companies

And here is a list of FCPA red flags for recordkeeping and accounting violations:

- Vague, nonspecific description for payments made in entries
- Documents conceal the true identify of an in-country representative or agent
- Payment descriptions that do not correspond to the appropriate account
- General purpose or miscellaneous accounts that can be used to hide improper payments
- Over-invoicing or false invoices
- Unrecorded accounts or transactions
- Travel and expense forms with incomplete information that are used to obtain cash for improper payments
- Submission of false or inaccurate expense account reports
- Misstatement of transactions, e.g., recording a payment to the wrong payee."[43]

A third-party agent's bad reputation is a significant red flag. Parties should be able to document the good reputation and experience of their third-party agents.[44] If a foreign partner seeks to monopolize control of native government approvals, seeks a relationship outside the boundaries of local

---

43. Sharie Brown, *Identification of "Red Flags" for Possible Violations of Key U.S. Laws for Companies Operating Overseas*, CORPORATE COMPLIANCE INSIGHTS (Oct. 14, 2010), http://www.corporatecomplianceinsights.com/2010/red-flags-fcpa-violations-compliance-risk-overseas-operations/.
44. *The Foreign Corrupt Practices Act of the United States FCPA Checklist*, *supra* note 19, at 12.

law, or otherwise has nothing to offer but influence, these, too, are red flags.[45] Requests for unusual bonuses, unorthodox up-front payments, and substantially inflated commissions or foreign partner asset contributions should also arouse suspicion and inquiry.[46] Cohen points out that companies can ask the U.S. Commercial Service to do background checks on indigenous entities, and should the DOJ come calling later in connection with that vendor, a report from an arm of the U.S. government might go towards demonstrating appropriate diligence. Such a report would not be conclusive whatsoever though, Cohen cautions.

Various past prosecutions can also be mined for circumstances and fact patterns that the DOJ deems red flag worthy and can provide important practical lessons. One commentator noted a number of these involved in the Baker Hughes case from 2007. The prosecution highlighted the importance of due diligence on not just the agent but their family and personal relationships as well.[47] Likewise, there is no *de minimis* exception to provisions regarding payments under the FCPA; in a matter that spawned $44 million in sanctions, a portion of the charges involved a $9,000 payment.[48] The DOJ does not care if an illegal practice is commonplace for purposes of the FCPA; the practice is still deemed illegal.[49] When an agent's actions are found inconsistent with the Act, all payments need to be terminated immediately—there is no room for accrued compensation or severance.[50] Finally, the Baker Hughes case yields the very important reminder that the mere existence of company procedures will not provide protection where they aren't followed.[51]

Lee Nelson, formerly of Hewlett-Packard (HP), relates a real-life red flag lesson. While he was stationed in Singapore on behalf of a predecessor company, a member of the sales department claimed to have an "in" to a

---

45. *Id.* at 13.
46. *Id.* at 13–14.
47. *Baker Hughes Settles FCPA Charges with DOJ and SEC*, HUGHES HUBBARD FCPA ALERT, 2 (May 2007), http://www.hugheshubbard.com/files/Publication/a9b9b892-4665-4d7b-99ef-5e3a0dfc7d1a/Presentation/PublicationAttachment/8ca38e39-d1ff-4186-9830-5eac85d4a135/FCPA%20Alert.pdf.
48. *Id.*
49. *Id.* at 3.
50. *Id.*
51. *Id.*

state-owned enterprise and that as a result the company would not need to pay a 10 percent commission. Nelson took this as an FCPA red flag and had outside counsel investigate the reference given by this inside person; the reference claimed to have never even heard of the person. Quick recognition of suspicious circumstances and prompt follow-through with a simple investigation saved the day.

Enforcement of FCPA

The SEC and DOJ each have complimentary roles in enforcing the FCPA. The SEC has civil jurisdiction over those parties registered with or in a reporting relationship with the Commission, whereas the DOJ maintains civil FCPA jurisdiction over parties with no relationship to the SEC and criminal jurisdiction related to parties accountable under the statute.[52] Where their jurisdictions overlap, the two agencies generally coordinate their investigations and enforcement activities.[53]

One might wonder why, if the FCPA has been law since 1977, it has only in recent years been garnering so much attention? The answer is that for the first quarter century or so of its existence, there were relatively few investigations under the FCPA, largely due to the difficulty the government had in gathering the necessary information.[54] This began to change with the passage of the Sarbanes-Oxley Act of 2002 (SOX), which required companies to tighten internal controls and mandated that chief executive officers (CEO's) and chief financial officers (CFO's) personally certify the accuracy of financial reporting.[55] Additionally, SOX requires prompt investigation of "material weaknesses" of internal controls.[56] It is not difficult to understand that in a post-SOX business environment, the costs of hiding suspicious

---

52. Joseph P. Covington, Thomas C. Newkirk & Jessica Tillipman, *FCPA Enforcement in a Sarbanes-Oxley World*, 20 CORPORATE COUNSELOR, 1–2 (Aug. 2005), *available at* http://jenner.com/system/assets/assets/2462/original/LJN_Corporate_Counselor_August2005.pdf?1319063342.
53. *Id.* at 2.
54. *Id.*
55. *Id.*
56. *Id.*

transactions suddenly became much greater.[57] Add to this the Federal Sentencing Guidelines (among other regimes), which have created incentives for establishment of FCPA reporting within companies and self-reporting to authorities of bribery and other corruption-related acts as a means of mitigating potential sanctions, and it becomes obvious that prosecutors no longer have difficulty obtaining the evidence needed to prosecute.[58]

Recent trends point to significantly more aggressive enforcement efforts. It is clear that the emphasis of the authorities has shifted from mere detection of corruption to enforcement of the law.[59] This translates into more cases being brought, higher fines and penalties, and a greater number of cases involving jail time for individuals. [60]

How many more cases are being brought? After trending upward for several years, in the first quarter of 2010 alone, the U.S government brought or resolved FCPA charges against 36 companies or individuals, compared to 6 in the first quarter of 2009 and 4 in the first quarter of 2008.[61] This increase makes sense when taking into account a report from the *Los Angeles Times* in January 2009 that quoted Justice Department officials as saying that their "enforcement of the FCPA is second only to fighting terrorism in terms of priority."[62] It's not for nothing that then-Assistant Attorney General Lanny Breuer commented on November 16, 2010, that "we are in a new era of FCPA enforcement."[63]

The new era of which Breuer spoke is marked with significantly higher penalties and fines. Of the top ten largest settlements tracked by The FCPA

---

57. Id.
58. Id.
59. *Best Practices in Preventing Fraud and Corruption in a Global Business*, supra note 2.
60. *Restoring Balance: Proposed Amendments to the Foreign Corrupt Practices Act*, supra note 32, at 2.
61. *Sharp Increases in Recent FCPA Enforcement*, Harvard Law School Forum on Corporate Governance and Financial Regulation (May 9, 2010) (posted by Scott Hirst, co-editor, based on a Willkie Farr & Gallagher LLP client memorandum by MartinWeinstein, Robert J. Meyer & Jeffrey D. Clark), http://blogs.law.harvard.edu/corpgov/2010/05/09/sharp-increases-in-recent-fcpa-enforcement/.
62. *Best Practices in Preventing Fraud and Corruption in a Global Business*, supra note 2.
63. T. Markus Funk, *Another Landmark Year: 2010 FCPA Year-In-Review and Enforcement Trends for 2011*, Bloomberg Law Reports (2010), http://www.perkinscoie.com/files/upload/11_01_03_FunkArticle.pdf (referencing DOJ, *Assistant Attorney General Lanny A. Breuer Speaks at the 24th National Conference on the Foreign Corrupt Practices Act* [Nov. 16, 2010], http://www.justice.gov/criminal/pr/speeches/2010/crm-speech-101116.html).

Blog as of April 2011, eight were entered into either in 2010 or early 2011, each with a value between $70 million and $400 million.[64] And continuing a seven-year trend, 2013 saw a continued surge in activity on the FCPA front; there were more enforcement actions brought by the Justice Department by July of 2013 than had been instituted in all of 2012.[65] As of December 31, 2013, 92 companies were known to be the subject of ongoing and unresolved FCPA-related investigations.[66]

Moreover, investigators are utilizing increasingly proactive and aggressive methods likely to result in even more indictments and more trials.[67] To better illustrate what "aggressive" means in a practical context, consider the settlement reached between the SEC and NATCO Group, Inc. in January 2010. NATCO had made payments to immigration officials in Kazakhstan—where the Kazakh officials extorted the company with threats of prison and deportation. Even under these seemingly exculpatory facts, the SEC still insisted on a $65,000 civil penalty against NATCO.[68]

Another example of what this new era of FCPA enforcement looks like is illustrated by the arrest of 22 military and law-enforcement supply company employees in a two-and-a-half-year-long undercover sting operation generally reserved for organized crime bosses.[69] Federal Bureau of Investigation (FBI) special agents posed as officials of the West African nation of Gabon. Wire taps, videotapes of the defendants, and a cooperating witness were all part of the government's efforts in setting up the sting, which culminated in arrests at a gun industry trade show in Las Vegas.[70] The government

---

64. Thomas O. Gorman, *SEC Enforcement Trends 2011: The New Era of FCPA Enforcement*, SEC ACTIONS (April 15, 2011), http://www.secactions.com/sec-enforcement-trends-2011-the-new-era-of-fcpa-enforcement/.
65. Greg Deis, William Michael, Jr., Simeon M. Kriesberg & Sean P. McDonnell, *FCPA Update: Mid-Year 2013*, MAYER BROWN (Aug. 15, 2013), http://www.mondaq.com/unitedstates/x/258152/Securities/FCPA+Update+MidYear+2013.
66. Richard L. Cassin, *The Corporate Investigations List (January 2014)*, FCPA BLOG (January 8, 2014), http://www.fcpablog.com/blog/2014/1/8/the-corporate-investigations-list-january-2014.html#.
67. Funk, *supra* note 61.
68. *Sharp Increases in Recent FCPA Enforcement*, *supra* note 59.
69. Thomas Fox, *Top FCPA Investigations of 2010, Part I*, FCPA COMPLIANCE AND ETHICS BLOG (Dec. 28, 2010), http://tfoxlaw.wordpress.com/2010/12/28/top-fcpa-investigations-of-2010-part-i/.
70. *Id.*

charged the defendants with "plotting to bribe the minister of defense for Gabon to sell military and law enforcement products."[71]

Additionally, federal prosecutors have been known to utilize another, previously used statute first enacted in 1961, the Travel Act, to expand on the already broad parameters of the FCPA. For instance, the FCPA does not reach commercial bribery involving purely private parties, whereas many state statutes do. To the extent the bribery transaction touches a state with such a commercial bribery prohibition, the Travel Act allows the prosecution to be "federalized."[72]

The more cynical members of the international business community might imagine that there are reasons for this "full-on" prosecutorial drive other than the stated goals of preventing bribery from undermining the integrity of foreign governments. After all, in an era of governmental cutbacks and austerity, these actions have transformed units of the SEC and DOJ into veritable profit centers, with efforts that "seem to have abundantly reimbursed the national treasury."[73] Not only do civil actions increasingly bring millions (if not hundreds of millions) of dollars to federal coffers at a clip, but they also often do so from non-U.S.–based companies.[74] If this is thought of as a form of indirect taxation, perhaps it is not surprising that the OECD Council in 2009 simply recommended that member states raise taxes on firms engaged in international corrupt practices.[75] A slightly less cynical view would note that foreign governments have been slow to follow the U.S. lead on corruption prosecutions, and actions taken against foreign companies might represent a less-than-subtle hint to various governments that more can and should be done.[76]

---

71. Richard L. Cassin, *Shot-Show Trial Opens in DC*, FCPA BLOG (May 16, 2011), http://www.fcpablog.com/blog/2011/5/16/shot-show-trial-opens-in-dc.html.
72. Adele Nicholas, Travel Advisory: *DOJ Dusts Off Little-Used Travel Act to Strengthen FCPA Prosecutions*, INSIDE COUNSEL, July 2013, http://www.insidecounseldigital.com/insidecounsel/july_2013/?pg=24&pm=2&u1=#pg24.
73. Carrington, *supra* note 5, at 136.
74. Funk, *supra* note 61.
75. Carrington, *supra* note 5, at 148.
76. Philip Urofsky & Danforth Newcomb, *Recent Trends and Patterns in FCPA Enforcement*, SHEARMAN & STERLING LLP FCPA DIGEST, 6 (Jan. 20, 2011), http://www.shearman.com/~/media/Files/NewsInsights/Publications/2011/01/Shearman%20%20Sterlings%20Recent%20Trends%20and%20Patterns%20i__/Files/View%20January%202011%20Recent

The Department of Justice has not shown reticence about bringing criminal charges against individuals either. The thought behind this is fairly straightforward: with no little justification, that potential personal criminal liability will have a deterrent effect on executives.[77]

To illustrate the breadth of DOJ targets, prosecutions in 2009 ran the gamut from Frederick Bourke's one-year sentence for bribery in his attempted acquisition of the state-owned oil company of Azerbaijan, to Rep. William Jefferson's (D-La.) thirteen-year sentence for, among other things, bribing former Nigerian officials, to two Hollywood film executives who were convicted of bribing the head of the Thai Tourism Authority to obtain the rights to run the Bangkok Film Festival.[78] On April 19, 2010, Charles Jumet was sentenced to a record 87 months in prison for his part in payments of over $200,000 made to former Panamanian officials to obtain maritime contracts and for making false statements to federal agents.[79] The targets of this campaign have been laid out in public statements by top Justice Department officials; they include" "mid-level to senior level corporate officers and employees, CEO's, CFO's, [and] heads of international sales."[80]

On top of FCPA civil and criminal liabilities, it is important to note that other, collateral damage can result from corrupt activities. To the extent that a violation of the FCPA can be shown to have resulted in harm to a competing firm, the violator may be found civilly liable under the Racketeer Influenced and Corrupt Organizations Act (RICO), or under the tort law of most U.S. states, which could involve the imposition of punitive damages.[81] Shareholder derivative suits and even the failure of the company due to losing key leadership to criminal convictions are also quite possible under such a scenario.

%20Trends%20and%20Patterns%20in%20__/FileAttachment/January%202011%20Trends%20%20Patterns.pdf.
77. Funk *supra* note 61, at 5–6.
78. Lanny A. Breuer, Prepared Address to the 22nd National Forum on the Foreign Corrupt Practices Act 3 (Nov. 17, 2009), http://www.justice.gov/criminal/pr/speeches-testimony/documents/11-17-09aagbreuer-remarks-fcpa.pdf.
79. *Virginia Resident Sentenced to 87 Months in Prison for Bribing Foreign Government Officials*, U.S. Dep't of Justice Office of Public Affairs (April 19, 2010), http://www.justice.gov/opa/pr/2010/April/10-crm-442.html.
80. *Restoring Balance: Proposed Amendments to the Foreign Corrupt Practices Act*, *supra* note 32, at 2.
81. Paul D. Carrington, *supra* note 5, at 134.

As in any enforcement endeavor, there will always be organizations that will draw more attention than others. In the FCPA enforcement landscape until recently, those organizations were generally thought to be, not surprisingly, industries that typically have significant contact with foreign government officials, including healthcare, pharmaceuticals, medical devices, transportation, entertainment, and energy.[82] Then in 2010 the SEC created specialized enforcement units to develop in-depth knowledge of industry and regional practices.[83] In 2013, it became apparent that compliance attention was being shifted somewhat, with an unidentified senior SEC enforcement official identifying retail, consumer products, insurance, private equity, and technology as areas of current emphasis.[84] Perhaps the focus on retail helps explain reports that Wal-Mart recently spent some $200 million on revamping its compliance operations and investigating possible violations of U.S. antibribery laws in Mexico, China, India, and Brazil.[85]

Not finding their industries listed might lead some executives, particularly in smaller businesses, to conclude that their overall FCPA exposure is minimal, and that not only their compliance spending but their time commitment to the issue can be reduced accordingly. Every indication in the recent, actual enforcement of the Act, however, suggests that any businesspeople potentially liable under the Act who take a cavalier attitude about the U.S. government's willingness to pursue violations are playing a game of Russian roulette with their careers—not to mention the risks of criminal conviction.

Simply put, the DOJ and SEC are not ignoring small and mid-sized companies that, whether they have bothered to seriously assess their compliance risk or not, might be conducting billions of dollar in overseas transactions.[86]

---

82. *Best Practices in Preventing Fraud and Corruption in a Global Business*, *supra* note 2.
83. Funk, *supra* note 61.
84. Robertson Park & Timothy P. Peterson, *Federal Agencies Target New Industries for FCPA Enforcement* INSIDE COUNSEL (June 12, 2013), http://www.insidecounsel.com/2013/06/12/regulatory-federal-agencies-target-new-industries?eNL=51c09d2a160ba0b55e000051?utm_source=IC_Commentary&utm_medium=eNL&utm_campaign=InsideCounsel_eNLs&_LID=82107898.
85. Shelly Banjo & R. Jai Krishna, *Wal-Mart Curbs Ambitions in India*, WALL ST. J. (Oct. 10, 2013), http://online.wsj.com/news/articles/SB20001424052702303382004579124703326968442.
86. Jeffrey Cramer, *Commentary: The FCPA Game Has Changed: Trends in Enforcement*, MAIN JUSTICE (April 23, 2010), http://www.mainjustice.com/2010/04/23/commentary-the-fcpa-game-has-changed-trends-in-enforcement/.

That said, billions of dollars in controversy are not needed to trigger the government's interest in this area. In a case resulting in two convictions for conspiracy to make corrupt payments to Panamanian officials, the total amount of payments over a six-year period was a relatively small $331,000.[87]

Moreover, as attorney Thomas Fox points out, there is no *de minimis* exception to the FCPA's book and recordkeeping requirements. This principle was illustrated in very concrete terms in the case of Texas-based Team Industrial Services, which provides services for mechanical and piping systems across a variety of industries. In 2009, Team conducted an internal investigation that revealed $50,000 of payments that potentially violated the FCPA. As Fox reported in his blog, the company self-reported the potential violation to the DOJ and then spent in excess of $3 million in investigatory costs.[88] It is no wonder that in summing up her thoughts on FCPA enforcement today, Kathryn Woodward says simply, "no one is safe."

So how does a case typically begin? Jessie Liu, a partner with Jenner & Block and herself a former federal prosecutor, acknowledges that "it is a huge endeavor for DOJ to do one of these cases." Before gearing up, prosecutors have to have some indication that a party is worth investigating, whether by anonymous tip, a newspaper article, or otherwise. At that point, Liu explains, a prosecutor has one of two choices. She may simply make an informal request to the target company—that is, the company gets a phone call from an FBI agent. The agent will ask directly whether the company will allow its people to voluntarily meet or give up documents. The other option is a grand jury subpoena, which only requires some probable cause that leads to evidence of a crime. Usually corporations are pretty cooperative with informal requests, Liu observes, since the bar to getting a grand jury subpoena is not that high. "Corporations have a general understanding that the government can get what it is asking for," Liu explains.

If you find yourself in the unfortunate position of being a target of an FCPA investigation, Liu counsels that the best way to deal with it is "to get ahead of it." You do that, Liu says, by conducting a parallel internal investigation. This involves engaging outside counsel who take an aggressive look

---

87. *Id.*
88. Fox, *supra* note 67.

at the area in question. Ideally, you find any problem first, before the government does. You then let the government know what you have discovered. When you take this approach, Liu explains, you are attempting to show the DOJ that you are proactive and that you take the matter seriously. As she logically points out, in situations where the government is already investigating you, there is really no downside in disclosing a violation to them.

Whether to voluntarily disclose becomes a much harder question, however, if the government doesn't know of and might never find out about any potential violation. The key issue comes down to one question: How much does cooperation buy you? Liu reminds us that you have to be realistic. "If you disclose," she posits, "it is extremely unlikely that you will end up with the DOJ saying, 'Thanks, you can go on your way.'" At a minimum, the government will ask follow-up questions.

There are conflicting views on the extent to which voluntary disclosure, with an eye toward mitigating fines and penalties, may actually be increasing the number of investigations and enforcement actions on FCPA violations. Critics of current enforcement policy suggest that the internal investigations that in many instances lead to self-disclosure represent "the effective outsourcing of investigations by the government to the private sector."[89] On the other hand, former Assistant Attorney General Lanny Breuer has stated directly, "the majority of our cases do not come from voluntary disclosures."[90]

You ultimately have to ask yourself the following when deciding whether to disclose: How serious is the violation you are looking at? Are any violations widespread? Are any defenses available? If you find yourself without a defense, and the government is likely to find out about the violation anyway, Liu concludes that you should probably end up disclosing, since there would be no justification for not having done so at that point. Even if a company does not disclose, however, it should remediate the problem, which could involve terminating parties who engaged in wrongdoing, providing additional anticorruption training to employees, and implementing enhanced anticorruption policies and procedures.

---

89. *Id.*
90. Breuer, *supra* note 76.

Liu points out that there is no law in place that requires you to voluntarily disclose potential violations. For the DOJ's part, Breuer was recently quoted as saying "there is no doubt that a company that comes forward on its own will see a more favorable resolution than one that doesn't."[91] Yet one commentator suggests the benefit of cooperation in terms of being charged with a crime component is unclear.[92] At the same time, he notes that the calculation of the criminal fine in the largest recent cases shows an obvious reduction below the range as it would be calculated under the Sentencing Guidelines.[93]

Since most fact scenarios encountered in the real world contain shades of grey, whether to voluntarily disclose is often a really difficult decision. A business has always had to consider whether a government investigator or perhaps a competitor might gain evidence of potential violations and turn it over to prosecutors. Now, however, Liu singles out the new Dodd-Frank Wall Street Reform and Consumer Protection Act of 2010 as something that may change the calculus for many businesses.

When the Dodd-Frank Wall Street Reform and Consumer Protection Act was enacted in 2010, many observers thought it would dramatically change the disclosure calculus for many businesses. The Dodd-Frank legislation, among many other things, permits whistleblowers to receive 10 to 30 percent of the total recovery that the government receives in an FCPA action. Authorities in the field are wondering whether this will result in more prophylactic disclosures by companies, since the government will potentially have many more vehicles by which to obtain information that might otherwise escape attention. Amazingly, the law is written in such a way that employees involved in the violations themselves may profit by the whistleblower bounty. Liu explains that, as the law is written, anything short of a conviction allows you to be a whistleblower. An SEC proposed rule would at least link the amount of recovery within the 10 to 30 percent range to the culpability of the putative whistleblower. A participant

---

91. *Assistant Attorney General Lanny A. Breuer Speaks at the 24th National Conference on the Foreign Corrupt Practices Act, National Harbor, Md. – Tuesday, Nov. 16, 2010*, U.S. DEP'T OF JUSTICE, http://www.justice.gov/criminal/pr/speeches/2010/crm-speech-101116.html.
92. Gorman, *supra* note 62.
93. *Id.*

in the activity deemed a violation might be limited to 10 percent, whereas an innocent party might receive 30 percent. In any event, the effect of how these potential multimillion dollar incentives for employees to turn in their employers will play out will need to be factored into the disclosure analysis. This would seem to encourage self-disclosures. But, Liu says, relatively few of the tips submitted to the SEC have concerned the FCPA, and it appears that Dodd-Frank has had minimal effect on businesses' decisions on whether to disclose potential FCPA violations.

If you determine that you should self-report, you may wish to consider doing so sooner rather than later:

> One of the most crucial elements of the decision to self-report is timing. No company wants to walk in to the government with half-formed allegations and underdeveloped facts; however, companies hoping to maximize their cooperation credit should consider that the government wants and expects voluntary disclosure of potential FCPA issues relatively soon after the issues come to light. For example, the recent DOJ and SEC non-prosecution agreements with Ralph Lauren Corp. both trumpeted the company's timely self-reporting—apparently only two weeks after the company uncovered the existence of a potential issue. Companies are best served by addressing the question of self-reporting at the earliest stages of an FCPA investigation. Ideally, this type of initial evaluation can be conducted in a quick and efficient manner, without engaging in a costly and fully-blown investigation. Companies should respond swiftly to corruption-based concerns, master the relevant facts in as effective a manner as possible, and quickly evaluate their potential liability in order to determine whether voluntary disclosure is appropriate.[94]

---

94. Timothy P. Peterson & Robertson Park, *Regulatory: Deciding Whether to Voluntarily Disclose a Potential FCPA Violation*, INSIDE COUNSEL (May 29, 2013), http://www.insidecounsel.com/2013/05/29/regulatory-deciding-whether-to-voluntarily-disclos?eNL=51a63bbc160ba0546900008f&utm_source=ic&utm_medium=email&utm_campaign=icscoopenews&_LID=91536800.

Of course, you should not report until you have considered the logical collateral consequences, which include civil liability, potential involvement by foreign enforcement officials, and effects on investors, personnel, other lines of business, and foreign business relationships.[95]

When top officials like Lanny Breuer warn the business community "you are right to be more concerned" about more aggressive enforcement,[96] it may appear that there are no serious limitations to FCPA enforcement. That may not be entirely true, however. As Professor Paul Carrington points out, international politics do occasionally play a part in prosecutions. One example Professor Carrington gives of this phenomenon is the case of James Giffen. Giffen was accused of bribing the President Nazerbaev of Kazakhstan, described as "a friend of American foreign policy in the Middle East," on behalf of several oil companies.[97] Nazerbaev was reportedly critical of the FCPA prosecution of Giffen,[98] and Giffen argued that he had served as a de facto agent of several U.S. government agencies. In any event, in late 2010 the DOJ agreed to a plea agreement dropping all but two minor counts against Giffen.[99] Any type of cloak and dagger scenario would seem to be a relatively uncommon occurrence, however, and of little practical benefit to the vast majority of potential FCPA defendants.

FCPA Defenses

Activity that might otherwise qualify as an FCPA antibribery violation may fall under the one exception directly contemplated by the statute: "facilitating payments," otherwise known more colloquially as "grease payments." These payments to foreign officials, made to expedite or secure the performance of routine actions of a governmental authority, are limited to

---

95. *Id.*
96. Gorman, *supra* note 62.
97. Carrington, *supra* note 5, at 138.
98. *Id.*
99. Steve LeVine, *James Giffen's Trial Ends: A Slap on the Wrist, and the Triumph of American Putinism*, FOREIGN POLICY (Aug. 6, 2010), http://oilandglory.foreignpolicy.com/posts/2010/08/06/james_giffens_trial_ends_a_slap_on_the_wrist_and_the_triumph_of_american_putinism.

nondiscretionary actions such as processing forms and mail delivery.[100] The exception does not embrace payments made to influence foreign officials to award business or continue a relationship with a given business entity.[101] Even if payments fall within the exception, they must still be properly accounted for in relevant books and records.[102]

It is important to note however, that there is growing disfavor with the "grease payment" exception. The reason for having the exception in the first place is straightforward enough. Eric O'Neill of The Georgetown Group explains that "the U.S. government understands that in some places in the world, you need facilitation payments to do business." That being said, more critics are rising up and asserting that even small amounts paid to "grease the wheels" in developing countries are doing too much harm to allow the practice to continue. In February 2010, the OECD's Anti-Bribery Convention recommended that its 38 member states prohibit or discourage them, citing the "corrosive effect of small facilitation payments, particularly on sustainable economic development and the rule of law."[103]

Even in the United States, there is a growing trend to read the grease payment exception more narrowly than in the past. In fact, the Fifth Circuit Court of Appeals decision in *United States v. Kay*,[104] could arguably serve as a rallying point for those seeking to end any official distinguishing between facilitation and other payments made to foreign officials. Notwithstanding the definition of "routine governmental action" as set forth in the statute, the Fifth Circuit declared the exception fell into "very narrow categories of largely non-discretionary, ministerial activities performed by mid- or low-level foreign functionaries," such that payments to an official to issue documents or provide inspections might not qualify.[105] The U.S. Supreme Court refused to grant certiorari in 2008, allowing the Fifth Circuit's ruling to stand. The result: one commentator concludes that under the logic of *Kay*,

---

100. *The FCPA Explained, FCPA Enforcement, supra* note 18.
101. *Id.*
102. Cheryl A. Krause & Elisa T. Wiygul, *FCPA Compliance: The Vanishing "Facilitating Payments" Exception?*, 2 FINANCIAL FRAUD LAW REPORT (Sept. 2010), http://www.dechert.com/files/Publication/53b317c3-d963-4ca6-9cbc-23cc76fa60d2/Presentation/PublicationAttachment/12e5a22a-daea-4d72-adc1-3048bfa33fb2/FCPA%20Compliance.pdf.
103. *Id.*
104. No. 05–20604, 2007 WL3088140 at *7 (5th Cir. Oct. 24, 2007).
105. Krause & Wiygul, *supra* note 101, citing *U.S. v. Kay*, 359 F3d 738, 751 (5th Cir. 2004).

"*any* payment made to a foreign official to secure a business advantage of any sort assists in 'obtaining or retaining business,'" and thus is now arguably in violation of the FCPA.[106]

It is not that surprising then that a TRACE International survey released in October 2009 revealed that over 70 percent of respondents believed their companies' employees either never or rarely made facilitation payments, even when company policy allowed them.[107]

The best policy, Woodward concludes, is to adopt a policy that allows no facilitation payments at all. There is good reason for her to take that position, even beyond the fact that the legal parameters for acceptable grease payments have been under attack. The problem with a policy that allows "a little grease" is the gray areas it creates. Exactly how much grease is permissible? "A common mistake is a policy that has thresholds but still confuses," says O'Neill. It's problematic for you if your policy allows people to use their own judgment. As O'Neill observes, "if you leave a door open, someone is going to walk through."

As noted above however, there are still countries where it will be virtually impossible to do business without some facilitation payments being made. The Transparency International 2013 Global Corruption Barometer reported that of the more than 114,000 people they surveyed in 107 nations, more than 1 in 4 had paid a bribe within the past year.[108] To the extent possible, companies would be well advised to avoid doing business in the countries with the worst corruption. For some businesses though (for example, companies in the energy and mining sector), that may not be an option. For them, O'Neill advises, "DOJ understands that in some places business can't be done otherwise—and will allow culturally acceptable payments in certain countries. Prudent companies will seek a letter from the U.S. government allowing the grease payment. But it's best to keep such decisions to seek permission for such payments at the executive and general counsel level."

---

106. *United States Supreme Court Denies Certiorari in Controversial Foreign Corrupt Practices Act Case: Expansive Enforcement of the FCPA Likely to Continue*, CHADBOURN & PARKE LLP (Oct. 13, 2008), http://www.chadbourne.com/clientalerts/2008/fcpa/.
107. *TRACE Facilitation Payments Benchmarking Survey* (Oct. 2009), http://traceinternational.org/data/public/documents/FacilitationPaymentsSurveyResults-64622-1.pdf.
108. *Global Corruption Barometer 2013: Report*, TRANSPARENCY INT'L, http://www.transparency.org/gcb2013/report.

There are two affirmative defenses to an antibribery violation, and it is the defendant individual or company that has the burden of proof to establish them. The first requires a showing that the payment to the official is lawful under the written laws of the foreign country. This will be a difficult defense to assert, given that grease payments almost always violate the law of the foreign country in question.[109] The second requires a reasonable and bona fide expenditure directly related to the promotion, demonstration, or explanation of products or services or the execution or performance of a contract.[110] If in fact the *Kay* decision is read as broadly as suggested above on what constitutes "obtaining or retaining business," the practical use of this defense may also be very limited.

Although not a formal defense to an FCPA charge, a demonstrably effective compliance program can potentially decrease sentences under the U.S. Sentencing Guidelines, while the failure to establish one can yield a harsher result.[111] Based on the observations of former U.S. Deputy Attorney General Paul McNulty, the DOJ will do more than just look at the program as it exists on paper:

> More than just having the policies, procedures and processes in place, did the Company provide training on these and were they actively used in business going forward, such as in the area of due diligence on foreign business partners, including agents, resellers, distributors and vendors? . . . [T]he DOJ would look to see if a company had tested its FCPA compliance systems, for instance, was a test case sent up through the hotline; was training in FCPA compliance confirmed or at least tested; were FCPA compliance audits conducted of both employees and foreign business partners; and were the results of the monitoring catalogued and maintained?[112]

---

109. Krause & Wiygul, *supra* note 101.
110. *FCPA 101*, *supra* note 29.
111. Covington, Newkirk & Tillipman, *supra* note 50, at 2.
112. Thomas Fox, *FCPA Compliance and Continuous Controls Monitoring*, INFOSEC ISLAND (May 9, 2010), https://www.infosecisland.com/blogview/3950-FCPA-Compliance-and-Continuous-Controls-Monitoring.html.

Given the importance of demonstrating the effectiveness of its programs to the regulators, written documentation of compliance efforts cannot be overstated.[113]

What is clearly not an effective defense is "conscious avoidance," that is, pleading ignorance of what your business colleagues and outside partners are doing. Frederick Bourke was convicted on what the jury found that he merely suspected.[114] Whatever else top management does with regards to their company's compliance efforts, they need to stay on top of what people are doing in the name of the company.

Fines and Penalties

The numbers involved in FCPA enforcement are significant enough to merit the attention of businesses of all sizes. For antibribery violations, individuals are subject to a $250,000 criminal file and a five-year jail term. Companies are subject to a $2 million criminal fine. For the books and recordkeeping portion of the statute, individuals may be criminally fined up to $5 million and receive a 20-year prison sentence, and companies may be criminally fined up to $25 million. In the cases of both individuals and companies, the Alternative Fines Act may increase the criminal fine to double the gain or loss resulting from the corrupt payment.[115] The SEC may also seek disgorgement of profits received from contracts obtained with illegal payments.[116]

There are many other costs that accompany resolution of cases brought by the government. These include fees for internal investigation and costs involved in replacing terminated employees and development of new procedures,[117] not to mention debarment from lucrative government

---

113. *Best Practices in Preventing Fraud and Corruption in a Global Business, supra* note 2.
114. *Restoring Balance: Proposed Amendments to the Foreign Corrupt Practices Act, supra* note 32, at 3.
115. *FCPA Penalties*, WORLDCOMPLIANCE, http://www.worldcompliance.com/en/resources/due-diligence-legislation/fcpa-legislation/fcpa-penalties.aspx (last visited June 25, 2011).
116. Sasha Kalb and Marc Alain Bohn, *Disgorgement: The Devil You Don't Know,* MILLER & CHEVALIER (April 12, 2010) http://www.corporatecomplianceinsights.com/disgorgement-fcpa-how-applied-calculated.
117. Gorman, *supra* note 62.

contracts.[118] Management must also consider the loss of earnings and revenue that will result—in the case of corruption charges related to Avon's business operations in China, this exceeded $84 million.[119]

Additionally, a corporate monitor may be appointed for a period of years, which can add millions in costs and in some instances helps to develop other leads for regulators.[120] Lanny Breuer defends these monitors as playing "a crucial role . . . in ensuring proper implementation of effective compliance measures," even while conceding they "can be costly and disruptive to a business, and are not necessary in every case."[121] When asked to approve a plea agreement in the Innospec case in 2010, U.S. District Judge Ellen Segal Huvelle is quoted as saying "It's an outrage, that people get $50 million to be a monitor. . . . I'm not comfortable, frankly, signing off on something that becomes a vehicle for someone to make lots of money."[122]

Whether monitors are a necessary part of enforcement from the standpoint of the federal government or not, no company would likely want to assume the expense of one unless it is necessary to forestall a worse outcome. If the appointment of a monitor can be avoided, it stands to reason most companies should look for a way to accomplish that. Jessie Liu, of Jenner & Block, provides the best formula I have yet heard for doing so:

> First, you need to conduct a very, very thorough internal investigation. This would proactively look at and suggest changes in compliance procedure indicated by any violation. The best thing is to admit the company needs stronger, more clear policies—and provide the government with a new, improved policy. Show the prosecutors that the company disciplined or let go offending employees. Announce that the company is creating an oversight committee, a new audit function,

---

118. *FCPA Enforcement, The FCPA Explained, supra* note 181.
119. Thomas R. Fox, *What Is the Cost of FCPA Compliance? Or What Is the Cost of Noncompliance?*, FCPA COMPLIANCE AND ETHICS BLOG (May 3, 2010), http://tfoxlaw.wordpress.com/2010/05/03/what-is-the-cost-of-fcpa-compliance-or-what-is-the-cost-of-non-compliance/.
120. *Id.*
121. Breuer, *supra* note 76, at 4.
122. *Sharp Increases in Recent FCPA Enforcement, supra* note 59, citing Christopher M. Matthew, *Judge Blasts Compliance Monitors at Innospec Plea Hearing*, CORRUPTION & COMPLIANCE (Mar. 18, 2010), http://www.policypoint.com/2010/03/judge-blasts-compliance-monitors-at-innospec-plea-hearing.

etc. The point is: take any actions that the DOJ would expect that a monitor would take. If you do, what practical need is there for a monitor then?

FCPA Opinion Procedure

Recognizing that there are any number of scenarios in which a legitimate question might arise regarding whether given conduct will run afoul of the DOJ's enforcement of the FCPA, procedures have been put into place that allow a request for a written opinion from the Justice Department, pursuant to 28 C.F.R. part 80.[123] In order to be eligible, the request must be submitted by an issuer or domestic concern that is a party to the subject transaction, and the conduct must be prospective, involve an actual transaction, and be accompanied by all relevant and material information bearing on the conduct.[124] Each request must be signed by an appropriate senior officer, or the CEO, if required by the DOJ, certifying that it contains a true, correct, and complete disclosure of the conduct and surrounding circumstances.[125] Within 30 days after receiving an appropriate request (or, if additional information is requested by the department, 30 days after such is received), a written opinion will be issued, and the DOJ will also take such other positions and action as deemed appropriate.[126] If a written opinion holds that the conduct is in compliance with present enforcement policy, a rebuttable presumption is created that the conduct is in compliance with the FCPA.

Potential liability under the FCPA arising from the acquisition of overseas companies was the subject of one such opinion, which created an approved set of procedures for avoiding vicarious FCPA liability derived from the target company's pre-acquisition activities, under circumstances where there are "foreign legal impediments to robust pre-acquisition due

---

123. *Foreign Corrupt Practices Act Opinion Procedure*, U.S. DEP'T OF JUSTICE, http://www.justice.gov/criminal/fraud/fcpa/docs/frgncrpt.pdf (last visited June 27, 2011).
124. *Id.*
125. *Id.*
126. *Id.*

diligence."[127] As the opinion was requested by the Halliburton Company, these procedures are sometimes referred to as the "Halliburton process." The procedures outlined by the DOJ require a great deal of disclosure and communication on the part of the acquiring company:

> Halliburton promised (1) to meet with the Justice Department immediately after closing to disclose any information learned before closing concerning any potential FCPA violations by the Target; (2) within 10 days after closing, to present and seek the Justice Department guidance on an FCPA due diligence work plan addressing from high to low risk the Target's use of agents, dealings with state-owned entities, joint ventures, customs and immigration matters, tax matters, and licenses and permits; (3) within 90 days, to report to the Justice Department on the high-risk due diligence; (4) within 120 days, to report on the medium-risk due diligence; (5) within 180 days, to report on the low-risk due diligence; (6) to provide continuing reports on its due diligence and to complete all investigations within one year after closing; (7) to retain outside counsel and consultants to conduct the due diligence including a review of financial and accounting records and e-mails and interviewing relevant employees; (8) to require all agents of the Target who have no compliance issues to sign new contracts with appropriate FCPA representations and warranties and terminate any agent that refuses to do so; (9) within 60 days, to train all officers and relevant employees holding management, sales, accounting, and financial control positions on FCPA and other anticorruption laws; (10) to train all other employees within 90 days; and (11) to disclose to the Justice Department all FCPA, corruption, and related internal controls and accounting issues revealed during the 180-day due diligence period.[128]

---

127. *Foreign Corrupt Practices Act Review, No. 08-02*, U.S. DEP'T OF JUSTICE (June 13, 2008), http://www.justice.gov/criminal/fraud/fcpa/opinion/2008/0802.pdf.
128. Joseph Spinelli & Steven D. Feldman , *Foreign Corrupt Practices Act Due Diligence in Mergers & Acquisitions Deals* (August 16, 2011), http://www.herrick.com/siteFiles/News/D54DC55EE00A9AC2DCD516FA670B51B8.pdf.

Fair to say that in a world in which there is still a relative dearth of settled authority in the FCPA realm, past DOJ opinions are required reading, and requests to the DOJ for an opinion on contemplated actions, particularly in situations where the law could create a catch-22 situation for a company or individuals with potential liability under the FCPA, should be carefully considered by your legal team.

Moreover, there is hope that the relatively strenuous requirements laid out by the DOJ in the Halliburton case may not be universally required. One commentator cites the recently issued *A Resource Guide to the U.S. Foreign Corrupt Practices Act* (the Guide), which notably suggested that "demanding standards" and "prescriptive timeframes" involved in that circumstance related to the fact that "due diligence was severely limited pre-acquisition and, therefore, greater efforts had to be made to successfully complete it after closing."[129] Recent settlements also do not adopt the burdensome 30-day phased timeframes of the Halliburton opinion.[130]

The Guide's "best practice" mergers and acquisitions (M&A) due diligence is divided into three parts:

> First, it is expected that the acquiring company's legal, accounting, and compliance departments should work together to review the target company's sales and financial data, its customer contracts, and its third party and distributor agreements. The government especially emphasizes that the target's customer base must be analyzed (i.e., to determine how much of that base is comprised of state-owned or controlled entities—both government agencies, departments and ministries, and the less obviously identified state commercial enterprises—and what protocols have been, or will be, put in place to identify and manage that risk). The second part of the equation is the participation of the audit function in the process. The government expects to see evidence of selected transaction testing for specific corruption-related

---

129. Joan Meyer, *Anti-Corruption Due Diligence in Mergers and Acquisitions: Are Enforcement Authorities Moving Toward a More Flexible Approach?* BLOOMBERG LAW (2013), http://about.bloomberglaw.com/practitioner-contributions/anti-corruption-due-diligence-in-mergers-and-acquisitions/.
130. *Id.*

issues as part of any audit plan. Third, the government anticipates that the acquiring company will interview key personnel, such as the target's general counsel and the department heads of sales and internal audit, to better understand the target's corruption risks and its compliance efforts, and to identify corruption-related issues that have arisen in the past. The government suggests that the target be required to disclose to its acquirer all corruption-related issues that have surfaced over the last ten years before the proposed acquisition.[131]

Criticism and Potential Reform of the FCPA

Not everyone is comfortable with the amount of ambiguity that still exists in the context of FCPA enforcement. As pointed out in a paper submitted by the U.S. Chamber Institute for Legal Reform in late 2010, "judicial oversight and rulings on the meaning of the FCPA is still minimal" and the primary statutory interpretive function still lies with the DOJ and SEC.[132] The Chamber argued that the problem with the prosecutors being the default arbiters of the meaning of ambiguous or grey areas within the statute is that a "chilling effect" is created within U.S. businesses, who have to consider whether—given the penalties they face if they guess wrong—they should continue their foreign operations.[133] In support, reference is made to a 1999 Congressional Research Service report that estimated that the FCPA's antibribery provision cost up to $1 trillion in lost U.S. exports annually.[134]

These criticisms have not fallen on deaf ears in the halls of Congress. On June 14, 2011, Rep. Jim Sensenbrenner (R-Wis.), Chair of the Crime, Terrorism and Homeland Security Subcommittee of the House Judiciary Committee, held a hearing that centered around five possible reforms to the FCPA:

---

131. *Id.*
132. *Restoring Balance: Proposed Amendments to the Foreign Corrupt Practices Act, supra* note 32, at 2.
133. *Id.* at 6.
134. *Id.*, citing Michael V. Seitzinger, Cong. Research Serv., RL 30079, Foreign Corrupt Practices Act (March 3, 1999).

(1) clarification of the definition of "instrumentality;" [in the definition of "what constitutes a "foreign official"] (2) clarification of what constitutes benign facilitation payments; (3) whether a state-of-the-art compliance program may provide an affirmative defense against criminal liability; (4) raising the *mens rea* requirement for companies from "willful blindness" to "willful;" and (5) limiting successor liability.[135]

It should come as little surprise that some on the opposite end of the political spectrum were opposed to such amendments. Ben Freeman at the Project on Government Oversight responded to business criticism of the status quo by arguing that "FCPA enforcement, while on the rise, is hardly excessive, and FCPA enforcement has, at least recently, placed a greater burden on foreign firms than American firms."[136]

In May 2013, critics addressed many of the same issues before the House Committee on the Judiciary's Over-Criminalization Task Force. In written testimony, former DOJ Deputy Attorney General George Terwilliger suggested instituting "long overdue reforms" including institution of a formal affirmative defense for having adequate procedures in place; immunity for entities that conduct adequate and prompt post-acquisition due diligence and voluntary disclosure of discovered noncompliant conduct; and greater clarity for key provisions in the Act such as definitions of "foreign official," "instrumentality" of a foreign government, and "facilitation payment."[137] That said, as of early 2014, there is still no particular indication that calls for reform are being seriously considered for debate, much less passage by Congress.[138]

---

135. Shawn M. Wright & Jennifer Peru Gary, *United States: Possible Amendments to the FCPA Considered During Recent House Judiciary Subcommittee Hearing*, BLANK ROME LLP (June 29, 2011), http://www.mondaq.com/unitedstates/x/137008/White+Collar+Crime+Fraud/Possible+Amendments+To+The+FCPA+Considered+During+Recent+House.
136. Ben Freeman, *Corrupt Arguments in Opposition to the Foreign Corrupt Practices Act*, PROJECT ON GOVERNMENT OVERSIGHT (July 1, 2011), http://pogoblog.typepad.com/pogo/2011/07/corrupt-arguments-in-opposition-to-the-foreign-corrupt-practices-act.html.
137. Mike Koehler, *Over-Criminalization and FCPA Reform Return to Capital Hill*, FCPA PROFESSOR (June 24, 2013), http://www.fcpaprofessor.com/over-criminalization-and-fcpa-reform-return-to-capital-hill.
138. William H. Devaney, Lindsay B. Meyer, Jan L. Handzlik, Joanna P. Breslow Boyd, & Victoria R. Danta, *United States: FCPA Snapshot 2013* (March 10, 2014), http://www.mondaq.com/unitedstates/x/298126/Corporate+Governance/FCPA+Snapshot+2013.

FCPA Resource Guide

Perhaps in part as a response to criticism over the lack of clarity on a variety of topics involved in the corruption sphere, in late 2012, the SEC and DOJ released the Guide. The Introduction of the Guide states that it

> addresses a wide variety of topics, including who and what is covered by the FCPA's anti-bribery and accounting provisions; the definition of a "foreign official"; what constitute proper and improper gifts, travel and entertainment expenses; the nature of facilitating payments; how successor liability applies in the mergers and acquisitions context; the hallmarks of an effective corporate compliance program; and the different types of civil and criminal resolutions available in the FCPA context.[139]

While compiling materials into a single reference volume, giving information on cases the DOJ declined to prosecute and various hypothetical discussions related to gifts, travel, and entertainment, it has been noted the Guide is nonbinding on the DOJ and SEC.[140]

U.K. Bribery Act

Ironically, as the debate over the extent to which the FCPA is disproportionately disadvantaging U.S.-based businesses continued, a major new compliance regime from outside America was coming online: the U.K. Bribery Act. "The FCPA used to be seen as the U.S. forcing its laws on the world, but now it's the Brits too," observes Charles Hallab, of Baker McKenzie. Effective on July 1, 2011, the new British statute has been hailed as "the

---

139. *A Resource Guide to the U.S. Foreign Corrupt Practices Act*, Criminal Division of the U.S. Dep't of Justice & Enforcement Division of the U.S. Securities and Exchange Commission (Nov. 14, 2012), http://www.sec.gov/spotlight/fcpa/fcpa-resource-guide.pdf.
140. Julie Beck & Melissa Maleske, *Cheat Sheet: A Quick Guide to the New FCPA Guidance*, Inside Counsel (Jan. 22, 2013), http://www.insidecounsel.com/2013/01/22/cheat-sheet-a-quick-guide-to-the-new-fcpa-guidance.

toughest anti-corruption legislation in the world."[141] While the United States continues to prosecute the majority of corruption cases globally, enactment of the U.K. Act can be seen as the latest in a series of actions taken by foreign governments to follow the lead of the United States in deterring illicit payments that date back to the 1990s.[142] Between 1995 and 2000, the European Union, Organization of American States, OECD, United Nations, World Bank, and International Monetary Fund all acted in various capacities to combat corruption.[143] More recently, in June 2013, Canada amended its antibribery laws to significantly expand the grounds for corporate liability, and in August 2013, Brazil enacted a new anticorruption law dealing with corrupt acts involving Brazilian and foreign public officials or government bodies.[144]

The U.K. Act and FCPA differ in some important respects. First, there is no limitation to bribery of "foreign officials," such that the bribery of purely private individuals and companies still results in criminal violation of the U.K. Act.[145] This obviously broadens the scope of potential enforcement dramatically, even though the U.S. DOJ has utilized the U.S. Travel Act, wire fraud statutes, and the books and records provisions of the FCPA to reach some commercial bribery in the past.[146]

Second, there is no need to show, as under the FCPA, a corrupt intent or even "conscious avoidance" on the part of any party; the U.K. Act explicitly imposes strict criminal liability upon companies that negligently fail to prevent "associated persons" such as employees or agents from engaging in

---

141. Kayleigh Roberts, *Curbing Corruption*, INSIDE COUNSEL, 34 (July 2011), http://www.insidecounseldigital.com/insidecounsel/201107?#pg1.
142. Carrington, *supra* note 5, at 139.
143. *The Foreign Corrupt Practices Act of the United States FCPA Checklist*, *supra* note 19, at 17–18.
144. Kevin Cooper, *U.K. Anti-Corruption Initiatives: Bribery Act Update, Deferred Prosecution Agreements and New Sentencing Guidelines*, INCE & CO. (Aug. 29, 2013), http://www.mondaq.com/x/260314/Corporate+Crime/UK+AntiCorruption+Initiatives+Bribery+Act+Update+Deferred+Prosecution+Agreements+And+New+Sentencing+Guidelines.
145. *The U.K. Bribery Act 2010 What U.S. Companies Need to Know*, DLA PIPER (June 1, 2010), http://www.dlapiper.com/the-uk-bribery-act-2010-what-us-companies-need-to-know/.
146. *Landmark U.K. Bribery Act to Have Far-Reaching Effects*, BASS, BERRY & SIMS PLC, INTERNAL INVESTIGATIONS AND COMPLIANCE UPDATE (April 19, 2010), http://www.bassberry.com/files/Publication/30be0733-5bf9-4c4e-9cd1-0a9f6b488f7a/Presentation/PublicationAttachment/991c61df-9887-443f-8a74-0d8d44f43420/InternalInvestigations19April2010.pdf.

bribery. This makes a company's genuine lack of knowledge of such activity irrelevant for the purposes of triggering the statute under the U.K. statute.[147] The U.K. Act does provide for one affirmative defense: the ability to demonstrate implementation of "adequate procedures" to prevent bribery.[148]

Third, to whatever extent there may be some practical safe harbor remaining under FCPA for grease payments, they are prohibited under the U.K. Act.[149] Fourth, the U.K. Act unequivocally holds the receipt, as well as the delivery, of bribery payments as an offense.[150] Given these fundamental differences from U.S. law, it is clear that a company's established FCPA compliance policy may be insufficient in meeting the demands of the U.K. Act, such that companies who haven't yet examined their activities and policies through the lens of its heightened scrutiny need to do so.[151]

The penalties under the U.K. Act match the aggressive reach of prohibited activity. Individuals indicted under the new regime may face up to ten years in prison, and corporations may have unlimited penalties imposed upon them. This is of course in addition to the same kind of collateral damage that also is inflicted in the context of an FCPA action, such as debarment, asset confiscation, and loss of key executive personnel and director disqualification.[152]

One thing that the U.K. Act has in common with the FCPA, however, is ambitious jurisdictional reach. Whether headquartered there or not, a company's mere presence inside the United Kingdom, whether as a subsidiary, office, or operations, is enough to create jurisdiction. Moreover, the U.K. Act on its face applies even if offenses take place offshore, whether related to U.K. operations or not. So, if a U.S. company has a U.K. presence and engages in prohibited acts in Asia, it could be prosecuted in the U.K. pursuant to the Act.[153]

---

147. *Id.*
148. *Id.*
149. Dionne Searcey, *U.K. Law on Bribes Has Firms in a Sweat*, WALL ST. J. (Dec. 28, 2010), http://online.wsj.com/article/SB10001424052748704118504576034080908533622.html.
150. *The U.K. Bribery Act 2010 What U.S. Companies Need to Know*, *supra* note 143.
151. *Landmark U.K. Bribery Act to Have Far-Reaching Effects*, *supra* note 144.
152. *The U.K. Bribery Act 2010 What U.S. Companies Need to Know*, *supra* note 143.
153. *Id.*

As of 2013, the international business community was still unsure of just how aggressively the U.K. Serious Fraud Office (SFO) would ultimately enforce the provisions of the Act. Implementation of the Act was actually postponed for three months after various business interests "complained the rules were too strict and lacked guidance."[154] In particular, improved guidance regarding the extent of liability through the supply chain, joint ventures, due diligence, and corporate hospitality was requested.[155]

Various experts weighed in. Mike Koehler, Assistant Professor of Business Law at Butler University and author of the blog FCPA Professor pointed out, "as with any new law, there is likely to be a learning phase for both the enforcement agencies and those subject to the law."[156] David Clark, head of Financial Crime Intelligence and Analysis at Barclays Wealth, similarly opined that the "full meaning" of the U.K. Act will not likely be apparent until "the first criminal prosecution in which a firm relied on an adequate procedures defence had taken place."[157]

As of December 2013, no corporate bribery cases had yet been brought under the Act.[158] But SFO initiated its first individual criminal cases against three executives and a financial advisor from Sustainable AgroEnergy in September 2013, and reports suggested SFO and City of London Police were in the midst of investigating up to 25 more cases.[159]

A leading voice, Barry Vitou, partner at Pinsent Masons LLP, observed that the SFO has no choice but to vigorously prosecute as "it has fought and won the battle for its survival on a ticket which includes tough but fair Bribery Act enforcement."[160] Indeed, SFO Director David Green has

---

154. Luke Balleny, *Expert Views: U.K. Bribery Act Enforced*, TRUSTLAW (July 1, 2011), http://www.trust.org/trustlaw/news/expert-views-uk-bribery-act-enforced/.
155. *Id.*
156. *Id.*
157. *Bribery Act Not Rocket Science for MLROs, Conference Hears*, TRUST LAW (June 9, 2011), http://www.trust.org/trustlaw/news/bribery-act-not-rocket-science-for-mlros-conference-hears/.
158. John P. Cunningham & Geoff Martin, *Global Anti-Corruption Enforcement Trends: The U.K. Serious Fraud Office—A Year-End Snapshot* (December 9, 2013), http://www.lexology.com/library/detail.aspx?g=27f3a995-0334-440f-acc8-138c971cca9f.
159. John Bray, *U.K. Anti-Corruption Efforts Are Getting Serious*, CONTROL RISKS (September 19, 2013), http://www.forbes.com/sites/riskmap/2013/09/19/uk-anti-corruption-efforts-are-getting-serious.
160. *Bribery Act Not Rocket Science for MLROs, Conference Hears*, TRUST LAW (June 9, 2011), http://www.trust.org/trustlaw/news/bribery-act-not-rocket-science-for

continued to reinforce and reiterate the SFO's commitment, priorities, and areas of progress. For example, in a recent speech in October 2013, Mr. Green emphasized that:

- Direct comparisons with current levels of corporate FCPA enforcement can be misleading;
- There is a pipeline of corruption cases that still include pre-Bribery Act matters;
- There are corporate Bribery Act cases under active investigation by the SFO;
- Once available, the SFO will look to make proactive use of DPAs;
- The SFO encourages self-reporting and will take into account any genuine corporate disclosure in assessing whether or not it would be in the public interest to prosecute a company;
- There will be no guarantees, however, of prosecution declinations; and
- The SFO will take any attempt to cover up a violation of applicable law, rather than self-disclose, very seriously—the consequences will be significant if the SFO becomes aware of the facts by alternative means.[161]

Speculation aside, until a sufficient sample of cases are resolved under the new law, the best place to divine the parameters of the Bribery Act is various guidance releases received via the Ministry of Justice. The Minstry's March 2011 Guidance contains six principles that are meant to inform subject companies how they should put forth procedures to avoid commission of bribery on their behalf.[162] By their own terms, the six principles are not prescriptive, but they are meant to be flexible and outcome focused, to allow for the variety of scenarios and types of companies to which they will be applied.[163] The six principles are (1) proportionate procedures based on the bribery risks faced; (2) top-level commitment to prevent bribery; (3) risk assessment that is periodic, informed, and documented; (4) due dili-

---

-mlros-conference-hears.
161. Cunningham & Martin, *supra* note 156.
162. *The Bribery Act 2010 Guidance*, MINISTRY OF JUSTICE, 20 (March 2011), http://www.justice.gov.uk/guidance/docs/bribery-act-2010-guidance.pdf.
163. *Id.*

gence both as risk assessment and mitigation tool; (5) internal and external communication, including training that ensures policies and procedures are embedded and understood throughout the organization; and (6) monitoring and review of procedures, with adjustments made as necessary.[164]

A further Guidance was issued by SFO on October 9, 2012. As noted above in connection with SFO Director Green's October 2013 comments, the revised Guidance made clear that SFO was less likely to forego prosecution in case of self-reporting as had been communicated previously. A company's decision to self-report was said only to be a "relevant consideration" that " is no guarantee that a prosecution will not follow."[165] More specifically, the Guidance provided that "for a self-report to be taken into consideration as a public interest factor tending against prosecution, it must form part of a 'genuinely proactive approach adopted by the corporate management team when the offending is brought to their notice.'"[166] Finally, the revised Guidance also suggested that the SFO will continue to exercise significant discretion in deciding whether to prosecute cases involving modest and infrequent facilitation or bribery payments disguised as business expenditures.[167] Where that dividing line is precisely of course will only become clear with time, though it has been suggested that SFO budget constraints may limit enforcement.[168]

In yet another development that may affect Bribery Act enforcement, Deferred Prosecution Agreements (DPAs) became available for use in the United Kingdom on February 24, 2014. Taken together with the publication of the Code of Practice for the U.K.'s DPA system, Guidelines for Sentencing corporate offenders, and various changes to the criminal procedure rules, the framework for DPAs in the United Kingdom is now complete.[169] As in

---

164. Id. at 21–31.
165. Mark F. Mendelsohn & David E. Ferster, *The SFO Issues New Guidance: More Sticks Than Carrots*, Paul, Weiss, Rifkind, Wharton & Garrison LLP (October 12, 2012) http://www.lexology.com/library/detail.aspx?g=a7eec467-2547-435c-81aa-698650209c4b.
166. Id.
167. Id.
168. Id.
169. Tony Lewis & Hannah Piper, *United Kingdom: Deferred Prosecution Agreements: A Brave New World for Commercial Organisations*, Field Fisher Waterhouse (March 14,2014), http://www.mondaq.com/x/299692/White+Collar+Crime+Fraud/Deferred+Prosecution+Agreements+a+brave+new+world+for+commercial+organisations.

the United States, a DPA is discretionary on the part of prosecutors and voluntary on behalf of defendant business entities.[170]

It should be noted however that, unlike in the United States, any DPA in the United Kingdom will have to be approved by a judge before it is finalized.[171] Companies must consider what might happen if a court does not approve a DPA, as prosecutors could still use materials disclosed during the DPA process and the law requires defendants issue a warranty that the information provided in support of the DPA is complete, raising protection of privileged material concerns.[172] Yet another issue raised in the current DPA scheme in the United Kingdom is that as they are not extended to individuals and thus disclosure may incriminate various employees, who would then be criminally prosecuted.[173]

Yet Another Layer: Local Anticorruption Laws

Complicating compliance efforts still further is the fact that other foreign governments appear ready to step up their own anticorruption efforts. While these laws may in large part attempt to mirror or complement the FCPA and U.K. Bribery Act, their peculiarities and enforcement may well create issues of their own.

China for instance amended its Criminal Code effective May 1, 2011, in what has been described as an effort to create "China's FCPA," but critics sounded warnings about the vagueness of certain provisions, including whether the law would be applied to state-owned enterprises.[174] The Chinese

---

170. Id.
171. Kevin Cooper, *U.K. Anti-Corruption Initiatives: Bribery Act Update, Deferred Prosecution Agreements And New Sentencing Guidelines* Ince & Co. (August 29, 2013), http://www.mondaq.com/x/260314/Corporate+Crime/UK+AntiCorruption+Initiatives+Bribery+Act+Update+Deferred+Prosecution+Agreements+And+New+Sentencing+Guidelines.
172. Lewis & Piper, *supra* note 167.
173. Id.
174. David W. Simon & Robert H. Iseman, *Domestic Anti-Bribery Enforcement May Be on the Rise in China: Multinationals Must Focus on Anti-Corruption Compliance*, FOLEY & LARDNER 2013 EYE ON CHINA QUARTERLY NEWSLETTER (May 1, 2013), http://www.foley.com/spring-2013-eye-on-china-newsletter-04-29-2013/, citing Christopher Matthews, *China Releases Guidance on Anti-Bribery Enforcement*," BLOGS.WSJ.COM (Jan. 3, 2013), http://blogs.wsj.com/corruption-currents/2013/01/03/china-releases-guidance-on-anti-bribery-enforcement/.

government, not unlike the U.S. DOJ, sought to clarify its antibribery regime by issuing a guidance, effective January 1, 2013. Unlike the U.S. example however, the Chinese Guidance carries the force of law.[175] It remains to be seen whether the Chinese government's recent efforts will herald a change in what some observers claim is "inconsistent and sometimes politically motivated enforcement" that is often biased against foreigners.[176] As rightly stated in one article, "the anti-bribery climate in China seems particularly perilous at the moment, and although multinationals do not currently seem to be principal targets, it would be wise to avoid being the first."[177]

Global economist David Hale suggests that a likely consequence of the emphasis on anticorruption enforcement might be a significant dip in the purchase of luxury goods in China, which had been growing at a rate of roughly 20 percent per year. Given estimates that 25 percent of luxury items purchased in China are given as gifts, Hale reasonably believes dips in those sales as well as in banquets are in the offing.[178]

In the meantime, Brazilian anticorruption stirred to life in a momentous way as reports were released indicating a joint U.S.-Brazilian investigation of Brazilian aircraft giant Embraer, in connection with possible bribery of Dominican Republic officials in return for a $90 million aircraft purchase. Brazil has never prosecuted an individual for paying bribes overseas, according to the anticorruption group Transparency International, but as the *Wall Street Journal* noted, "the country picked a high-profile target."[179]

All in all, it seems that compliance departments of the future will need to square their programs not only with their home regimes, but also with those of the overseas jurisdictions they operate within as well. The traditional headache associated with scoping an internal investigation is now likened

---

175. *Id.*, citing Eric Carlson, *China Releases New Judicial Interpretation on Bribery Enforcement*," FCPA BLOG (Jan. 3, 2013).
176. *Id.*, citing *Strong Arm of the Law: China's Commercial Corruption Laws Are Undermined by Politically Driven Enforcement*," CHINA ECON. REV. (July 2012).
177. *Id.*
178. David Hale, Speech before the Federal Reserve Bank of Asia, *What's Next in Asia? Ten Things You Might Not Be Expecting in 2013* (Jan. 9, 2013), http://www.frbsf.org/banking-supervision/programs/asia-program/events/2013/january/us-asia-relationship-implications-american-economy/.
179. Joe Palazzolo & Paulo Winterstein, *Plane Maker Embraer Faces Bribery Inquiries*, WALL ST. J. (Nov. 1, 2013), http://online.wsj.com/news/articles/SB10001424052702303618904579172070636222040?mod=WSJ_hp_LEFTWhatsNewsCollection.

to a migraine with diverse and complex symptoms, given that governmental investigations and enforcement of as many as 40 OECD signatories can now be involved—including almost all of the important jurisdictions with business growth opportunities.[180]

Building Effective Compliance Programs

Based on the legislation and prosecutorial preferences of both the United States and United Kingdom, it is clear enough that a company's international compliance program requires significant attention from senior management. For them, and whoever is acting in the capacity of Chief Compliance Officer, how to determine the scope and particulars of the program is the fundamental line of inquiry.

Both the U.S. Department of Justice and U.K. Ministry of Justice advocate the use of risk assessment in developing compliance programs. The DOJ sets forth its risk assessment guidelines as

> addressing the individual circumstances of the Company, in particular the foreign bribery risks facing the Company, including but not limited to, its geographic organization, interactions with various types and levels of government officials, industrial sectors of operation, involvement in joint venture arrangements, importance of licenses and permits in the company's operations, degree of governmental oversight and inspection, and volume and importance of goods and personnel clearing though customs and immigration.[181]

---

180. Robertson Park & Timothy P. Peterson, *Regulatory: Investigating Potential Bribery Means Looking Beyond the FCPA*, INSIDE COUNSEL (July 10, 2013), http://www.insidecounsel.com/2013/07/10/regulatory-investigating-potential-bribery-means-l?eNL=51dda3c1140ba06923000195&utm_source=ic&utm_medium=email&utm_campaign=icscoopenews&_LID=91536800.
181. Thomas R. Fox, *FCPA Settlement Day: DOJ Guidance on the Best Practices of a Corporate Compliance Program*, FCPA COMPLIANCE & ETHICS BLOG (Nov. 5, 2010), http://tfoxlaw.wordpress.com/2010/11/05/fcpa-settlement-daydoj-guidance-on-the-best-practices-of-a-corporate-compliance-program/.

FCPA expert and attorney Thomas Fox adds that supply chain vendors, who are often overlooked by compliance professionals, should be classified into one of four risk categories: high-risk suppliers; low-risk suppliers; nominal risk suppliers; and suppliers of general goods and products, with an appropriate due diligence protocol applied to each.[182]

And in order to do a practical, realistic risk assessment, it is wise, as Eric O'Neill, of The Georgetown Group, counsels to first understand the *culture* of the company. And no, this is not yet another corporate buzzword utterly devoid of real-world meaning, but a concrete factor in understanding compliance risk and the corresponding programs needed to address it. According to Randall Hansen, at its most basic,

> [corporate culture is] described as the personality of an organization, or simply as "how things are done around here." It guides how employees think, act, and feel. Corporate culture is a broad term used to define the unique personality or character of a particular company or organization, and includes such elements as core values and beliefs, corporate ethics, and rules of behavior.[183]

It's not hard to understand that the particular command chains, risk tolerance levels, and even historical development of a company might significantly affect how things get done—and thus require focused consideration in compliance training and program formation.

This is especially true in light of the observation of Chari Aweidah, Senior Vice President, FactRight LLC, that FCPA violations are in some ways not unlike incidents of sexual harassment. In both situations, the perpetrators often fail in the beginning to recognize that they have crossed a line. Rationalization is a prominent part of the fraud triangle, a concept credited to Donald Cressey. In the FCPA context, these violators think they are just being sophisticated by creating transactions that they see as serving the

---

182. Thomas R. Fox, *Risk-Based Due Diligence For Supply Chain Vendors Under The FCPA*, FCPA COMPLIANCE & ETHICS BLOG (Nov. 24, 2009), http://tfoxlaw.wordpress.com/2009/11/24/risk-based-due-diligence-for-supply-chain-vendors-under-the-fcpa/.
183. Randall S. Hansen, *Uncovering a Company's Corporate Culture Is a Critical Task for Job-Seekers*, QUINTESSENTIAL CAREERS, http://www.quintcareers.com/employer_corporate_culture.html (last visited Aug. 20, 2011).

company's purposes. As Aweidah puts it, "they think they are just smarter than the next guy."

It is also worth mentioning at this juncture that adequate resources need to be expended in funding compliance program and training initiatives. Lanny Breuer put not too fine a point on it when in a speech he said, "as our recent prosecutions show, failing to adopt and maintain a real compliance structure will have serious consequences."[184] As Thomas Fox further relates, it wouldn't look very good to prosecutors when they look at an underfunded compliance budget and then ask, "and how much did you spend on Post-it® notes last year?"

"Underfunded" is, of course, a relative term. A smaller company simply does not have revenues that would support the complex type of compliance program expected of a Fortune 500 multinational. That does not mean, however, that a smaller company should have no compliance program. An effective compliance program can be implemented with a small investment, argues Roy Snell, CEO of the Society of Corporate Compliance and Ethics, Health Care Compliance Association, "if you know what you are doing."[185] After all, the same type of management tools that help make a given company successful can be used to ensure it is run legally and ethically.[186] And a commitment to doing the right thing, the very heart of successful compliance, costs nothing.[187]

In fact, in some respects smaller companies have an advantage over larger concerns, in that it is much easier to communicate ethical business practices to every company employee when you have 50 employees instead of 15,000.[188] There are many low-cost or no-cost resources a smaller company can take advantage of to build a risk appropriate program. Networking with other companies' compliance experts, studying online codes of conduct of similar businesses, participating in programs offered by trade associations

---

184. *Assistant Attorney General Lanny A. Breuer Delivers Keynote Address at Money Laundering Enforcement Conference, Oct. 19, 2010*, U.S. DEP'T OF JUSTICE, http://www.justice.gov/criminal/pr/speeches/2010/crm-speech-101019.html.
185. Joseph E. Murphy, *A Compliance & Ethics Program on a Dollar a Day: How Small Companies Can Have Effective Programs*, Society of Corporate Compliance and Ethics, 1 (Aug. 2010).
186. *Id.* at 4.
187. *Id.* at 6.
188. *Id.*

or chambers of commerce, and making sure your accountants or auditors have training in compliance are just a few examples.[189]

It can be argued that the overriding theme behind an effective compliance program should be an emphasis on company core values, since strict rules-based training can be easily misinterpreted by employees, and developing black letter rules that cover all contingencies is difficult.[190] Thomas Fox, however, argues for a combination of rules-based "ethics" training and values-based training, given typical expectations for bright line prohibitions.[191]

Once a risk assessment informed by an adequate examination of corporate culture and core values is completed, codes of conduct, policies, and supporting processes and procedures should be developed, clearly setting out

- "Basic rules, standards and behaviors expected regardless of geography or circumstance
- The company's fundamental values and principles
- The company's position on bribery, corruption and facilitation payments
- The company's rules on competition and antitrust and how they affect commercial operations and transactions
- Policy and procedures for business entertainment and gifts
- Policy and procedures for political and other donations or grants
- Policy, process and procedures on conflicts of interest"[192]

A common-sense approach for those new to compliance who are putting together programs, offered by Dorene MacVey, of Rockwell Collins, is to study the U.S. Federal Sentencing Guidelines and the U.K. Bribery Act—these lay out what needs to be proven or justified. Past DOJ enforcement actions have laid out 13 parts to what they consider to be the "minimum" in the way of internal controls, procedures, and policies:

1. "A clearly articulated, written code of conduct;

---

[189]. *Id.* at 9–10, 20.
[190]. *Best Practices in Preventing Fraud and Corruption in a Global Business*, supra note 2.
[191]. Thomas R. Fox, *Effective Compliance Training*, FCPA Compliance and Ethics Blog (Jan. 19, 2010), http://tfoxlaw.wordpress.com/2010/01/19/effective-complinace-training/.
[192]. *Best Practices in Preventing Fraud and Corruption in a Global Business*, supra note 2.

2. Strong, visible commitment from senior management ("tone at the top")
3. Anti-corruption policies and procedures (dealing with gifts, hospitality, travel, etc.)
4. Use of risk assessment
5. Annual review
6. Senior management oversight and reporting
7. Internal controls to ensure fair and accurate books and records
8. Periodic training
9. Ongoing advice and guidance
10. Disciplinary procedures
11. Due diligence and compliance requirements for retention and oversight of agents and business partners
12. Contractual compliance terms and conditions
13. Ongoing assessment to evaluate and improve effectiveness"[193]

The standards for corporate codes of conduct are growing more sophisticated in response to more demanding inquiries from regulators, notes Fox. Initially, codes were short, written statements distributed in hard copy form; today they are often detailed enough to require a table of contents. Fox argues that the state of the art in codes of conduct will revolve around an interactive and dynamic model, hosted on the Internet so that it can be quickly edited when necessary, customized to account for different locations, job functions and degrees of risk, and easily accessed by employees anywhere around the world. This "future code" will include interactive activities such as quizzes for employees, corporate policies, case studies, and reporting resources. The point of these resources, Fox concludes, is to provide an ongoing education for all employees, up to and including senior management.

When considering policies specifically surrounding travel, gifts, and entertainment, special care is advisable. While an affirmative defense exists under U.S. Federal Statutes for a "payment, gift, offer or promise of anything of value," where it was a "reasonable and bona fide expenditure" and "directly

---

193. Fox, *supra* note 176.

related to . . . the promotion, demonstration, or explanation of products or services; or . . . the execution or performance of a contract with a foreign government or agency," a violation of the FCPA can still be found if corrupt intent to obtain or retain business is found.[194] There are no clear guidelines in the statute or the legislative history and no *de minimis* provision.[195] Moreover it appears that the DOJ has not issued guidelines on the subject since the early 1980s.[196]

What can be gleaned from these 30-year-old advisory opinions suggests the following:

- "The gift should be provided as a token of esteem, courtesy or in return for hospitality.
- The gift should be of nominal value but in no case greater than $250.
- No gifts in cash.
- The gift shall be permitted under both local law and the guidelines of the employer/governmental agency.
- The gift should be a value which is customary for country involved and appropriate for the occasion.
- The gift should be for official use rather than personal use.
- The gift should showcase the company's products or contain the company logo.
- The gift should be presented openly with complete transparency.
- The expense for the gift should be correctly recorded on the company's books and records."[197]

Scott Cauwels, of Best Buy, notes that, with respect to his company's operations in China, only preapproved, nominal-value gift giving is permitted and is subject to a strict policy that is communicated and trained on regularly. The policy places limits on the circumstances under which gifts can

---

194. Thomas L. Fox, *When a Rose Is Not a Rose But an FCPA Violation*, FCPA COMPLIANCE AND ETHICS BLOG (July 2, 2010), http://tfoxlaw.wordpress.com/2010/07/02/.
195. *Id.*
196. Thomas L. Fox, *Gifts and Business Entertainment under the FCPA*, FCPA COMPLIANCE AND ETHICS BLOG (June 18, 2010), http://tfoxlaw.wordpress.com/2010/06/18/gifts-and-business-entertainment-under-the-fcpa/.
197. *Id.*

be given, the value and types of gifts permitted, and "involves an approval, record-keeping, and reporting process such that there should be complete transparency in our relationships with government officials."

MacVey notes that to the extent that a company's business model uses sales representatives or agents, there is a compliance risk. The key question in those businesses, according to MacVey, is what you do to educate both your own people and third parties on what is and is not permissible under company policy and the law.

MacVey would also focus on the specific risks endemic to the market they are entering, the kinds of due diligence in place as to third parties, what processes need to be monitored, and what ongoing monitoring is needed. This analysis needs to be undertaken at the beginning of an international transaction, MacVey warns: "It really is necessary to spend time doing background checks on third parties." It appears more companies should be heeding her wise advice and otherwise engaging third parties in compliance generally. For instance, this author can point to a 2010 Society of Corporate Compliance and Ethics benchmarking survey that found that fewer than half of businesses disseminated their code of conduct to third parties, almost three of four did not require certification of third parties to their own codes, and just 17 percent had a third-party code of conduct.[198] To the extent that companies fail to augment their policies, it could be a very costly mistake. As Fox notes, the expectations of the authorities have changed from a "know your customer" standard to a "know your supply chain" standard. Fox emphasizes that those responsible for compliance should not fall into the trap of ignoring suppliers and vendors after completing the initial due diligence—instead, forcing vendors to follow the same protocols you do is the best policy to follow. Recent cases involving the DOJ declining to prosecute Morgan Stanley and reaching a nonprosecution agreement with Ralph Lauren Corp. are examples of the real value of

---

198. Thomas Fox & Scott Moritz, *Finding the Worm in the Apple—The Identification and Management of the FCPA Risk of Third Parties*, MAIN JUSTICE (April 21, 2010), http://www.mainjustice.com/2010/04/21/finding-the-worm-in-the-apple-%E2%80%94-the-identification-and-management-of-the-fcpa-risk-of-third-parties-2/print/.

having robust compliance programs and internal procedures in place when corruption activities are detected.[199]

Once an appropriate set of policies and procedures has been hammered out, thought needs to be given on how to best communicate them, MacVey relates. This is true enough since, as Fox observes, companies such as Enron and Siemens both had "gold standard" ethics and compliance codes, yet the training given on them clearly did not prevent major negative headlines for both.[200]

Education and training programs utilizing a flexible, multi-faceted approach that is tailored to specific business's risks and the local cultures the company is operating in are lauded as the most effective.[201] A number of resources can be brought to bear to support a given program: in-person seminars, webinars, targeted issue training, e-mail blasts, and certification programs.[202] The point of using varying training tools is simply to reach the widest possible target audience.[203] Attendance and results records should be carefully maintained for evidentiary purposes.[204]

Practitioners who have actually provided this training in the field have many words of advice for those who are new to the process. Nelson, formerly of HP, emphasizes the importance of training people in the local language. The necessity of clear communication in this area makes this step a critical line item despite the extra costs involved. MacVey advises that particular attention should be paid to grey areas, such as hospitality gifts. Is a $50 bottle of wine ok? What about a $200 or $300 bottle? How should grease payments be handled? Scott Cauwels, of Best Buy, reminds us that it is essential to design tailored training so that it is highly relevant

---

199. Shanti Adkins, *Lessons from Ralph Lauren: Designing Better Ways to Manage Third Party Risk*, NAVEX GLOBAL (May 20, 2013), http://www.navexglobal.com/blog/2013/05/20/lessons-ralph-lauren-designing-better-ways-manage-third-party-risk.
200. *Thomas Fox on Effective Ethics and Compliance Training for Foreign Corrupt Practices Act Sentencing Guidelines*, LEXISNEXUS LEGAL NEWSROOM (July 22, 2010), http://www.lexisnexis.com/legalnewsroom/top-emerging-trends/b/emerging-trends-law-blog/archive/2010/07/22/effective-ethics-and-compliance-training.aspx.
201. *Best Practices in Preventing Fraud and Corruption in a Global Business*, supra note 2.
202. *Id.*
203. Thomas Fox, *Effective Compliance Training—Part 2*, MAIN JUSTICE (Jan. 29, 2010), http://www.mainjustice.com/2010/01/29/guest-contributor-effective-compliance-training-pt-2/.
204. *Id.*

to your company's operations and to make abstract principles concrete for the target employees.

Kathryn Woodward revised Sara Lee Corp.'s compliance policy and guidelines and put a training strategy in place for the company in 2010. When evaluating policies and guidelines, she first recommends that the policies be revised so that they are in line with those of peer companies. In terms of training strategy, Woodward points to the high corruption risk countries as defined in the Transparency International Index, suggesting you compare that list to those countries in which your company operates. She organized live training sessions and argues that it is best if training is interactive, as this allows for questions. She advocates reliance on in-country lawyers to conduct this training, not just because of the language barrier but also from an efficient use of resources perspective.

Woodward also emphasizes training on the "red flag" level issues. This includes real-world items ranging from bills that just don't seem right to making sure that there is an understanding of what expectations underlie the contractual language being used. Woodward observes that in difficult economic times, it is even more important than ever to be vigilant about corruption.

The difference between policy and guidelines, Woodward maintains, is that the policy must be brief enough for employees to understand, while guidelines have to be detailed enough so that employees know what the company's expectations are and when to involve the compliance team. The guidelines should be built around due diligence lines of inquiry. Woodward further emphasizes the importance of clarity in policy documents: "You have to be clear to get through the static."

In-house training is needed at least once a year, and it needs to be situation specific, Cauwels recommends. Custom training content is not only more effective but also a reflection of the fact that the sentencing guidelines focus on how robust a program you actually have. In his experience in China, it can sometimes be more effective to have separate training for management. Because of the business culture in China, having executive officers out of the room allows lower-level employees to feel at liberty to participate actively and give more feedback. "If the aim is to encourage a candid discussion, this format is more likely to produce a genuine conversation about the real-life challenges with dealing with the government and getting permits and licenses," Cauwels recounts.

In Cauwels' experience, Best Buy has usually had local in-house or outside counsel involved in training, supported by a U.S. in-house lawyer and in many cases also by their company's Chief Ethics Officer or Chief Compliance Officer. Training topics have included antibribery, anticorruption, protection of information (confidentiality, data protection), and overall ethical considerations such as avoiding conflicts of interest along with a reminder of policies pertaining to gifts and gratuities. In recent years, the strategy has shifted to provide more focus on antibribery compliance in particular through live, in-depth training to a wider audience of employees, including those not previously getting in-person training in regional offices.

In terms of getting employees' attention, as with everything else, it is important to look at what drives behavior. "Salespeople are motivated by money," observes Lee Nelson, formerly of HP. In that vein, MacVey advises that a compliance officer must approach employees with an attitude of "How can I help you make profit the right way?" Attorney Thomas Fox notes there are plenty of real-world examples that one can point to in making such an argument. After all, he explains, "Siemens is more profitable now that it's *not* bribing."

Another point worth passing on to employees who might otherwise be tempted to make prohibited payments to get something done "just this once": it never ends up being limited to an individual transaction.

"We don't even think about paying bribes," Jed Hepworth of Cargill relates, "as our CEO said many years ago, long before the FCPA became front-page news: it's not only illegal, and against our values, it's just bad business. The day you start paying, there is no end." So, how does one get things done in developing countries without resorting to facilitation?

Hepworth, advocating patience and persistence, gives an example: "Once we had a manager go to an official's office every day for several months to follow-up on a permit that wasn't being issued—even though there was no question we were entitled. Ultimately, our manager wore the official down. He finally said, 'If I give you your permit, will you go away?' After that, the ministry staff finally believed that we would never "smooth the path," and we got our permits processed on a more timely basis."

Hepworth also offers another important, if subtle, warning related to compliance: be careful what message you send others about your values in conversations with your business partners, in negotiations, and in training exercises with your employees. Hepworth asks: What message does your local partner hear when he tells you that a bribe can solve a big permitting problem that threatens to derail progress of your joint venture and hears from you, "We cannot approve or pay a bribe because it is prohibited by the FCPA and the fines and penalties are horrible"? What he hears is that your primary concern is the cost of being caught and that if you don't know or have to pay, you don't object. He didn't hear, "We don't do business that way ever, and you must not pay a bribe to get the permit, even if it is out of your pocket." What are you communicating about your values?

When you assert your values as part of your negotiation with prospective distributors or partners, Jed Hepworth of Cargill reports, you will get one of several reactions:

> Some partners who want to do business the old familiar way won't want to work with you. Others will simply not take what you are saying seriously until the conflict over values creates a crisis in the relationship. Then there are the "sophisticated" ones: they will tell you, "I completely understand and I'll be responsible for taking care of the problem the right way," without the slightest intention of changing how they solve problems. Finally, if you are patient and transparent, you will find people who actually share your values. Those are the partners with whom you can build a sustainable relationship and the ones who won't keep your CEO awake at night."

This sort of communication and certification needs to be had with all of your partners, Harvey Cohen, of Dinsmore Shohl, warns. In some developing countries, he notes "even local counsel could be engaging in bribery."

Additional Coming Challenges from Whistleblowers?

Given the significant amount of time and money many companies have devoted to setting up internal hotlines and other procedures to encourage employees aware of corrupt activities to step forward and give companies an opportunity to take corrective action and self-report, changes that encourage whistleblowing employees to become government informants are a concern going forward. As Jessie Liu, of Jenner & Block, notes, the Dodd–Frank Wall Street Reform and Consumer Protection Act of 2010 in particular permits whistleblowers to receive a bounty equal to 10–30 percent of the total recovery the government ultimately gets. With the threat of employees looking to personally profit from disclosures, experts are divided on the extent to which the new provisions change the calculus for companies on whether to voluntarily disclose potential violations of anticorruption laws as a prophylactic measure.

Amazingly, Liu explains, the Dodd–Frank legislation is written in such a way that even employees involved in the violations they are reporting may collect a whistleblowing bounty. Liu points out that the law is written in so that any behavior short of a conviction allows someone to be a whistleblower. The SEC has proposed a rule that would at least link the amount of recovery to the individual culpability of the putative whistleblower. A participant might be limited to the minimum 10 percent share of the total recovery, while a wholly innocent whistleblower could potentially receive as much as 30 percent.

What is clear is that the whistleblower policy is not an overlooked or unintended consequence; the SEC means to encourage parties close to fraudulent behavior to come forward, and early reports suggest a positive response.[205] It should be noted that under the SEC's proposed rules, the whistleblower must provide original information that leads to the SEC obtaining monetary sanctions totaling more than $1 million, and employees are discouraged from bypassing their own company's internal compliance programs.[206]

---

205. Funk, *supra* note 61, at 5.
206. *Id.*

Moreover, whistleblowers in the United States are not the only concern. Whistleblowing in China, for instance, has made the news in connection with investigations into the pharmaceutical industry, despite much more limited financial incentives available to citizens there under local law.[207]

Preparing for Post-Closing Anticorruption Compliance Needs

Successor liability in the M&A context is a critical potential exposure to the FCPA. On the condition of anonymity, I had a candid discussion on this topic with a senior executive of a globally known Fortune 500 company. He noted that one cannot overestimate the risk of corruption in a potential target or partner—even in higher stature or highly regarded organizations. Why? Because, he pointed out, few people are actually putting boots on the ground in developing countries. There is little interest on the part of expatriates to go to such places, and it is even difficult for auditors to travel to some of them. Additionally, the natural loyalties of society are stronger than those given to the organization. Also, as always, language differences play a part. What this all means is that "controls" in developing world locations may be horrendous.

Especially challenging, this executive noted, is a target or partner that has operations in multiple countries. From the perspective of diligence, where do you start? Certainly, countries with a low Transparency International score represent some risk. Naturally, too, the audit team needs to dig deeper into any transactions that come back from initial diligence with multiple red flags.

Specific due diligence steps recommended prior to acquiring a target company to avoid corruption related liability include

1. "identifying the jurisdictions the target has done business in over the past five years and evaluating applicable anti-corruption laws in each;

---

207. Henry Chen, Glenn Englemann, Frederic Firestone, John Huang & Leon C.G. Liu, *Whistleblowing in China and the United States*, McDermott Will & Emery (Aug. 30, 2013), http://www.jdsupra.com/legalnews/whistleblowing-in-china-and-the-united-s-71050/.

2. questioning executives and compliance, accounting, and sales departments at the target regarding their anti-corruption programs and applicable laws;
3. examining policies, controls, compliance programs, and any investigations, allegations, or reporting related to corruption related to the company;
4. conducting thorough reviews of third-party agreements, due diligence files, and course of dealings with third parties to verify FCPA compliance;
5. instituting forensic reviews of financials and the past five years' auditors' reports; and
6. inserting representations and warranties regarding FCPA and related compliance in the operative merger agreement."[208]

The executive I spoke with highlighted the Halliburton process discussed earlier in this chapter, pointing out that pharmaceutical companies acquire companies that deal with foreign governments all the time, and thus are more likely to do both pre- and post-closing due diligence. In any context, he stressed the importance of remembering that no one involved in this work expects perfection. What is expected is a set of reasonable processes proportionate to a company's individual risk profile. Given that third-party due diligence is a clear focus of the DOJ, an acquiring company needs to have a systematic way of reviewing vendors proportionate to risk. That being said, he warns that you need to accept significant dollar expense on diligence as a one-time expenditure or you are asking for trouble. Reminding senior leadership and the board of the manifest trouble that others have gotten into by failing to do this may be warranted in some circumstances.

Woodward focuses on the need for strong anticorruption programs in both the acquiring and target companies in the M&A context. In her view, companies need to have a "no tolerance" anticorruption policy, because as she puts it, "you don't want to sacrifice ethics to make your numbers." Otherwise, the issues will eventually be found out and put the entire company at risk.

---

208. *Best Practices in Preventing Fraud and Corruption in a Global Business*, *supra* note 2.

There are numerous third-party agencies that assist in gathering information on companies, Arvind Vij, of JPMorgan Chase, notes. They prepare a detailed report that allows for an informed decision on whether a party has violated or is likely to violate anticorruption laws and on its general reputation. Vij adds, however, that "speaking to locals on the ground helps; something that many miss doing." Eric O'Neill, of The Georgetown Group, notes that while many smaller and medium-sized companies retain him to do such external investigations, many larger and seemingly more experienced firms think they are sophisticated enough that they don't need help. One observation perhaps worth interjecting here is that many of the companies highlighted in DOJ and SEC press releases include these same larger, seemingly more experienced companies.

One simple place to start for contractual terms needed to protect your client's interests is the operative set of formation documents. Harvey Cohen puts FCPA language in with the export control clause. In fact, Cohen muses, your first element of defense of many in an FCPA charge involves "put[ing] an FCPA provision into the contract—and set[ting] things up to enforce it." The documents should include a representation on the part of the putative business partner that the partner will make no payment or offer of anything of value to any "foreign official" in order to gain or retain business or obtain an improper business advantage.[209] Additionally, although undoubtedly not to be taken as an all-inclusive list, attorney Thomas Fox recommends the following additional terms be considered:

- Indemnification: The foreign business partner must provide full indemnification for any FCPA violation, including all costs of the underlying investigation.
- Cooperation: The foreign business partner must agree to full cooperation with any ethics and compliance investigation, including the review of foreign business partner emails and bank accounts relating to a company's use of the foreign business partner.

---

209. Fox & Moritz, *supra* note 196.

- Material breach of contract: This clause must include any FCPA violations, with no notice or opportunity to cure. Such a finding would be grounds for immediate cessation of all payments.
- No sub-vendors (without approval): The foreign business partner must agree that it will not hire an agent, subcontractor or consultant without the company's prior written consent (to be based on adequate due diligence).
- Audit rights: These audit rights must exceed the simple audit rights associated with the financial relationship between the parties and allow a full review of all FCPA-related compliance procedures, such as those for meeting with foreign governmental officials and compliance related training.
- Acknowledgment: The foreign business partner should specifically acknowledge the applicability of the FCPA to the business relationship, as well as any country or regional anti-corruption or anti-bribery laws which apply to either the foreign business partner or business relationship.
- On-going training: The top management of the foreign business partner and all persons performing services on a company's behalf should be required to participate in FCPA compliance training.
- Annual certification: This should state that the foreign business partner has not engaged in, or is aware of, any conduct that violates the FCPA or any applicable laws.
- Re-qualification: The foreign business partner must be required to re-qualify as a business partner at regular intervals, not exceeding a three year period.[210]

In his practice, Lee Nelson, formerly of HP develops template agreements and processes, an investigation protocol, and a consulting agreement. These are attached as an exhibit to a signed statement from subject employees that is renewed every six months in which the employee avers they have not violated the FCPA.

---

210. *Id.*

Monitoring and auditing are also key to FCPA risk management, advises Eric O'Neill, of The Georgetown Group. Monitoring allows a company to allocate compliance resources.[211]

In setting up your control framework, keep in mind that clear documentation of formalized responsibilities, defined procedures, and testing methodology are critical as evidentiary proof to regulatory authorities that an appropriate compliance program is in operation.[212]

In terms of auditing, a regional general counsel stresses both its importance and limitations:

> If you are in a country where the head of your local subsidiary is king, then you have to audit regularly and vigorously. But remember that harsh experience suggests audits are usually a look backward and far from the complete answer. You have to ask yourself some fundamental questions. Does the head of your local subsidiary have the authority under local law or the by-laws of the company to unilaterally sell off the assets of the company or commit the company to multiyear contracts? What practical checks and balances do you have in place? Who does the controller report to? If the "king" determines who gets hired and fired and who gets bonuses and raises, you should not expect to hear bad news from the "king's" team. Make sure your audit team reviews governance as well as controls and the control environment. Local Law and Finance should report directly to their home office's functional leadership, not to local business leadership.

If fraud is discovered through auditing or otherwise, Aweidah states that the first task of a fraud investigation is to quantify the fraud. Is it limited to the area of the business where it was discovered? For instance, if a kickback scheme with a vendor is discovered, are you sure similar behavior isn't systemic?

The next step is then to scope out the duration of the fraudulent practices. Domestically, Aweidah reflects, the average fraud goes on for 18 months

---

211. *Best Practices in Preventing Fraud and Corruption in a Global Business*, *supra* note 2.
212. *Id.*

before it is discovered. So she often begins an investigation that goes back at least one year, and if the results of the investigation warrant, she might extend it to two years back, and so on. As with many other things in diligence, a cost-benefit analysis on extending the length of the investigation further must be utilized.

A Few More Thoughts on International Compliance Issues

Every company with current and planned international operations must not only carefully assess which statutes and regulations currently apply to their industry and act accordingly, they must also ensure that their policies and procedures will be modified as needed to *remain* in compliance with new and modified laws as they are promulgated. In particular, regulations that are created and adjusted based on political considerations must be monitored on a regular basis. A good example of this are the sanctions regimes overseen by the Office of Foreign Assets Control (OFAC), an agency of the U.S. Treasury Department.

OFAC Basics and Where You Fit In

OFAC is responsible for the administration and enforcement of economic and trade sanctions that are created to further U.S. national security and foreign policy goals.[213] The sanctions are levied against foreign countries, terrorists, drug traffickers, proliferators of weapons of mass destruction, and other threats to the United States.[214] OFAC is authorized to act under presidential national emergency powers and other enacted legislation.[215] Many of the sanctions, which often impose limitations on transactions and freeze assets under U.S. control, are based on United Nations or other international mandates and require close cooperation with other foreign governments.[216]

---

213. *Office of Foreign Assets Control): Mission*, U.S. Dep't of the Treasury (March 31, 2011), http://www.treasury.gov/about/organizational-structure/offices/Pages/Office-of-Foreign-Assets-Control.aspx.
214. *Id.*
215. *Id.*
216. *Id.*

How broad is OFAC's jurisdiction? The answer is quite broad. All U.S. citizens and permanent residents, as well as all companies located inside the United States and overseas branches of U.S. companies, are generally accountable for sanctions violations. In the case of Cuban and North Korean programs (as of the date this book went to press) OFAC jurisdiction extends to overseas subsidiaries as well.[217]

Given the heavy emphasis on fund transfers involved in the sanctions regimes OFAC oversees (discussed further below), one can immediately appreciate that entities within the financial services industries, such as banks and insurance companies, necessarily have significant responsibilities to fulfill within this sphere of compliance. But as one executive of a U.S.-based Fortune 500 multinational consumer products company advised, the reach of OFAC goes far beyond financial services. One must recognize that the sanctions regimes also seek to limit commercial transactions involving various nations and targeted groups of individuals. This implicates any company involved in import or export of goods and services.[218] Also, by the nature of their business, travel-related companies are at greater risk for noncompliance.[219] OFAC prohibits transactions related to travel to some targeted countries.[220] Additionally, it maintains a list of vessels that U.S. persons may not lease due to their connection to sanctioned countries or individuals, and U.S. companies or their branches may incur OFAC liability by hiring nationals of targeted countries or specially designated nationals (SDNs, discussed in the next section) as employees or agents for their overseas operations.[221]

Moreover, applicability of this compliance area isn't necessarily limited to for-profit activities either. As discussed further below, while most OFAC sanctions programs provide exemptions for certain donated goods, such as

---

217. Frederick J. Pomeranz, *Applicability of Foreign Assets Control Regulations to Insurance Producers*, WILSON ELSER CORPORATE REGULATORY REPORT (Spring 2004), http://www.wilsonelser.com/files/repository/Applicabilityforeignassets_Spring2004.pdf.
218. *Resource Center, OFAC Information for Industry Groups*, U.S. DEP'T OF THE TREASURY (Sept. 15, 2011), http://www.treasury.gov/resource-center/sanctions/Pages/regulations.aspx.
219. Carol M. Beaumier, *OFAC Compliance: The Role of Internal Audit*, 3 FSA TIMES 2 (2004), http://www.theiia.org/FSAarchive/index.cfm?iid=256.
220. Edward L. Rubinoff & Tamer A. Soliman, *Developing and Implementing an Internal Compliance Program to Address Economic Sanctions Concerns—Part I*, METROPOLITAN CORPORATE COUNSEL (April 1, 2007), http://www.metrocorpcounsel.com/articles/8135/developing-and-implementing-internal-compliance-program-address-economic-sanctions-con.
221. *Id.*

articles to relieve human suffering, this is not universally true. In the past, if you wished to donate food to Sudan, for example, you would have been directed to apply for a specific license to do so.[222]

It is important to note that OFAC does not enforce anti-money laundering provisions contained in the USA PATRIOT Act's amendments to the 1970 Bank Secrecy Act. OFAC generally requires a company to inform any person whose assets are being blocked by operation of sanctions; by contrast, where money laundering is suspected, companies are advised to make a report to the Treasury Department and not to advise the suspect.[223]

Regulations on Blocked Persons and Specially Designated Nationals

A "blocked person" is defined as "a citizen of a blocked country or business owned and controlled by the government of a sanctioned country."[224] SDNs, by contrast, are "blocked individuals and entities that could be located anywhere, not just within a blocked country."[225] They either are affiliated with a sanctioned government or have otherwise been identified by OFAC as international narcotics traffickers or terrorists.[226] OFAC makes an updated listing of blocked persons and SDNs available to the public.[227]

Generally, OFAC regulations require those operating under its jurisdiction to block accounts and other property of, and prohibit or reject unlicensed trade and financial transactions with, designated nations, entities, and individuals.[228] Assets and property are broadly construed and defined within each sanctions regime but generally include "anything of direct, indirect,

---

222. *Resource Center, OFAC, Frequently Asked Questions and Answers*, U.S. DEP'T OF THE TREASURY (Dec. 12, 2011), http://www.treasury.gov/resource-center/faqs/Sanctions/Pages/answer.aspx#54.
223. Scott Ostericher, *OFAC Compliance: How to Minimize the Threat of Costly Violations*, 6–7 (April 17, 2008), http://www.hww-law.com/161E02/assets/files/lawarticles/OFAC%20Presentation.ppt#290,1,Slide 1.
224. *Overview of OFAC Regulations*, EQUIFAX OFAC ALERT CUSTOMER GUIDE, 3 (Nov. 2002), http://www.e-cbi.com/pdf_forms/eq_ofac_alert.pdf.
225. *Id.*
226. *Id.*
227. *Id.*
228. *Office of Foreign Assets Control—Overview*, BANK SECRECY ACT ANTI-MONEY LAUNDERING EXAMINATION MANUAL, Federal Financial Institution Examination Council Bank Secrecy Act/Anti-Money Laundering InfoBase, https://www.ffiec.gov/bsa_aml_infobase/pages_manual/manual_online.htm (last visited Jan. 2, 2012).

present, future or contingent value."[229] Again, it is the broad definitions involved in these regimes that potentially implicate companies operating outside the financial industry. For example, Sudanese sanctions regulations prohibit, "transactions in support of commercial activities in Sudan," even if the transaction does not specifically involve the Sudanese government or listed SDNs as parties to it.[230]

Moreover, depending upon the course of events in given nations, new entities and states can be added or subtracted from the sanctions list—and it is the responsibility of businesses and individuals subject to OFAC jurisdiction to monitor these changes. For example, on April 12, 2010, President Barack Obama issued Executive Order 13536 in response to the "deterioration of violence in Somalia, and acts of piracy and armed robbery at sea off the coast of Somalia" and violations of various UN Security Council Resolutions.[231] As OFAC's definitions of the terms "property," "interests in property," and "U.S. person" are very broad in the Somalian sanctions regime, the regulations prohibit virtually any transaction by U.S. persons or involving property interests in the United States of listed individuals or the entities they own.[232]

Current Sanctions Programs

As of September 2013, the U.S. Treasury website had sanctions listings for the following: Balkans-, Belarus , Burma , Ivory Coast, counter narcotics trafficking, counterterrorism, Cuba, Democratic Republic of the Congo, Iran, Iraq, Lebanon, former Liberian regime of Charles Taylor, Libya, Magnitsky sanctions, nonproliferation, North Korea, rough diamond trade controls, Somalia, Sudan, Syria, transnational criminal organizations, Ukraine, Yemen, and Zimbabwe.[233]

---

229. Id.
230. Id.
231. Kay Georgi & Valentin Povarchuk, *OFAC Announces a New Sanctions Program on Somali Pirates*, ARENT FOX (May 27, 2010), http://www.arentfox.com/newsroom/alerts/ofac-announces-new-sanctions-program-somali-pirates#.UvJHn-BKbHw.
232. Id.
233. *Sanctions Programs and Country Information*, U.S. TREASURY DEP'T (March. 13, 2014), http://www.treasury.gov/resource-center/sanctions/Programs/Pages/Programs.aspx.

Licensure

Despite the sanction regimes in place, exceptions can be requested from OFAC through the process of licensure, provided OFAC determines the transaction in question does not undermine the stated policy behind the sanctions or otherwise can be justified in terms of other U.S. national security or foreign policy objectives.[234] Specific licenses can be granted for a particular transaction or set of transactions; general licenses that authorize certain categories of transactions are found in the regulations underlying the individual sanction programs.[235]

Penalties

While occasionally companies that run afoul of OFAC may receive a cautionary warning,[236] as with the FCPA and U.K. Anti-Bribery Act, the reason companies need to take this area of compliance so seriously is the fact that both substantial monetary penalties and criminal liability attach to violations. For instance, even if the violations are committed *without* knowledge, a U.S. person could be assessed a fine of up to $250,000 or twice the value of the subject transaction, whichever is greater.[237] Willing violations could trigger up to $1 million in criminal fines and 20 years imprisonment.[238] As we have seen in other compliance areas, existence of a viable compliance program and self-discovery of violations are considered when penalties are meted out, as is a failure to take remedial action.[239]

Designing and Monitoring Appropriate OFAC Compliance

Although OFAC regulations do not strictly require a dedicated compliance program,[240] the penalties above and opportunities for mitigation clearly demonstrate that no matter what size the company, no matter what industry, and no matter whether your operations deal directly with a sanctioned

---

234. *Office of Foreign Assets Control—Overview*, *supra* note 226.
235. *Id.*
236. Beaumier, *supra* note 217, at 2.
237. John B. Reynolds, III, Amy E. Worlton & Carl N. Stinebower, *OFAC Sanctions Come Calling on the Insurance Industry*, Wiley Rein LLP (April 17, 2008), http://www.lexology.com/library/detail.aspx?g=a7dfe437-d9cd-4074-9da8-e43393893497.
238. *Id.*
239. Beaumier, *supra* note 217, at 2.
240. *Office of Foreign Assets Control—Overview*, *supra* note 226.

government, putting in place controls appropriate to your risk profile is only common sense. Designing the right system requires evaluating the same risk criteria developed in the due diligence phase and applying sanctions exposure to them.

As Dr. Michael Faske, of Ernst & Young Switzerland, puts it, "the key to complying with the OFAC regulations is to understand the sanctions and how they apply to your operations."[241] And that of course requires you to go back and look at how you defined your operations and determine what types of transactions those operations entail.[242]

Next, again, is defining who your customer is. Particularly, who are your highest risk customers?[243] And who are *their* customers? A thorough customer base review can also identify whether the company's business and particular products or services attract high-risk customers.[244]

This assessment should assist in developing policies and procedures that allow your company to identify and review suspicious transactions.[245] Higher risk transactions may require specially designed software to cull for close name derivations; in lower risk areas, manual searches may be acceptable.[246] To the extent OFAC compliance is outsourced, adequate controls must be enforced.[247] Nevertheless, as with the anticorruption areas above, in general companies will want to designate an individual to act in the capacity of a compliance officer who will designate compliance responsibilities to various managers as appropriate and oversee communication of OFAC-relevant information and updates throughout the company.[248]

Once these policies and procedures are in place, it is important to frequently review the most up-to-date OFAC listings to monitor transactions.[249] Compliance with OFAC regulations requires

---

241. Michael Faske, *OFAC Sanction Regulations: The Underestimated Risk for Insurance Companies* (April 1, 2008), http://www.in-sure.org/en/expert-corner/ofac-sanction-regulations_-the-underestimated-risk-for-insurance-companies.
242. Id.
243. Id.
244. Rubinoff & Soliman, *supra* note 218.
245. *Office of Foreign Assets Control—Overview*, *supra* note 223.
246. Id.
247. Id.
248. *Overview of OFAC Regulations*, *supra* note 219, at 3.
249. Faske, *supra* note 239.

(1) checking the names of new customers or parties to a new transaction against the existing OFAC list and (2) screening an existing customer or counterparty database against updates to the list. Finding a match may necessitate blocking a transaction or freezing assets and filing reports with OFAC. All matches, or "hits," must be investigated and cleared before a transaction can be completed. Clearing the transaction may require, in the case of certain programs, confirming that the customer has obtained a license from OFAC to conduct a transaction that involves a sanctioned country or, in the instance of a match with a name on the list, confirming that the company's customer is not the same person, entity, or business. With respect to the latter, such factors as the customer's address and date of birth for individuals may be considerations used to "clear" the hit. When a company is not comfortable that it has sufficient dispositive information to conclude the names are not a true match, then it should contact OFAC directly at its telephone or e-mail hotlines. The company's investigation should be documented and maintained in the event questions arise in the future.[250]

When subject transactions are self-identified, they should be reported to OFAC as required.[251] Regular training, reinforcement through internal communications, and a program of internal audits round out the basics of a sound program.[252]

Looking forward, OFAC compliance faces a number of challenges, including the explosion of growth in e-commerce, which can complicate the screening process. There are, however, tools for dealing with this challenge. Software may be adapted to scan Web purchases prior to authorization, and Web purchasers can be required to provide additional data that could reveal possible OFAC issues.[253] Also, businesses with significant e-commerce

---

250. Beaumier, *supra* note 217, at 2.
251. Faske, *supra* note 239.
252. *Id.*
253. Rubinoff & Soliman, *supra* note 218.

operations may build protections into shipping procedures to thwart sales destined for prohibited destinations.[254]

Likewise, the danger of inheriting OFAC violations in new business partnerships must be considered.[255] Companies concluding joint ventures should therefore have processes designed to elicit the partner's connections and dealings with sanctioned countries or SDN's and forward them to a compliance officer for review.[256]

Contemplating the Bigger Compliance Picture

In bringing this chapter to a close, it must be noted that there are many, many more potential compliance areas to consider depending on the nature of your operations and where you operate. If you are expanding to the European Union for instance, anticompetition regulation and data privacy legislation leap to mind as areas to carefully review and develop.

Entire volumes are written about how to develop an appropriate strategy as to each area of a company's compliance exposure. For the purposes of this short guide, I simply return you to where we began this chapter: there is no worse bad day than staring down a headline-grabbing fine, reputational damage, significant stock price decline, and criminal prosecution for failure to have thought through your compliance risks and create a system to manage those risks. You must not necessarily eliminate the risks, but just intelligently manage them, as you must manage all the other business risks you face day to day. If your budget is small and your resources are limited, you must work within them and not use them as an excuse to avoid doing what is necessary based on your risk profile.

There are many seemingly Herculean tasks in business today that can be met with even limited resources. An appropriate compliance program is one. A system of protecting your company's intellectual property is another. That is the subject of the next chapter.

---

254. Id.
255. Id.
256. Id.

Chapter 8

International Intellectual Property: Issues and Its Essential Value in Twenty-First Century Business

It is only to be expected that as commerce becomes increasingly global in scope, not only the nominal but also the practical value of intellectual property (IP) would grow exponentially. The reasons for this are straightforward enough. First, the development of a truly global marketplace has caused an explosion of competitive forces that have led to a paradigmatic shift of economic activity toward developing nations.[1] Second, widespread use of computer technology, particularly in lower cost nations, has been driving a commoditization of goods and services via digitized design, manufacturing, and distribution.[2] This in turn causes competitive advantage in the current landscape to be decided by a firm's capacity to manage, harness, and protect key data, and its ability to safeguard unique and innovative business models. As restated by Jaime Stapleton, Associate Research Fellow at the University of London,

> the necessity to protect the value-added components in consumer products, together with the general value of intellectual property licences,

---
[1]. Siemens 2010 Annual Report, Section I, at 29, http://www.siemens.com/investor/pool/en/investor_relations/siemens_ar_2010.pdf.
[2]. *See* Langdon Morris, *The Driving Force of Change*, INNOVATION MANAGEMENT (Aug. 26, 2011), http://www.innovationmanagement.se/2013/07/18/the-driving-forces-of-change.

has pushed intellectual property to the top of foreign policy agendas in the developed world.[3]

In a knowledge-based business climate where protecting such assets is so critical, it is little wonder that informed observers describe an emerging "global IP battlefield" where literally billions of dollars are spent in acquiring cutting-edge patent portfolios.[4] The number of global patent applications has exploded, from 800,000 in the early 1980s to 1.8 million in 2009.[5] Similarly, the volume of trademark applications worldwide has increased from 1 million per year in the mid-1980s to 3.3 million in 2009, while industrial design applications globally have more than doubled over the period from 2000 to 2009.[6] And there is little sign of this trend slowing. Despite an overall decline in litigation spending, IP litigation is expected to grow by 2.8 percent, to hit approximately $3 billion, according to BTI Consulting Group's Litigation Outlook report for 2014.[7]

Whether one discusses the largest and most advanced high-tech conglomerates or a more humble small to medium-sized enterprise (SME) taking its first steps into international operations, the fundamental benefits of building and protecting IP assets are largely the same. Understanding these benefits—and the challenges you face in trying to secure them in a cross-border context—is a crucial part of planning and executing profitable overseas ventures. Ownership of IP rights can constitute, for instance, a key component of your marketing and branding strategy, allowing you to meaningfully differentiate your company from your competitors'.[8] It can also be used strategically. It can be used on one end of the spectrum to

---

3. Jaime Stapleton, *Art, Intellectual Property and the Knowledge Economy*, Doctoral thesis, Ch. 5 at 218, University of London (2002), http://www.jaimestapleton.net/aipkefive.pdf.
4. Steven Andersen, *The Global IP Battlefield*, INSIDE COUNSEL, 2 (Jan. 1, 2012), http://www.insidecounsel.com/2012/01/01/extended-version-the-global-ip-battlefield.
5. *2011 World Intellectual Property Report*, WORLD INTELLECTUAL PROPERTY ORGANIZATION 8, http://www.wipo.int/export/sites/www/econ_stat/en/economics/wipr/pdf/wipr_2011_intro.pdf.
6. *Id.* at 9.
7. *High-Stakes IP Work Continues Its Steady Climb, GCs Say*, BTI CONSULTING GROUP (Sept. 13, 2013), http://www.bticonsulting.com/press/2013/9/12/high-stakes-ip-work-continues-its-steady-climb-gcs-say.html.
8. *Intellectual Property Rights and Marketing*, World Intellectual Property Organization, http://www.wipo.int/sme/en/ip_business/marketing/ip_rights.htm.

stop rivals from making, using, or selling items incorporating the protected property,[9] while on the other, to collaborate to produce jointly owned IP or to utilize "patent pools" to ease the burden of negotiating with a fragmented group of rights holders.[10]

Additionally, however, IP assets can often be monetized. They can be sold, licensed, or used as collateral or security for debt finance.[11] This is particularly important for start-up companies for whom intellectual property may be the only significant asset of value that they have.[12] Intermediaries such as IP clearinghouses, exchanges, auctions, and brokerages have slowly begun to establish themselves in the business of bringing together buyers and sellers of intangibles.[13]

Types of IP: The Four Traditional Categories and Beyond

The following is a listing of the four classically recognized classes of intellectual property:

1. **Patents:** Patents cover tangible things and confer the legal right to exclude others from manufacturing or marketing the subject items. Patents can also be registered in foreign countries as part of a global IP protection strategy. Even when patented, though, others can generally apply to license your product.
2. **Trademarks:** Generally, trademarks constitute a name, phrase, sound, or symbol exclusively associated with the holder's services or products.
3. **Copyrights:** Copyrights are protections for written or artistic expressions of ideas (but not ideas themselves) fixed in a tangible medium,

---

9. J.D. Harriman, *Patent Enforcement Best Practices, The Implications of Intellectual Property Protection, in* PATENT ENFORCEMENT BEST PRACTICES (2007).
10. *2011 World Intellectual Property Report, supra* note 5, at 12–13.
11. S.K. Verma, *Financing of Intellectual Property: Developing Countries' Context* (January 2006), http://nopr.niscair.res.in/bitstream/123456789/3550/1/JIPR%2011%281%29%2022-32.pdf.
12. Jon M. Garin, *Start-Ups 101: Intellectual Property: Reflecting Value in Intangible Assets*, CALLAGHER, CALLAHAN & GARTELL (May 2008), http://www.gcglaw.com/resources/business/intangible_assets.html.
13. *2011 World Intellectual Property Report, supra* note 5, at 9.

such as novels, video games, songs, or movies. The copyright owner has the right to reproduce, make derivative works, or sell, perform, or display the protected work to the public.
4. **Trade secrets:** Trade secrets are formulas, patterns, devices or compilations of data that grant the user a business advantage over competitors. The owner must prove that the secret adds value and that appropriate measures have been taken to safeguard it.[14] Processes such as marketing plans and franchise management protocols, modifications to improve equipment, and test results all potentially qualify as trade secrets.[15]

IP can extend beyond these four categories, however.[16] For instance, know-how is a related concept to trade secrets (and sometimes overlaps with that category) but consists of "an accumulation of information, knowledge, and experience" that enables one to achieve practical results that cannot be obtained in its absence.[17] Even information that demonstrates what does *not* work (such as unsuccessful product testing)—so called "negative know how"—may be protected in some circumstances.[18]

In some cases, more than one potential IP protection can apply to a single item. For example, software can involve not only copyright but also patent, trade secret, and know-how.[19]

---

14. Derek Slater, *Intellectual Property Protection: The Basics*, CSOONLINE.COM (Feb. 14, 2011), http://www.csoonline.com/article/204600/intellectual-property-protection-the-basics.
15. Andrew J. Sherman, *Understanding the Various Types*, ENTREPRENEURSHIP RESOURCE CENTER (2006), http://www.entrepreneurship.org/en/resource-center/understanding-the-various-types-of-intellectual-property.aspx.
16. Slater, *supra* note 14.
17. *Id.*
18. Natalie Flechsig, Trade *Secret Enforcement After Tian Rui: Fighting Misappropriation Through the ITC*, BERKELEY TECHNOLOGY LAW JOURNAL, Vol. 28:449 (2013) at 450–51. http://btlj.org/data/articles/28_AR/0449-0482_Flechsig_091113_Web.pdf.
19. Rajiv P. Patel, *Seven Sins—Intellectual Property Mistakes Start-Up Technology Companies Should Avoid*, FENWICK & WEST LLP, 2 (Feb. 23, 2010), http://www.fenwick.com/docstore/publications/ip/2010_seven_sins.pdf.

TRIPS and Attempts to Create International IP Protection

As the current phase of globalization began to take hold in the early to mid-1990s, it became increasingly obvious that both the scope of protection and the capacity to enforce IP rights varied widely from country to country, and that tensions created by the lack of uniform standards endangered efforts at further liberalizing world trade.[20]

As part of the General Agreement on Tariff and Trade talks that set up the World Trade Organization (WTO), known commonly as the "Uruguay Round" (1986–94), the Trade-Related Aspects of Intellectual Property Rights Agreement (TRIPS) was negotiated. TRIPS was the first attempt at applying IP rules to the multilateral trading system[21] and represents a multilateral agreement that applies to all current WTO member states and any nations that choose to accede in the future.[22]

TRIPS address five areas: (1) how basic trading system principles and international IP agreements should be applied, (2) what constitutes adequate IP protection, (3) what constitutes adequate enforcement within WTO member nations, (4) how to settle IP disputes among WTO signatories, and (5) transitional arrangements for selected members.[23] The agreement breaks IP into the following seven categories, rather than the four described earlier: (1) copyright, (2) trademarks, (3) geographical indications, (4) industrial designs, (5) patents, (6) integrated circuit layout designs, and (7) undisclosed information, including trade secrets.[24]

---

20. *Intellectual Property: Protection and Enforcement*, WORLD TRADE ORGANIZATION (2012), http://www.wto.org/english/thewto_e/whatis_e/tif_e/agrm7_e.htm.
21. *Id.*
22. Carsten Fink, *Intellectual Property and the WTO* (Nov. 2004), https://docs.google.com/viewer?a=v&q=cache:OJW585yGM0MJ:siteresources.worldbank.org/INTRANETTRADE/Resources/Topics/Accession/438734-1109706732431/IPRs_Russia.doc+&hl=en&gl=us&pid=bl&srcid=ADGEESgEPjgoCZrJDbOZXqdQcgQPUs3a_xeIkmud49Aey1BO6QwrdkVRxWtAiObXt-yopb1uxZ5WC9uXPwzcda3al7SSrwbo-fuU71kp6qCH_luUwJGE2wWXNCuowr-Ico3SEZZq-uOhW&sig=AHIEtbRIcZ5mPZNZl4URQklZbd8LIkObTA&pli=1.
23. *Intellectual Property: Protection and Enforcement*, supra note 20.
24. *Id.*

Enforcement: Limitations on the International IP Paradigm

While TRIPS is a solid first step toward creating a set of uniform standards in relation to intellectual property, one must consider that the agreement itself sets up no overarching international enforcement mechanism. That is, a party who seeks to have an IP right acknowledged, protected, or acted upon must still do so within individual member states' legal systems.[25]

This can be, to put it colloquially, a bit of a crapshoot in many locales. Despite the significant multilateral efforts made to date, in some countries IP protection is still arguably nonexistent.[26] To the extent that at least some local legal framework for enforcement exists in a foreign nation, the degree of protection may vary for different types of IP rights; it may even vary for different products covered by the same IP right.[27] Although stated in a slightly different context, perhaps the best expression of what American lawyers face in this regard is this succinct appraisal from Littler Mendelson shareholder Paul Weiner: "A lot of people don't fully appreciate the severe restrictions and significant sanctions that come from applying U.S. concepts in a foreign country."[28]

Further, cultural attitudes in a given nation toward the whole concept of intellectual property certainly may affect enforcement efforts. For attorneys trained in the West, where thought on intellectual property has developed and coalesced over centuries, there is no serious challenge to the basic assumptions that support the IP system. However, this attitude is hardly universally held—particularly in many developing countries. As a common sense proposition, regardless of what laws a country has agreed to enact, if its culture doesn't respect the underlying concept of intellectual property, its

---

25. Michael Fitzgerald, *Big Savings, Big Risks*, CSOONLINE.COM, 41 (Nov. 2003), http://books.google.com/books?id=WmAEAAAAMBAJ&pg=PA36&dq=big+savings+big+risk+cso+online+2003&hl=en&sa=X&ei=uQByT_7HM6qB0QGu8enVAQ&ved=0CEkQ6AEwAA#v=onepage&q=big%20savings%20big%20risk%20cso%20online%202003&f=false.
26. Bernard J. Casey, *Are Some Patent Holders More Equal Than Others?*, IP WATCHDOG.COM (March 8, 2012), http://www.ipwatchdog.com/2012/03/08/are-some-patent-holders-more-equal-than-others/id=22669/.
27. Donna Ghelfi, *The "Outsourcing Offshore" Conundrum: An Intellectual Property Perspective*, WIPO, http://www.wipo.int/export/sites/www/sme/en/documents/pdf/outsourcing.pdf.
28. Alex Vorro, *The Challenges of Collecting Data Outside the U.S.*, INSIDE COUNSEL (Jan. 1, 2012), http://www.insidecounsel.com/2012/01/01/the-challenges-of-collecting-data-outside-the-us.

courts are unlikely to enforce whatever nominal rights have been recently created.[29] A significant number of nations suffer from generalized corruption, but enforcement efforts are even more likely to be frustrated in those nations that have consciously decided as a matter of policy to use foreign-owned IP to help close the gap between themselves and leading competitors: "Over the years France, China, Latin America and the former Soviet Union have all developed reputations as places where industrial espionage is accepted, even encouraged, as a way of promoting a country's economy."[30]

Finally, even if a mechanism exists that will ultimately allow for successful litigation of an IP rights-based claim in an overseas location, if the system in practice involves significant delays before an injunction is available—or is otherwise inordinately expensive, complicated to navigate, or provides a limited scope of relief—it might well act as more of a deterrent to the rights holder than the infringer.[31]

Protecting Your IP Rights

As with other aspects of cross-border deal making and operations management, the most critical steps in dealing with the challenges of protecting your crucial IP on a global basis should take place prior to negotiation and implementation. The four components to a well thought out strategy are (1) forming an IP security steering committee, (2) mapping out a complete, enterprise-wide IP inventory, (3) Formulating an IP protection strategy based on a cost-benefit analysis, and (4) intelligent execution of the strategy.

Forming the IP Security Steering Committee

If thorough planning is the key to success in protecting your company or client's IP assets, the reasonable follow-up question suggested is, who should do this planning? Much as discussed in earlier chapters in connection with

---

29. Slater, *supra* note 14.
30. *Id.*
31. *Injunctions in Intellectual Property Rights*, EUROPEAN OBSERVATORY ON COUNTERFEITING AND PIRACY 2–8, http://ec.europa.eu/internal_market/iprenforcement/docs/injunctions_en.pdf (last visited March 28, 2012).

due diligence generally, it needs to be conducted by a steering committee of responsible stakeholders selected for the task based on their experience and occupational relation to the subject matter. As a matter of course this would include senior management such as the chief executive officer, chief strategy officer, and chief operating officer, but it would also likely include representatives of the human resources, marketing, sales, legal, production, and research and development departments.[32]

Mapping Out the IP Inventory

The committee's work begins, as you might imagine, with a thorough review of the company's products and processes top to bottom, in order to get a complete picture of all the various kinds of intellectual property it uses, from the four traditional categories or otherwise. Keep in mind that this will require breaking down each of the products or processes into their constituent or component parts, with special attention paid to those that add the most value, most significantly differentiate, and which cannot be reverse engineered.[33] Also remember that more than one type of IP right can potentially apply to a given product or process.[34]

Organizing so-called "directed invention brainstorming sessions" in house before a vendor or business partner begins working with your company's IP may allow for anticipation of likely incremental improvements, and set the stage for claiming and retaining ownership of the IP rights associated with them.[35] Likewise, to the extent that valuable intangible assets need to be shared in furtherance of a given initiative, give thought to whether they should be broken up such that no one outside entity has enough information to reproduce or disseminate anything that would harm your interests.[36]

Note, however, that simply identifying and documenting all the various kinds of intellectual property assets you use only scratches the surface of

---

32. Slater, *supra* note 14.
33. Michael Bielski, *Lowering Intellectual Property (IP) Risk When Outsourcing Manufacturing*, VENTUREOUTSOURCE.COM (June 2007), http://www.ventureoutsource.com/contract-manufacturing/benchmarks-best-practices/outsourcing-pitfalls/lowering-intellectual-property-ip-risk-when-outsourcing-ma.
34. Patel, *supra* note 19, at 1.
35. Bielski, *supra* note 33.
36. *Id.*

the task at hand; the next key inquiry is who invented/authored/created these assets, and who has legal ownership of them?[37] The reason for that is your inventory process should capture IP that you actually use via license or assignment that is owned by third parties or even employees, or intangible assets of yours that others utilize via a technology transfer agreement for example.[38]

Once you have uncovered any such assets, the next logical step is obvious: pull all the contractual agreements that affect your rights and obligations as to that property—including confidentiality and noncompete agreements.[39] Compare the contract to how the IP is actually being used—are provisions being breached, rights infringed, fees or other obligations being ignored, or proprietary information being disclosed to unauthorized users without senior management even realizing it?[40] Running this to ground is important for many reasons. Not the least of these, advises Darren Gardner, a partner at Seyfarth Shaw, is to confirm whether the entity you are dealing with actually has the legal rights to the IP you are buying from them.

Finally, note for future reference as to each intangible asset what law applies, what type of resolution mechanism applies to this property and what provisions exist to obtain indemnification or other relief in case of infringement.[41] A failure to inventory and understand the strengths and weaknesses of applicable contracts now could lead to expensive litigation and a potential loss of rights in the future.[42] What is worse, even if it is ultimately successful, litigation could take years of effort, while the damage from infringement is immediate.[43]

---

37. Ghelfi, *supra* note 27.
38. *Id.*
39. *Id.*
40. *Id.*
41. *Id.*
42. Adam Haller & Jordana Sanft, *Buyer Beware: IP Is Not Just Another Asset*, NORTON ROSE IP MONITOR (Dec. 2011), http://www.nortonrose.com/files/ip-monitor-buyer-beware-ip-is-not-just-another-asset-pdf-83kb-60779.pdf.
43. Rob Ramer, *The Security Challenges of Offshore Development*, SANS INSTITUTE, 4 (2001), http://www.sans.org/reading_room/whitepapers/securecode/security-challenges-offshore-development_383.

Formulation and Implementation of a Security Plan

The sum total of information gathered above is useless if simply locked up in a drawer somewhere and not acted upon. The next task of the committee is to create a plan that incorporates the necessary procedures to protect the intangible assets identified, at a price that reflects the economic realities the company faces. This is particularly true in the case of SME's, since while risks to them are essentially the same as with a larger entity, they actually may suffer disproportionately from the effects of a security breach.[44] Moreover, to the extent your company has reporting responsibilities to the Securities and Exchange Commission (SEC), planning may be more than just a good idea. An October 2011 guidance from the SEC's Division of Corporate Finance suggests entities under its authority may be expected to disclose that they have done a risk assessment, including consequences of a cyber attack and potential responses.[45]

Consistent with advice provided in other chapters of this text, when faced with the likely prospect of a limited budget to accomplish the critical task of protecting IP assets, the solution will come by way of a cost-benefit analysis. To the extent that the committee determines what information, if misappropriated or disseminated, would cause the most damage to the organization and what assets are the most vulnerable to threat, spending priorities can be agreed upon.[46] Additionally, regulations applicable to certain industries or to certain items (such as personal data in the European Union) will require a certain security spend regardless of other considerations.[47]

Some basic measures involve little or no cost, such as labeling physical and electronic documents as confidential or proprietary, locking up document storage areas, and limiting access to key databases.[48] It is also true that "security is a process," not a product.[49] Software packages that track the location and access to sensitive documents are available and worth

---

44. Jeff Herbert, *Introducing Security to the Small Business Enterprise*, SANS INSTITUTE, 4 (April 28, 2003), http://www.sans.org/reading_room/whitepapers/basics/introducing-security-small-business-enterprise_1066.
45. Melissa Maleske, *Life's A Breach*, INSIDE COUNSEL (Jan. 1, 2012), http://www.insidecounseldigital.com/insidecounsel/201201?pg=6#pg32.
46. Slater, *supra* note 14.
47. *Id.*
48. *Id.*
49. Herbert, *supra* note 44, at 6.

consideration, but as in any security scenario, it is generally the humans in the system that are the weakest link.[50] This means that any plan the committee approves should involve employee training to avoid creating unnecessary vulnerabilities and true cooperation and coordination between departments so that all are made aware of individual instances of activity that when viewed as a whole reveal a security threat.[51] And, as recommended in the due diligence portion of this text, gaming out the vulnerabilities that someone practicing industrial espionage against your company would be able to exploit, from sensitive documents in the trash to trade secrets carelessly released in a speech or trade publication, will help you close them before damage is done.[52] It will also help you to hone a country-by-country strategy where appropriate.

Even with all of this, the committee's work is not necessarily done. To the extent that your operations incorporate those of a foreign vendor or business partner, the threats to shared assets and the access to your systems must also be accounted for. All too often, the uninitiated forego doing an independent security review of a vendor or partner, simply assuming that whatever policy is listed on paper is actually enforced.[53] As mentioned elsewhere, however, despite the cost involved, there is no substitute for boots on the ground; it is important to visit the partner or vendor's physical location and observe the security and access controls they have in place.[54] Be aware of the extent to which the partner or vendor's business model allows contact between teams working for competing firms, employees to work from home or off of portable computers, and liberal access to sensitive data, all of which might create greater risk.[55] Security guarantees should be included in the contract with the vendor or partner, with strict and enumerated financial penalties for violation and mandatory regular security

---

50. Slater, *supra* note 14.
51. *Id.*
52. *Id.*
53. Ramer, *supra* note 43, at 5.
54. Slater, *supra* note 14.
55. *Id.*

reviews to ensure appropriate enforcement.[56] Of course, confidentiality is part of this regimen.[57]

Contracting for Ownership of IP

While a customer company may understandably believe it should get the rights to IP created by virtue of a customer/vendor relationship (having paid for the associated service), vendors in some jurisdictions can potentially point to moral rights and ownership assignment requirements to challenge ownership in works created within a given contractual relationship.[58] While the rights themselves are important, there are underlying concerns at play that drive the conversation. For the customer, it amounts to a recognition that allowing the vendor to maintain ownership of these rights might lead to a much longer working relationship than they had in mind—since the customer may wish to move the process or product development in-house or to another vendor.[59] As to the vendor, they in large part want to be able to recycle items in their "toolbox" that they may have developed prior to the instant relationship—and will resist capitulation on the disputed IP that will impinge on their ability to do business with other, future clients.[60]

A firm may also partner with a local concern that more closely represents a relationship among equals, with each party contributing unique expertise to the project. Under such circumstances, IP resulting from their joint efforts may be owned by the party that bore the expense for creating

---

56. Ramer, *supra* note 43, at 5.
57. Bielski, *supra* note 33.
58. Fred Greguras, Steven Levine, & S.R. Gopalan, *Legal Structures for Outsourcing*, 3 Fenwick & West (2004), https://www.fenwick.com/FenwickDocuments/Outsourcing.pdf.
59. Richard Nicholas and Sara McNeil, *Protecting Intellectual Property Rights throughout an Outsourcing/Shared Services Project* SSON (January 10, 2012), http://www.ssonetwork.com/business-process-outsourcing/articles/protecting-intellectual-property-rights-throughout/.
60. Chris Falkowski, *Negotiating Intellectual Property Rights in Software Related Contracts*, Michigan Bar Journal, August 2012 at 32, http://www.michbar.org/journal/pdf/pdf4article2071.pdf.

the innovation, or the parties may decide on joint ownership.[61] Regardless of what arrangement is decided upon, it must be clearly defined in the agreement.[62]

Where joint ownership is contemplated, the parties' agreement should describe the responsibilities of each entity to maintain the IP rights and what each party is permitted to do or not do with the rights they hold.[63]

To the extent joint ownership cannot be agreed upon, one common way to address the parties' respective interests and concerns is for one party to maintain ownership and the other to be granted a license for continued use. Ideally, in negotiating such an arrangement, both parties will recognize the value the other has to offer, such as skilled employees, a market that can be commercially exploited, know-how, research facilities and commitments, and, of course, some form of IP.[64] The licensor's interest is in narrowing the definition of what is being licensed while the licensee's interest is in having a broad definition of the technology.[65] It is important for the parties to communicate with relevant stakeholders to clearly delineate what they need in order to design the agreement so the parties can make effective business and technological use of the subject of the agreement.[66] Often forgotten in the context of licensing negotiations are associated nonproprietary items such as service and support, spare parts, know-how, and training.[67]

If modifications to the subject of the agreement are necessary to adapt it to particular systems or technology, the agreement should specify who will own the modifications.[68] In that context and in general, it is most important to contemplate how the agreement sets out what duties and obligations

---

61. Monika Hussell, *Outsourcing Intellectual Property: Do Risks Outweigh Potential Awards?*, NAT. L. REV. (Dec. 17, 2010), http://www.natlawreview.com/article/outsourcing-intellectual-property-do-risks-outweigh-potential-rewards.
62. *Id.*
63. Patel, *supra* note 19, at 1.
64. *Sucessful Technology Licensing*, World Intellectual Property Organization, 6 (September 2004), http://www.wipo.int/export/sites/www/freepublications/en/licensing/903/wipo_pub_903.pdf.
65. *Id.* at 16.
66. *Id.*
67. *Id* at 36.
68. *Id.*at 22.

end or continue past the effective date of the agreement, including final accounting and reporting activities. [69]

When crafting contractual provisions regarding IP rights, Darren Gardner, partner with Seyfarth Shaw, reminds us that a key question for the parties to ask themselves is whether the granting entity even has the relevant legal rights to the IP involved. Statutory presumptions of ownership can change both based on the type of intellectual property rights in question as well as the jurisdictions involved.[70]

Moreover, it is important to fully think through just which grantees of rights should be included in a contract. That is, in many instances, it is not only the entity that directly engaged a vendor or signed a joint venture agreement; it is all the other related corporate entities that will have need of the IP, and perhaps even the grantor's competitors who might well be engaged in other aspects of the grantee firm's operations and yet still require the grantee's rights to complete certain tasks.[71]

Another point worth noting in terms of securing IP rights is that, where permitted under local law, employees (or other individuals) developing improvements or innovations should be required under the applicable contract to assign over their intellectual property rights to their employer:

> In the United States, rights in an invention first rest with the individual employee—unless there is a written agreement, or an expectation of innovation, the employer may receive no more than "shop rights" to the innovation. In this case, employees are free to license the patented innovation to competitors, for their own profit.[72]

If you don't structure things properly and make any appropriate payments required by the laws of the appropriate jurisdiction, as Darren Gardner warns, "you might find you'll be paying a license fee to employees—for IP they developed for you—forever."

---

69. Cory J. Furman, *Drafting Intellectual Property License Agreements: Issues Overview*, MacPherson Leslie & Tyerman LLP (2010) at 18, http://documents.jdsupra.com/a34ab85c-6f3d-4e5e-ab93-1672de75d0b2.pdf.
70. *Id.* at 34.
71. *Id* at 4.
72. Hussell, *supra* note 61.

There are a number of ways to structure employment agreements to maximize protection for the U.S.-based customer. For instance, as a protection against employees or business partners inserting any malicious coding in embedded product software, a provision incorporating the language of the U.S. Computer Fraud and Abuse Act (CFAA) may be inserted into private employment contracts.[73] Doing so provides a company a private right of action under the statute against the violating foreign employee—a right that may have real teeth, in that in appropriate circumstances a U.S. federal court arguably can assert subject matter jurisdiction over the foreign employee to deter and punish violators.[74]

Availing oneself of CFAA protection leads us to a consideration of choice of law in the employment contract setting. For a U.S. company to ensure it can benefit from the private right of action in the CFAA, the company must explicitly choose U.S. law as the governing law in any foreign-related contract. In addition, the company should choose the United States or arbitration as the forum.[75] Of course in some circumstances, you may not have the ability—for either legal or business reasons—to insist on U.S. law applying to a particular contract. In that instance, it may still be possible to incorporate key language of the CFAA into the agreement. If for instance the terms hold that programming malicious code into embedded software constitutes unauthorized access, a breach may trigger enforcement under applicable foreign law.[76]

Dissemination of proprietary information can take place either accidentally or intentionally; a different strategy is required to combat these two scenarios.[77] One weapon in combating inadvertent disclosure is a well-drafted social media policy that identifies categories of information the company seeks to protect in specific terms but utilizes the broadest possible

---

73. Carrie Greenplate, *Of Protection and Sovereignty: Applying the Computer Fraud and Abuse Act Extraterritorially to Protect Embedded Software Outsourced to China*, 57 AM. U. L. REV. (Oct. 2007), http://digitalcommons.wcl.american.edu/cgi/viewcontent.cgi?article=1024&context=aulr.
74. *Id.*
75. *Id.*
76. *Id.*
77. Michelle Sherman, *Protecting Trade Secrets in a Post-WikiLeaks World*, LEXOLOGY.com (April 6, 2011), http://www.lexology.com/library/detail.aspx?g=62814c70-4c8f-4842-9ea9-f23223db6576.

definition of trade secrets, which can found in the Economic Espionage Act (EEA).[78] The EEA defines trade secrets as information, however stored or maintained, concerning which the owner has taken reasonable measures to keep secret and that has independent economic value.[79] Employee training in this regard should be tailored to individual departments so applicable trade secrets can be identified and the ways in which they should be safeguarded can be discussed.[80]

Also worth remembering is the fact that competitors who might later interview a former employee for a position may ask for a copy of any confidentiality agreement entered into with their previous employer.[81] Therefore, confidentiality agreements should clearly list the categories of trade secrets to be safeguarded without disclosing the specific trade secret information itself, while including clear language asserting that you will pursue all civil and criminal remedies available against employees and third parties for disclosure or inducement of disclosure of trade secrets.[82] Additionally, including terms in the agreement evincing that the business treats protection of its trade secrets as the highest priority and that the company will pursue all civil and criminal legal remedies against the employee or any third party who induces or enables the disclosure of trade secrets can add a deterrent effect.[83] Finally, background checks on employee assigned access to trade secrets are a sound precaution, assuming they are done with the employee's consent and in accordance with applicable laws.[84]

Arvind Vij, of JPMorgan Chase Bank, notes that, again in the context of software issues, many arrangements now potentially include the use of open source software. Clearly, open source software carries many potential benefits. Nevertheless, Vij cautions counsel to consider what the rights of each party would be to ensure that your client is protected and whether one would even want to work with open source software, given the potential issues that surround it. These include the possibility that someone in the

---

78. 18 U.S.C. § 1831 *et seq.* Sherman, *supra* note 77.
79. 18 U.S.C. § 1839. Sherman, *supra* note 77.
80. Sherman, *supra* note 77.
81. *Id.*
82. *Id.*
83. *Id.*
84. *Id.*

process causes infringement by inserting proprietary code.[85] Even where a given program is designated as open source, the open source license may not be enforceable, allowing an erstwhile IP owner to appear who seeks to enforce its rights against both developers *and* users.[86] Open source licenses shift the risk of infringement to the licensee and generally do not contain representations and warranties of quality or fitness for a particular purpose that one would expect in a proprietary setting.[87] A company that utilizes open source software and thinks that it has rights because of a "value add" they designed might find that their efforts are considered a derivative work that under the open source license must be distributed for free.[88] Additionally, an open source license may be deemed to convert once-proprietary programs into open source software, even if only a portion began as open source.[89]

Vij further recommends that for software code that is being licensed, consideration should be given to whether the code should be parked with a third-party escrow agent. Software or technology escrow involves the use of a third-party agent who holds IP (generally of a technical nature) for the benefit of the licensee.[90] Besides software, this could include diagrams or drawings for circuit boards, formulas, production processes, and complex product specifications.[91] The agent maintains the IP until one of a set of defined events in the escrow agreement occurs.[92]

If for instance the licensor—for example, a code developer—suffers extreme financial hardship, files bankruptcy, and terminates a licensing agreement or is acquired by a competitor of the licensee, the licensee is

---

85. *An Overview of "Open Source" Software Licenses*, Software Licensing Committee of the American Bar Association's Intellectual Property Section, http://archive.is/Uqp86.
86. John R. Thomas, *Intellectual Property, Computer Software and the Open Source Movement*, Congressional Research Service (March 11, 2004), http://www.consumidoreslibres.org/cafta/RL32268.pdf.
87. *An Overview of "Open Source" Software Licenses*, *supra* note 85.
88. *Id.*
89. *Id.*
90. Jonathan Reuvid, Managing Business Risk: A Practical Guide to Protecting Your Business 95 (2010), http://books.google.com/books?id=4aNO5PmbEtEC&pg=PA95&lpg=PA95&dq=intellectual+property+escrow+explained&source=bl&ots=sPq67NFMGu&sig=RPhQmiDosJRgf36gfiWOhXqEHZs&hl=en&sa=X&ei=p-F9T6GrJePX0QGJ_tHuCw&ved=0CDIQ6AEwAA#v=onepage&q=intellectual%20property%20escrow%20explained&f=false.
91. *Id.*
92. *Id.* at 97.

threatened with a loss of perhaps a critical component of their business operation.[93] Likewise, if there is a decision to terminate a given product offering, maintenance standards slip below a predetermined metric, or key personnel responsible for the product leave the licensor's employ, this might also trigger the escrow agreement.[94] Vij emphasizes that counsel focus on clarity in terms of the specific conditions for the release of the code through the escrow agent, as well as careful monitoring of the financial well being of both the licensor and escrow agent. Additionally, experts recommend monitoring of what is actually deposited in the escrow account to confirm terms such as associated material being provided are met and requiring regular updates as new versions of the product are developed and released.[95]

There will always be risks to your IP portfolio that are difficult to predict. Still, knowing that IP laws are territorial and decentralized, a practitioner must develop an understanding of how variations in applicable local laws can affect critical portfolio components involved in a given cross-border deal. [96] This has significant implications for negotiation and drafting of final agreements on issues such as representations and warranties, indemnification and confidentiality provisions, covenants, and closing conditions, which must be tailored to the jurisdictions in which the client is located and does its business.[97]

Dealing with Contract Breach

When drafting IP agreements, one approach to consider is defining key provisions in terms of a material breach from the beginning. This may avoid a supplier's argument of wrongful repudiation—that the customer is only claiming a breach to justify termination for unrelated reasons—but

---

93. Rajiv Patel, *Software Escrows as Part of an Intellectual Property Strategy*, FENWICK & WEST LLP (Feb. 15, 2005), http://www.fenwick.com/FenwickDocuments/Software_Escrows.pdf.
94. REUVID, *supra* note 90, at 98.
95. Patel, *supra* note 19.
96. Anne Cappela, Charan Sandhu, & Marisa B. Geiger, *IP Rights Are Wildcard in Cross-Border Transactions*, TODAY'S GENERAL COUNSEL (Dec/Jan 2014) at 19, http://digital.todaysgeneralcounsel.com/Vizion5/viewer.aspx?shareKey=VvbvEe#issueID=22&pageID=21.
97. *Id* at 20.

consider whether mandatory local laws might affect or override your contractual rights.[98] Additionally, indemnification clauses can be drafted to specifically address failures of a target entity to adequately establish and protect its IP rights.[99] Covenants and closing conditions can be utilized to ensure sellers rectify any IP issues prior to closing of a transaction.[100] This is especially important when the indemnifying company might not have adequate resources to pay an adverse judgment later, leaving the holder of indemnification rights with nothing more in practical terms than the right to bankrupt the nominally indemnifying entity should a third party make an infringement claim.[101]

Confidentiality and Conflicts with IPR and Licensing Provisions

A confidentiality agreement is in reality the creation of a confidential relationship, the terms of which are defined in the agreement.[102] It is particularly important when a party intends to apply for IP rights (IPR), such as a patent, as it prevents any written description from being considered as published.[103] Providing written proof that a company considers the subject disclosed information as being confidential, the settlement enables the parties to state how and where a dispute will be settled.[104] Drafters who not only clearly spell out confidentiality obligations and expressly identify the protected information but also set out restrictions on use, access, and disclosure of it put the party seeking to enforce the agreement into the best possible legal

---

98. Tania L. Williams, *Thinking of Terminating Your Outsourcing Agreement?* SOURCINGSPEAK.COM (January 13, 2012), http://www.sourcingspeak.com/2012/01/thinking-of-terminating.html.
99. Cappella, *supra* note 96 at 20.
100. *Id.*
101. Thomas M.S. Hemnes, *Intellectual Property Indemnity Clauses*, BOSTON COLLEGE INTELLECTUAL PROPERTY & TECHNOLOGY FORUM (2013) 4, http://bciptf.org/wp-content/uploads/2013/04/Hemnes_final.pdf.
102. *Intellectual Property Rights, About Confidentiality Agreements*, ESA (Dec. 8, 2004), http://www.esa.int/esaMI/Intellectual_Property_Rights/SEMOGY9DFZD_0.html.
103. *Id.*
104. *Id.*

posture to accomplish that.[105] Further, the parties may negotiate a specific period (five or ten years for example) after which the duties of confidentiality cease,[106] or whether use and disclosure restrictions against former employees should continue for an unlimited time to protect the long term value of the IP in question.[107]

Staffing

Certain terms relating to employee or vendor staffing can also have an impact on your IP program. These terms can include, for instance, a provision prohibiting key personnel working on the customer's account from also working on the account of a competing firm.[108] Critical information should only be distributed on a "need to know" basis, and adequate procedures to maintain it in a confidential manner, both during and after employment, should be mandated.[109] A vendor may further be prohibited from engaging in the manufacture or sale of competing products during the term of your venture and for a reasonable period thereafter.[110] This provision can of course be combined with the step of withholding information regarding a critical component or step.[111]

Keep in mind that while a useful tool, there are limits to the utility of confidentiality agreements, depending upon the circumstances. For example, the U.S. Labor Department's Administrative Review Board in September 2011 handed down its decision in *Vannoy v. Celanese Corp.*,[112] holding that firing an employee who steals confidential information to support a whistleblower report to the Internal Revenue Service or SEC may constitute

---

105. *Id.*
106. Julianne M. Hartzell, *Time Limits in Confidentiality Agreements*, INTELLECTUAL PROPERTY LITIGATION (Spring 2009) 1, http://www.marshallip.com/media/pnc/7/media.7.pdf.
107. *Id.*
108. *Id.*
109. Hussell, *supra* note 61.
110. *Id.*
111. *Id.*
112. ALJ Case No. 2008-SOX-00064, ARB Case No. 09-118 (ALJ July 24, 2013).

retaliation under the Sarbanes-Oxley Act, even though it may also violate the Computer Fraud and Abuse Act.[113]

Protecting IP from Infringement by Third Parties

Naturally, threats to your intangible assets do not stem from only your own employees, vendors, and business partners. In this digitized age, individuals wrongfully distribute copyrighted works to perhaps millions of computer users across the globe. Illicit operations utilizing so-called "rogue websites" misappropriate trademarks and sell inferior knockoff products that dilute an upstanding company's brand. Competitors seek a way around key patents. And, as paranoid as it sounds at first blush, even foreign governments may target unsuspecting firms of all sizes for theft of their confidential information and know-how. Recognizing the scope and severity of all the potential threats to your IP assets is of the highest priority for your IP security steering committee.

In a situation when actual infringement is discovered, a multi-stage investigation is necessary. First, what is the extent of the infringement?[114] Second, who are the infringers and what is the extent of their distribution network?[115] Third, what are the likely implications of the infringement on the business model? It is necessary to know this to determine how to respond (i.e., how much has the infringing activity cost and how much will it likely cost in the future?).[116] If the damage is *de minimis*, a wait-and-see approach may be warranted; if it is the result of unintentional behavior, a licensing agreement might be negotiated.[117] Issues that arise in licensing negotiations may be worked out through the auspices of a mediator, or even through

---

113. Mary Swanton, *Does SOX Protect Whistleblowers Who Steal Confidential Information?*, INSIDE COUNSEL (Jan. 1, 2012), http://www.insidecounsel.com/2012/01/01/does-sox-protect-whistleblowers-who-steal-confiden.
114. *Dealing with Violators of Intellectual Property Rights*, WIPO MAG., 10 (Jan./Feb. 2004), http://www.wipo.int/export/sites/www/sme/en/documents/wipo_magazine/1_2004.pdf.
115. *Id.*
116. *Id.* at 10–11
117. *Id.* at 11

arbitration.[118] If legal action is warranted, consideration should be given to obtaining injunctive relief where available, both to stop the infringing activity and to allow for evidence gathering before the infringer can destroy it.[119] Keep in mind that prosecuting an infringement case requires the owner to prove the existence and ownership of its IP rights; proof of infringement; and, pragmatically, enough value in winning the suit to justify the costs.[120]

While it is not the only region of concern in terms of IP infringement, Asian nations tend to get the most attention on the topic, particularly in the popular press. Jeffrey Paulsen, former Vice President and General Counsel at Brunswick Bowling and Billiards Corp. Corporation, reminds us all of an important lesson in looking at any issue at a regional level. Some executives are tempted to analyze any issue, including IP concerns, by viewing all nations across a continent as one and the same and then conclude rather offhandedly, "That's Asia." Experienced practitioners however stress that one needs to remember there are distinct cultures across a continent—you can't just lump all cultures and peoples together. To illustrate this point, Paulsen relates an amusing true story. He was in China during a business trip and happened to be sitting with one British and one Australian colleague. A Chinese man came up to them and said, "You guys all look the same to me." Of course, they didn't think that they looked that much alike; it merely served as an unintentionally ironic juxtaposition of a classically American conceit. The point is simple enough: just remember Asian peoples are *not* all the same. In fact, given their respective histories, many Asian peoples have manifold reasons they might not even like one another very much.

In keeping with this maxim, Brent Caslin, partner with Jenner & Block, scores the IP threat in various Asian nations on a spectrum from most IP friendly to least. On one end of the spectrum is Japan, which Caslin classifies as very modern and generally respectful of IP rights. In the middle of the spectrum are nations such as South Korea and Singapore. At the far end of Caslin's scale are what he terms "IP renegades," a group of countries that includes China. These last nations are, in his experience, "a huge mess for IP."

---

118. *Enforcement of Intellectual Property Rights*, WIPO INTELLECTUAL PROPERTY HANDBOOK: POLICY, LAW AND USE 208 (2004), http://www.wipo.int/about-ip/en/iprm/pdf/ch4.pdf.
119. *Dealing with Violators of Intellectual Property Rights*, *supra* note 114, at 12.
120. *Id.* at 13.

Caslin explains that in these renegade nations, there are deeply rooted cultural issues at play. People in these countries have generally never been taught the value of intellectual property—simply put, they oftentimes just "don't get it." This can extend to the leadership class as well, with the result that it often takes a lot of time to get leaders within these nations to even pay attention to the issue.

As a result, clients can have tremendous issues with IP, Caslin notes. He gives the example of one client that bought a company in China, including its IP and customer lists. The sellers then set up an identical company just blocks away, using virtually the same trademark. Caslin advises clients to consider adding a contractual clause to sales agreements that prohibits the seller setting up a competing company from using similar IP. Additionally, Caslin believes it is better to have an arbitration provision when you are doing business in a country new to the concept of IP, even though arbitration can sometimes be slow in practice and have issues with enforcement. When looking at your rights in the courts, "you have to recognize what jurisdiction you will be in," he admonishes, and you have to honestly discern if you can "expect fair treatment in that court."

There are signs that the IP climate in China may be improving, at least marginally. In 2011, China surpassed both the United States and Japan in number of patents filed, and one of its largest Web service providers, Baidu, Inc., was removed from the U.S. Trade Representative's Notorious Markets list for positive actions taken toward eliminating piracy and counterfeiting.[121]

One cannot limit one's attention on IP to the Asia-Pacific region only, however. Ed Bathelt, Vice President and General Counsel at Komatsu America, notes companies should have concerns with IP issues in South America, particularly in connection with trademark and patent issues. This is because the methods for registering them in Latin America can themselves transfer proprietary rights.

What can happen, Bathelt explains, is that local business partners may offer to register your trademark or patent in their local jurisdiction—but

---

121. Amer Raja, *Greater Protection in China?: China's Intellectual Property Rights Developments in 2011*, AM. U. WASH. COLLEGE OF L. INTELLECTUAL PROPERTY BRIEF (Jan. 3, 2012), http://www.ipbrief.net/2012/01/03/greater-protection-in-china-china's-intellectual-property-rights-developments-in-2011/.

in doing so, they may gain local rights in the mark. The concerns raised by the local business partners are valid enough in Bathelt's estimation: Chinese and other Asian businesses have been using others' trademarks in South America with more ease because there is typically less enforcement there.

On the one hand, you certainly don't want the local business partner to gain rights in your IP, but at the same time, you do need someone to fight the infringing importer. Bathelt concludes that in the final analysis, you probably want to go down yourself and handle such matters on your own, directly with local counsel, particularly where your trademark is a global mark. You simply don't want someone else to gain a foothold there. This strategy can be complicated however by any dearth of legal talent with requisite knowledge of a given venue's procedures and holdings. Bathelt notes he has found it difficult at times to locate local counsel with IP expertise in South America.

In Latin America too, however, there are some signs that things may be changing for the better, if slowly. Roger Correa, Compliance Marketing Director of the international information technology industry group Business Software Alliance, finds that while in 2011 Latin America had a 64 percent software piracy rate, up slightly from 2010, the importance of IP rights to local economies is recognized by the Latin American business and legal communities there.[122] Correa points to Brazil's anti-software piracy laws that carry the potential for treble damages and the use of local tax authorities to combat piracy in nations such as Mexico and Colombia.[123]

Even the European Union (EU), which obviously has a long-standing history of intellectual property rights protection, confronts businesses with challenges. For example, small businesses in particular are said to have been disadvantaged by the complexity and cost incumbent on protecting their IP rights across the EU.[124] In response, the European Commission is proposing a strategy—"A Single Market for Intellectual Property Rights"—that

---

122. Dan Berthiaume, *Latin America Makes Progress on Intellectual Property Rights*, NEARSHORE AMERICAS (Oct. 10, 2011), http://nearshoreamericas.com/latin-america-progress-intellectual-property-rights/.
123. *Id.*
124. *Citizens' Summary: A Single Market for Intellectual Property Rights*, EU SINGLE MARKET, INTELLECTUAL PROPERTY, http://ec.europa.eu/internal_market/copyright/docs/ipr_strategy/citizenssummary_en.pdf (last visited April 21, 2012).

sets a blueprint for various actions on trademarks, patents, copyright and enforcement strategy for IP rights both within the Union and in conjunction with non-EU countries.[125]

Whatever region you are concerned with, however, part of the difficulty in addressing intangible asset threats is that, in a globalized world, there is a tension between maintaining security and simultaneously retaining the openness that customers expect and that collaborative innovation demands. While recognizing that real world business concerns mean that airtight security is impossible as a practical matter, there are reasonable steps that companies who operate internationally can take to minimize infringement risk. The remainder of this chapter considers these steps as to each category of intellectual property.

Trade Secrets

Mark Halligan, a partner at Nixon Peabody, notes that in information security today, there is a greater emphasis on what is leaving the enterprise than what is entering. This relates to a change from "trade secrets at rest" to "trade secrets in motion." Halligan explains that it used to be that research and development (R&D), manufacturing, and marketing functions within a company were all performed within one building. In that world, where trade secrets were "at rest," they could be kept safe in a filing cabinet. Today however, trade secrets are "in motion": quality control, manufacturing, and R&D can be located in different parts of the world. The key now, Halligan says, is to track and follow trade secrets in motion as they move to a variety of third parties.

Halligan points out that companies have a right to copy what their competitors do—except for materials protected by patent, trademark, copyright, and trade secret. By far, he reckons, the United States has the best protection for trade secrets. The inevitable disclosure doctrine serves as the basis for emergency injunctive relief in the United States before a tort happens. Decisions such as *BF Goodrich v. Wohlegmuth*[126] and *Pepsico v. Redmond*[127]

---

125. Id.
126. 117 Ohio App. 493, 192 N.E.2d 99 (Ohio Ct. App. 1963).
127. 54 F.3d 1262 (7th Cir. 1995).

discuss the doctrine. Of course, once one is outside the United States, the rules of enforcement change.

Generally, systems based on common law have well-developed and predictable protections for trade secrets. According to Halligan, the United Kingdom solved 90 percent of its trade secret issues with two things: (1) the *Anton Piller* order—essentially an ex parte seizure order that deals with the ease of erasing relevant evidence off of computers; and (2) Garden Leave—where employees leaving the company remain subject to noncompete agreements for 1–2 years after leaving company, but the employees remain on the payroll during this period. U.S. courts prevent spoliation of evidence via preservation orders. Even in India, Halligan finds that there is some good law on the books, although litigants may not get to trial for 20 years. One can, however, get injunctive relief in India.

By contrast, civil law systems have swift and effective remedies upon requisite factual showing. For instance, Italy is one civil law jurisdiction that has a strong national trade secrets statute. In many civil law jurisdictions however, discovery is virtually nonexistent. For instance, Brazil recognizes trade secrets, but little or no discovery is available. That constitutes a big problem in Halligan's view because without American-style discovery, you cannot ferret out who it is that is stealing your client's trade secrets.

As discussed elsewhere in this chapter, Asian legal systems have not historically recognized IP rights. For instance, Halligan explains, in China, you have to supply evidence of damage suffered by misappropriation before recovering.

So, how to protect trade secrets there? Halligan offers a few practical suggestions. First, he advises clients to avoid putting their current generation of products into China. Even so, one does have to recognize that trade secrets today have a shorter shelf life generally. Second, he advises putting key provisions ("the guts") of U.S. Uniform Trade Secrets Act into your contract. That is, utilize the statute's definitions of trade secrets and misappropriation, the right to interim injunctive relief, procedures for international arbitration and dispute adjudication, liquidated damages and remedies for violations, and the right to conduct discovery including inspections to safeguard one's IP rights. Regarding this strategy, Halligan notes that every nation, including China, recognizes the legal right to make a contract.

The question in China's case is whether they actually enforce the contract. Third, Halligan advocates the use of "carrots and sticks." The carrots are incentives to the foreign business partner that it must protect. Such incentives can be as effective as penalties, especially with individual employees and small businesses in developing countries. The sticks are penalty clauses with high U.S. dollar amounts assigned to each violation.

When budgets are tight and resources limited, Halligan points to what he refers to as the "Two Cardinal Rules of Trade Secret Protection." In his view, fully 80 percent of your goal to protect trade secrets can be reached simply by following these two rules. The first rule is that you should permit access to trade secrets only on a "need to know" basis. The second rule is compartmentalization: that is, to break up the pieces of the puzzle so that a given individual only has access to their piece of the puzzle. That being said, Halligan warns clients to be careful of establishing multiple security levels, as it puts into question whether the information at the lower level will receive protection. He explains that this is because courts have held that information available at lower security levels was not protected by "reasonable measures" in light of more secure environments available.

A reader might be concerned by the seeming contradiction in this advice; after all, to the extent that access to information is on a "need to know basis," doesn't that create multiple security levels that then leave whatever is not at the highest level potentially exposed? In response, Halligan explains that in his experience, no more than about 5 percent of a company's information will be properly classified as "top Secret, "and perhaps another 45 percent will qualify as "confidential." That means that roughly 50 percent of a given company's information will cause no meaningful impact if released.

So Halligan concludes, if you handle your security classifications correctly, you don't really worry about the possibility that lower-level information might be disclosed. He does however attach one last warning: classifications may not be static. That is, what is considered low-level information today might be deemed top secret tomorrow, and vice versa. This merely suggests that your IP inventory, like many other aspects of your international operation, is never a "one and done" task. It needs to be revisited often by your IP steering committee.

To the extent a client determines it needs to file suit to protect its trade secrets, venue will naturally be a key decision. Some counsel recommend bringing such cases before the International Trade Commission (ITC). While proceedings will not involve a jury, damages awards are unavailable, and preliminary relief is rare, ITC rulings can exclude products from the U.S. market and are generally delivered in less than a year.[128] Others prefer the familiar environs of U.S. district court, pointing out that certain "rocket dockets" such as the Eastern District of Virginia have an average filing-to-trial period of just nine months.[129]

Eric Hagen, partner with McDermott Will & Emery, LLP, adds that to the extent a company begins a joint venture (JV) overseas in which it is sharing know-how and trade secrets, it needs to carefully keep track of what is happening to that confidential information. He warns that it is not enough to simply include confidentiality and nondisclosure agreements into contract language. Hagen gives the example of a client company operating in both the United States and Germany. A JV involving the company went into bankruptcy. The company found to its horror that its trade secrets were to be sold off as an asset! Naturally, the company sought and obtained an injunction to prevent the sale. The point is you must ask yourself when sharing proprietary information, "What happens if the joint venture splits up?"

Hagen further notes that there is an interplay between trade secrets and patent infringement strategy. You must decide to keep something secret (e.g., the Coke formula and KFC's blend of secret spices) or to disclose it to the public via a patent filing in order to get patent protection. The latter has its benefits, including twenty years of legal monopoly and the ability to collect licensing fees and exercise rights to exclude anyone else from unauthorized manufacture. It is important to remember that you cannot have your proverbial cake and eat it too in this context. As Hagen reminds us, if you file for a patent in even one foreign jurisdiction, you can't claim trade secret anywhere anymore.

---

128. Ashley Post, *Tackling International Trade Secret Cases*, INSIDE COUNSEL (Jan. 1, 2012), http://www.insidecounsel.com/2012/01/01/tackling-international-trade-secret-cases.
129. *Id.*

Patents

Jeffrey Paulsen, of Brunswick Bowling and Billiards Corp. , reiterates that the key to your entire IP strategy has to be protecting your IP "crown jewels." These could include not just the traditional inventions commonly thought of in this context but such things as business processes.[130] To fully protect your patents across borders, you generally need to go country by country. This fact illustrates a basic tension, of course. Paulsen recounts that at Brunswick Bowling and Billiards Corp., IP spend was a big item. Still, it was not economically feasible to try to protect patents in every single country on Earth.

This leads to the fundamental question: How do you deal with this tension between the need for protection and budgetary limitations? Paulsen advises that you ask a basic question: What are you selling? That is, are you selling products based primarily on your technology, or those based primarily on a brand and trademark? If the latter, it's more important for you to protect your brand and trademark than the patent.

A second question to ponder is what the purpose of your entry into a particular country is. Once again, a company needs to do a cost-benefit analysis. The analysis has to involve both business and legal planning. Since the reasons to enter a given market may not be the same across the board, Paulsen reasons, so too enforcement strategy can vary from country to country, depending on where sales are particularly strong. It is also worth considering that patents protect against not only the manufacture but also the importation of infringing products. Thus, if you obtain patents in countries where the sale of your product will be profitable, you have little need for patent protection in countries where infringing products may be manufactured but not sold for any significant profit.[131]

Paulsen highlights a third related concern: If you discover there is ongoing infringement, what will you do? Utilizing a patent-pending warning (what Paulsen refers to as "pretending to do something") is a strategy in itself, but you still need to know what to do if "your bluff is called." For instance, what if the cost to actually enforce your IP rights through litigation is $500,000? Foreign litigation may entail more costs than onshore

---

130. *Business Method Patents*, Russ Weinzimmer & Associates P.C. (2014), http://www.strategicpatentlaw.com/business-method-patents.
131. Hussell, *supra* note 61.

litigation. Translation services, travel costs, and extra logistical steps needed to obtain whatever discovery is permissible need to be factored into the budget.[132] Moreover, extra time may need to be set aside in document review, to search for evidence of spoliation in countries where U.S.-style document retention is not common.[133]

Further, Paulsen relates, a company needs to determine how practically enforceable its rights are in a given set of circumstances. While some counsel might prefer litigating in a U.S. courtroom, as discussed above, Paulsen suggests that companies attempt to bring any IP disputes to a neutral venue. It is important to remember, he holds, that a Chinese business, for instance, might like a neutral spot as well. The U.S. court system might be pretty intimidating to that foreign business. Also, choosing a third-party country as your dispute venue imparts a feeling of mutual respect.

There are ways to get a better bang for your patent enforcement buck, according to Hagen. He recommends filing an application via the World Intellectual Property Organization's Patent Cooperation Treaty, which is subscribed to by 144 participating nations. Down the line, after the type of analysis described above, you can choose which of these nations you choose to designate. The European Patent Office also has a common system that will save time and money on the search portion of the patent process. Likewise, there is an African Regional Intellectual Property Organization (ARIPO) that serves a similar function for 17 sub-Saharan nations, though at the time of application, the applicant must designate to which states the application will apply.[134] An application can be filed in any ARIPO member state or directly with the ARIPO office.[135]

An important consideration when contemplating your patent strategy is that filing a foreign application may have repercussions on U.S. patent litigation. In the United States, it is not uncommon to file a patent application and then abandon all or part of it. In some instances, an abandoned patent application is picked back up by means of a continuation application,

---

132. Post, *supra* note 128.
133. *Id.*
134. African Regional Intellectual Property Organization, *Legal Framework (2014)*, http://www.aripo.org/index.php/about-aripo/legal-framework.
135. *Id.*

which is a second application for the same invention claimed in a prior non-provisional application, filed before the original prior application becomes abandoned or otherwise patented.[136] Additionally, multiple patents may claim priority off of a single application. Hagen cautions that in light of all of this, arguments you are making in a foreign application may hamstring your position in enforcing a U.S. patent if, say, in the foreign jurisdiction you make arguments that limit the scope of your invention to avoid the issue in the foreign locale. In Hagen's view, patent efforts in both the United States and abroad require careful coordination, so that you can ensure you are making consistent arguments across jurisdictions.

Much has been written on the subject of so-called "patent trolls," which are generally understood as individuals or companies who leverage a patent portfolio to obtain cash from a technology's existing uses rather than by manufacturing or adapting it in new ways. While once generally a U.S. phenomenon, Hagen notes that in the last two years, patent trolls have been springing up in Japan. It is easy to disparage such activity, but Hagan says that to some extent, who is a "patent troll" today may be in the eye of the beholder. Because the patent market today is as liquid as it is, large multinationals often hold patents on items they don't make. In the event that a company finds itself in litigation with a patent troll (still most likely in U.S. federal court), Robert J. Gaybrick and Robert J. Hollingshead, of the Morgan Lewis firm, recommend strategies such as demanding reexamination of the patent owners' asserted patents; filing of declaratory judgment actions; engaging in joint defense arrangements with other troll targets, and, where factually appropriate, using defenses such as antitrust violation, equitable estoppel, and standing.[137]

Hagen recently visited Uganda and notes that various African nations will soon lose their TRIPS exception regarding obtaining generic drugs from domestic producers in a health crisis (e.g., HIV/AIDS, malaria). From Hagen's observations in Uganda, the patent offices of many African nations

---

136. 201.07 Continuation Application [R-3]—200 Types, Cross-Noting, and Status of Application, U.S. Patent and Trademark, http://www.uspto.gov/web/offices/pac/mpep/documents/0200_201_07.htm (last visited April 29, 2012).
137. Robert J. Gaybrick & Robert J. Hollingshead, *Fighting the Patent Troll* (Sept. 27, 2007), http://www.morganlewis.com/pubs/fightingpatenttroll_gaybrickhollingshead20070927.pdf.

will have a lot of catching up to do. In Uganda's office, there were no electronic records and no computers. When the TRIPS exception expires, pharmaceutical companies that are cranking out a significant volume of product there will come calling to patent their products. Hagen questions, will it overwhelm the system there?

Trademark

There is little doubt that there is a fair amount of counterfeiting going on today, as has been documented by various journalists, business leaders, and government officials. In-house counsel who have spoken to this author acknowledge some success in stopping this by businesses working with authorities and conducting raids. In their opinion, a company simply can't afford not to engage in that sort of deterrent action—IP owners have to show people it doesn't pay to infringe. Interestingly, many companies may not be as concerned about cheap knockoffs of their product. Instead, analysts say the closer in quality and price the knockoffs are to the genuine products, the more the counterfeit goods chip away at a company's sales. Companies are increasingly analyzing which parts of their supply chain are most vulnerable to counterfeiters and who has access to their product designs, according to Violet Ho, a senior managing director for investigative-services firm Kroll.[138]

While a lot of attention has focused on the problem that big brands such as Columbia Sportswear have with counterfeits on Chinese shopping sites like Alibaba.com and its sister site Taobao.com, it may actually be that small businesses and entrepreneurs are hardest hit, says Joel Shulman, a professor of entrepreneurship at Babson College in Wellesley, MA. They lack the financial and technological resources that large companies have to deter or fight offenders, especially those based overseas where U.S. patent laws don't apply. While cease and desist letters and registration of trademarks in foreign markets are recommended to SME's, Shulman says a small business's

---

138. Kathy Chu, *Foreign Brands Battle Counterfeiters in China*, WALL STREET JOURNAL (April 29, 2014), http://blogs.wsj.com/corporate-intelligence/2014/04/29/foreign-brands-battle-counterfeiters-in-china/?KEYWORDS=counterfeit+goods

best defense is "to constantly update your product to distinguish it in the marketplace. Unfortunately, it's the cost of doing business," he says.[139]

One of Eric Hagen's clients is a U.S.-based business selling consumer products. He recounts that they were having success in the United States and wanted to expand to Europe, Asia, Australia, and other countries. In Hagen's experience, it is not uncommon for a company to expand into a number of European markets simultaneously, as success in one country tends to bleed into another. As such, it made sense to Hagen to file a community trademark in Europe as a cost-effective tool—it allows you to file one application, but when issued, protects your mark in all 27 EU countries. In the end, it saves a lot of money. A similar procedure can be utilized in Australia and New Zealand, where one can file for trademark jointly for these two countries. Hagen has local counsel in New Zealand who work at lower rates than Australian attorneys, so joint filing in New Zealand then saves both filing and attorneys' fees.

As with patent enforcement, a lot of companies have more than a few brands or tag lines to protect. It can become expensive to register all of them in multiple markets. Filing trademarks in foreign countries is generally more difficult from a practical point of view than filing in the United States, Hagen contends. With overseas applications, however, one can at least search the official records. Once an application is filed, it is reviewed by the foreign trademark office. In some instances, Hagen's clients have gotten an answer right away—almost a rubber stamp. Others required a response to official inquiries.

One country where Hagen experienced a delay was Thailand. In that instance, his client filed an application for a mark where the local business partner had applied for the same mark previously. Thus, the client's application was denied. Hagen handled the matter through local counsel. In that situation, his clients had some important decisions to make. Should they appeal the decision? Was it possible to change the mark? Or should the client simply withdraw from that market? In the end, the client's local business partner was persuaded to withdraw its application.

---

139. Sarah E. Needleman & Kathy Chu, *Entrpreneurs Bemoan Counterfeit Goods*, WALL ST. J (April 28,2014), http://online.wsj.com/news/articles/SB10001424052702304163604579529790140841718?KEYWORDS=counterfeit+goods&mg=reno64-wsj.

Although in this chapter we deal with trade secrets and patents first, Hagen cautions that operationally, it makes the most sense to put the trademark in place and register relevant domain names for that country first, then deal with patents. He finds it common that many U.S.-based businesses go to trade shows overseas, see an opportunity, and start laying the groundwork by dealing with restrictions, disclaimers, and approvals that may be required by local regulatory regimes (e.g., food, drugs, etc.). In the meantime, after sometimes waiting 18 to 24 months to get their mark registered, they decide to pull out of the market and or forego the opportunity. This cautionary tale reminds us yet again of the value of careful feasibility studies and cost-benefit analysis, rather than a shoot-from-the-hip mentality when entering new markets.

When seeking to register a mark, Hagen suggests that a logical starting point is a list of countries where you are distributing or doing business. Again, it is important to ask what your reasons are for seeking trademark protection. Are you trying to scare off competitors from knocking off your brand? What is the cost of actually enforcing your rights via a lawsuit? If you determine the cost of protection to be expensive relative to your resources, do you register all your brands or limit application to only the most recognized ones? You may decide to register now and make a decision on whether to actually take the next step of enforcement actions later.

One consideration if you choose to do business in an emerging country with few existing brands is that it is possible to run into the problem of "genericide, which is where a brand name or trademark has been transformed through popular usage into a common noun." In Uganda, for instance, any brand of toothpaste is known as "Colgate." It is possible if you are a brand leader that your mark in such a locale may suffer the same fate as "aspirin."

In terms of trademark litigation costs, Hagen points out that in the United States, attorneys' fees and the costs of discovery drive costs. Outside the United States, however, trademark dispute resolution procedures may be primarily administrative, be streamlined, and involve no discovery. Hagen advises clients to discuss with local counsel the costs of proceedings in specific locations. But costs are not the sole consideration. Clients also have to consider how proceeding might hamper ongoing business. What travel costs will be incurred? How much time of key people must shift away from their core functions?

A pivotal consideration is to identify in which of these jurisdictions there is an issue with locals "knocking off stuff"—i.e., counterfeiting problems. Where there are problems, it may be harder to prosecute infringement. An important consideration is whether criminal prosecution is an option in the specific jurisdiction or jurisdictions involved. In some Latin American countries, Hagen relates, governments are seemingly on the defensive about infringement. Authorities will say they are vigilant when something is actually brought to their attention. So you may well want to research what the enforcement regime is in the subject country.

Copyright

Copyright can be said to be similar to the other types of intellectual property discussed above in that virtually all nations have their own individual laws—that often materially differ from one another—that must be understood prior to making any key business decision involving rights affected by them.[140] Likewise, should infringement occur, legal action would need to be pursued in the venue where the infringement occurred.[141] Generally speaking, the rights holder will seek to demonstrate a causal connection between the copyrighted work and alleged infringement that explains the similarity between them.[142]

It is also true that in this area, a host of nations have entered into international treaties (including the Berne Convention of 1886, Rome Convention of 1961, and Phonograms Convention of 1971) that have made it possible for copyright owners to benefit from their rights without any formalities or requirement of registration.[143] It is not surprising then that Hagen suggests

---

140. *Creative Expression: An Introduction to Copyright and Related Rights for Small and Medium-sized Enterprises* 6 WIPO (2006), www.wipo.int/freepublications/en/sme/918/wipo_pub_918.pdf.
141. *How Can I Enforce Copyright?* Intellectual Property and Copyright in the Digital Environment, University of Cambridge (Sept. 12, 2005), http://www.caret.cam.ac.uk/copyright/Page148.html#Topic134.
142. *Enforcement of Intellectual Property Rights*, WIPO INTELLECTUAL PROPERTY HANDBOOK: POLICY, LAW AND USE 226 (2004) http://www.wipo.int/about-ip/en/iprm/pdf/ch4.pdf.
143. *Creative Expression: An Introduction to Copyright and Related Rights for Small and Medium-sized Enterprises*, *supra* note 140, at 6.

that the first question you should ask yourself in terms of your defensive strategy is whether you really need to have a registered copyright. To help figure this out, he advises clients to determine what the process for registration is in the subject country. For example, is the process in the subject location purely administrative, requiring only a form and a fee? Perhaps more importantly, to the extent that infringement becomes an issue, can registration be "done on the fly?" By way of example, a certificate of registration (or rejection of copyright application) is a prerequisite for U.S. owners seeking to initiate a suit for copyright infringement in federal district court.[144] However, the U.S. Copyright Office allows for expedited processing of registration when litigation is pending or anticipated.[145]

If someone uses copyrighted material without permission, and no defense such as fair use applies, in most countries the owner may use any remedies available under the civil law of the country in which the infringement occurred.[146] Naturally, remedies will vary from one jurisdiction to the next, but they may include injunctive relief, seizure of infringing articles, actual damages, lost profits or statutory damages, and attorneys' fees.[147] One can potentially consult with industry-specific organizations that monitor and prosecute copyright violations.[148] Additionally, where infringement is intentionally committed on a commercial scale, referring the matter for a criminal prosecution may be an option.[149] Clients who become aware of infringement may also work closely with customs officials to prevent unauthorized copies from entering a given nation's borders.[150]

A client whose copyright is actively being violated will want to put an end to the infringement as soon as possible and seek compensation for that which has already taken place. This can be more complicated in the digital age, when so-called "rogue websites" are specifically set up by bad actors who utilize Internet service providers (ISP's) domiciled outside the U.S. in

---

144. *Stopping Copyright Infringement*, U.S. COPYRIGHT OFFICE, http://www.copyright.gov/help/faq/faq-infringement.html (last visited May 5, 2012).
145. *Id.*
146. *How Can I Enforce Copyright?*, *supra* note 141.
147. Henry James Fasthoff IV, *Copyright Infringement Litigation FAQ*, AVVO.COM, http://www.avvo.com/legal-guides/ugc/copyright-infringement-litigation-faq (last visited May 7, 2012).
148. *Stopping Copyright Infringement*, *supra* note 144.
149. *Id.*
150. *Enforcement of Intellectual Property Rights*, *supra* note 142, at 216.

an effort to avoid application of existing U.S. law. Cease and desist letters and even take-down notices pursuant to the Digital Millennium Copyright Act (DMCA) often run into practical and jurisdictional hurdles when rogue sites are set up utilizing offshore ISP's. That's not to say that it might not be worth sending a take-down notice to an offshore ISP, as it is possible that the jurisdiction it sits in has a law similar to DMCA that will cause the provider to respond.[151] You may also attempt to send take-down notices to the firm that registers the offending site's URL and to major search engines such as Google and Yahoo.[152] Unfortunately though, in many instances when rogue sites are successfully shut down, they reappear soon after, utilizing a new domain name.[153]

Because current law has been deemed inadequate to the task of dealing with the avalanche of Web-based piracy, legislative efforts both in the U.S. Congress and via treaty have been undertaken—but with little success to date. In Congress, this took the form of the Protect IP Act (PIPA) in the Senate and the Stop Online Piracy Act (SOPA) in the House. A primary purpose of PIPA was "enhancing enforcement against rogue websites operated and registered overseas."[154] It allowed for the Attorney General to bring *in rem* actions when a registrant, owner, or operator of a site cannot be found within U.S. jurisdiction.[155] Injunctive relief would have been available as to sites that conduct business directed to U.S. residents and are "dedicated to infringing activities" that harm holders of U.S. IP rights.[156] Operators of systems hosting such rogue sites would be required to "take the least burdensome technically feasible and reasonable measures" to take down the sites, but the Act specifically maintains the limitation of liability afforded to the under section 512 of the DMCA.[157] Financial transaction providers,

---

151. Sarah Bird, *Four Ways to Enforce Your Copyright: What to Do When Your Online Content Is Being Stolen*, THE MOZ BLOG (Jan. 14, 2008), http://moz.com/blog/four-ways-to-enforce-your-copyright-what-to-do-when-your-online-content-is-being-stolen.
152. *Id.*
153. Jennifer Martinez, *Feds Shut Down Rogue Websites*, POLITICO.COM (Nov. 29, 2010), http://www.politico.com/news/stories/1110/45674.html.
154. David A. Steiger, "COUNTERFEIT.COM: Congressional and Plurilateral Responses to Global Internet Piracy," paper presented at 84th Annual Meeting of the State Bar of California, Sept. 17, 2011, citing "PROTECT IT Act of 2011," (S.968), sec. 3.
155. *Id.* sec. 3(a)(2).
156. *Id.* sec. 3(b).
157. *Id.* sec. 3(d)(2)(A)(i).

Internet advertising services, and information location tools would have been similarly required to take reasonable measures to suspend payments; cease making advertisements, links, or other placements; and disable access to offending sites, respectively.[158]

Section 4 of PIPA would have added an even more controversial new weapon to the battle: a private right of action for intellectual property holders against infringers.[159] Under a qualifying court-issued order pursuant to this section, financial transaction providers and Internet advertising services would again be required to take reasonable measures vis-à-vis the offending site.[160]

SOPA was deemed if anything perhaps even more troubling to critics. It arguably requires websites with user-generated content to actively police all material posted and remove infringing items.[161] Concern has been raised that this would drive many smaller user-generated content sites from the Web because of the cost of such monitoring.[162] Critics of the two principal bills drafted an alternative piece of legislation in the House, the Online Protection and Enforcement of Digital Trade Act, which employs a "follow-the-money strategy" and would involve the auspices of the ITC rather than the Justice Department.[163] None of these three bills have yet come up for a vote before the full membership of the Senate or House.

In the meantime, on November 15, 2010, the final text of the Anti-Counterfeiting Trade Agreement (ACTA) was released. In some ways, one could argue that ACTA seeks to have similar effects as PIPA and SOFA, on a global basis. According to the Office of the United States Trade Representative, the aim of the negotiations on ACTA is

---

158. *Id.* sec. 3(d)(2)(B)(C) and (D).
159. *Id.* sec. 4.
160. *Id.* sec. 4(d)(2)(A) and (B).
161. Steven Seidenberg, *Congress Takes Steps to Shut Down Rogue Websites*, Inside Counsel (Jan. 1, 2012), http://www.insidecounsel.com/2012/01/01/congress-takes-steps-to-shut-down-rogue-websites?page=3.
162. *Id.*
163. Juliana Gruenwald, *Critics of Online-Piracy Bills Release Their Own Draft Legislation*, Nat. Rev. (Dec. 8, 2011), http://www.nationaljournal.com/tech/critics-of-online-piracy-bills-release-their-own-draft-legislation-20111208.

to establish a state-of-the-art international framework that provides a model for effectively combating global proliferation of commercial-scale counterfeiting and piracy in the 21st century. The agreement will also include innovative provisions to deepen international cooperation and to promote strong enforcement practices.[164]

The initial provisions make it clear that ACTA is meant to support the objectives and principles of existing agreements, specifically including TRIPS.[165]

None of the 38 nations involved in the construction of the agreement fall within the category of "large emerging economies." Nevertheless, the European Trade Commission has expressly stated:

The ultimate objective is that large emerging economies, where IPR enforcement could be improved, such as China or Russia, will sign up to the global pact. ACTA is not intended to isolate these countries or point the finger at their enforcement efforts. In light of the growing international consensus on IPR enforcement, the Commission is confident that more countries will join ACTA when they feel the time is right.[166]

The text of the agreement sets forth provisions for both civil and criminal enforcement. Civil proceedings must permit injunctive relief, including cease and desist orders and prevention of infringing goods from entering the stream of commerce.[167] Judicial authorities must have authority to impose damages adequate to compensate the rights holder on an infringer who "knowingly or with reasonable grounds to know" engaged in infringement.[168] Where appropriate, prevailing parties can be awarded court costs and attorneys' fees.[169] The agreement further provides for *inaudita altera*

---

164. Steiger, *supra* note 154, citing *Anti-Counterfeiting Trade Agreement (ACTA)*, OFFICE OF THE UNITED STATES TRADE REPRESENTATIVE, http://www.ustr.gov/acta.
165. *Id.*, citing *Anti-Counterfeiting Trade Agreement*, Dec. 3, 2010, ch. I, sec. 1, art. 1 & 2.
166. *Id.*, citing *Anti-Counterfeiting Trade Agreement (ACTA) Fact Sheet*, EUROPEAN COMMISSION-TRADE (updated Nov. 2008), http://trade.ec.europa.eu/doclib/docs/2008/october/tradoc_140836.11.08.pdf.
167. *Id.*, citing *Anti-Counterfeiting Trade Agreement*, Dec. 3, 2010, ch. II, sec. 2, art. 8.
168. *Id.* art. 9.
169. *Id.*

parte provisional measures when delay might cause irreparable harm to the rights holder; however authorities can require reasonably available evidence to "satisfy themselves with a sufficient degree of certainty" of imminent or ongoing infringement and to provide security or equivalent assurance to protect defendants and prevent abuse.[170]

The signatories are required to provide for criminal procedures and penalties in cases of "willful trademark counterfeiting or copyright or related rights piracy on a commercial scale," and in the course of trade and on a commercial scale, willful use of labels and packaging identical to or indistinguishable from a trademark registered in its territory intended to be used in trade of goods or services identical to those for which the trademark is registered.[171] Criminal penalties shall include imprisonment and fines "sufficiently high to provide a deterrent to future acts of infringement."[172]

ACTA has specific provisions related to enforcement of IPR in the digital environment, including a requirement to make available procedures permitting "expeditious remedies" to prevent and deter infringement.[173] The procedures are to be implemented so as to avoid creation of "barriers to legitimate activity, including electronic commerce," and be consistent with the signatory nations' laws to preserve "fundamental principles such as freedom of expression, fair process, and privacy."[174] ACTA specifically allows for orders against online service providers to expeditiously disclose to a rights holder with a legally adequate claim of infringement information sufficient to identify a subscriber whose account was allegedly used for infringement, where such information is being sought for the purpose of protecting or enforcing those rights.[175]

Given that it is an international agreement involving an approval process involving dozens of sovereign governments, passing ACTA involved a fair amount of impassioned debate. The United States, European Union, and nine other sovereign nations ultimately signed the agreement ahead of the May 1, 2013, deadline, but there is no corresponding deadline for

---

170. *Id.* art. 12.
171. *Id.* sec. 4, art. 23, para. 1 & 2.
172. *Id.*
173. *Id.* sec. 5, art. 27, para. 1.
174. *Id.* para. 2.
175. *Id.* para. 4.

ratification, and the agreement will only actually enter into force when six of the sovereign governments ratify it.[176] Critics fear the combination of a ratified ACTA and the conclusion of the Trans-Pacific Partnership will cause significant violations of free expression rights solely to satisfy Hollywood and other content industry interests.[177] Regardless of how one comes out in the debate over these measures, what is clear is that at least as this book goes to press, owners of intellectual property are still mainly on their own in terms of protecting themselves from counterfeiters and pirates and for now will have to make plans accordingly.

Unfair Competition

In connection with all IP infringement cases, counsel would be well advised to consider whether to pursue a claim based on unfair competition practices.[178] Unfair competition is not generally seen as an independent IP right but as part of protection of recognized IP rights.[179] For instance, taking advantage of third-party efforts in a manner that leads to confusion is at the heart of unfair competitive practices law, such as section 10bis of the Paris Convention and section 39 of TRIPS.[180] Unfair competition law in part seeks to punish "free riding" behavior such as slavish imitation, parasitic competition, and dilution of a mark holder's reputation and goodwill.[181] Disclosure of trade secrets is another focus of unfair competition.[182]

---

176. *Anti-Counterfeiting Trade Agreement (ACTA)*, Swiss Federal Institute of Intellectual Property (June 28, 2013), https://www.ige.ch/en/legal-info/legal-areas/counterfeiting-piracy/acta.html.
177. Maira Sutton, *U.S. Trade Office Calls ACTA Back From the Dead and Canada Complies*, Electronic Frontier Foundation (March 1, 2013), https://www.eff.org/deeplinks/2013/03/us-trade-office-calls-acta-back-dead-and-canada-complies.
178. Daniel Zuccherino, *Unfair Competition and Comparative Advertising Legal Regimes*, Int'l L. Office (June 15, 2009), http://www.internationallawoffice.com/newsletters/detail.aspx?g=a291939e-fc96-4a23-a085-9c6a5bf7524f#unfair.
179. Maria Teresa Lo Greco, *Unfair Competition and IP*, WIPO (Oct. 9, 2008), http://www.wipo.int/edocs/mdocs/sme/en/wipo_kipo_kipa_ip_ge_08/wipo_kipo_kipa_ip_ge_08_www_109885.ppt#282,1,Slide 1.
180. Zuccherino, *supra* note 178.
181. Lo Greco, *supra* note 179.
182. *Id.*

A Word About Economic Espionage by Foreign Governments

It's at this point in the text that many readers will smile and say to themselves, "Seriously? There is absolutely *no way* that any foreign government is interested in my business." This is precisely why you need to read on. Industrial espionage is much more common than you think, and failing to prepare for this contingency is as dangerous as leaving any other detail to chance.

The scale of the problem is quite shocking. A Federal Bureau of Investigation study of 173 countries reports that 100 of them spent money to acquire U.S. technology and of those 100, 57 engaged in covert operations against U.S. corporations.[183] Former Central Intelligence Agency (CIA) Director and Defense Secretary Robert Gates declared that governments in Asia, Europe, the Middle East, and Latin America have been involved in intelligence activities detrimental to our economic interests.[184] A declassified CIA report from 1996 determined that governments who "extensively engaged in economic espionage" were not only expected players such as China, Russia, Iran, and Cuba, but also France and Israel.[185] Are you surprised to see our erstwhile foreign allies included on this list? Former French intelligence chief Pierre Marion pointed out, "it is an elementary blunder to think we're allies. When it comes to business, it's war."[186]

Not surprisingly, foreign intelligence agencies are most interested in high technology and defense-related industries; however, that does not mean that nontechnology-intensive industries are not also at risk.[187] Foreign agents can target industries when they provide products that serve both military and private sector applications or that are critical to maintaining economic security.[188] Among the industries that are considered most of interest to foreign governments are aerospace, biotechnology, telecommunications, computer hardware and software, transportation technology, defense and armaments technology, automobiles, energy research, semiconductors,

---

183. Hedieh Nasheri, Economic Espionage and Industrial Spying, 92 (2005).
184. *Id.*
185. *Id.*
186. *Id.*
187. *Id.* at 93.
188. *Id.*

advanced materials, basic research, and lasers.[189] And even if your business is not bristling with cutting edge technology, intelligence agents may seek seemingly mundane but proprietary business information such as pricing data, customer lists, product development data, proprietary software, sales figures, marketing plans, and strategic plans.[190] This information is not necessarily being collected by our traditional conception of "spies." The U.S. House of Representatives' Cox Report found that in the case of China, professional intelligence agents account for only a small share of data collection; the bulk of the theft is mostly by students, scientists, researchers, and other visitors to the West.[191]

It is worth pointing out that many traditional spying techniques are being used in these situations. These include one of the oldest tricks in the trade, "the honey trap." Simply put, an attractive woman or man is recruited to provide sexual favors or enter into a romantic relationship in order to extract information or blackmail the target. This technique remains popular because, well, it works very well—in both espionage and business. As the East German spymaster Markus Wolf is quoted as saying, "it opens up channels of communication more quickly than other approaches."[192] One's character, cleverness, and even patriotism are sometimes no defense.[193]

Now again, many readers will sit back and think, "This is all very interesting, but I don't live and work in a James Bond movie." True, perhaps, but as author Ira Winkler puts it, "'It won't happen to me' or 'I have nothing that anyone would want' are all too common beliefs floating around the business world without solid foundation."[194]

Surprisingly, some of the biggest victims of economic espionage are smaller businesses, and the reason follows logically: small businesses have

---

189. *Id.*
190. *Id.*
191. *Id.*
192. Phillip Knightley, *The History of the Honey Trap*, FOREIGN POLICY (March 12, 2010), http://www.foreignpolicy.com/articles/2010/03/12/the_history_of_the_honey_trap?hidecomments=yes.
193. *Id.*
194. IRA WINKLER, CORPORATE ESPIONAGE 13 (1997).

the largest number of competitors and thus face the largest number of spies.[195]

At the same time of course, a business cannot overreact to such threats. In what by now might be considered a recurrent theme of this text, a cost-benefit analysis needs to be conducted to measure your realistic risk. Winkler provides a simple risk equation:

RISK = Threat × Vulnerability/Countermeasures × Value of Information to the Company[196]

Winkler describes a small manufacturing company that develops a new process for creating a part much cheaper than foreign competitors can. Assume the threat of theft in this scenario is medium to high. An examination of procedures shows some weakness, indicating medium vulnerability. The value of the process is clearly high. Assuming no countermeasures are in place, plugging in these variables to the equation obviously suggests increasing countermeasures.[197]

It is obvious that you cannot do business today in a bubble, and you will never be totally risk-free. But many highly effective countermeasures are simple, inexpensive, and largely unobtrusive to operations.[198] Winkler provides over 60 pages of such measures in his comprehensive text *Corporate Espionage*. They range from security awareness programs and requiring identity verification before releasing sensitive information, to creating strict guidelines for marketers and salespeople and monitoring Internet activity, to bug and wiretap sweeps and use of encryption.[199]

Part of protecting IP involves protecting executives traveling abroad who often have access to the most critical secrets of the company. At its most basic, this involves your employees doing their homework on their chosen destination before they go, remaining alert, and above all using common

---

195. STEVEN FINK, STICKY FINGERS: MANAGING THE GLOBAL RISK OF ECONOMIC ESPIONAGE xv (2002).
196. WINKLER, *supra* note 194, at 13.
197. *Id.* at 15.
198. *Id.* at 16.
199. *Id.* at 276–338.

sense while on the ground.[200] A solid and simple tip is to consult the U.S. State Department website for its most recent list of security incidents that have occurred the destination country.[201] By way of example, in one Latin American nation, criminals used the technique of copying the name of a traveler from a legitimate greeter onto their own sign. They then moved closer to the front of line and intercepted the unsuspecting target, who was then kidnapped, robbed, and/or murdered.[202] In that context, the simple precaution of creating a spoken password or codeword seems less Sean Connery than it does being sensible.

Taking everything together that we have seen in this chapter, I would summarize the effective construction of any successful international business operation as requiring **PIP**: a detailed **P**lan, innovative **I**ntellectual property, and **P**eople to apply that intellectual property according to the plan. At this point, we have a plan and have set up protection for our non-tangible assets. It's time to think about how we get the right people to the right place and what law will apply to them when they are there. That is the focus of our next chapter.

---

200. F. W. RUSTMAN, JR., CIA, INC.: ESPIONAGE AND THE CRAFT OF BUSINESS INTELLIGENCE 188 (2002).
201. *Id.*
202. *Id.* at 190–91.

Chapter 9

Cross-Border Labor Law and Global Mobility Issues

If we accept the well-established proposition that intellectual property (IP) has become one of the most important assets of 21st-century companies, then we probably have to pay at least some heed to the corresponding, oft-related notion that the people who generate and apply the IP to daily business are a critical part of, if not the key to, success. Michael Milken, chairman of the Milken Institute, has declared, "any analysis of capital structure should recognize that most balance sheets are dramatically inaccurate because (with the exception of professional sports franchises) they fail to include the value of human capital."[1]

Milken illustrates just how much more true this is today than ever by pointing out that in the 1920s, 60 percent of the cost of producing the high-end technology of the time, such as automobiles, was in raw materials and energy, compared to less than 2 percent of the cost of producing computer chips today.[2] It is not very surprising then that Darren Gardner, a partner with Seyfarth Shaw, relates that employment issues have gone from being a "dirty afterthought" to assuming an upfront position in many international deals—particularly in the tech sector. "Unless you are acquiring a company for licenses or physical assets it holds," Gardner concludes, "the biggest asset of companies now is its employees."

---

1. *Human Capital*, Quotes by Mike Milken, http://www.mikemilken.com/quotes.taf (last visited May 28, 2012).
2. *Id.*

Unfortunately, executives and counsel used to dealing with human resources (HR) issues solely from a U.S. legal perspective are in for a rude awakening when they venture overseas. It is likely that wherever else you want to do business, regulations will exist that you must take into consideration before you begin, lest you inherit unexpected costs and obligations that could change a profit-making operation into a vortex of losses and legal uncertainty.

The Challenges of "International Labor Law"

Because employment disputes represent one of the primary risks facing a company operating across borders, it is critical to understand how to operate within what legal authority that has been built up.[3] For the uninitiated, let's start with a basic point of reference: almost no U.S. employment law applies in an international context.[4] Some of the few exceptions are certain federal antidiscrimination in employment laws, which apply only where U.S. citizens are employed abroad by non-U.S. entities that are nonetheless "controlled" by a U.S. company.[5]

It is also important to understand as an initial matter that no formal international labor law system is in place.[6] What does exist is really an informal regulatory system, comprised of international treaties and conventions, International Labor Organization (ILO) standards, voluntary codes of conduct, nongovernmental organizations' (NGOs) guidelines, and domestic enforcement mechanisms, among others.[7] On the ground, labor laws and regulations vary greatly between jurisdictions, often with substantial

---

3. Jennifer L. Hagerman, *Navigating the Waters of International Employment Law: Dispute Avoidance Tactics for United States-Based Multinational Corporations*, 41 VALPARAISO U. L. REV. 898 (Winter 2007), *available at* http://scholar.valpo.edu/cgi/viewcontent.cgi?article=1177&context=vulr.
4. *Id.* at 864.
5. *"Going Global": An Overview of International Employment Issues*, BAKER & MCKENZIE, 3 (2010), http://www.bakermckenzie.com/files/Uploads/Documents/Going%20Global%20-%20An%20Overview%20of%20Int'l%20Employment%20Issues%20(2010).pdf.
6. Hagerman, *supra* note 3, at 860.
7. *Id.* at 860–62.

differences in application and penalties for violation.[8] To complicate matters further, regional differences can also exist within the borders of a given nation or state.[9]

The cacophony of the often-inconsistent demands of the various stakeholders can be very confusing to U.S.-based executives who are used to the law generally speaking with "one voice."[10] Still, Gardner holds that there is no place around the globe that he would not do business solely because of labor and employment issues. A logical starting point in getting one's arms around this area of law is the ILO core labor standards.[11] As it happens, in a number of jurisdictions, ratified international treaties are applied automatically at the national level.[12]

Gardner reckons that he has personally dealt with the employment laws of over 120 different countries. While he admits that the United States has a complex enforcement system and large potential liability for employers, he points out that the relatively laissez-faire, at-will environment prevalent in the United States simply doesn't exist anywhere else. What is more, most foreign jurisdictions will not honor a "choice of law" provision in an employment contract where the employer's desired terms and conditions differ significantly from local employment laws and regulations.[13] An employer in China must generally conclude a written employment contract with its full-time employees no later than 13 months after hire, or the employer must pay double wages to the employee for every month that it has failed to sign a contract.[14] Further, current Chinese employment law makes short-term (e.g., yearly) employment contracts less advantageous

---

8. Stephen J. Hirschfeld & Ginger D. Schroeder, *Global Employment Law Compliance*, N.Y. L.J. (Sept. 14, 2009), http://www.chklawyers.com/images/ps_attachment/attachment46.pdf.
9. *Id.*
10. Hagerman, *supra* note 3, at 899, http://scholar.valpo.edu/cgi/viewcontent.cgi?article=1177&context=vulr.
11. *Id.* at 900.
12. *How International Labour Standards Are Used*, INT'L LABOUR ORG. (2012), http://ilo.org/global/standards/introduction-to-international-labour-standards/international-labour-standards-use/lang--en/index.htm.
13. Hirschfeld & Schroeder, *supra* note 8.
14. *The 2011 Global Employer: Highlights of Littler's Fourth Annual Global Employer Institute*, LITTLER MENDELSON, P.C., 50 (Feb. 2012), http://www.littler.com/files/press/pdf/TheLittlerReportThe2011GlobalEmployerHighlightsofLittlersFourthAnnualGlobalEmployerInstitute.pdf.

than previously; fully 80 percent of employment contracts executed there since 2008 are for a three-year period.[15] Moreover, new amendments to the Chinese Employment Contract Law that went into effect as of July 1, 2013, and Interim Provisions effective March 1, 2014, will significantly limit the use of "dispatched" or temporary workers after July 1, 2015.[16]

Throughout Europe, Asia, and South America, most employees not only have an employment contract, but they may also enjoy varying degrees of statutory notice and termination benefits, including generous severance where no serious wrongdoing is involved.[17] In Germany, for example, in connection with companies of more than five employees, after six months' probation, an employer might find itself having to give a one to seven-month-long notice on termination of an indefinite employment contract, effective at of the end of the calendar month.[18] Special termination protection against unlawful dismissal applies to a German employee who is an officially acknowledged handicapped person, an employee on three years' maternity leave, or a pregnant employee; prior approval of various German authorities is required (but is usually very difficult to obtain).[19] Chinese law prohibits termination without cause outright, even during probation.[20] In Japan too, the employer is typically exposed to one or more years of negotiated severance pay and benefits.[21]

In fact, in the vast majority of foreign jurisdictions, "good cause" is required to terminate the relationship.[22] French courts, for example, can intervene if specific time periods for consultation and agreement on a social plan are not met in the layoff context.[23]

---

15. *Id.*
16. Philip Cheng, Daniel Fogarty & Sherry Y. Gong, *Developments in China's Labor Dispatch Regulations*, HOGAN LOVELLS (March 31, 2014), http://www.lexology.com/library/detail.aspx?g=1c88186c-1e17-4dd6-b9df-de3bd35598a9.
17. Barbara Roth, *Labor: When Laws and Cultures Collide*, INSIDE COUNSEL (May 16, 2011), http://www.insidecounsel.com/2011/05/16/labor-when-laws-and-cultures-collide.
18. Wilmer Hale, *Features of German Labor and Employment Law* (October 8, 2003), http://www.wilmerhale.com/pages/publicationsandnewsdetail.aspx?NewsPubId=90463.
19. *Id.*
20. Isabelle I. H. Wan & Peter A. Susser, *10 Tips for Employers with Operations in China*, GLOBAL EMPLOYMENT LAW (Dec. 16, 2010), http://www.globalemploymentlaw.com/2010/12/articles/cross-border/the-continuing-growth-of-the/.
21. *"Going Global": An Overview of International Employment Issues*, *supra* note 5, at 9.
22. *Id.* at 8–9.
23. *Id.* at 9.

Chinese law further provides that in cases of wrongful termination, the affected employee may choose as a remedy either reinstatement or two times the applicable severance pay.[24] Even in cases where termination is for incompetence, Chinese law requires the employer first provide either additional job training or a new position, and then to demonstrate that the employee is still unable to perform satisfactorily.[25] Only then is termination allowed, by providing a 30-day written notice or by paying the employee one month's salary in lieu of notice.[26]

The very hiring process itself is affected by different rules than U.S. employers have come to expect. Rules regulating interviewing procedures, selection criteria, reference checks, and pre-employment testing and exams can vary by location as well.[27]

Civil law jurisdictions are heavily codified, Gardner observes, and therefore more complicated. Many Latin American systems have significant bureaucracies with which to contend. France and Germany exhibit idiosyncrasies in compliance, coupled with a high level of regulation. In Gardner's view, Indonesia and Korea incorporate protectionism into their systems. You need governmental approval in connection with many labor-related decisions in China.

Labor Law and M&A Scenarios

Cross-border merger and acquisition (M&A) transactions give rise to a host of employment-related issues that can impact transaction structure and overall costs and liabilities.[28] The fundamental difference in how employment is viewed by foreign courts and cultures requires careful consideration of ongoing human capital management as well as exit strategy, recognizing that there may substantial costs in discharging employees there that

---

24. Wan & Susser, *supra* note 19.
25. *Id.*
26. *Id.*
27. Hirschfeld & Schroeder, *supra* note 8.
28. Erika C. Collins & Michelle A. Gyves, *Employment Issues in Crossborder M&A Transactions*, *in* EMP. L. REV. 1 (3d ed. 2012), http://www.paulhastings.com/assets/publications/2163.pdf.

do not exist at home.[29] Gardner advises a review of business transfer rules and cautions that enough time needs to be built in to get the right process in place. If not properly managed, these issues can delay or even prevent a deal from progressing.[30]

The core labor-related question that arises in most cross-border deals is: "What happens, after closing, to the seller's employees?"[31] While a buyer of a U.S.-based business has relative freedom to make only those employment offers to employees of the target that it chooses, such practices may not be practicable in many foreign jurisdictions and may even be unlawful.[32] Impulsive hiring decisions or staffing beyond the company's needs may result in not only significant statutory obligations to the employee but also notification to and negotiations with work councils or other collective bargaining representatives.[33] It is important to realize that some foreign jurisdictions purposely make plant closures so painful that employers must carefully consider every conceivable alternative to collective termination.[34]

Before determining the structure of an international merger or acquisition, the buyer needs to decide to what extent it will continue to employ acquired workforces into ongoing operations.[35] That decision can be based on many things, but should primarily rest on understanding and reconciling differences in corporate cultures.[36] This is because while there are generally significant incentives to streamline and seek economies of scale, these at best only potentially increase value to shareholders.[37] The synergy that results from the full buy-in of both parties' employees is how innovation

---

29. *"Going Global": An Overview of International Employment Issues*, supra note 5, at 13.
30. *Id.*
31. Donald C. Dowling, Jr., *Employment Law Toolkit for Cross-Border M&A Deals*, White & Case, 1 (May 2010), http://www.whitecase.com/files/Uploads/Documents/article_CrossBorder_byline_v2.pdf.
32. *"Going Global": An Overview of International Employment Issues*, supra note 5, at 11.
33. *Id.* at 13.
34. *Id.*
35. Dowling, *supra* note 30, at 8–9.
36. *Conducting Successful Transactions*, Deloitte, 57 (2008), http://www.deloitte.com/assets/Dcom-SouthAfrica/Local%20Assets/Documents/ZA_MAbrochurecomplete_180508.pdf.
37. Nils Bohlin, Eliot Daley & Sue Thomson, *Successful Post-Merger Integration: Realizing the Synergies*, IMAA Institute, 1–2, http://www.imaa-institute.org/docs/m&a/adlittle_02_Successful%20Post-Merger%20Integration%20-%20Realising%20the%20Synergies.pdf (last visited Oct. 25, 2012).

thrives and the knowledge capital of key employees is maintained.[38] These "people issues" do not simply "take care of themselves" however; the key is a theme addressed repeatedly in this text: careful planning by appropriate staff utilizing scenario building that can be appropriately classified as "cultural due diligence."[39]

So what does this entail? It should start with selection of a merger executive committee that is responsible for establishing the initial strategy and performance metrics for the new operation, monitoring implementation of planned activities, and handling any transaction-related issues as they arise.[40] This committee, as with the others we have discussed in this book, will be required to plan not only in the short and medium term, but in the long term as well in order to be successful.[41] The committee's diligence involves a thorough review of core business cultural elements, including everything from critical human resource policies and procedures to activities that employees view as important for maintaining morale and institutional cohesion.[42] Playing out various reorganization and strategic scenarios can help management understand the effects planned changes will have on the workforce.[43] A key focus of this process should be seeking out ways in which employees' existing attitudes and beliefs can be acknowledged and also utilized as a bridge to new, "out-of-the-box" skills that allow for growth of the individual and new organization.[44]

During post-merger integration, one way to work through potential conflicts between the parties is to utilize what are referred to as "clean teams," or objective third parties, who can also be utilized in situations where open sharing of information between the parties is not possible.[45] As the new organization is being laid out, Deloitte advises that you remain flexible: "Design organizations with pencil, not pen."[46] Other key objectives in the process that Deloitte identifies include articulating why change is necessary,

---

38. *Id.*
39. *Id.* at 2.
40. *Id.* at 4.
41. *Conducting Successful Transactions*, *supra* note 35, at 57.
42. Bohlin, Daley & Thomson, *supra* note 36, at 3–4.
43. *Id.* at 2.
44. *Id.* at 5.
45. *Conducting Successful Transactions*, *supra* note 35, at 56.
46. *Id.* at 57.

creating optimism about the future, retaining key employees, designing in cooperation with labor unions and work councils, minimizing disruption to existing operations, capturing institutional knowledge, and carrying all this out in a spirit best described as "kind but confident."[47]

Assuming it can be done in a cost-effective manner within the confines of local law, some existing employees may be let go. Companies may elect in certain situations to enter into a post-termination separation agreement with a former employee to release that employee's claims against the employer.[48] In such situations, the U.S. entity should ensure that the agreement provides for a release of claims against not only the parent but all subsidiaries and affiliates as well.[49]

Besides requiring the payment of minimum severance pay, which is either negotiated or prescribed by local law, statutes may also set out the selection criteria employers should apply when deciding which employees to terminate due to economic or organizational reasons.[50] In some countries the law restricts disclosures about terminated staff. For example, in Botswana, the required certificate of termination "shall contain nothing unfavorable to the employee," while in Malawi, the employer may only include the reason for firing or an evaluation if the worker expressly requests it.[51]

Where the seller has employees in more than one country, the law's treatment of subject employees may be different across the various jurisdictions involved.[52] Brock Smith, a partner at the Vancouver-based firm Clark Wilson LLP, reminds practitioners that you have to be careful of transactions involving employees in different jurisdictions within a given country as well. He cites a Canadian example: say 99 percent of a company's employees are based in Vancouver. However, they have one person in Toronto and another in Calgary. These last two cannot be treated the same as the rest, as different provincial-based rules may apply to them. This is why it is so

---

47. *Id.* at 58.
48. *"Going Global": An Overview of International Employment Issues, supra* note 5, at 11.
49. *Id.*
50. *The 2011 Global Employer: Highlights of Littler's Fourth Annual Global Employer Institute, supra* note 14, at 47.
51. *Id.* at 48.
52. Dowling, *supra* note 30, at 1.

important to identify all locations where the employees are, and factor in location-specific rules that may apply, Smith notes.

Darren Gardner, of Seyfarth Shaw, notes that employees are often deemed part of the goodwill acquired in a transaction. Deals sometimes contemplate the seller laying off some or all employees before closing, although in the European Union (EU) such a move is treated largely the same as any other reduction in force.[53] Any pre-closing lay-off must comply with each affected jurisdiction's applicable notice, termination, and severance laws, including local labor laws that require information, consultation, and bargaining with employee representatives.[54]

This is particularly true in Europe by virtue of the provisions of the EC Acquired Rights Directive 2001/23/EC, which apply where an entire business or part of it is acquired or sold, but may also effect outsourcing or "insourcing" transactions and reorganizations that transfer employees to a different corporate entity.[55] Protections afforded to employees by the Directive include the following: the purchaser must take on the seller's employees; the purchaser and seller are both required to inform and consult employee representatives; and the prohibition of dismissals effected to avoid the Directive, except for economic, technical, or organizational reasons.[56]

As an aside, most non-U.S. jurisdictions will not permit an employer to make detrimental modifications unilaterally, and employees who are subject to such detrimental modifications may be able either to claim constructive dismissal or to bring claims for unpaid wages or benefits.[57] While in most jurisdictions, employees can consent to the modification of their terms and conditions, Brazil, for instance, adheres to a nonwaiver principle of labor rights, meaning that an employer cannot, under *any* circumstances, modify employment terms to an employee's detriment, regardless of consent.[58]

---

53. *Id.*
54. *Id.*
55. *"Going Global": An Overview of International Employment Issues, supra* note 5, at 11–12.
56. *Business Transfers Across Europe*, HOGAN LOVELLS, 3 (May 1, 2010), http://emp-navigator.hoganlovells.com/download/Business_Transfer_across_Europe.pdf.
57. Collins & Gyves, *supra* note 27, at 5.
58. *Id.* at 6.

Under the EC Directive, the purchaser is deemed liable for pre-transfer acts of the seller relating to the transferred employees.[59] Failure to consult as required under the Directive can result in sanctions up to and including injunctive proceedings to stop the transfer.[60] In the United Kingdom under their version of the Directive—the Transfer of Undertakings (Protection of Employment) Regulations 2006, or "TUPE"—there is a penalty of up to 13 weeks' pay per employee.[61] There is no ability to contract out of the terms of the Directive.[62]

Individual EU states do have some discretion in applying certain issues under the Directive, including the consequences of employees' refusal to be transferred and sanctions imposed for failure to inform and consult and for dismissing on transfer.[63] Because different jurisdictions took their own approaches to implementing the Directive, conflicting answers to the same question have been generated.[64] Knowing the differences from state to state can be critical. For instance, in Germany, employees have the power to refuse the transfer.[65] Moreover, issues raised by the Directive may have application outside of the EU. At least one U.K. decision suggests a transaction between U.K. and Israeli entities might be subject to the Directive.[66] Additionally, legislation with similar provisions to the Directive exists in many countries outside Europe,[67] such as Brazil, Colombia, India, Singapore, and South Korea.[68]

Where such laws exist, a fact-specific inquiry to determine whether the proposed transaction amounts to a "business transfer" is undertaken.[69] In general, a business transfer is found where "an independent business unit

---

59. *"Going Global": An Overview of International Employment Issues*, *supra* note 5, at 12.
60. *Id.*
61. David Ludlow, *The Risks Created by Employment Law on Mergers, Acquisitions and Other Business Transfers*, Barlow Robbins, http://www.barlowrobbins.com/site/library/legalnews/the_risks_created_by_employment_law_on_mergers_and_acquisitions (last visited Sept. 1, 2012).
62. *Business Transfers Across Europe*, *supra* note 55, at 3.
63. *Id.*
64. *Id.*
65. Dowling, *supra* note 30, at 4.
66. *Transfer of Undertakings Guide*, Ius Laboris, 15 (Dec. 2009), http://www.iuslaboris.com/files/documents/Public%20Files/Publications/2008_Publications/transfers-of-undertaking.pdf.
67. *"Going Global": An Overview of International Employment Issues*, *supra* note 5, at 11.
68. Collins & Gyves, *supra* note 27, at 3.
69. *Id.*

is transferred and the activities of such unit continue with the buyer."[70] In some countries, employees transfer automatically, while in others—such as Australia, China, Japan, and Hong Kong—they must consent to a transfer.[71] Even in a nation such as India that does not have a statute that explicitly answers what happens when employees transfer from one company to another, the employees' consent is deemed a prerequisite to transfer their employment.[72] Where consent is mandated, the transacting parties must consider what retention bonuses or other sweeteners should be offered to induce key employees to consent and what to do with those who refuse.[73]

In analyzing these transfers outside the United States, typically a distinction is drawn between share purchase and asset purchase transactions.[74] In a stock sale or a merger scenario, the buyer generally steps into the shoes of the seller and assumes the seller's liabilities as a matter of law unless specifically agreed otherwise, while in an asset sale, a buyer contracts to purchase certain enumerated assets and does not typically assume liabilities unless they are expressly set out in the purchase agreement.[75] Care should be taken when applying this general rule to specific situations, however. In Venezuela, for instance, absent statutory publications, an asset purchase in the form of a bulk sale renders the purchaser jointly and severally liable for seller liabilities, unless otherwise limited to those expressly assumed in the asset acquisition agreement.[76] By contrast, in a stock acquisition there, in principle there is no change to the company's liabilities and responsibilities, and the new shareholder's responsibility is limited by the amount of capital held in the target company.[77] And if instead the transfer is accomplished by

---

70. *Id.*
71. *Id.*
72. *Outsourcing in Europe: What Employers Need to Know*, EMPLOYMENT LAW ALLIANCE at 19-21 (April 10, 2010), http://www.employmentlawalliance.com/Templates/media/files/Power%20Point%20Documents/April20-Outsourcing.pdf.
73. Collins & Gyves, *supra* note 27, at 3–4.
74. Dowling, *supra* note 30, at 3.
75. Gavin Johnson, *Purchase and Sale of a Business: Structuring the Transaction*, The iVLG Blog (August 30, 2013), https://www.invigorlaw.com/purchase-and-sale-of-a-business-structuring-the-transaction/.
76. *Acquiring Businesses in Venezuela*, BAKER & MCKENZIE, 6 (2010), http://www.bakermckenzie.com/files/Uploads/Documents/LATAX%202010/09_General%20Publications/ab_06_venezuela.pdf.
77. *Id.*

a merger, the merging and surviving entities are deemed jointly and severally liable for payment of all employment-related obligations incurred prior to the substitution of employers, for a one-year period.[78]

Outside of U.S. borders, many times upon closing a stock transfer the buyer is subject to "indefinite employment" rules or their equivalent.[79] Under this doctrine, fired employees are afforded some cause of action for a dismissal without notice, good cause, or following mandated procedures.[80] The upshot is that stock buyers outside the United States cannot lay off employees after closing unless they comply with legal restrictions; pay legally imposed costs; and heed local notice, termination, and severance laws.[81] Smith observes that perhaps 90 percent of the employment disputes he sees in Canada center around whether the correct notice period was observed or whether termination was for cause. Still, there is more: under the related restrictions to constructive discharge, a stock buyer, after closing, faces obstacles restructuring; transferring workers to new locations; realigning job titles; and discontinuing bonuses, benefits, and equity plans absent employee consent.[82]

Indonesian law can also be instructive here. A definite term of employment can be transformed into an indefinite term in several ways by statute in Indonesia, including that the original agreement was not made in the Indonesian language or that the original agreement's provisions in the requirements of type of work to be done are not fulfilled.[83]

As noted above, however tempted a buyer might be to attempt sidestepping these issues by simply casting the transaction as an asset purchase rather than a stock acquisition, hold on. Many jurisdictions mandate that however a deal is structured, the buyer steps into the seller's shoes as employer and assumes a legal obligation to perpetuate existing employment terms absent employee consent.[84] In other nations, sometimes referred to as de facto

---

78. *Id.*
79. Dowling, *supra* note 30, at 3.
80. *Id.*
81. *Id.*
82. *Id.*
83. *An Indefinite Employment Agreement*, Leks & Co. (Aug. 16, 2012), http://www.indonesialaborlaw.com/an-indefinite-employment-agreement/#more-36.
84. Dowling, *supra* note 30, at 3.

firing jurisdictions, the law imposes a presumption that a seller's employees continue on as before until they have been lawfully terminated and paid out notice and severance pay.[85] That is even, in many cases, where the asset buyer agrees to hire them at closing; smart asset sellers who plan to institute a layoff factor the severance expenses into sales prices. Alternatively, the parties can offer each employee a choice between either a full severance package or a comparable job with the buyer—but not both—in some instances via "employer substitutions" or other mechanisms.[86] Of course, as Smith points out, how major a factor severance becomes is a function of the extent to which it is a $40,000 problem and not a $4 million one.

There are a host of other considerations involved in choosing which entity structure should be adopted, ranging from the buyer's overall business strategy to local legal requirements.[87] A more specific listing of factors includes the following:

- Expected size of the business in overseas location, turnover and number of employees and/or contractors
- The type of activity
- Initial share capital requirements
- The number of shareholders
- The presence of partners
- The responsibilities of the management
- The revenue model
- The tax regime, including planning, accounting, compliance, and risk management concerns:
  - Do you know which activities (or thresholds) constitute taxable presence?
  - If there is a Permanent Establishment, how much profit should be allocated to it?
  - Are there any discriminatory taxes on particular industries or types of investment?

---

85. *Id.*
86. *Id.* at 4.
87. *Entity Structuring Checklist*, HIGH STREET PARTNERS (May 24, 2012), http://www.hsp.com/knowledge/country-updates/2012/5/entity-structuring-checklist.

- Are there unusual withholding taxes on fund transfers or sale of goods?
- Can the U.S. parent "check-the-box" for U.S. tax entity classification purposes?
  - Human Resources/Employee considerations, including items such as the following:
    - Hiring locally? Expatriate employees?
    - Structure of compensation and required and expected benefits?
    - Payroll Options?
  - Available tax credits and history of unexpected withdrawal of those exemptions.[88]

The resources of the acquirer, the financial health and viability of the target company, and the relative simplicity of acquiring specified assets or stock may also factor into the decision.[89]

Another issue that can affect choice of entity is a scenario in which, in the asset sale context, only certain target business units are purchased, resulting in transferred employees being directly employed by the acquiring, foreign-based owner.[90] Some jurisdictions, such as Spain and Italy, require an onerous registration process with local taxation and social security authorities; in such locales, where permissible, setting up a subsidiary or branch may be prudent.[91] This may be time consuming in its own right, however: in India, for example, it can take six to eight weeks to set up a company or a branch/liaison office.[92] As this can interfere with closing, the buyer may consider engaging third-party service providers or using a transition services agreement with the seller; however, some countries prohibit employee leasing.[93] Further, where employment of individuals requires registration or a formal business presence, failure to comply can lead to criminal fines

---

88. *Id.*
89. *Asia Pacific Guide to Mergers & Acquisition*, BAKER & MCKENZIE, 294 (2013), http://www.bakermckenzie.com/files/Uploads/Documents/MA_Guide_.pdf.
90. Collins & Gyves, *supra* note 27, at 6.
91. *Id.*
92. *Doing Business in India*, AMARCHAND & MANGALDAS & SURESH A. SHROFF & CO., 5 (Sept. 2009), www.lexmundi.com/Document.asp?DocID=4684.
93. Collins & Gyves, *supra* note 27, at 6.

and penalties for the unregistered employment, and failure to pay taxes and social charge contributions as well.[94]

In sum, the choice of method of business acquisition will have an important impact on personnel issues, tax planning, the buyer's responsibility to former creditors, and other potential risk factors.[95] Again, understanding the peculiarities of the law in the location or locations that you are in is key in thinking about how to structure the transaction. In Lithuania, for example, a share transfer is impossible in transactions involving partnerships, individual enterprises, and farms.[96] Further, the Lithuanian Labor Code provides that in the transfer of a business or a part of it, employment contracts remain with the seller, which is the opposite outcome from EU Directive 2001/23/EC.[97]

Due Diligence in the Labor Context

As Darren Gardner relates, at this point it is important to do the necessary diligence before signing on the dotted line. Doing your diligence in this respect serves the same purposes as documented in other parts of this book, i.e., developing a thorough knowledge base about the seller's operations, uncovering issues that could prevent a successful conclusion to the deal, confirming that representations and warranties made are accurate, demonstrating that the purchaser has discharged its fiduciary duties,[98] and, of course, improved identification and measurement of net assets obtained in a transaction and better understanding of risks of ownership.[99]

---

94. *Id.* at 7.
95. Giedrius Kolesnikovas, *Lithuania: Share Purchase versus Asset Purchase in Lithuania*, IFLR (April 1, 2012), http://www.iflr.com/Article/3001474/Lithuania-Share-purchase-versus-asset-purchase-in-Lithuania.html.
96. *Id.*
97. *Id.*
98. *Labor and Employment Issues Triggered by Mergers and Acquisitions in the U.S.*, EMPLOYMENT LAW ALLIANCE (Oct. 19, 2010), http://www.employmentlawalliance.com/Templates/media/files/Power%20Point%20Documents/Oct19powerpoint.pdf.
99. Daniel D. Wangerin, *M&A Due Diligence and its Consequences for Post-Acquisition Financial Statements* (November 23, 2010) 1, http://www3.nd.edu/~carecob/Workshops/10-11%20Recruiting/Wangerin%20Road%20Paper%20Draft%2011-23-10.pdf.

While there are some important differences, by and large, cross-border due diligence inquiries are often similar to those done on a domestic deal.[100] Buyer's counsel must determine whether the transaction features any aspects that are beyond the client's risk tolerance.[101] That said, U.S. attorneys and executives tend to expect a significantly higher level of disclosure than is traditionally found in other jurisdictions, which can create a conflict in expectations in terms of both how much time and attention is devoted to diligence generally and the resulting product.[102] While differences in business culture need to be understood and respected, it is fairly said that the importance of due diligence has only increased as investors' confidence in sellers' documentation decreases.[103] Thus, cross-border transactions often require the use of reliable local counsel and other supporting professionals.[104]

A letter of intent typically furnishes a buyer with the right to conduct wide-ranging due diligence.[105] Buyers will usually seek to maximize the diligence period, which allows them the greatest opportunity to raise issues and negotiate more favorable terms or a lower purchase price; sellers typically seek to negotiate the diligence period down.[106] Sellers can expedite diligence through common-sense steps such as disclosing risks up front, providing financials audited by a reputable firm, ensuring that managers who might be the subject of isolation interviews have a common understanding of strategic direction and key facts surrounding operations, and developing a list of customers willing to act as references.[107]

---

100. *Outsourcing Technology Booklet, Appendix C: Foreign-Based Third-Party Service Providers*, FEDERAL FINANCIAL INSTITUTIONS EXAMINATION COUNCIL, http://ithandbook.ffiec.gov/it-booklets/outsourcing-technology-services/appendix-c-foreign-based-third-party-service-providers.aspx (last visited Nov. 14, 2012).
101. Peter Samuels, Yuval Tal & Ryan Searfoorce, *Chapter 24: Dispute Resolution Issues in Drafting Agreements in the International Context*, PROSKAUER ON INT'L LIT. AND ARB.: MANAGING, RESOLVING, AND AVOIDING CROSS-BORDER BUSINESS OR REGULATORY DISPUTES, http://www.proskauerguide.com/law_topics/24/III (last visited Sept. 29, 2012).
102. *Id.*
103. Peter Mindenhall, *Property Investment Due Diligence*, IPIN GLOBAL (Jan. 27, 2011), http://www.ipinglobal.com/ipin-live/article/358417/property-investment-due-diligence.
104. Samuels, Tal & Searfoorce, *supra* note 100.
105. Eric King, *The Purchase Agreement—A Primer for Business Owners*, AXIAL (March 21, 2011), http://www.businessinsider.com/the-purchase-agreement-a-primer-for-business-owners-2011-3.
106. John Warrillow, *How to Get What Your Business Is Worth*, INC. (Nov. 30, 2010), http://www.inc.com/guides/2010/11/how-to-get-what-your-business-is-worth.html.
107. *Id.*

As has been discussed elsewhere, what is required in terms of diligence will vary by industry, jurisdiction, and other specifics of the deal involved. A good starting point for general employment diligence topics includes the following:

1. a census of all employees worldwide (anonymized where necessary), including part-time and contract employees, preferably including date of hire, complete compensation, and job category;
2. all agreements and information concerning employee benefits, prerequisites, and retirement plans. Information regarding the value of plans and how plans are funded is critical because in many countries a plan is considered legally funded with mere book reserves as opposed to cash. Unfunded or underfunded pension liabilities discovered during due diligence can be an employment-related deal killer because of the potentially high costs involved;
3. information regarding change-in-control, golden parachute and other M&A-related clauses in any employment contract or other agreement;
4. any agreements (such as from a target's prior business acquisitions) that affect or limit employment flexibility (e.g., agreements limiting reductions in force);
5. text of all employment agreements, whether individual, collective, or with works councils, including contracts designated "noncompete," "confidentiality," "indemnification," or "expatriate" agreements;
6. pay information, including data on salary administration (to, among other things, establish that withholdings are proper and that the target complies with any legally mandated payroll requirements such as payroll frequency, form of payment, etc.) and incentive/bonus plans;
7. information on stock options or employee ownership programmes (the transfer or replication of which can be particularly complicated);
8. information regarding any pending employment-related lawsuits, disciplinary proceedings, potential claims, government investigations and unpaid judgments;
9. information on any layoffs or other reductions in force conducted in the past several years; and

10. any social plans or severance plans from previous reductions in force.[108]

Representations and warranties may assist in the diligence process by giving both parties a basic understanding of the transaction.[109] Seller's representations may also function as a substitute for further due diligence where the information to be verified is unavailable or cannot be confirmed in a cost-effective manner.[110]

Once the basic diligence materials have been compiled, the principal task of the employment task force is to construct a system for identifying potential labor compliance issues and developing a plan to ensure said issues are appropriately handled going forward.[111] This is done by means of an employment law audit, which is a thorough review of all personnel policies, procedures, and practices from recruiting through employment to post-termination, overseen by legal counsel.[112] Yes, using counsel, particularly experienced employment counsel, will cost more, but doing so confers multiple benefits. First, involving counsel may help protect audit results from disclosure during a lawsuit or governmental proceeding.[113] Second, the in-house human resource team may not maintain the same level of objectivity when determining whether policies and practices comply with all applicable law, and audit findings may be more carefully considered by senior management when delivered by outside experts.[114] Additionally, the possibility that an in-house audit may not be privileged and may lead to disclosure of sensitive information must also be considered.[115] That being

---

108. Collins & Gyves, *supra* note 27, at 2–3.
109. David J. Roettgers, *Representations and Warranties in Business Transactions*, Weiss, Berzowski, Brady LLP (August 14, 2013), http://www.wbb-law.com/multimedia/blog/representations-and-warranties-business-sale-transactions.
110. Tai Chu Wei and Benjamin Kong, *Business Strategy in Cross Border Transactions: The Need for Due Diligence,* LEGAL500.COM, http://www.legal500.com/assets/images/stories/firmdevs/raja_article_by_tcwben.pdf.
111. Hirschfeld & Schroeder, *supra* note 8.
112. *Id.*
113. *Id.*
114. *Id.*
115. Tyler M. Paetkau & Jennifer Garber, *Conducting Self-Audits Without Creating a Roadmap*, ABA Section of Business Law, 1, http://apps.americanbar.org/buslaw/newsletter/0047/materials/pp4.pdf (last visited Nov. 14, 2012).

said, involvement of HR is also important to spot and address company-specific issues that might otherwise be missed.[116]

The employment task force (likely a combination of HR executives, local management, and outside counsel) develops a questionnaire that identifies critical HR policies and practices to be reviewed, typically focusing on four key issues:

> (a) Pre-employment Actions: determining local recruitment practices, application forms utilized, interviewing procedures, selection process and criteria, offers made, and any reference checks or pre-employment testing, screening and examinations conducted; (b) Employment Relationship: reviewing standard employment contracts utilized including noncompete and trade secrets agreements, probationary periods used, evaluation procedures, codes of conduct and other personnel policies utilized, wage and hour practices, mandatory training, your company's complaint and investigation procedure, process used and reasons for terminations and dismissals; (c) Post-employment Conduct: required notice for terminations, layoffs and redundancies, mandatory benefits provided post-termination, providing post-employment references, mandatory severance benefits and record retention requirements; (d) Past and Pending Litigation: careful review of current and past legal disputes involving employees is critical in determining whether there are lessons to be learned from this litigation.[117]

The internal audit results will help the task force drill down into which policies and practices need to be scrutinized and thus determine how to set priorities.[118] Avoiding employee complaints and governmental audits are natural top priorities.[119] Without a doubt, even the most thorough due diligence process won't catch every acquisition risk and liability.[120] Still, a

---

116. Everingham & Kerr, Inc., *Snake in the Grass: Employee-Related Liabilities Can Poison Your Deal*, MERGER & ACQUISITION FOCUS, 4 (Feb./March 2009), http://www.everkerr.com/files/Feb_March%20Newsletter.pdf.
117. Hirschfeld & Schroeder, *supra* note 8.
118. *Id.*
119. *Id.*
120. Everingham & Kerr, Inc., *supra* note 115, at 4.

focused and thorough diligence effort that addresses foreseeable issues will maximize your chances to conclude a transaction successfully and profitably.

Understanding the Target and the Local Environment—General Considerations

From an employment diligence perspective, potential buyers need to identify all the locations of the target's businesses that will be involved in the transaction.[121] This requires not only a general understanding of the location of the seller's various corporate entities throughout the world, but also that of any related "service company" and a list of part-time and "seconded" employees.[122] If only part of the target operation is targeted, develop a list of only those employees that will transfer, including any that work for both acquired and nonacquired entities.[123] Additionally, for both diligence and compliance purposes, it is important at this stage to identify independent contractors, consultants' agents, and sales personnel that work with the target.[124]

Questions that Gardner, of Seyfarth, recommends you ask include: what do you need to do to change anything in the new location's workforce? Should you proceed unilaterally or attempt to reach agreement in order to change terms of employment? Does the subject location mandate expensive social security or accrued leave, termination or retirement benefits? Is this too much liability to make the deal profitable? Gardner also advises that provisions specific to the structure of a company and its obligations, including warranties and indemnities, are a function of what the transaction is and what role the client is playing in it. If you have 300 contractors in a location, you as a buyer probably don't want to purchase shares, Gardner reasons. Instead, the buyer will look to pick up assets and transition people—and leave liability with the seller.

---

121. Garvey Schubert Barer, *Taking Sherlock Shopping- International Due Diligence Garvey Schubert Barer* (2001), http://www.gsblaw.com/news/publication/taking_sherlock_shopping_-_international_due_diligence.
122. Dowling, *supra* note 30, at 6.
123. *Id.*
124. *Id.*

Gardner points out that it is in the course of structuring and pulling together the deal that you have the best opportunity you'll ever have to manage your work force issues strategically. Otherwise, he concludes, you are "forever fighting rear-guard actions."

Brent Caslin, of Jenner & Block, has seen just how critical a role cultural issues in employment can play in practical terms. In one instance, he was working on a potential international merger between a U.S. and a Japanese company. They planned to combine operations. The deal fell through halfway through the process however, when it was determined that under Japanese law, the new entity would not be able to lay off a large number of Japanese workers. Understanding that, the U.S. company would not go through with the deal. Interestingly, however, when the Japanese found out that layoffs had been part of the plan, they were not interested in moving forward either. As Caslin relates, "they didn't want to lay people off."

For many in-house lawyers, labor issues are indeed one of the more important considerations in any acquisition. They know that when you go into a brand new country, you want to do some diligence on not just the laws but the labor climate as well, asking questions such as "What will people do and exploit? How will the courts enforce labor agreements?"

Failing to do the appropriate diligence may mean buying a business but then not being allowed to do what you had planned to do with it. One in-house employment lawyer described diligence in the labor sphere as "living with and making the best of (labor regulations) by understanding what it is going to cost you to pull out." One should consider having the labor team be involved in diligence right away, and each step of the way, including in the implementation, integration, and augmentation phases. Specifically, savvy in-house attorneys seek to incorporate the potential cost of shutting down and moving operations into their model, unless that proves to be prohibitively expensive.

Participative management with work councils and unions can be another option. Does the applicable work council have a history of working rationally? Part of the diligence process is factoring in the need to work with unions and work councils that don't always see eye to eye, as many in-house counsel have observed. If you don't know what you are getting into with the personalities involved, it may be necessary (where possible) to get pre-approval from them. Of course the problem with that approach is that the seller may not want the buyer to know about discussions before the deal is closed. In that event, one in-house labor counsel cautions, "you may be walking a fine line." How to get a feel for it is to investigate what cooperation they have shown others.

Western Europe (particularly Germany, the Netherlands, and France) often has the reputation of being the region where the biggest labor issues are. That said, in-house counsel have occasionally observed that labor issues may in some instances be more predictable in Europe than elsewhere, since the nations there function within a statutory framework. Of course, having access to internal labor and employment attorneys in different regions, when available, gives decision makers additional insight into whether the outside advice they are receiving on a particular locale is good.

Arvind Vij, Managing Director, Associate General Counsel, and Head of Legal at JPMorgan Chase Bank, India, has a slightly different take on these issues. He agrees that to operate in a new jurisdiction, it is important to look into labor issues such as whether the jurisdiction is "labor or employer friendly," whether the courts are corruptible, the length of time it takes to have cases heard and disposed by the court, and the overall sophistication of labor laws. But when asked whether those laws should ever be a deciding factor in determining where operations are located, he responds,

> technically, these laws should be an important factor in the determination but in practicality, they are looked into as part of the due diligence at a much later stage . . . so if there is an overriding business decision to start operations in a new jurisdiction, unless the labor laws and landscape are so difficult, we as lawyers need to learn to adapt and manage the exposure. Net net, labor laws do not become a determining factor in reality.

Locations that Vij cites as having more "business friendly labor policies" include more developed economies in Asia such as Hong Kong and Singapore. Vij typically sees the development of such policies as a function of the sophistication of these economies and their advancement; as an effort on the part of these jurisdictions' governments to attract foreign corporations by paying attention to these issues. By contrast, Vij suggests that countries such as India and the Philippines, though in the process of opening up their economies, are still more influenced by their ruling political parties' needs to appeal to the "common man," such that their labor policies are still relatively "employee/labor friendly."

Overall, Vij concludes that companies who want to operate in "labor-friendly" economies need to manage the attendant risk with suitable policies, procedures, and benefits. This includes procedures for dealing with employee investigations, terminations, and general personnel decisions "that are sensitive to the local legal environment." Additionally, Vij states that his firm ensures that HR staff are trained on the "dos and don'ts of dealing with employees," educated on what the employees' rights are vis-à-vis the employer, and instructed on when they should escalate issues to the legal department. What Vij describes as "very local matters," such as dealing with "show cause" actions from labor inspectors, nuisance actions, and labor cases litigated in court all serve as triggers to hire external counsel and labor law consultants. Indeed, Vij's concern over local issues is well-founded. Due diligence in employment is complicated because employment issues can fairly be said to be inherently local.[125]

Issues Affecting the Deal

Purchase Agreement Drafting and Employment Issues

Choice of law will affect the purchase agreement in a fundamental way.[126] The common law tradition, emphasizing the importance of representations and warranties, will require a much longer agreement than one written to the dictates of a civil law system that reads in a duty to negotiate in good faith.[127]

Even where a buyer does not intend to employ any of the seller's workforce, a purchase agreement's representations, warranties, covenants, and schedules should address employment issues across the seller's worldwide

---
125. Id.
126. King, *supra* note 104.
127. Id.

operations, since employment liabilities often transfer at closing.[128] Three of the key issues involved in the negotiation of the agreement include which parties make representations on the part of the seller, the materiality of data requested in support of various schedules to the representations and warranties, and how "materiality" and "knowledge" are defined in the agreement.[129]

While the parties to an M&A transaction usually agree that pre-closing employee-related liabilities remain with the seller and post-closing liabilities rest with the buyer, as we have seen, local laws in many jurisdictions can hold both parties liable for employment claims that accrue in the months before, or after, a deal.[130] The actions of the parties post-agreement but pre-closing can also cause potential liabilities for one another. Post-agreement pay raises that raise the buyer's post-closing employment costs or the buyer's failure to match employment terms or conditions that trigger implied terminations by the seller can be anticipated through the use of indemnification or set-aside funds to cover post-closing claims.[131] Disputes in negotiating indemnifications often arise in the context of the breadth of actions covered, who provides the indemnification and for how long, damage caps, and relationship to escrow.[132]

An interesting, pro-buyer development in apportioning responsibility for a target company's liabilities in an M&A transaction is known as a "materiality scrape."[133] Inserted into a purchasing agreement, this provision causes a representation and warranty that states "the target company is not party to any *material* litigation" to be read, in determining whether a breach of that representation and warranty has occurred for indemnification purposes, as if it said "the target company is not party to *any* litigation."[134] Such a term may be either a "double" materiality scrape that applies to both whether a breach has occurred *and* the amount of indemnified losses resulting from

---

128. Dowling, *supra* note 30, at 9.
129. King, *supra* note 104.
130. Dowling, *supra* note 30, at 9.
131. *Id.*
132. King, *supra* note 104.
133. Daniel Avery & Daniel H. Weintraub, *Trends in M&A Provisions: The "Materiality Scrape"*, Bloomberg Law Reports (2011), http://www.goulstonstorrs.com/portalresource/lookup/wosid/contentpilot-core-6-16806/media.name=/avery%20_weintraub_Bloomberg%20Law%20reports.pdf.
134. *Id.*

the breach or a "single" scrape that deals with only losses resulting from a breach.[135] Occasionally a "knowledge scrape," which eliminates knowledge qualifiers, may also be used.[136] A buyer might seek a materiality scrape to avoid a scenario where a series of otherwise "immaterial" breaches amounts to significant losses in the aggregate; a seller would likely argue that the term would greatly increase (unnecessarily) its disclosure burden and would allow the buyer to harass the seller with minor claims.[137] As with all other parts of the agreement, compromises reflecting the facts of the individual transaction and particular interests of the parties can be crafted.

Assumedly, the diligence process will have gone beyond merely identifying pending employee claims and delved into the target entity's past labor-related litigation and disputes, with an eye toward discovering compliance issues in discrimination, harassment, and safety violations, among others.[138] While buyers will generally seek representations regarding labor compliance, potential claims, and other issues, a useful supplement that can be considered is the purchase of representation and warranty insurance.[139] Typically providing coverage for a three-to-seven-year term, the noncancelable policy is triggered when a breach of a representation or warranty is discovered and also addresses contingent liabilities.[140] Another benefit of purchasing this coverage is the protection of relationships with key employees, in that with the policy in place, the buyer will not act as a potential adversary in future claims against them.[141]

Permanent Establishment

Tax officials in given jurisdictions use the concept of permanent establishment to assert jurisdiction over any entity deemed to be "doing business"

---

135. *Id.*
136. *Id.*
137. *Id.*
138. Everingham & Kerr, Inc., *supra* note 115, at 5.
139. Everingham & Kerr, Inc., *M&A Insurance Can Shield Your Deal From Risk*, MERGER & ACQUISITION FOCUS, 5 (Feb./March 2009), http://www.everkerr.com/files/Feb_March%20Newsletter.pdf.
140. *Id.*
141. *Id.*

within their sphere of authority.[142] When purchasing or merging with an entity already acknowledged to have a formal presence in a given country, the tax, filing, reporting, licensing, registration, and related fee requirements can be adequately planned around.[143] What is harmful to profits in an international operations context is permanent establishment coming about through unexpected and unplanned means.

For example, perhaps a target operation has undisclosed expatriates in its employ in another jurisdiction. If they are found to be "doing business" in that foreign state, where the seller is neither properly licensed nor paying applicable fees and taxes, it could cause unplanned-for costs and legal issues.[144] A branch, office, factory, workshop, or other place of management could all potentially trigger obligations.[145] And we are talking *significant* obligations, in the worst case, a multinational concern might find itself paying higher taxes on a worldwide basis.[146]

The importance of doing an employee census, as discussed above, is put in stark relief when one considers that a single individual can create a permanent establishment issue, even in the absence of a true physical location.[147] Just some of the scenarios that can engender governmental interest include the following:

- High level assignees retaining global responsibilities,
- Assignees or agents concluding contracts on behalf of their home country employer,
- Projects or contracts that continue or last for more than six months,
- Inter-company assignments without the proper secondment documentation,
- High numbers of short term assignees or business travelers into one location,

---

142. Chris Hall, *Permanent Establishment and the International Assignee*, INT'L HR FORUM (Feb. 3, 2012), http://www.internationalhrforum.com/2012/02/03/permanent-establishment-and-the-international-assignee/#more-3587.
143. Id.
144. Dowling, *supra* note 30, at 6–7.
145. Hall, *supra* note 141.
146. "Going Global": An Overview of International Employment Issues, *supra* note 5, at 3.
147. Hall, *supra* note 141.

- Cross border remote workers ("e-commuters"), and
- Initial start up assignees or agents (i.e. Advance sales forces).[148]

Maintaining technical support services outside the United States or other revenue-producing operational activities outside the United States can also serve as triggers.[149] In a foreign country, individual agencies and applicable tax treaties may have differing definitions as to a given activity or scenario.[150] As a result, consultation with an expert on the location or locations at issue is critical.[151]

In order to avoid the permanent establishment problem, many companies will set up a foreign-based subsidiary or a U.S.-based holding company to hire and manage overseas employees and generate employment-related documents, but to the extent the parent retains a "right of control" over the foreign personnel, they may still unwillingly be found a joint employer.[152]

Labor Organization Issues

As mentioned above, outside of the United States and particularly within Europe, business transfers trigger various legal provisions that confer notification and consultation duties upon employers.[153] These duties do not entail direct consultation with individual employees but rather with their "appropriate representatives."[154] While the form of the representative body may vary by location or industry, one of the simplest is the works council, which is appointed by employee election.[155] In Germany, for instance, a company with more than five workers may form a works council that must be

---

148. *Id.*
149. *"Going Global": An Overview of International Employment Issues, supra* note 5, at 3.
150. Hall, *supra* note 141.
151. *Id.*
152. *"Going Global": An Overview of International Employment Issues, supra* note 5, at 2–3.
153. *Employment Law for People Managers*, CHARTERED INSTITUTE OF PERSONNEL AND DEVELOPMENT, UPDATE 12, sec. 11.2, at 3 (May 2007), http://www.cipd.co.uk/NR/rdonlyres/570EE068-6A58-4FB7-856F-CB0BAA854DE4/0/ELfPM_samplechapter.pdf.
154. *Id.* sec. 11.3.1, at 4.
155. Oliver Dörfler & Maximilian Gröning, *Investment in Germany*, IFLR (Sept. 1, 2012), http://www.iflr.com/IssueArticle/3084656/Supplements/Investment-in-Germany.html?supplementListId=86566.

involved in decisions such as the termination of employees.[156] Members of the works council and employees who prepare their elections are afforded additional protection against termination.[157]

Other than works councils, unions in Germany are rarely involved in a company's day-to-day issues. However, collective bargaining agreements between a trade union and an individual employer or between a trade union and an employers' association can contain comprehensive provisions governing the conditions of employment.[158] Collective bargaining agreements are legally binding upon the parties of the employment contract when both parties are members of the parties that negotiated the collective agreement and the collective bargaining agreement is declared "generally binding" by the authorities or it refers to the collective agreement.[159]

Depending on the jurisdiction involved, there may be a variety of entities to which notice and consultation may apply. These include health and safety committees, staff consultation committees, and ombudsmen.[160]

Notice and consultation protections have been legislatively in place in some EU member nations since the 1970s.[161] Americans might mistakenly think these protections were created as "stand-alone" requirements; in fact they are meant as parts of a complex system of collective relations whose aim is to influence the most crucial management decisions.[162] In this mind set, alliances with unions and workers are particularly valued by companies seen as vulnerable during periods of profound restructuring, and this commonly translates to workers and their representatives who become increasingly associated with decision-making at the enterprise level.[163]

---

156. *European Employment Law Checkpoint*, WRAGGE & CO, 2012, http://www.wragge.com/eelc_3504.asp.
157. Norma Studt, Matthias Rubner, & Gretchen Lennon, *Works Councils and Union Strike Action in Germany, France, and the U.K.*, THE WORKING WORLD (November 2011), www.lw.com/thoughtLeadership/working-world-november-2011.
158. Id.
159. *European Employment Law Checkpoint*, supra note 155.
160. Dowling, *supra* note 30, at 7.
161. Gianni Arrigo & Giuseppe Casale, *A Comparative Overview of Terms and Notions on Employee Participation*, INT'L LABOUR ORG.—GENEVA, 7 (Feb. 2010), http://www.ilo.org/wcmsp5/groups/public/---ed_dialogue/---lab_admin/documents/publication/wcms_123713.pdf.
162. Id.
163. Id.

The scope of the duty to consult varies by jurisdiction, but it can extend to transactions that not only directly impact employee conditions, such as layoffs or changes in employment terms and conditions, but even those that may *ultimately* affect them, such as large capital outlays.[164] By virtue of common pre-closing restructuring that takes place prior to stock transfers, consultation may be required in that context as well as in asset transfers.[165] Notice and consultation rights can apply to not only the target company's employees but also those of the purchaser, and duties can potentially apply to both buyer and seller.[166]

Consultation regarding an M&A deal must generally take place before a purchase agreement is finalized, but this creates a dilemma, notes Brock Smith, of Clark Wilson. The parties, he notes, have several reasons to keep negotiations confidential. Despite the difficulties, the penalties for failing to comply with these duties may be catastrophic. In Holland, for instance, the affected work councils can apply for injunctive relief to halt the deal until obligations are fulfilled.[167] Outside Europe, collective bargaining agreements commonly insert notice and/or consultation clauses where transfer of ownership or employees takes place.[168]

While it may be necessary, disrupting confidentiality can create its own headaches. Smith relates an example of a chief executive officer and a chief financial officer in the process of selling a company to its biggest competitor. Some salespeople in that company had previously left the buyer's employment because they hated working there. The buyer sought to have the seller include a provision that the seller certified its top people would transfer to the buyer after sale. In fact, on closing, the buyer may want assurance that those employees will sign a contract. The seller is in a tough spot after disclosure is made. What the seller can do, Smith explains, is to seek dilution of the purchase agreement's terms to state that the seller need only make reasonable efforts that X percent of employees will transfer.

---

164. Collins & Gyves, *supra* note 27, at 4.
165. Id.
166. *Employment Law for People Managers, supra* note 152, sec. 11.2, at 3.
167. Collins & Gyves, *supra* note 27, at 5.
168. Id.

In many jurisdictions, consultation results in a "social plan," which seeks to ease any financial consequences for the employees, especially through use of severance payments.[169] Governmental notification and approval may add still further time and money to the process, and if a mass layoff is contemplated, still more requirements may be triggered.[170]

When it comes to health and safety matters, consultation does not end with workers' representatives having some amorphous right to know and be heard. Rather, representatives should

> (a) be given adequate information on safety and health matters, enabled to examine factors affecting safety and health matters, and encouraged to propose measures on the subject. They should also: (b) be consulted when major new safety and health measures are envisaged and before they are carried out and seek to obtain the support of the workers for such measures and (c) in planning alterations to work processes, work content or organizations of work, which may have safety or health implications for the workers.[171]

While this may not rise to the level of joint decision making, both International Labour Organization (ILO) and European Council legislative texts suggest workers' representatives in this context are not merely informed by management but can also comment and expect justification from management in the event of differing opinions.[172] To underscore this point, the information-consultation procedures are designed to "achieve an agreement." such as those which must be performed in the case of collective layoffs.[173]

---

169. Jonathan Maude, *A Highlight on How to Carry Out a Reorganisation and Redundancies in the U.K., the U.S., France and Germany*, EMPLOYMENT & INDUSTRIAL RELATIONS LAW, 23 (Sept. 2009), http://www.hoganlovells.com/files/Publication/892e2919-0d1a-4248-9c92-cd04a5c7a174/Presentation/PublicationAttachment/0184b85d-1604-45df-8e8c-50771aab5c6f/Employment_and_Indus_Relations_Law_Sept_2009.pdf.
170. Collins & Gyves, *supra* note 27, at 5.
171. Arrigo & Casale, *supra* note 160, at 16–17.
172. *Id.* at 17–18.
173. *Id.* at 18.

Labor Compliance Issues

Dealing with Conflicts Between U.S. and Local and Foreign Law

A general, overarching consideration when striving to maintain a coherent, consistent labor compliance program across borders is the fact that the strictures of U.S. law and those of foreign jurisdictions will sometimes operate at cross purposes. A crucial point in developing your compliance program is to avoid the all-too-common mistake of assuming that you can simply take an offer letter, employee handbook, or policy vetted for the U.S. market and simply "cut and paste" it for use with your foreign operations.[174] The uninitiated may mistakenly believe, particularly in the case of developing countries, that U.S. law must necessarily grant stronger employee protections than the target locale;[175] as we have already seen, this is not necessarily borne out in reality. In addition, differences in local laws might, for instance, cause an employee handbook that is compliant with the authorities in Shanghai to run afoul of requirements in Beijing.[176]

Expatriates working in a foreign location raise another set of issues. First, as noted above, several U.S. discrimination statues, including Title VII of the Civil Rights Act, the Age Discrimination in Employment Act (ADEA), and Americans with Disabilities Act (ADA) can apply to U.S. citizens working abroad for U.S.-controlled operations.[177] A four-pronged test is used to determine whether the U.S. parent maintains sufficient control over the foreign subsidiary in order for the statutes to apply:

> (1) interrelation of operations; (2) common management; (3) centralized control of labor relations; and (4) common ownership or financial control. When these four factors are present, the U.S. citizen, even though employed by the non-U.S. subsidiary, will carry with him or her extraterritorial application of Title VII, the ADEA and ADA.[178]

---

174. *"Going Global": An Overview of International Employment Issues, supra* note 5, at 4.
175. Wan & Susser, *supra* note 19.
176. *Id.*
177. *Id.*
178. *"Going Global": An Overview of International Employment Issues, supra* note 5, at 3.

Employers can assert a defense to the extent the U.S. statutes directly conflict with foreign law, though more indirect tension, such as Title VII's mandate regarding prompt remedial measures versus many foreign statutes featuring good cause requirements for discipline or termination requires cross-border employers to take great care in running afoul of one or both systems.[179] Outside of these discrimination statutes, U.S. citizens working for either a U.S. parent or U.S.-controlled foreign subsidiary may be able to assert the protection of local law as well.[180]

Be advised as well that seeking an employee waiver of foreign labor rights may not always be availing. In China, absent prior approval for a special working-hours system, employment contracts will be wholly or partially invalid where the employer seeks to limit its legal liabilities or curtails an employee's rights.[181] Recently the Brazilian Superior Labour Court held that an employee cannot waive individual labor rights deemed absolute such as minimum wages or health and safety standards.[182]

Employee Monitoring and Data Privacy

It is fair to say that foreign jurisdictions, particularly European ones, also have a completely different set of priorities than the United States when it comes to data privacy, monitoring, and surveillance in the workplace.[183] The guiding U.S. federal statute on workplace surveillance, the Electronic Communications Privacy Act, places few restrictions where employee consent is obtained or where activities are carried out in the ordinary course of business; in fact, it actually gives employers a perverse incentive to monitor to cut off potential claims that later, sudden introduction of such actions affected a previous expectation of privacy.[184] It could be argued that this simply reflects a proto-typical American suspicion of State activity, whereas in much of Europe there is an expectation that a system of binding legal

---

179. *Id.*
180. *Id.*
181. Wan & Susser, *supra* note 19.
182. *The 2011 Global Employer: Highlights of Littler's Fourth Annual Global Employer Institute*, *supra* note 14, at 59.
183. Shelley Wallach, *The Medusa Stare: Surveillance and Monitoring of Employees and the Right to Privacy*, 1 INT'L J. OF COMPARATIVE LABOUR LAW & INDUST. RELATIONS 190 (2011), *available at* http://ilera2012.wharton.upenn.edu/RefereedPapers/WallachShelley.pdf.
184. *Id.* at 191.

arrangements will be imposed to safeguard fundamental rights.[185] It has been observed that European law deals far more extensively with privacy claims between individuals and business entities, and that regulatory systems there contemplate much more comprehensive rights in that area than in the United States.[186] To that end, the EU has already enacted a directive binding all 27 member states on "the protection of individuals with regard to the processing of personal data and on the free movement of such data."[187] The European approach limits data disclosure to particular purposes with explicit consent required and prohibits further data transmission without further permission. [188]

To the extent that U.S.-based employers would seek to monitor EU-based employees' Internet use and e-mails, or utilize video cameras or location data in the workplace, they should be aware that Directive 95/46/EC is read to prohibit those activities there.[189] In a 2011 decision, the French *Cour de Cassation* specifically held

> employees have the right, even during working hours and in the workplace, to respect for the privacy of their private lives. This entails the secrecy of correspondence in particular: the employer therefore cannot, without violating this fundamental freedom, examine the contents of personal messages sent and received by employees using computer equipment made available to them for their work, even in cases where an employer has forbidden non-business use of the computer.[190]

Suffice to say that general, unspecified notice to employees about potential surveillance is legally insufficient in EU member states; notice on all

---

185. *Id.* at 192.
186. Allen E. Shoenberger, *Privacy Wars: EU Versus U.S.: Scattered Skirmishes, Storm Clouds Ahead*, 17 IND. INT'L & COMP. L. REV. 358, 393 (2007), *available at* http://lawecommons.luc.edu/facpubs/29/.
187. *How Proposed EU-Wide Data Protection Regulation Will Affect U.S. Based Businesses*, COOLEY LLP (Jan 12, 2012), http://www.cooley.com/showalert.aspx?Show=66023.
188. Shoenberger, *supra* note 185, at 393.
189. Wallach, *supra* note 182, at 200.
190. *Id.*, citing www.out-law.com, 2052.

monitoring aspects must be given to applicable works councils and union representatives, and consent must be explicit.[191]

Likewise, it is unlikely that a U.S. company can simply use its standard job application forms or advertisements, since seemingly innocuous inquiries such as whether someone can drive a car, let alone whether they have a criminal record, can run afoul of data privacy and antidiscrimination statutes in many locations.[192] Pre-employment physicals and drug and alcohol screenings also raise cultural and legal issues.[193] Transfer of employee information in connection with benefits outside the boundaries of the EU can also violate a host of data privacy statutes absent very specific written consent or compliance with safe harbor safeguards.[194]

Efforts are underway to assist U.S. companies with compliance in this area. On July 26, 2012, acting U.S. Secretary of Commerce Rebecca Blank announced that the Joint Oversight Panel of the Asia-Pacific Economic Cooperation (APEC) had approved the United States' request to participate in its Cross-Border Privacy Rules System.[195] Once a U.S. accountability agent has been approved, U.S. companies will be able to submit their cross-border privacy rules to be recognized as meeting the APEC standard[196] and engage in data sharing with Member Economies in APEC, without additional data privacy protection hurdles.[197]

In the meantime, the same Europeans who have been on the leading edge of protection in this area are looking at revisions to the laws they have had in place since 1995, both to achieve consistency across EU member states and to account for the many changes that have occurred over the past two

---

191. *Id.* at 208.
192. *"Going Global": An Overview of International Employment Issues*, *supra* note 5, at 6.
193. *Id.*
194. *Id.*
195. Hunton & Williams LLP, *United States Approved for Participation in APEC Cross-Border Privacy Rules System*, Privacy and Information Security Law Blog (July 27, 2012), http://www.huntonprivacyblog.com/2012/07/articles/united-states-approved-for-participation-in-apec-cross-border-privacy-rules-system/.
196. *Id.*
197. White & Case LLP, *United States Joins the APEC Cross Border Privacy Rules System*, JD Supra (Sept. 13, 2012), http://www.jdsupra.com/legalnews/united-states-joins-the-apec-cross-borde-50366/.

decades, including social networking and cloud computing.[198] Proposed changes include giving individuals more control over personal data, including the right to delete it if no valid reason to keep it exists; ensuring EU rules will be enforced wherever in the world the data is transferred; imposition of substantial fines for noncompliance; requiring companies and public organizations to appoint data protection officers; and mandating notification of data breaches within 24 hours.[199] For all types of marketing, the opt-in system contemplated by this new regime is in direct opposition to the current U.S. system, which generally allows a user to opt-out.[200]

The cross-border enterprise is well advised to start to adapt to these anticipated changes now. A corollary to the IP inventory and risk analysis discussed in Chapter 8 is a personal data assessment that surveys current security around both employee and customer data.[201] For those who are starting from scratch in doing such a data assessment, the ISO 27002 standards are recommended as a good initial resource.[202] Regardless of the size of the enterprise, a data protection officer should be appointed who will have accountability for updating the policy to maintain compliance with applicable statutes, investigating and reporting on data breaches, setting protocols for dealing with breaches, and setting appropriate controls on employee information.[203]

A specific policy for employees, including contractors and temporary staff, needs to be formulated and implemented as well to spell out their rights and obligations in this area.[204] This must include what notice is to be furnished concerning what personal information the employer holds in terms of salary, pension details, and occupational health records; employees' rights to access their own personal data; and the conditions that must be met before

---

198. Ricky M. Magalhaes, *Compliance, Data Protection and Keeping Safe Online in 2012*, WINDOWSECURITY.COM (Feb. 29, 2012), http://www.windowsecurity.com/articles/Compliance-data-protection-keeping-safe-online-2012.html?printversion.
199. *Id.*
200. *How Proposed EU-Wide Data Protection Regulation Will Affect U.S. Based Businesses*, *supra* note 186.
201. Magalhaes, *supra* note 197.
202. *Id.*
203. *Id.*
204. *Data Protection*, PERSONNEL TODAY (June 22, 2006), http://www.personneltoday.com/Articles/22/06/2006/36007/Data-protection.htm.

such data can be processed.[205] The employer should seek explicit consent to processing employee information by a clear and sufficiently detailed clause in all employment contracts, rather than by a passive statement of policy.[206] The policy must also explicitly set forth employees' responsibilities when handling customers, clients, or colleagues' personal information, identify those positions that will require more detailed guidelines, and incorporate regular training schedules.[207] Knowing or reckless disclosure of personal information must be appropriately penalized; the publicly posted privacy policy of Dallas-based Dava Oncology advises, "should it be found that confidential information was knowingly or recklessly disclosed with disregard of the Company policies by a Company employee, said employee may be held criminally liable and will be subject to Company disciplinary action."[208]

Brock Smith, of Clark Wilson, maintains that data privacy is an issue you can manage by having the right language in your employee contracts. Suppose you have a client multinational with an HR department in Country A and employees in Countries A, B, C, D, and E. The contract will need to contain a provision that the employee understands that human resources is in Country A and that he or she expressly consents to share personal information.

A further data privacy problem arises when you have to "backfill," as Smith puts it. In a share deal you typically inherit existing employment agreements. If all target employees are in Country A, their existing contracts never needed to contemplate a data sharing consent clause. Except the buyer is headquartered in Country B. Perhaps current employees can sign new contracts, but what about former employees? Will you be able to track them all down? Can you keep all HR information on them in Country B? Is that practical?

Smith notes still further complexity can develop if payroll or HR is outsourced to another country or to the cloud. In that event, you must make sure the vendor has appropriate safeguards in their contracts with you. So, he concludes, first nail down employees, then nail down vendors.

---

205. *Id.*
206. *Id.*
207. *Id.*
208. *Privacy Policy*, Dava Oncology LP (2012), http://www.davaonc.com/privacy-policy.

HR Policies

When evaluating an existing foreign enterprise's overall HR framework, it is critical to look beyond written policies, handbooks, and work rules and take into account what if any unwritten guidelines are in place.[209] Likewise, in examining whether the local company is in compliance with its home jurisdiction's minimum terms of employment, the HR professional should not neglect a review of any special terms or benefits extended beyond those that are legally mandated.[210]

In terms of attempting to adapt U.S.-based HR policies to foreign jurisdictions, not only is it obvious that there are too many differences to expect complete standardization across borders, but also overseas locales will often present issues that are without precedent in the United States and within that location itself.[211] Creative solutions developed with the in-house HR team, outside counsel, local attorneys, and local employees may be needed. Being open to locally based, outside-the-box solutions, provided they do not violate your client's overarching legal or ethical responsibilities, is more than political correctness: it's just smart.[212]

Performance management is a particularly significant part of any HR program and an important area to consider in the cross-border context.[213] Educating yourself on the legal implications of actions you intend to take when you determine an employee is not performing to standard is the necessary first step.[214] Combining that knowledge with an understanding of how cultural differences affect the ability of local employees to engage in frank exchanges with senior management is no less important.[215] It is only by ensuring an employee can clearly understand your expectations that a performance management system is truly objective.[216]

---

209. Dowling, *supra* note 30, at 7.
210. *Id.*
211. Warren Heaps, *Seven Characteristics of Highly Effective International HR Professionals*, Int'l HR Forum (Aug. 12, 2012), http://www.internationalhrforum.com/2012/08/12/seven-characteristics-of-highly-effective-international-hr-professionals/.
212. *Id.*
213. *Id.*
214. Carol Tissiman, *Managing Poor Work Performance*, GetSmarter (May 2010), http://www.getsmarter.co.za/blog-labour-law/244-managing-poor-work-performance.
215. Heaps, *supra* note 210.
216. Tissiman, *supra* note 213.

The absence of detailed "corresponding punishment" provisions in Chinese labor law for misconduct for example has significantly undermined an employer's position in labor disputes there.[217] To prevail under such a regime, an employer must not only be able to prove the misconduct, but also demonstrate that the employee both knew that the conduct was prohibited and was aware of the consequences.[218]

Employee handbooks also represent yet another trap for the unwary, as many countries outside the United States treat employee handbooks as binding contracts, regardless of any disclaimer language the employer interposes.[219] Nor in some locations can employers impose conditions via handbook by fiat; to be admissible evidence in a Chinese labor disputes, for example, the handbook must be formulated through the "democratic procedures" set forth under the ECL and proactively published to the covered work force.[220]

Payroll and Benefits Compliance

Yet another point about which U.S.-based HR departments must be mindful is that most non-U.S. jurisdictions have statutorily mandated holidays and vacation requirements; France requires more than one month's paid vacation plus national holidays. Brazil requires payment of a "thirteenth" or "fourteenth month salary."[221] Common U.S. practices such as vacation caps, "cashing out" accrued but untaken vacation, and "personal leave" may be banned overseas by statutes or rules imposed via works councils or collective bargaining.[222] Additionally, most EU countries have significantly greater parental leave requirements that insulate employees from potential discrimination before, during, and after such a furlough.[223]

China in particular has seen a massive increases in employee labor disputes, with almost 35 percent of a reported 1.28 million filings cited in a 2011 Littler Global employment report based on compensation-related

---

217. Wan & Susser, *supra* note 19.
218. *Id.*
219. Hirschfeld & Schroeder, *supra* note 8.
220. *Id.*
221. *"Going Global": An Overview of International Employment Issues*, *supra* note 5, at 6.
222. *Id.*
223. *Id.*

compliance issues.[224] Once an employee has provided testimony of having worked overtime, it is the employer who has the burden of proving otherwise.[225] Considering that 85 percent of claims are resolved in the employee's favor, failing to develop overtime management or a simple time punch system can easily lead to an assessment of significant costs against a foreign employer.[226]

In an M&A context, the buyer must make the necessary filings and acquire taxpayer identification numbers to make payroll in each applicable jurisdiction and put new benefit plans in place to the extent that the seller's plan does not automatically transfer.[227] Further, plans must be made to add the target employees into the buyer's HR information system and, as noted above, ensure data is appropriately transferred and safeguarded.[228]

Employment Agreements

Even in nations outside the European continent, written employment contracts are often used, whether or not strictly mandated. For instance, in South Africa, most employers use written contracts even though statutory employment rights attach regardless.[229] South African law, in the form of the Basic Conditions of Employment Act, mandates basic conditions of employment; while contracts can provide more generous terms, even collective bargaining agreements cannot set lower requirements as to certain conditions.[230] Written notice to employees of key terms is a basic requirement at commencement of the employment relationship, but South African law can recognize oral contracts in absence of a written one, and even conduct can in principle form the basis for a contractual right.[231] The South African

---

224. *The 2011 Global Employer: Highlights of Littler's Fourth Annual Global Employer Institute, supra* note 14, at 52.
225. *Id.*
226. *Id.*
227. *"Going Global": An Overview of International Employment Issues, supra* note 5, at 6.
228. *Id.*
229. Susan Stelzner, Stuart Harrison, Brian Patterson & Zahida Ebrahim, *Legal Compliance in South Africa*, INT'L LABOUR AND EMP. COMPLIANCE HANDBOOK, 3 (Nov. 2010), http://www.ens.co.za/images/news/South-Africa.pdf.
230. *Id.* at 2.
231. *Id.* at 3.

example underscores yet again the importance of understanding the nuances of a jurisdiction's labor laws in order to avoid unwelcome surprise outcomes.

Two more areas of concern in relation to employment contracts involve choice of law and the language in which the contract is written. While U.S. lawyers understandably seek to impose the law of their home jurisdiction on the employment relationship and have the contract finalized in English rather than Mandarin or Arabic, for example, they can violate local law. Employment relationships in Mainland China must be governed by People's Republic of China law, and only the Chinese version of the contract is legally binding.[232] The French, too, are particular about the language utilized in an employment contract. In one decision in France, the court awarded a full bonus and refused to consider whether a terminated employee had met his sales targets because the incentive plan was written in English rather than French, notwithstanding that the employee had understood the document as drafted.[233]

Still another problem can result from the American tendency to assume that the employer in an overseas locale has control over where employees will be located. In point of fact, most non-U.S. jurisdictions require that the specific location where the employee is to provide services be set out in the employment contract, and to the extent that the employer seeks to transfer the employee either across town or to another country, the move may be construed as an invalid unilateral change.[234] Assuming no written consent had been obtained, such an action can give rise to a "constructive termination" claim, potentially resulting in liability and an award of severance benefits.[235] Merely reserving the employer's rights to transfer the employee in the contract may not avoid the constructive termination finding in some jurisdictions.[236] Employers should identify which employees might be affected by the contemplated changes and determine if there is

---

232. Wan & Susser, *supra* note 19.
233. *The 2011 Global Employer: Highlights of Littler's Fourth Annual Global Employer Institute*, *supra* note 14, at 58.
234. *"Going Global": An Overview of International Employment Issues*, *supra* note 5, at 9.
235. *Id.*
236. *Id.*

significant "push back" from any of them; if so, employers should consult local counsel to gauge the risk of a constructive dismissal in that context.[237]

Noncompete agreements can be enforceable in many jurisdictions around the world; however, in many jurisdictions they are often conditioned on the subject employee or agent receiving "adequate compensation."[238] This may translate to 50 percent of the employee's total compensation package for the term of the noncompete.[239] Foreign courts, just like their U.S. counterparts, may narrow the scope of a noncompete it finds too broad (as in the Netherlands, for example), or refuse to apply the agreement at all (as has occurred in Canada and the United Kingdom).[240]

Finally, companies are advised to delete references to stock options or stock grants in offer letters or employment agreements, to avoid not only negative tax, corporate, and securities ramifications but also the use of these stocks in calculation of severance.[241] A side letter from the U.S. parent is sometimes used in support of this strategy, although in Spain, the value of such options is used in calculating severance regardless.[242]

Dispute Avoidance

Even the casual reader understands that labor disputes are not uncommon overseas. What may be at least somewhat surprising to those not closely following events on the ground in China is that even workers there have been showing an increasing willingness to engage in collective labor stoppages since at least 2010.[243] It has been suggested that Chinese workers have begun to strike proactively not only to further economic demands and improve

---

237. Robert K. Smithson, *Managing The Risk of Constructive Dismissal*, BCJOBS.CA (May 21, 2009), http://www.bcjobs.ca/hr-advice/managing-the-risk-of-constructive-dismissal/.
238. Donald C. Dowling, *Global HR Hot Topic—June 2012: Non-Competes and Other Restrictive Covenants in a Foreign Jurisdiction* (June 2012) White & Case LLP, http://www.whitecase.com/hrhottopic-0612/
239. *"Going Global": An Overview of International Employment Issues*, supra note 5, at 9.
240. *Id.*
241. *Id.* at 7.
242. *Id.*
243. Manfred Elfstrom & Sarosh Kuruvill, *The Changing Nature of Labor Unrest in China* (July 2012), http://ilera2012.wharton.upenn.edu/NonRefereedPapers/Kuruvilla,%20Sarosh%20and%20Elfstrom,%20Manfred.pdf.

working conditions, but also in a desire for more respect from their employers.[244] The workers' actions have not been without effect: after stoppages of up to two weeks, striking workers in Guangdong successfully negotiated themselves wage increases of better than 30 percent.[245] The Freshfields law firm anticipates that the All-China Federation of Trade Unions will continue to push for increased collective bargaining in 2014 and that, in particular, Fortune 500 companies may be targeted particularly in relation to wage increases with their employees.[246] And, indeed, the ACFTU has reportedly been leading at least one protest involving the closure of a Wal-Mart store in the city of Changde in Hunan province.[247] In April 2014, Chinese show manufacturer Yue Yuen (supplier to Nike and Adidas) saw some 30,000 workers strike at its factory in Dongguan province over inadequate contributions to social insurance and housing payments. Direct losses from the strike were calculated at $27 million, with increased benefits to add another $31 million in 2014 alone.[248] Meanwhile, in India, 4,200 union members at Toyota's Bangalore factories went on strike in March 2014 seeking a better deal on wages, holidays, and housing.[249]

Whether in China or elsewhere, there are a number of common-sense steps to prepare for and potentially prevent labor disputes. These include management familiarizing itself with current local employment law, including any provisions on collective bargaining; establishing clear lines of communication with employees and/or union representatives; and, particularly with respect to wage and overtime claims, seriously consider adopting time clock

---

244. *Id.* at 2–3.
245. *Id.*
246. *The Asia Employment Landscape in 2014,* Freshfields Bruckhouse Deringer (January 22, 2014), http://www.freshfields.com/en/knowledge/The_Asia_employment_landscape_in_2014/?LanguageId=2057#china:developmentsincollectivebargaining.
247. Tom Mitchell & Barney Jopson, *Official China Union Raises Stakes in Walmart Closure Programme,* FINANCIAL TIMES (March 23, 2014), http://www.ft.com/cms/s/0/2038fd78-b262-11e3-b891-00144feabdc0.html#axzz2wuP5IlpA.
248. Liyan Qi, *Yue Yuen Strike Is Estimated to Cost $60 Million,* WALL ST. J (April 28, 2014), http://online.wsj.com/news/articles/SB10001424052702304163604579528504234144092?KEYWORDS=shoe+factory+strike&mg=reno64-wsj.
249. Santanu Choudhury & Dhanya Ann Thoppil, *Toyota Sputters in India,* WALL ST. J (March 28, 2014) at B4.

procedures for any employees eligible for overtime to verify exactly when an employee is working.[250]

To the extent a company seeks to terminate an individual employment contract, notification of applicable union or work council organization is likely required. Turning again to the Chinese example, the governing national employment law gives trade unions there the authority to demand remedies to any violation of law or an employment contract.[251] The Supreme People's Court per its Interpretation 4, effective February 1, 2013, indicates that an employee may seek damages for unlawful dismissal if an employer has not provided advance notice to the relevant labor unions.[252]

A grievance procedure can often forestall labor litigation. The backbone of such a procedure generally includes the following:

(a) An attempt should be made initially to settle the grievance directly between the worker or group of workers and their immediate supervisor;
(b) Where an attempt at settlement has failed at the initial level, the worker should have the right to have the case considered at a higher level, depending on the nature of the grievance and structure of the enterprise;
(c) Grievance procedures should be so formulated and applied that there is a real possibility at each step for the dispute to be settled;
(d) Grievance procedures should be rapid and simple;
(e) Workers concerned in a grievance should have the right to take part directly in the grievance procedure. During the procedure, workers may be assisted or represented by a trade union representative or any other person of their choosing, in conformity with national law and practice;
(f) Employers should have the same right to be assisted or represented by an employers' organization or by any other person of their choosing;

---

250. Elfstrom & Kuruvill *supra* note 242.
251. Wan & Susser, *supra* note 19.
252. Kevin L. Jones, *Three Major Changes to China's Labor Landscape* (Dec. 3, 2013), http://www.faegrebd.com/webfiles/3%20Major%20Changes%20To%20Chinas%20Labor%20Landscape.pdf.

(g) No co-worker who assists or represents an aggrieved worker during the examination of his or her grievance should suffer any prejudice on that account;
(h) Workers concerned in a grievance, as well as their representatives if they are co-workers in the same enterprise, should be allowed sufficient time off to participate in the grievance procedure, without loss of remuneration;
(i) If the parties consider it necessary, minutes of the proceedings should be drawn up by mutual agreement. Copies of the minutes should be made available to both parties to the dispute;
(j) The grievance procedure and practices governing it should be brought to the knowledge of the workers;
(k) Any worker who has submitted a grievance should be kept informed of the steps being taken under the procedure, and the action taken on the grievance.[253]

Where a grievance cannot be settled within the company, alternatives such as applicable provisions within collective agreements or conciliation and arbitration procedures may be utilized prior to resorting to litigation.[254]

Human Rights Issues

Code of Conduct

As disgruntled, foreign-based employees have attempted to apply U.S. laws extraterritorially and pursue litigation in U.S. courts with increasing frequency, self-regulation in the form of a corporate code of conduct has become commonplace.[255] As with many other items previously discussed in this chapter, a code of conduct must be implemented with careful consideration of the differences between local laws and those of the parent

---

253. Arrigo & Casale, *supra* note 160, at 14.
254. *Id.*
255. Jennifer L. Hagerman, *Navigating the Waters of International Employment Law: Dispute Avoidance Tactics for United States-Based Multinational Corporations*, 41 Valparaiso U. L. Rev. 97 (Winter 2007), *available at* http://scholar.valpo.edu/cgi/viewcontent.cgi?article=1177&context=vulr.

company's home jurisdiction.[256] For instance, one jurisdiction's law may prohibit certain forms of discrimination, while in other countries the same behavior may not only be allowed but encouraged.[257] Many of the largest multinationals have adopted codes that refer back to ILO standards.[258]

Another important trend in recent years driving companies to develop codes of conduct involves increasing consumer interest in the ethical dimensions of their supply chains.[259] Following very public controversies involving Kathie Lee Gifford, Nike, and Reebok, among others, companies denying responsibility for the behavior of licensees and third-party suppliers has generally given way to accepting responsibility for and seeking to influence them into more socially acceptable operating procedures.[260] The obvious reason for the shift is the desire of companies to protect their brands, reputations, and international images from the scorn and scrutiny of activists and media alike.[261] Whether firms would otherwise take an interest in promoting human rights, because of the potential public relations downside, companies must take vendor labor practices into account, even where arbitrage would otherwise yield less costs.[262] Doing so often has the added benefit of avoiding imposition of formal regulation by outside authorities.[263]

Dozens of countries and provinces have enacted employment discrimination and sexual harassment laws.[264] It is beyond the scope of this text to offer any sort of comprehensive overview of what a code of conduct for overseas application should contain. It is fair to say however, that prohibited behavior should be defined, effective training and grievance procedures must be put into place, retaliation should be expressly prohibited, and independent investigations should be adopted, particularly if the accused is a

---

256. Hirschfeld & Schroeder, *supra* note 8.
257. *Id.*
258. *How International Labour Standards Are Used, supra* note 12.
259. *Id.*
260. Debora L. Spar, *The Spotlight on the Bottom Line: How Multinationals Export Human Rights*, 77 FOREIGN AFFAIRS 7(6) (March–April 1998), http://sandovalhernandezj.people.cofc.edu/index_files/egl_33.pdf.
261. *Id.*
262. *Id.*
263. Hagerman, *supra* note 254, at 911–12.
264. Ellen Pinkos Cobb, *Emerging Workplace Health and Safety Issues*, THE ISOCELES GROUP, 1 (April 2011).

high-ranking member of the organization.[265] Accurate and detailed records should be kept at each step of the process.[266] As with other policies and procedures, these should be seen not as a "one and done" phenomenon but as something that should be continually reexamined and reassessed.[267]

Workplace Bullying

Workplace abuse known as workplace bullying, psychological harassment, moral harassment, victimization, or mobbing has only been gaining attention in the United States in recent years but has been the focus of significant attention in many overseas jurisdictions for decades.[268] There does not appear to be a set definition for behaviors that constitute workplace bullying; they can include verbal threats, personal attacks, humiliation, innuendo, and attempts at deliberately isolating a colleague.[269] Still other examples involve false accusations of errors or insubordination, imposing arbitrary standards, and imposing unrealistic demands and deadlines.[270]

What is clear is that workplace bullying is increasingly seen as relevant across professions and national borders.[271] A Monster Global Poll conducted in May 2011 surveyed over 16,000 workers worldwide, and 55 percent of Asian respondents reported that they had been emotionally or physically bullied at work; that figure was 65 percent for Americans and 83 percent for Europeans.[272] Illnesses ranging from anxiety disorders and sleep disturbances to digestion problems and even fibromyalgia have been attributed

---

265. Keith A. Fink & Jennifer H. Yeung, *Harrassment and Bullying Laws: An International Perspective*, INT'L EMP. & BUS. IMMIGRATION L. SYMPOSIUM, 3 (Oct. 10, 2009), http://www.finksteinberg.com/files/Harassment%20and%20Bullying%20Laws,%20An%20International%20Perspective.pdf.
266. Hagerman, *supra* note 254, at 914.
267. *Id.* at 912.
268. Katherine Lippel, *The Law of Workplace Bullying: An International Overview*, 32 COMPARATIVE LABOR LAW & POL'Y J. 1 (2010).
269. Ellen Pinkos Cobb, *Workplace Bullying: A Global Issue*, INT'L HR FORUM (July 5, 2011), http://internationalhr.wordpress.com/2011/07/05/workplace-bullying-a-global-issue/.
270. *The 2011 Global Employer: Highlights of Littler's Fourth Annual Global Employer Institute*, *supra* note 14, at 34.
271. Cobb, *supra* note 268.
272. *Id.*

to bullying.[273] A 2007 British study calculated the annual cost of bullying in the United Kingdom as in excess of 13 billion pounds.[274]

A number of countries are addressing the issue by introducing new legislation, amending existing statutes, or using extra-regulatory means such as codes of practice or collective agreement provisions.[275] Bullying is illegal in some jurisdictions in which it is deemed contrary to the idea of dignity at work.[276] Sweden was the first EU nation that defined bullying behaviors as a threat to occupational health and safety in 1993.[277] Since then France, Belgium, New Zealand, the state of South Australia, and three Canadian provinces have passed antibullying laws, and the courts in other nations such as the United Kingdom and Germany have handed down decisions against such behavior.[278] In January 2011, the Turkish Parliament amended the Debts law to create an offense for commission of or failing to prevent verbal insults, belittling, and intentional isolation.[279]

For the international practitioner, the conclusion is obvious: adding provisions against employment-based bullying into an overseas health and safety program is progressing from the realm of "a wise precaution" to a basic requirement in many locales.[280] This is especially evident in Spain and France, which have instituted criminal or penal recourse explicitly targeting bullying by employers.[281] Moreover, if bullying involves elements of sexual harassment or discrimination, employees may also take action under some jurisdictions' health and safety laws.[282] Employees have had recourse to workers' compensation claims for exposure to bullying in Australia and certain Canadian provinces for a number of years.[283] Remedies for constructive dismissal for exposure to such behavior have been used in countries

---

273. *The 2011 Global Employer: Highlights of Littler's Fourth Annual Global Employer Institute*, *supra* note 14, at 33.
274. *Id.*
275. Cobb, *supra* note 263, at 1.
276. *The 2011 Global Employer: Highlights of Littler's Fourth Annual Global Employer Institute*, *supra* note 14, at 33.
277. *Id.*
278. *Id.* at 33–34.
279. Cobb, *supra* note 268.
280. Cobb, *supra* note 263, at 2.
281. Lippel, *supra* note 267, at 10.
282. Cobb, *supra* note 263, at 2.
283. Lippel, *supra* note 267, at 7.

such as Argentina, Chile, and Germany.[284] Evidence of intent is often not required in either tort or contractual contexts.[285]

Given this backdrop, the question becomes: What kinds of policies should employers adopt, at home or abroad? As with other matters discussed here, where the line should be drawn between legitimate and abusive management strategy will likely vary from one jurisdiction to another.[286] One guiding principle that should apply across borders is the critical goal of establishing a respectful workplace culture.[287] Still another is the importance of addressing organizational factors such as role conflicts and ambiguities, job insecurity, and leadership to prevent bullying behaviors before they start.[288]

A number of practical steps employers can take are offered from a variety of sources. The following is a sampling, not meant as comprehensive by any means. First, the employer should publicize the addition of prohibitions against bullying behaviors to the code of conduct, with specificity as to the types of conduct banned.[289] Second, a written reporting process should be put in place that accounts for local practices of collective bargaining, works councils, and staff delegates and recognizes those jurisdictions that prohibit anonymous submissions.[290] Third, thorough investigations and timely remedial action akin to the process followed for sexual harassment and discrimination claims should be instituted.[291] Fourth, victims should be protected from retaliation and bullies should be disciplined and, where appropriate, terminated.[292] Fifth, employers should consider purchasing employment practices liability insurance coverage.[293] Sixth, policies should be drafted by a labor lawyer familiar with the subject jurisdictions and disseminated in the local language.[294] Seventh, periodic training provided by a

---

284. *Id.* at 9.
285. *Id.* at 12.
286. *Id.* at 9.
287. *The 2011 Global Employer: Highlights of Littler's Fourth Annual Global Employer Institute, supra* note 14, at 38.
288. Lippel, *supra* note 267, at 3.
289. *The 2011 Global Employer: Highlights of Littler's Fourth Annual Global Employer Institute, supra* note 14, at 38.
290. *Id.*
291. *Id.*
292. *Id.*
293. Fink & Yeung, *supra* note 264, at 6.
294. *Id.* at 9.

knowledgeable party is advisable.[295] Such training should be instituted with care to foster clear communication and mutual respect with local offices and to avoid ethnocentric mistakes.[296]

Alien Tort Claims Act Litigation

The Alien Tort Claims Act (ATCA) was included as part of the Judiciary Act of 1789, investing in the federal district courts original jurisdiction of any civil action by an alien for a tort committed in violation of the law of nations or a treaty of the United States.[297] When initially implemented, actionable offenses were limited to violations of safe conduct, infringement of the rights of ambassadors, and piracy.[298] Over the succeeding two centuries, jurisdiction was successfully invoked in only two cases.[299]

ACTA emerged from obscurity in 1980 with the decision of *Filártiga v. Peña-Irala*,[300] a case involving a Paraguayan boy who was tortured to death in Paraguay by a Paraguayan police officer who subsequently moved to New York.[301] The Second Circuit expanded applicable jurisdiction of ACTA beyond state officials to private actors for purely private acts in its 1995 decision in *Kadic v. Karadzic*,[302] regarding genocide and war crimes alleged against Serbian leader Radovan Karadzic.[303] The upshot of the *Kadic* decision was that it allowed United States' courts to adjudicate crimes committed overseas, many times by non-U.S.–based multinational corporations.[304] In 1997, the District Court's decision in *Doe v. Unocal*[305] further

---

295. *Id.* at 10.
296. Hagerman, *supra* note 254, at 915.
297. Marion Weschka, *Human Rights and Multinational Enterprises: How Can Multinational Enterprises Be Held Responsible for Human Rights Violations Committed Abroad?*, MAX-PLANCK-INSTITUT FÜR AUSLÄNDISCHES ÖFFENTLICHES RECHT UND VÖLKERRECHT, 635 (2006), http://www.zaoerv.de/66_2006/66_2006_3_a_625_662.pdf.
298. Theresa Adamski, *The Alien Tort Claims Act and Corporate Liability: A Threat to the United States' International Relations*, 34 FORDHAM INT'L L. J. 1511 (2011), *available at* http://ir.lawnet.fordham.edu/cgi/viewcontent.cgi?article=2311&context=ilj.
299. *Id.* at 1512.
300. 630 F.2d 876 (2d Cir. 1980).
301. Weschka, *supra* note 296, at 635.
302. 70 F.3d 232 (2d. Cir. 1995).
303. Weschka, *supra* note 296, at 635–36.
304. Adamski, *supra* note 297, at 1517.
305. 963 F. Supp. 880 (C.D. Cal 1997).

extended personal jurisdiction pursuant to the Act to include multinational corporations.[306]

Activists began to see ATCA as a type of "impact litigation" and an advocacy tool that could be used to generate large settlements and further fund public interest group activities.[307] Suits filed against oil companies, food and beverage producers, and others alleged solicitation of violence against union organizers, pollution, or practices resulting in physical harm to foreign workers.[308] Allegations in the extractive sector stemmed primarily from excessive acts under corporate security arrangements, whereas those in the manufacturing sector focused mainly within the supply chain and infringed on labor standards in the workplace.[309]

The activists' hand was strengthened in September 2002, when the 9th Circuit Court of Appeals reversed the District Court's dismissal of *Doe v. Unocal*, holding that plaintiffs need only show that defendant Unocal "knowingly assisted" Burmese army units in their abuses.[310] A confidential settlement was reached in March 2005.[311] The settlement was seen by some observers as encouraging to plaintiffs' lawyers and an event putting corporations on notice of the threat that ATCA litigation could ultimately represent.[312] Unocal's joint venture partner Total found itself in further litigation in the Belgian courts stemming from the same project, even after it had settled French litigation on similar charges.[313] A Total subsidiary had been dismissed from the *Doe* case, underscoring that ACTA requires at least some links with the United States in order for jurisdiction to attach.[314]

---

306. Weschka, *supra* note 296, at 636.
307. Theresa Harris, *Settling a Corporate Accountability Lawsuit Without Sacrificing Human Rights: Wang Xiaoning v. Yahoo!*, 15 Hum. Rts. Brief 10–11, 13 (2008) http://www.wcl.american.edu/hrbrief/15/2harris.pdf.
308. J. Russell Jackson, *Alien Tort Claims Act Cases Keep Coming*, Nat'l L. J. (Sept. 14, 2009), https://www.skadden.com/sites/default/files/publications/Publications1866_0.pdf.
309. Caroline Kaeb, *Emerging Issues of Human Rights Responsibility in the Extractive and Manufacturing Industries: Patterns and Liability Risks*, 6 Northwestern J. Int'l Human Rights 344 (Spring 2008), *available at* http://www.law.northwestern.edu/journals/jihr/v6/n2/5/Kaeb.pdf.
310. Weschka, *supra* note 296, at 636.
311. *Id.*
312. Adamski, *supra* note 297, at 1518–19.
313. Kaeb, *supra* note 308, at 345.
314. Weschka, *supra* note 296, at 642–43.

The Ninth Circuit's complicity standard in *Doe v. Unocal* drew heavily from the precedent conceived in international criminal tribunals requiring plaintiffs show that the corporation "knew or had reason to know" that its actions assisted the crime.[315] While there is no consensus on precisely what is required to satisfy the test, a number of indicators have been posited, including a corporation deriving economic benefits from the violations, the level of corporate control in a private-public joint venture, continuation of corporate assistance despite awareness of the violations, and the presence of a common goal.[316]

Succeeding decisions were a mixed bag for corporate interests. The District Court for the Northern District of California in March 2004 denied ChevronTexaco's motion for summary judgment in *Bowoto v. ChevronTexaco*,[317] finding that the parent company could be held responsible for torts committed by its Nigerian subsidiary, given what the court determined was an "extraordinarily close relationship between the two."[318] In June 2004, the U.S. Supreme Court issued a ruling in *Sosa v. Alvarez-Machain*[319] that was notable for underscoring that ACTA jurisdiction was limited to a small number of international norms that were definable, universal, and obligatory.[320] After the *Sosa* decision, *Bowoto v. Chevron Corp.*[321] in the Ninth Circuit and *Romero v. Drummond Company*[322] in the Eleventh Circuit went to trial; both cases resulted in defense verdicts, although at least in the case of Drummond, it may still have suffered adverse economic consequences as a result of the litigation.[323]

What may represent a critical turning point for ATCA litigation, however, occurred on September 17, 2010, when the Second Circuit issued its ruling in *Kiobel v. Royal Dutch Petroleum*.[324] In *Kiobel*, the court definitively held that multinational corporations could not be held liable for human rights

---

315. Kaeb, *supra* note 308, at 334.
316. *Id.*
317. 312 F. Supp. 2d 1229 (N.D. Cal. 2004).
318. Weschka, *supra* note 296, at 638.
319. 542 U.S. 692 (2004).
320. Weschka, *supra* note 296, at 640.
321. 621 F.3d 1116 (9th Cir. 2010).
322. 552 F.3d 1303 (11th Cir. 2008).
323. Adamski, *supra* note 297, at 1533.
324. 621 F.3d 111 (2d Cir. 2010).

violations under ATCA.[325] The basis of the 2–1 majority's ruling was that customary international law controls what claims are actionable under the ATCA and who may be a defendant, and that unlike American jurisprudence that permits corporate liability, the majority's reading of foreign authority was that it has not yet done so.[326]

The *Kiobel* decision did, however, set up a split among the circuits regarding ACTA jurisdiction, which the U.S. Supreme Court determined to address by accepting a writ of certiorari in the matter. Oral argument was had in February 2012, but additional argument was ordered for October 1, 2012, to allow for additional briefing of the crucial question of whether ATCA could apply to conduct outside of the United States.[327] On April 17, 2013, the Supreme Court affirmed the Second Circuit ruling, basing it on "a presumption against extraterritoriality."[328]

As welcome to multinationals as the Supreme Court's decision must have been, it was noted at the time the decision was released that it would not completely foreclose human rights-based litigation:

> Plaintiffs' lawyers are likely ... to assert that their allegations of overseas human rights abuses can go forward as common law tort actions alleging violations of state law. States are largely free to craft their tort law without interference from the federal government, so plaintiffs' lawyers barred from raising overseas human rights claims in federal court under the ATS [Alien Tort Statute] may well decide to file their lawsuits in state courts instead. Of course, most states are likely to decide, for many of the same reasons that motivated the Supreme Court in *Kiobel*, that it would be inappropriate for them to stand in judgment of events that took place in foreign countries. But if even one state makes known its willingness to hear suits alleging overseas

---

325. Adamski, *supra* note 297, at 1528.
326. *Id.* at 1530.
327. Rodger Citron, *Another Fine Mess: An Assessment of the Most Recent Supreme Court Oral Argument in* Kiobel v. Royal Dutch Petroleum, VERDICT (Oct. 23, 2012), http://verdict.justia.com/2012/10/23/another-fine-mess.
328. Rich Samp, *Supreme Court Observations:* Kiobel v. Royal Dutch Petroleum *& the Future of Alien Tort Litigation*, FORBES (April 18, 2013), http://www.forbes.com/sites/wlf/2013/04/18/supreme-court-observations-kiobel-v-royal-dutch-petroleum-the-future-of-alien-tort-litigation/.

human rights abuses, one can reasonably expect plaintiffs' lawyers to flock there. In sum, yesterday's *Kiobel* decision is likely to make it far more difficult for human rights activists to sue U.S. corporations based on the corporation's overseas activities. But the decision left activists with sufficient wiggle room that we can expect to see multinational corporations regularly being sued for their overseas activities for the foreseeable future.[329]

Additionally, major human rights cases have been brought in European domestic courts, and as noted above, France and Belgium are exceptions to the general rule that legal systems would not allow for the application of criminal liability to corporations.[330]

Global Mobility

General Considerations

The demands of a company's customers, strategic considerations, and overall business needs naturally drive decisions about the extent of its global reach and exactly how it will staff overseas operations.[331] Decision making concerning that staffing centers on a well thought-out international HR policy for expatriates, third-country nationals, and international travelers.[332] As with so many things, the time and money invested in this planning is seen by leading organizations not so much as an option as an absolute necessity, before the lack of forethought causes expensive, profit-killing problems.[333] These problems could potentially include civil and in some instances criminal judgments from "duty of care" failures, discrimination suits, and local and international labor law violations; ex gratia payments or unbudgeted payouts to employees resulting from poor policy or communication; and

---

329. *Id.*
330. Kaeb, *supra* note 308, at 327–28.
331. *"Going Global": An Overview of International Employment Issues*, *supra* note 5, at 1.
332. *A Best in Class Expatriate Policy & Procedure Manual, and a Way to Communicate This Information, Can Save Millions*, EXPAT POLICY & PROCEDURES GROUP (2009), http://www.expatpolicy.com/Expatriate%20Policy%20Shields%20Liability.html.
333. *Id.*

wasted time and expense in solving otherwise foreseeable issues.[334] As has been argued generally throughout this book in various circumstances, the return on investment of putting appropriate policies in place ahead of implementation will likely exceed any service, tax, security, relocation, or insurance program that could be otherwise adopted. [335]

Expatriate Policy

One in-house labor attorney notes that as things become more global, you don't have to move people around as much as you used to. You can, for instance, set up a design center anywhere in the world today. Still, many overseas operations require making a decision between sending employees of the U.S. parent (expatriates), hiring locals, or even utilization of independent contractors.[336] Expatriate assignments raise issues about the interplay between U.S. and foreign employment, tax, and immigration laws.[337] Given the complexities involved, prior to staffing an overseas operation, responsibility for this area should be concentrated in a mobility committee comprised of individuals responsible for corporate tax, finance, facilities, employment law, immigration, compensation and benefits, and payroll.[338] Depending on the size of the nascent overseas operation, appointing a dedicated mobility specialist may also be advisable.[339]

Prior to making any overseas placements, the terms of the assignment and an exit strategy for the employees need to be carefully thought out.[340] Defining the operational parameters of each job title involved is important for determining whether a works council needs to be consulted, among other potential employment law issues in the overseas location.[341] Affected employees' nationalities may add costs if, as with the United States, their countries of origin tax citizens when they work exclusively outside the

---

334. *Id.*
335. *Id.*
336. *"Going Global": An Overview of International Employment Issues, supra* note 5, at 1.
337. *Id.* at 14.
338. *The 2011 Global Employer: Highlights of Littler's Fourth Annual Global Employer Institute, supra* note 14, at 13.
339. *Id.* at 14.
340. *"Going Global": An Overview of International Employment Issues, supra* note 5, at 14.
341. *The 2011 Global Employer: Highlights of Littler's Fourth Annual Global Employer Institute, supra* note 14, at 14.

country or are subject to a lower visa cap.[342] A host of items need to be considered on a per-employee basis, including:

- Cost of living equalization
- Pension and social security obligations
- Insurances
- Potential needs of employee's family
- Local regulations regarding working conditions and terms of employment
- Duration of assignment
- Local conditions, including safety
- Housing
- Automobile
- Shipments of household goods
- Repatriation, including costs and placement of employee on return[343]

Additionally, as has been described elsewhere in the text, the committee should engage in gaming out responses to potential, foreseeable issues, ranging from political or business climate changes, to performance issues, illness, or injury and the need for emergency evacuation.[344]

To the extent that particular employees are under consideration for overseas assignments, they should be evaluated for their suitability in a variety of contexts. One novel approach in terms of setting up these criteria is to expatriate the HR or other personnel for a period of time to help them understand the challenges involved from a first-hand perspective.[345] This would include not just their assignment-specific skills, experience level, and language capability, but also their cultural adaptability and family circumstances.[346] This last point is important, as residency or work visas for

---

342. *Id.*
343. *Id.*
344. *Id.* at 14–15.
345. Geert Hofstede, *The Art of Family Management*, NET EXPAT (Jan. 2001), http://www.netexpat.com/news/200101.html.
346. *The 2011 Global Employer: Highlights of Littler's Fourth Annual Global Employer Institute*, *supra* note 14, at 12.

nonmarried or other family members may be denied or put under additional scrutiny.[347]

There are several ways an expatriate relationship can be set up, depending upon which factors are most favorable to the parent entity. An expatriate can remain employed by the U.S. entity but in an assignment to the foreign nation; this does open up the U.S. entity to the permanent establishment problems discussed above.[348] Another option is to transfer the U.S. employee to a foreign subsidiary and sever the employee's relationship with the U.S. entity, although this could interfere with the employee's benefits.[349] Still another method is a transfer followed by secondment of the employee for a definite period of time to an agency, vendor, or client who can sponsor him or her for a work visa, and handle all of the administrative tasks.[350] While this might avoid permanent establishment issues, if the U.S. parent continues to direct and control the employee's work, a joint employer relationship that triggers the employment laws of both jurisdictions can result.[351]

Recently, in an effort to avoid disruption of employee benefits and insulate the ultimate U.S. parent company from liability and, in particular, the risk of permanent establishment, many companies have chosen to establish a separate "holding" subsidiary to employ expatriates.[352] If, however, the U.S. parent seeks to direct the expatriate's work, joint employer liability can still result.[353] It is worth noting here that simultaneously trying to control a person's work while claiming her or she is an independent contractor can be construed as a violation of employment, tax, and social security laws, both foreign and domestic.[354] Which of the arrangements listed above should be used generally requires consultation with the company's tax or finance departments.[355]

---

347. *Id.*
348. *"Going Global": An Overview of International Employment Issues, supra* note 5, at 14.
349. *Id.*
350. *The 2011 Global Employer: Highlights of Littler's Fourth Annual Global Employer Institute, supra* note 14, at 13.
351. *"Going Global": An Overview of International Employment Issues, supra* note 5, at 14.
352. *Id.*
353. *Id.* at 14–15.
354. *Id.* at 2.
355. *The 2011 Global Employer: Highlights of Littler's Fourth Annual Global Employer Institute, supra* note 14, at 13.

Yet another consideration when contracting with expatriates is the place where the contract is deemed to have been made and what nations' law applies to it.[356] This naturally has direct effect on the rights of the employee, the obligations of the employer, and the extent to which the contract can be terminated easily and lawfully.[357] In that vein, it may be very important to terminate the employee's existing contract before moving him or her to another jurisdiction, to avoid the risk of inconsistent or multiple obligations on the part of the employer.[358] Further, assuming the expatriate remains an employee of the U.S. entity, a separate expatriate assignment letter should be drafted that sets out the terms of his or her assignment to ensure that there is no questions regarding severability and no alteration in employee status.[359] Finally, care should be taken to avoid careless statements about what will happen to the expatriate upon relocation, as a later failure to honor those statements may lead to liability.[360]

When sending employees overseas, it is expected they will be taxed in two different countries, which requires determination of tax domicile and the cost of any tax equalization that the company may need to provide.[361] The cost of obtaining tax advice should be factored into the overall cost of the assignment.[362] The timing of an assignment may also significantly impact tax and administrative costs associated with it.[363] In some jurisdictions, tax treaties may provide benefits if the assignee is in the country less than 183 days in a tax year, which translates to a start date after July 1 and end date before the following June 30 when using a calendar year for the tax year.[364] Conversely, starting an assignment just before year end or ending it shortly after the beginning of a new tax year can necessitate filing an

---

356. Roth, *supra* note 16.
357. *Id.*
358. *Id.*
359. *"Going Global": An Overview of International Employment Issues*, *supra* note 5, at 15.
360. *Id.*
361. *The 2011 Global Employer: Highlights of Littler's Fourth Annual Global Employer Institute*, *supra* note 14, at 12.
362. *Id.*
363. Eric Loff, *Two Tax Planning Strategies to Reduce Expatriate Costs*, INT'L HR FORUM (July 30, 2012), http://www.internationalhrforum.com/2012/07/30/two-tax-planning-strategies-to-reduce-expatriate-costs/.
364. Hall, *supra* note 141.

additional tax return.[365] It may also be possible to provide benefits such as housing, cars, and club dues on a tax-free basis.[366] The direct payment of certain expenses by an employer is considered a benefit-in-kind, which in many countries will not be fully taxable to the employee.[367]

An often-overlooked aspect of overseas assignments is the need for specialized insurance coverage. After a 60-day period living outside the country, covered perils to the employee's' vacant residence such as fire or vandalism may fall outside homeowners' coverage.[368] Similarly, while a U.S. employees' homeowners' policy might cover damage from a traffic accident overseas during a vacation, it will likely not do so in an expatriate assignment situation.[369] Due to the gravity of the employer's responsibilities in such a situation, diversity of legislation, and questions over choice of law, employers should be prepared for the highest prevailing duty of care standards to be applied against them.[370] One solution is to create an international specific insurance program that is voluntarily offered to expatriates at no cost to the employer and that, if declined by the employee, could in some instances help shield the company from liability.[371]

Attention must also be given to personal hazards that expatriates may face on foreign assignment. These can include mass uprisings, terrorist attacks, kidnapping and execution, natural disasters such as earthquakes and volcanoes, and the possibility of pandemic disease.[372] Regardless of the specific risk, employers must consider whether they will be seen to owe a legal or ethical obligation to prevent harm to employees that gives rise to

---

365. *Id.*
366. Loff, *supra* note 362.
367. *Id.*
368. *A Best in Class Expatriate Policy & Procedure Manual, and a Way to Communicate This Information, Can Save Millions*, *supra* note 331.
369. *Id.*
370. Dr. Lisbeth Claus, *Duty of Care of Employers for Protecting International Assignees, Their Dependents, and International Business Travelers*, INT'L S.O.S. (2009), http://www.internationalsos.com/en/files/Duty_of_Care_whitepaper.pdf.
371. *A Best in Class Expatriate Policy & Procedure Manual, and a Way to Communicate This Information, Can Save Millions*, *supra* note 331.
372. Nick Martindale, *Managing Expats in Dangerous Areas: What Employers Need to Know*, PERSONNEL TODAY (June 29, 2010), http://www.personneltoday.com/articles/29/06/2010/56081/managing-expats-in-dangerous-areas-what-employers-need-to.htm.

a duty to create a wide-ranging plan to protect them.[373] One of the most direct routes to creation of such a duty under U.S. law would likely begin through a straightforward application of a common law negligence theory.[374] To the extent that a company would seek to protect itself from such a cause of action, ensuring employees are given hostile environment training, relevant security briefings, personal protective equipment, appropriate medical advice and vaccines, private security personnel and transport arrangements, and relevant embassy or consulate details would be advisable. [375]

One must also consider the many jurisdictions that have enacted duty of care legislation, which is seen to be generally expanding in scope.[376] In the U.K., the outcome of duty of care cases often turns on whether the injury is found to have been foreseeable.[377] By contrast, in Australia, workers' compensation laws requiring a safe working environment can give rise to personal criminal liability to management and are expressly extraterritorial.[378] In the face of such requirements, a comprehensive strategy that involves consultation with experienced counsel on local legal obligations, together with a plan addressing the specific risks posed by the subject locale in conjunction with a qualified safety consultant and objective resources, must be developed.[379] In sum however, HR departments must be prepared to resist pressure from employees to travel if they reach the conclusion it is too dangerous.[380]

Immigration Issues

During times of corporate restructuring, counsel must not leave matters concerning overseas staff to the HR department, since foreign national workers must continue to be authorized by immigration authorities to work

---

373. Philip M. Berkowitz & Michael G. Congiu, *Managing The Global Workforce—A Legal and Practical Guide to Dangerous International Employee Assignments*, LITTLER REPORT, 1 (Feb. 2011), http://www.littler.com/files/press/pdf/WP_IntlAssignments_2-23-11.pdf.
374. *Id.* at 2.
375. Martindale, *supra* note 371.
376. Berkowitz & Congiu, *supra* note 372, at 1.
377. *Id.*
378. *Id.*
379. *Id.* at 4–7.
380. Martindale, *supra* note 371.

for the new employer.[381] In some cases, a previously granted work authorization will not automatically transfer to the new entity, and the employer will need to file additional paperwork.[382]

An expatriate assignment should not be designed without early and detailed immigration planning.[383] Among other reasons, this is because the nature and purpose of the job involved may be relevant to a particular jurisdiction's visa requirements.[384]

Angelo Paparelli, a partner at Seyfarth Shaw who advises clients from Fortune 10 multinationals to start-ups, has seen the same immigration drama play out many times. In the usual life cycle that he relates, the setting up of a website leads to customer inquiries and recognition of market opportunities not perceived before in another nation. Responding to this, some part of management travels to the location and engages in meetings to get a sense of local requirements, preferences, business partners and available sales representatives.

Senior management only gets serious when they are convinced of the market opportunity. But then many companies develop what Paparelli deems an ill-advised strategy—the notion that "foreign immigration is just a bunch of paperwork—and once you get past the border guard, no problem." This is what Paparelli calls the "stealth visitor" strategy. Essentially, the stealth visitor goes into a foreign country and makes claims to immigration officials there that are not fully accurate.

Generally, Paparelli observes, a foreign national is asked at the border if they are visiting for personal or business reasons. Legitimate personal reasons might include visiting friends or relatives, vacationing as a tourist, or even seeking specialized medical care. If however the foreign national is there to conduct business, this generally opens up a series of questions about whether he or she is working in violation of local immigration laws.

---

381. Megan Raesner & Elaine Martino, *"You're Fired!" or Maybe Not: The Effect of Restructuring on Foreign National Employees*, ACC Docket, 100 (July/Aug. 2010), http://paragongeoimmigration.com/press/The%20Effect%20of%20Restructing%20on%20Foreign%20Nationals.pdf.
382. *Id.*
383. *"Going Global": An Overview of International Employment Issues*, *supra* note 5, at 15.
384. *The 2011 Global Employer: Highlights of Littler's Fourth Annual Global Employer Institute*, *supra* note 14, at 13.

Some misguided employees claim they are visiting for personal reasons, then overstep their boundaries and engage in what is legally defined in the jurisdiction as "work." Another variation on the theme features the antsy manager who wants to get a "head start" in a foreign location and sends an employee with instructions to "just say you're a visitor." Unfortunately, it is often only after having done this that the rogue business seeks out Paparelli's advice.

The problem with thinking this way and trying to be too clever by half is that foreign border inspectors may actually ask more questions, learn the truth, and sanction the employer. Potential sanctions can include fines, a prohibition to change status unless the offending employees leave the country, deportation, and, in egregious situations, even incarceration. Categorically, Paparelli advises that wiser, sophisticated companies who would *never* violate U.S. law need to equally respect the laws of sovereign foreign countries. Clients should recognize that immigration law is not a bureaucratic process that can be transcended by cutting corners. Paparelli sternly warns,

> Remember that for any statements you make in writing or orally, you could be held accountable. If for instance your new international operation doesn't end up hiring as many people as you originally thought—and that you put down on official forms—it could be considered fraud by a foreign government, unless a satisfactory explanation is offered.

The lesson: be careful with what might be construed as possible misrepresentations. Put caveats in the representations you make in official declarations to leave yourself some wiggle room, particularly with newer ventures.

Although it may be a bit repetitious to say it again in this chapter, a company with cross-border operations must—wait for it—*map out a strategy* for global mobility, says Paparelli. Large companies are often very sophisticated in this regard, having appointed regional heads of global mobility and attorneys in-country to facilitate movement. Established multinationals may also utilize relocation companies who team with law firms to offer immigration services. Further, they often incorporate purpose-specific software developed to manage deadlines for visa and passport status, built out country by country. This is a wise precaution, as Paparelli points out that violation of visa expiration dates could be a crime in some jurisdictions. And, in keeping with this book's earlier discussion of FCPA/antibribery legislation, it should go without saying that you can't make questionable payments to obtain visas without unacceptable risk.

Just being a large multinational does not guarantee you won't run afoul of the rules, however. In October 2013, Infosys reportedly agreed to pay $34 million to settle a two-year federal investigation into whether the Bangalore-based company sent Indian workers to the United States on cheaper B-1 business visit visas instead of H1-B work visas. Infosys has denied any wrongdoing.[385]

When Paparelli began his practice in 1978, the United States had what he judged to be the most sophisticated immigration law in world. At that time, many jurisdictions employed broad categories that were unclear. This lead to conversations beginning with phrases such as, "I know this is the answer because I know a local immigration officer, and he interprets it this way." Increasingly, however, Paparelli is seeing overseas immigration law becoming as sophisticated as that in the United States in terms of both eligibility and penalties for violations. In fact, Paparelli reckons some other countries' systems have actually leapfrogged over the those in the United States. This is being driven by phenomena that includes changing demographics in Europe and Japan and aging in Canada and Australia—in other words, scarcity of qualified working age people.

The fascinating trend that Paparelli sees coming out of this evolution is that some countries are starting to use immigration the same way they use tax law—as a means of comparative advantage. India, Brazil, and China are competing for immigrants. At the same time, the rest of world outside of North America, the United Kingdom, and Australia, are clamoring for education. Can immigration policy making it easier to get educated in a country encourage people to stay? In Paparelli's view, U.S. immigration quotas cannot be stuck in limbo. If they are, perhaps these best and brightest will simply go back home.

---

385. Jochelle Mendonca, *After Infosys Visa Row, Other IT Companies under U.S. Scanner*, Economic Times of India (Nov. 4, 2013), http://economictimes.indiatimes.com/tech/ ites/after-infosys-visa-row-other-it-companies-under-us-scanner/articleshow/25190812.cms.

Jim King, a Seyfarth immigration partner, sees the economic downturn causing increasingly restrictive immigration in some places, such as in the United Kingdom, the Netherlands, and even Canada. Economic downturns are making some countries more protectionist, in his view. King's bottom line for businesses with global mobility needs is that, even though in some countries intracompany transfers can move quickly, "getting work permits and visas outside of that context takes longer than you think—two weeks to get a work permit is not sufficient!" The better practice is for the business to provide a three-to-four-month heads up—counsel may need it. You want to get the process started while still negotiating the contract.

Once you start the work-permit process, it might be possible to make intermittent visits while waiting for the work permit and visa to be issued. King warns, however, that during those interim visits you will need to limit client-facing meetings, and you typically can't pay the worker on local foreign company payroll.

Another issue that can arise is if the employee has some sort of problematic background or criminal record that isn't disclosed early in the process. Not surprisingly, King relates, the same kinds of entry standards are often applied in foreign countries as apply in the United States. Multiple criminal violations, or even a single DUI or shoplifting conviction, can at best be a red flag for foreign immigration officials. What is so vexing for companies and counsel is that very often in the real world, an executive doesn't disclose the problematic past history. While it may be routine for companies to do commercial background checks, the checks don't always pick up everything. A criminal matter surfacing at the eleventh hour can often disrupt the work-permit application process.

In terms of in-bound U.S. immigration, a foreign national may come in on a training visa. King notes, however, that training visas have lots of conditions and limitations that often don't work in the real world. Further, the annual quota on new "H-1B" permits is also a challenge within the U.S. immigration system; moreover, there are increasingly restrictive requirements on the use of H-1B work permits in third-party worksite situations.

Also, when dealing with the American immigration system, political correctness aside, security clearances can delay the process materially. The prototypical example is a Middle Eastern man who goes home for personal reasons and then finds himself stuck there. King advises clients to consider these kinds of delays when working through global mobility issues.

Russell Swapp, still another Seyfarth immigration partner, advises generally that the difficulty in immigration comes from being reactive, rather than proactive. Swapp opines that particularly when it comes to in-bound immigration to the U.S., a company must ensure that "the tail isn't wagging the dog."

How a company is structured can affect the difficulty in dealing with global mobility issues, Swapp adds. Certain visa classifications allow transfer from one country's office to another. It is just that common definitions of "affiliate," "subsidiary," and "joint venture" don't necessarily match up with how these entities are commonly set up. Swapp gives the example of an affiliate defined as two companies owned by the same shareholders with almost identical share of stock ownership. Such a company structure is typically shaped by tax considerations. The question for company management and their counsel is whether there is enough of an immigration implication in a given transaction that it might outweigh tax consequences such that the entity should be set up in line with the immigration statute? Or, at least to tweak the set-up? This is yet another reason to get immigration attorneys involved before an entity is even set up—if you don't, you end up having to react to the immigration system.

In the U.S system, it is quite common to have incoming workers apply for temporary visas first, come into the country, and then apply for permanent worker status, Swapp explains. Visas are for a finite period and focus on appropriate credentials. Seeking permanent residence involves a different analysis—you have to "test the labor market" to obtain a green card. You can only do this because of what is seen to be a legitimate business need.

Considering a company's out-bound immigration needs, Swapp advises that generally for a company that wants to be multinational, the best approach is to have centralized control over personnel. Immigration should not be managed by an in-country officer. And as noted above, timing is an important factor to consider. Simply put, Swapp states, "you have to remember the rest of the world isn't as efficient as the U.S." For example, a decision on a temporary transfer request in the United States might take 15 days; in Brazil, it might take five months just to process paperwork—and you never know how long it will ultimately take. In Switzerland, timing on immigration issues varies from canton to canton. In Germany, Swapp finds it can even vary from city to city. This highlights the need to rely on qualified local practitioners, because to know the likely timing at a particular locale, you have to "live immigration" in that system. Moreover, local counsel might have developed working relationships with regulatory agencies allowing for quicker responses to compliance questions and avoiding bureaucratic snafus.[386]

As discussed above in the section regarding data privacy, it is important to obtain an executed consent for sharing of personal data.[387] In more strict jurisdictions, intercompany data transfer agreements, participation in the Safe Harbor Privacy Agreement, and governmental filings may also be necessary.[388]

While as noted in previous chapters that it is always an ongoing process, we will now close out our discussions on diligence. By now, you have your plan and you have done your homework. Let's go negotiate your deal!

---

386. Hirschfeld & Schroeder, *supra* note 8.
387. *The Global Employer: Mobilizing the Work Force Globally*, GLOBAL EMPLOYER, 6 (May 2010), http://www.bakermckenzie.com/files/Uploads/Documents/North%20America/GlobalCitizenship/bk_theglobalemployer_may10.pdf.
388. *Id.*

Chapter 10

Negotiations

Having successfully navigated through the due diligence process, a talented and experienced lawyer or businessperson might be tempted to think that he or she does not need much advice in actually negotiating a deal, even if it is overseas. After all, aren't negotiations essentially the same anywhere—two individuals or groups of individuals who seek to come to a mutually acceptable agreement? While this is to some extent true, as we have seen in earlier chapters, negotiating transactions across borders complicates the working world you otherwise know. Once again, having the right people in the right place with the right information can be the difference between success and failure. It all starts with having the right team of people at the negotiating table.

Assembling Your Negotiating Team, or the Noah's Ark Principle: Every Specialist That You Need, None That You Don't

Howard Mills, of Deloitte, has a delightfully simple way of summarizing the negotiation of cross-border transactions: "Doing something international is going to be a team effort." According to Mills this is because in an international context, you are dealing with legal issues *and* people issues (including cultural issues) on both sides of the border. That begs the question, however: how do you determine who should be on your negotiating team?

Lest any of my friends, whether lawyers, consultants, or anyone else who bills on an hourly basis, get too excited, my answer to that question—the Noah's Ark principle—does *not* mean having two of every profession on Earth around the bargaining table. It means because of the ever-present need to keep costs under control, it is essential to recognize that there is only limited room on your negotiating "ark." So it is necessary to take great care in choosing whom you invite on board and being sure that you have the professionals that your particular deal requires, including appropriate in-house personnel, outside counsel, and, quite possibly, consultants of various stripes.

How do you recruit the negotiating team? At Caterpillar, Don Chenevert reports that once diligence is done, the deal is handed off to the transaction team that, logically enough, is made up of the same people who did the diligence. That way, a consistent approach and high familiarity with the target company's issues is maintained.

It is important to note, however, that the team that handles the due diligence phase is usually broader than the negotiating team. Chenevert will have a negotiating team consisting of a client manager, an in-house lawyer and his/her lieutenant, an outside accounting consultant, and an outside lawyer with expertise in handling acquisitions. The outside lawyer is typically someone who lives in the subject jurisdiction where the transaction is taking place. Paring down the negotiating team to the essentials is important because of the need for proportionality. Chenevert has found that if the other negotiating team has five members, it is important to bring only five people with you into meetings. If more than five people are needed over the course of a deal, there is nothing to prevent you from rotating people in and out of the team.

Successfully choosing the team members is a function of understanding which skill sets are necessary to properly attend to all the details of the given transaction.[1] An engineering expert with specialized knowledge of tolerances might be necessary if you are a manufacturing concern. Someone

---

1. Eric Lesser & Joanne Stephane, *Preparing for Human Resources Business Transformation Outsourcing*, IBM BUSINESS CONSULTING SERVICES, 10–11 (2005), http://www-935.ibm.com/services/multimedia/ge510-4015-hr-bto.pdf.

familiar with migration issues could be necessary if information technology (IT) is at the heart of a deal.

In order to control costs, it is likely that the in-house management and legal staff will choose the makeup of the negotiating team. Still, the counseling role should not be forgotten—outside counsel and consultants should advise their clients of the potential consequences of proceeding without key skill sets being represented. In his experience, Mills has found that the deals he has worked on have benefited from

> good lawyers on both sides, a good international accountant, a good banker, a finance person and a client that has some strong business and some strong international skills. Hopefully, the client is someone that understands a little bit of the culture or is willing to do some homework on it.

Harvey Cohen, of Dinsmore & Shohl, also stresses the importance of having "a detail person to handle the finance and accounting issues." Based on his experience, Cohen emphasizes the value of having that person physically with you at the negotiating table.

The type of transaction often dictates who the necessary parties to your negotiating team should be. In an outsourcing IT transaction, Vikas Bhalla, of EXL, notes that legal function, human resources, migration, quality, operations, and training issues are all involved. In a straightforward sales transaction, on the other hand, different parties are needed. Patricia Gill, formerly an in-house contract lawyer supporting Motorola sales teams, recalls that Motorola's proposal team generally included

> a sales guy, a proposal manager, an in-house attorney, technical/engineering staff, after market support, a tax guy and a financing guy to check on the buyer's creditworthiness. This did not include people who might be assisting the buyer with obtaining financing through the Export-Import bank or otherwise.

The takeaway here is that it is crucial to consider all the skill sets needed now and foreseeably in the future, and to line up appropriate professionals ahead of time. With all the other uncertainties and roadblocks that are likely to present themselves in the course of reaching an agreement, scrambling to find expertise in the midst of a tough negotiation is a problem that should be avoided through thoughtful planning.

In-House Team

If the steering committee has done its job, you should already have a good idea of which in-house experts (legal, operational, or managerial) have a stake in the transaction, and which individuals with these skills sets would be best able to represent the company around the negotiating table. For instance, a technical team that can answer questions about the many specifications involved should be assembled at the beginning of the project.

Identifying the necessary in-house people is not generally the problem. The problem is pulling them away from their regular duties when you need them. Outside lawyers are prone to forget that the transaction at hand may not consume the attention of everyone at the client organization. IBM Consulting wisely advises that a client company should "obtain the time and commitment of these individuals and their managers early in the process."[2] If nothing else, having "reserved" key in-house players ahead of time will make it much more likely that they will be available at crucial moments in the negotiations.

Finally, it seems that the one indispensable party around the table is *the boss*. Loring Knoblauch, of Underwriters' Laboratories (UL), asserts that in Japan, for instance, the chief executive officer (CEO) needs to be 100 percent involved in reaching the all-important initial handshake and broad outlines of the key elements of the deal. He or she stays out of the rest of the negotiations. Field your best negotiators for the details, and once the details are hammered out, bring them back to the CEOs for their blessing. The commitment of the company head is necessary not only in Japan, though. Former Aon Greater China CEO Dr. David Liu states that in China, "the entrepreneur himself has to come; everything gets done between the top guys." It is not hard to understand why this is true in many countries where there is a strong emphasis on business built on personal relationships.

---

2. *Id.* at 11.

The opposing CEO or leader wants to have some confidence, often through social interaction, in your leader's character.

This is one of the many reasons getting senior buy-in is necessary. CEOs need to be available for meetings and social gatherings, often for substantial amounts of time. This may come at a cost to otherwise normal operations, but it is a necessary investment.

Outside Legal Team

Ostensibly, unless your client company is well-staffed with in-house lawyers with experience in international transactions, it is likely that a coordinating outside law firm is involved prior to the due diligence phase. One of the key questions in terms of legal representation around the negotiating table is the extent to which you involve a local lawyer, and if you do, what type of local firm to use.

If your coordinating firm has lawyers with up-to-date knowledge of local regulations and legal developments (e.g., they have an office in the subject jurisdiction), you may be able to forego retaining a separate local law firm. In most instances, though, it is advisable to retain such a firm to assist you with the transaction, at least generally.

If you are retaining local counsel, what kind of firm should you choose? Here, reasonable minds differ. In China, Chenevert likes to use lawyers from larger firms with a longstanding presence there. In his opinion, smaller local firms often do not have the resources for the larger transactions with which he is involved. Big firms, on the other hand, have the capacity to pull in extra bodies if and when you need them. Not everyone agrees, however. Dr. Liu holds that you do not necessarily need a "big firm" lawyer—you need someone who knows the relevant officials.

In what circumstances should you actually involve local counsel around the negotiating table?

Ed Bathelt, of Komatsu America, has moved toward a model of seeking stateside assistance with a U.S. practitioner that has a high-level understanding of pan-South and Central American issues. The goal, he says, is to address 98 percent of potential issues with the U.S. practitioner before turning to local counsel to address truly local issues. Bathelt emphasizes that the local counsel he has worked with abroad have been professional, but "you just want to make sure that when working with them . . . you are actually agreeing to what you think you are agreeing to." That is, that the English version of the contract is really being translated and understood the same way be all stakeholders. You may find it difficult to retain the same level of specificity that you are used to when dealing in English with U.S. lawyers. Are you *sure* that you and local counsel are on the same page? Especially when dealing with complex issues?

Patricia Gill recalls that she would retain outside local counsel in her sales transactions if there were questions about labor regulations or if the equipment under contract was subject to local health and safety regulations. It would seem local counsel should be present (or at least available for quick consultations behind the scenes) when you expect that local law will have an effect on what position you are taking on a given issue.

Financial Team

Financial consultants take part in negotiations directly and behind the scenes, notes Mills. A lot of planning goes on behind the scenes. And, as with the legal team, it can help to have a financial consultant that is familiar with rules and laws on the ground in the subject jurisdiction.

Mills gives the example of an investment fund client exploring options on how to sell an investment in Mexico. Under some scenarios, withholding taxes would be imposed if profits were remitted from Mexico back to the United States. The lawyers involved were struggling with the question of how to structure the transaction so that there would be no withholding. Mills was asked how the client could get certified as a U.S. taxpayer under the rules. They could not because they were organized as a partnership.

Admittedly not an expert on Mexican withholding rules, Mills utilized one of the Deloitte partners from a different area of the world residing here in the United States, a member of what is known as the "international desk" program. Calling the partner in Chicago who heads up the Mexican desk, Mills organized a conference call with the client and its counsel in Mexico, which immediately led to a referral to the right expert in Mexico City, who, in turn, "bridged the gap." The expert was located and retained without having to incur the time and expense of intermediaries, more proof that having the right resources available will reduce frustration and save time, money, and perhaps even the very success of the deal itself.

Cultural Team

According to Mills,

> people from other cultures want us to understand how they work and what their culture is. I think they would welcome that and I think they are going to help you be a lot more successful if you take the time to understand where they are coming from rather than say "my way is the right way and the only way."

After all, as Charles Hallab, of Baker & McKenzie, puts it, "part of doing a successful deal is about understanding the person on the other side of the table." You can either determine what motivates that person—what their objectives are and what context they are operating in—or attribute to them a U.S. perspective that does not always translate well.

When doing business overseas, you have to remember that you have to change your mindset, says Jeffrey Paulsen, formerly of Brunswick Bowling and Billiards Corp.:

> The United States is contract driven—and our court system is geared to that. Going to China? You have to *think* Chinese. You have to adopt the mindset that I can't pound table and win every point for my client. Although in a deal with the Japanese, their lawyer wanted to win every single point on the deal because Japan is a culture that cares about the details. In Asia, it's about the relationship. A lot of food—eating and drinking. You can barely communicate, but you are still all there together. Getting to know you on a personal level is all about establishing trust and a win-win mentality. Without that, a JV [joint venture] is destined to fail. You have to learn what battles to fight and which ones not to. How to tell the difference? Ask, what is this relationship about? What are the chances you will actually end up litigating over this point?

Over the last 15 years, Mills has observed that successful Japanese companies that came over to the United States spent time learning about how to "Americanize" everything from the nicknames they would use instead of their Japanese names, to spending time with English and other "little niceties."

One of Mills' clients demonstrated how this principle works when you are a U.S. firm trying to acclimate to a foreign culture. In Japan, where you sit in a room depends on, or is a direct function of, your status. So if in the context of a meeting, one of the American delegation sat in the chairman's spot, the chairman would not be upset, but a little perplexed. This is because in his cultural context, the chairman should not have to sit near the door. That, of course, is foreign to American cultural custom. While this example is not something that could stop a deal in its tracks, other cultural faux pas certainly can. That being the case, having someone on the negotiating team who can help you avoid such unnecessary and embarrassing roadblocks, given all that has been invested to get you to this point, should be strongly considered.

Otherwise, you may find yourself in a situation similar to that recounted by Karen Klein, formerly of Kayak.com. Early in her career, her firm's client was buying a company from a foreign banking conglomerate. A partner for the law firm Klein was working for made what he thought was the innocuous remark, "assuming you have disclosed everything." The other side proceeded to pack their bags, insulted by the implication that they had not been forthcoming. The partner was not trying to be an "ugly American." He simply had no idea what effect his casual, offhand comment would have. Clemens Ceipek, of LexisNexis, says that from the European point of view, U.S. lawyers are perceived as having "a certain level of arrogance . . . that they believe the U.S. way is superior and that they just *know*." On the other hand, says Ceipek, "Europeans realize people aren't the same."

Cultural sensitivity is very important in India, as well, reports an expert at doing business in India. In one instance, a Western woman greeted an Indian man with a kiss on the cheek. She, of course, meant nothing sexual or offensive by it, but it literally broke down a meeting. The woman simply could not understand why the man became so aggressive. The lesson: do not play into foreign stereotypes by doing something that is taboo in another culture; take time to learn the social and cultural rules of the road in the venue in which you are operating.

In India, for example, it is not a good idea to call people by their first name. The culture values people being called by one's title and last name. The American custom of quick familiarity will leave many Indians ill at ease. That having been said, Indians like to acquaint their business partners with their family and friends.

In China, given the complexity of the business culture and many points of difference with American business practices, lawyer Richard Wageman argues simply "you need experienced local Chinese personnel on your team." Dr. Liu is perhaps a little less emphatic. From his perspective, "you have to have someone bicultural; someone who actually knows China and who has integrity. Chinese-Americans who have done business there for a long time are a good choice, but they don't necessarily need to be of Chinese ancestry."

Cohen explains that having someone on the team who is also familiar with *local* business culture is important, as well. Your Chinese partner, for instance, might tell you, "you don't have to do X," that is, they will just cut through the red tape for you. The problem is that their "tape cutting" does not necessarily get things done correctly under applicable laws and regulations. Many experienced businesspeople will tell you that the Chinese government might well treat enforcement issues against a Western company differently than it would where only a Chinese company is involved. In fact, says Cohen, "what you need is Chinese counsel on your side."

Pre-Negotiation Preparation

Once you have assembled your team, it is necessary to develop a negotiation strategy. The key is to develop flexible but defined goals based on the due diligence and strategic analysis described in previous chapters of this text. Chenevert observes that the entire due diligence process can be distilled to a book of issues that gets reviewed by in-house management. That book then can become the basis of negotiations between the parties. It includes issues such as necessary warranties, price, and potential liabilities.

It is important to identify the basic provisions that you want included in the contract so that you can push for concessions on these terms from the outset and evaluate where the other side is likely to generate resistance.[3] In other words, what are your "must haves"? Warren Reid suggests (at least in the context of IT outsourcing) that you especially consider the following:

> Scope of responsibilities and services; third-party services; project managers; project development standards and acceptance; project timetables and milestones; progress reports and meetings; problem resolution and escalation of differences; acquisition of systems and facilities; interim acceptance testing; final acceptance testing; service warranty; proprietary rights cross indemnity; documentation; training; fees; change orders; personnel; company's proprietary rights; exceptions; physical security and backup; customer access and copying rights; termination; general provisions including taxes, insurance, most favored provisions; *force majeure*, severability, right to offset, transfer of software licenses; ownership of developed software; . . . and specific concrete definitions and scenarios for those things with multiple interpretations."[4]

Again, this is hardly an exhaustive list: you need to return the strategic analysis of your own steering committee and the results of your due diligence to capture the most important terms and issues for your particular situation. Having developed these core issues, you can construct "best case," "acceptable case" and, if need be, "walk away" scenarios.

As you prepare for initial negotiations to begin, it also makes sense to conduct an analysis of the vendor or partner's position. What are their likely goals? What are their "must haves?" Are any of their "must haves" antithetical to yours, such that a deal is not practically possible? It is better for you to find that out sooner rather than later, so that an alternate vendor or partner can be located, if possible. Do they have any other—perhaps more attractive—options than working with you? If so, the extent to which you

---

3. Warren S. Reid, *Outsourcing: The 20 Steps to Success* 4 (1996), http://www.wsrcg.com/Articles/OutSourcing.pdf.
4. *Id.* at 5.

choose to be aggressive in your insistence on anything other than your "must haves" should perhaps be revisited.

Gill recalls that in the early 1990s, management would stress that there should not be any deviation from Motorola's standard terms of contract. The salespeople were instructed, "this is how we do business at Motorola." For instance, Motorola generally insisted that the governing law of the sales contract be U.S. law. Although there might be some customers that would push back and insist on Mexican law, for instance, the company could largely dictate terms.

This changed by the late 1990s. Customers started telling Motorola, "this is how *we* do business." What changed? By then they had someplace else to go. At that time, Gill attended an "auction" for a customer in Argentina that was putting together the first digital cell phone system in South America. Siemens was in Room A, Motorola was in Room B, and Lucent was in Room C. The buyers' representatives moved from one room to the next saying that "if you won't give us this price point, we'll just go down the hall." And the buyer's contract was in Spanish.

On the other hand, deal making is often about finding the proverbial "win-win" solution. Gill reflects that in her Motorola deals, if the standard warranty on a given product was 15 months and the buyer wanted one for 36 months, the team would either figure out what the cost of offering the longer warranty was and adjust the price accordingly, or say no and stay with the lower price. Likewise, the warranty might call for free replacement parts for 7 years, and the RFP might demand them for 21 years. Again, the team would need to calculate the cost and adjust the price. It is likely that such adjustments may need to be made in your own transaction. Identifying likely contention points and being prepared to make quick and accurate calculations on compromise points will assist you during negotiations. As always, preparation is key.

Understanding the Effects of Cross-Cultural Issues

A general manager of a manufacturing company doing business in China explains that to understand how cross-cultural issues affect transactions, it is useful to think of a cross-border transaction as the beginning of a personal relationship. In a business context, Americans, for example, rush right in with a proposal, "I want a joint venture with you." This gentleman cautions that in many cultures this is considered too abrupt. It is not unlike being on a first date and saying directly, "I want to sleep with you."

Knoblauch agrees. He advises that you have to spend weeks or months building personal relationships with potential business partners. Acquisitions in Japan have only been possible for the past 10 to 15 years. Until recently the tradition-bound Japanese culture could never begin to contemplate the sale of businesses to foreigners, because selling the businesses often involves handing over employees. If you, as a foreign buyer, cause the business to fail and jeopardize the employees, then the former Japanese business owners lose face in the community.

Americans often assume that the sole purpose of a corporation is to turn a profit, observes Chenevert. But outside of the United States, in Southeast Asia, for example, companies are perceived as units of societal governance. That is, they are a means of providing employment and goods and services to society. Companies there may have daycare facilities, nurseries, medical clinics, and schools for the benefit of employees. American companies like to avoid acquiring the responsibility for these facilities, but for the sellers, guaranteeing that such peripheral services will continue is often very important.

In India, where there is much more of a socialist societal arrangement, capitalism can be looked on as exploitative. How do you deal with this issue? Chenevert notes that you can negotiate adjustments to the selling price that will allow for the duty for these services to be shifted onto other providers.

"Some people are still doing business in China as if it was still the nineteenth century," Dr. Liu reflects. In the twenty-first century in China, Liu explains,

> if you try to generalize about anything, you fail. Be ready for anything and expect the unexpected. China is like a big elephant, and those who generalize are like blind men individually trying to figure out what it is. Some think it is all trunk, others that it is only a big body, and still others that it is just all feet. But China today ranges from the coastal areas that are ultramodern, to Tibet, which is in many ways just as it was in the 19th century. You need to understand the local customs or ethos.

Peoples in different regions of the world will act and react differently, says Paulsen:

> Asians tend to be more reserved. They will never say no. You have to figure out whether they meant yes or no. Latin Americans are more outgoing; they tend to wear their feelings on their sleeves. No matter where you are, the most important things to ask when trying to understand your foreign business partners is what drives them. What's their background and life experiences?

Assuming that your team negotiates at least a part of the deal in the foreign location, they probably will have a lot of adjustments to make. Chenevert observes that they may not be used to the local food, they may be suffering from jet lag, they may not be fluent in the local language, and in some instances, they may be intimidated to be the only Americans at the negotiating table.

Still, the team needs to focus objectively on the facts before them. As Klein points out, it is possible that the other side will attempt to use cultural differences to posture and drive a wedge between lawyer and client. It is important that American lawyers learn to ask more questions and get a feel for local customs. Do not just assume that everything works the same way as it does in the United States.

The vendor or partner's team has adjusting to do, as well. For instance, Klein noted that her European counterparts were not used to the same litigiousness that exists in the United States and were shocked by the detail of U.S. contracts. The Europeans had drafted a settlement agreement without a release, because in their jurisdiction, releases are not sought.

While cultural sensitivity is essential, it can be overdone—to your client company's detriment. "Sometime, U.S. firms go too far to acclimate and demonstrate vulnerability or weakness," warns Hallab. Being overly deferential opens the door to concessions. How do you know where the dividing line is between appropriate sensitivity and overcompensating? "This is an art, not a science," replies Hallab. His answer suggests that a good local counsel be relied on to discern when you are running into a legitimate cultural disconnect versus mere posturing for bargaining advantage.

Ability to Commit

Before negotiations begin, make sure that both sides either have the ultimate decision maker present, or at a minimum, have quick access to that person or group of people. Dr. Liu cautions that in China, nothing gets done unless you know the real decision maker. There are many pitfalls. With a state-owned enterprise, you might deal with one person and in a few months, he is gone—promoted—and you have to start over dealing with someone else. And that person might delay or table your deal if he is not happy. The Chinese central government might try to set up a system of laws, but at its essence, business in China is still about relationships. No government can regulate human nature.

The U.S. business team must also have authority to act, particularly if a compromise is necessary to save a deal. Gill recalls that the Motorola team would have a certain amount of authority to compromise on terms. There were occasions when the buyer's terms were such that they would have to call back to management and ask the ultimate question: "How badly do you want this deal?"

Choosing Location, Timing, and Language

Before negotiations can begin, logistics must be considered. Where will negotiations take place? On what schedule? In what language(s)?

In many instances, you may find your options limited. You may try to insist that negotiations take place in your offices so that disruptions to your management's schedule are minimized, and you may even be in the bargaining position to have your way. Consider, however, whether you achieve a pyrrhic victory by doing so. If having the negotiations in the United States causes the vendor/partner to leave behind key members of their negotiating team, the pace of negotiations may slow to a crawl, or even stop, as the team present has to seek authority or obtain information from halfway around the world.

On the other hand, some foreign entities may take active advantage of the venue (by way of jet lag, unfamiliar food, reduced communication capacity, etc.) in order to gain an unfair advantage in negotiations. Sometimes, choosing a neutral site can be an effective compromise. In others, your people will simply have to do their best in an unfamiliar forum but should adequately prepare themselves for it to the extent possible by adjusting arrival times, acclimating to local cuisine, and so forth.

The timing and pace of negotiations may also be outside of your control to a great extent. Many U.S. businesspeople are shocked by the relative slowness of business dealings in other cultures. Again, Americans' perceived impatience to move forward at breakneck speed with a deal can be used against them by shrewd foreign negotiators. In many instances, Americans just have to learn to adjust and make their plans accordingly. Bhalla, of EXL, points out that you have to consider the speed at which both organizations involved in a given transaction operate. Bhalla has seen rather small deals take many months to complete. He has also seen complex, large contracts get negotiated in 30 to 45 days.

There are also times when, because of local holidays or events, business will be virtually impossible to conduct. Dole gives the example of cricket in India. You do not schedule a meeting when there is a cricket championship going on, any more than you would schedule a meeting in the United States on Super Bowl Sunday.

Language, of course, can also present an issue in negotiations. Some experts insist that it is becoming less of an issue as transactions around the world are more often being done in English. That is not to say that you can always assume there will be no language gap between the parties. In China, Chenevert relates, a challenge can arise when the senior manager for the client is not fluent in Mandarin, for instance.

Cultural and language issues can slow things down, even if you do your best to prepare for them. "If you have a willing buyer and a willing seller though," says Chenevert, "you can get past a lot."

The Agenda: Who Proposes and Who Responds?

Sometimes for strategic reasons, a party may see value in attempting to set and control the negotiating agenda. Some view this tactic as maximizing their opportunities for wresting concessions from the other side. Indeed, as Mills points out, "everybody wants the controlling chip. Both sides of the table want the trump card." Still, control of the agenda may not be as advantageous as it might otherwise appear.

It is probably fair to say that the party with the greater bargaining power is likely to have the ability to unilaterally set the agenda—if it so chooses. Often it is the customer who sends the contract. The first level of negotiations takes place on a commercial level, relying heavily on schedules. Issues that then get discussed are ones the buyer is concerned about, like enforceability of intellectual property (IP) and circumstances that lead to awards of damages and injunctive relief. Still, do not become too surprised if you find more sophisticated vendors beginning to approach negotiations as the Western companies do.

The point is that even if you have the ability to dominate the agenda setting, it may be a bad idea. Clearly, it is important to make sure that the agenda is such that you are given an opportunity to raise your issues, questions, and concerns. It is equally important that the vendor/partner be given an opportunity to do the same, otherwise issues may arise in the implementation phase that should have been addressed in negotiations but were never recognized. In fact, given the predilection of some cultures to avoid open disputes and reach consensus, you may actually find it beneficial to set the agenda in such a way as to encourage the other side to raise issues and concerns in order to avoid nasty surprises later on, and to encourage a true sense of business partnership.

In putting together the agenda, consider what paradigm will most likely lead to reaching an agreement. Do you start with an attempt to reach an accord on the "big picture" level to gain momentum before dealing with details? Or does a slow build-up to the bigger issues make more sense? Hallab says that, as with many things in international transactions, it depends—in this case, on the nature of the deal on which you are working. "An infinite number of factors" go into the decision, Hallab says.

The leverage profile of the parties is a big factor, and at different stages in the negotiations, the approach you might take will morph. If either party *needs* a deal, this of course changes the landscape of the negotiation. Many parties initially have more leverage early in negotiations, but as opportunities dwindle, so does their bargaining advantage, notes Hallab. Overall, Hallab prefers to get big issues out of the way at the start. This tends to generate momentum that hopefully can enable the parties to overcome disagreements on small issues.

Six Tips for Negotiating the Cross-Border Deal

Months of preparation and planning have brought you to the negotiating table. Awareness of the following six general areas will help you master the intricacies and idiosyncrasies of the cross-border transaction.

Tip 1: Monitor Information Exchange

As noted above, in some instances, negotiations will be held mostly or entirely in English. In others, translators will be needed. Regardless, misunderstandings because of language are likely to occur unless you carefully and consistently make certain that both sides correctly understand what is being communicated to them.

When the opposing side does not have enough competence in English to conduct negotiations without a translator, the interpreter is a key player and must be chosen with great care. After all, all information in the negotiations goes through him or her. In one meeting that took place in China, for instance, the gentleman there on behalf of the U.S. company recognized that the interpreter was not accurately translating what the parties were saying. He was actually going beyond conveying what he was hearing and doing the actual negotiation himself by misrepresenting what the other side said!

Whatever country you are working in, a good translator needs to understand both the native culture and U.S. culture. Knoblauch relates that while at UL, he hired Ernst & Young investment bankers to facilitate financing and put together a deal, working with a bicultural colleague, Wayne Aoki, based in Honolulu. Aoki speaks both English and Japanese. He became so well trusted by the other side that by the end of negotiations, he had moved to the other side of the table! Knoblauch does not consider that a problem. In these kinds of transactions, he holds that a contract in a business relationship is like a prenuptial agreement is to a marriage. If you hold back anything from your partner, it is like putting poison in this system. In Japan, Knoblauch asserts, the deal will not hinge on the monetary terms. Instead, trust is built by sharing information.

Knoblauch recalls another occasion in which he was working on a venture in Amsterdam with a family-owned business. Seven children from the family were involved. The deal again involved complicated financing, as well as local regulatory issues. But this time, there was no colleague like Aoki to step in, and the transaction was infinitely more complicated.

Remember, however, that just because someone from another part of the world is fluent enough in English to be conversational, they might still be unaware of the cultural significance of words and phrases. Moreover, many cultures value consensus and harmony, and if you are not careful, you may believe you have reached agreement on a critical point while the other side is only politely listening to your position.

In dealing with potential partners from China, for instance, Michel Feldman, of Seyfarth, Shaw, notes that you might sit through a set of negotiations with them without hearing any objections to your points. That does not mean, however, that they are in agreement with your positions. They will later explain that their silence means that they neither agreed nor disagreed with your terms, part of a cultural value of saving face. So one thing that Feldman always does is to periodically stop and say, "Let me summarize what we have agreed to." If the parties are not on the same page, Feldman explains, "we can go back and address the open issues before more negotiation takes place on the assumption that there is agreement where there is none."

Similarly, when negotiating in India, Shrikar Dole, formerly of EEPC and now JD Director General of the Federation of Indian Export Organisations, cautions you to remember that "yes does not always mean yes." That is, saying yes does not always mean I agree; it may just be acknowledging what the other person is saying. Dole also recommends going back and making certain that your Indian counterpart actually understands and agrees with your point before you move on to the next one. Because this takes time, Dole concludes, expect the pace of negotiations to be slower than in the West.

Hand gestures, too, may have different meanings across cultures. For instance, nodding one's head up and down does not necessarily mean assent, and moving the head from side to side might not express disagreement in the culture with which you are dealing. Also, be careful that what to you may seem like an innocent gesture, such as the "thumbs up" sign, is not considered a disrespectful or obscene one by your counterparts.

A contrasting view is offered by Hallab. In his experience (involving East Asia, the Middle East, and Europe), translators are used less often than you would think—"it is extraordinarily rare today," Hallab says. He admits that translation is sometimes needed but warns that in Asia, for instance, it is important to be aware that the suggestion that someone cannot speak English well might cause him or her to lose face. The point is that the decision to involve translators needs to be made on a case-by-case basis and in consultation with your prospective business partner.

Tip 2: Engage in Creative Give and Take to Save Deals and Build Relationships

Not unlike business within the United States, sometimes to save a deal you have to get creative. Perhaps the payment terms have to be adjusted. This option depends on the price of providing the money for a given period of time. Other circumstances might involve modifying the terms of the transfer of title and the transfer of the risk of loss. Sometimes you can also provide something outside of the specific terms of the commercial arrangement—within the parameters of U.S. and local law, of course. In some circumstances, offering extra training classes for workers or a perk for the local community at a relatively low cost can help to develop the relationship. There are any number of examples, but the core issue is finding out what the other side cares about and addressing the need to build trust and move past potential snags on the commercial terms.

When talks break down, the key negotiators are the leaders of the respective delegations. Knoblauch recalls at least two or three situations he was involved with where both sides were frustrated enough that everybody was ready to give up and go home without a deal. According to Knoblauch, the fix in such a circumstance is

> having the two CEOs go play a round of golf, or go to dinner. At that point one or the other needs to face his counterpart and ask bluntly, "Do we want to do this deal or not?" Assuming they do, they will find a reasonable resolution to the sticking point, and then reconvene the negotiating teams to continue their work.

There will be instances, of course, where some other senior executive company is your representative, but the point holds true regardless—deadlocks are best broken up by the leaders of both organizations. Hallab notes that the best way to avoid the collapse of negotiations over a major point is to identify the key terms and have those agreed to before even beginning the principal-to-principal discussions.

Tip 3: Know When to Pause and Regroup

You will occasionally find yourself in a negotiating round with players from around the world who know how to use culture and bargaining techniques that will frankly set you back on your heels. Knoblauch, for instance, reflects that in his experience, Korean companies are extremely clever and skilled negotiators (even in Asia where many cultures pride themselves on their negotiating skills). As he puts it,

> They would employ various techniques to "jerk you around." They would set up a meeting for 9 a.m. and not begin until 2 p.m. They were constantly doing things to keep you off balance. They would send in a team that would hang on to certain parts on a deal, and finally give in. Then they would send in an entirely new team who would "forget" about the concessions the previous team had made. There were often 4–5 factions in their team. It was hard to keep them all happy; they tended to conflict with one another.

Much as a sporting team that finds itself "playing someone else's game" or style of play—and having trouble dealing with it—you may occasionally need to take a time out and redirect both the tempo and the focus of the negotiations so that a level playing field is re-established.

Tip 4: Factor in the Unanticipated

"International deals are fluid," says Mills, of Deloitte. You can always count on encountering something—perhaps many somethings—that do not work according to plan. Perhaps the CEO of the vendor or partner leaves, taking with them the understanding and emotional goodwill the parties have built up. Assuming that this departure does not affect the underlying premise for doing the deal, you must carry on negotiations that allow for a sustainable relationship with the new head of the company,[5] just as you would do in a deal at home.

It is a fast-changing world in many respects, whether we are talking about the demands of your customers, your vendor or partner's capabilities, or the regulatory climate in which you operate. Recognize that contract provisions need not only to incorporate defined metrics but a willingness to adapt the terms of the contract to reflect changing circumstances, because problems are bound to arise that could not be foreseen when the contract was awarded.[6]

Knoblauch relates that in Japan, for example, deals are still done primarily by a handshake. If circumstances change, then the relationship changes to take that into account. It is the ongoing relationship, not the contract, that is the focus of Japanese entities. That approach ought to, and does in his experience, lead to less litigation in Japan. German and Indian companies, Knoblauch observes, have been relatively more litigious than the Japanese and Chinese companies. (It is probably fair to say that no other society at this point compares to the United States in litigiousness.)

Tip 5: Know When to Come to Agreement on the Issues—or Not

"You shouldn't think of an international deal as if it were a U.S. deal," Knoblauch advises. The main question in an international deal, from his perspective, is: "Does the ongoing relationship have good profit potential?" If so, he continues,

> don't get completely focused on how much you are paying. A "really good deal" is good because of the fundamentals, the strategic fit, the chemistry, etc., not on the projected return on investment. Anyone can come up with attractive internal rates of return, but the critical relationships and chemistry will mean far, far more.

---

5. Mark Hollands, *Deal or No Deal*, 3 THE OUTSOURCING INSTITUTE (2005), http://www.outsourcing.com/content.asp?page=01b/other/oe/q405/dornod.html&nonav=false.
6. R.D. Elsey, *Contract Management Guide*, CHARTERED INSTITUTE OF PURCHASING & SUPPLY (October 2007) 4, http://www.cips.org/documents/cips_ki_contract%20management%20guidev2.pdf.

While this thinking may seem counterintuitive, and a far cry from current standard practice in the United States, Knoblauch says, "don't ignore the financial projections but don't become a slave to them either." The world of international business operates quite differently, with intuition and insight often more important than arithmetic. At the very least, even if you are typically an aggressive, "take no prisoners" type of negotiator, you may want to keep the bigger picture in mind as you haggle over nonessential terms.

"People new to these deals need help recognizing something else," adds Chenevert:

> Until the deal is done, you always have the option to pull the plug if it no longer seems worth doing. It's like buying a house. If you become psychologically committed too soon, you lose your negotiating leverage and accept aspects of the deal you never would have when you were thinking clearly. OK, so you may have invested months of sweat and incurred thousands of dollars in expenses on negotiations with someone; don't be afraid to shoot it in the head like a lame horse if you have to. Don't be afraid to walk away from a potential deal. A deal is only worth doing if it is a good deal for your company. Remember, the thorny problems that come to light during the negotiations will not go away after you close the deal.

Tip 6: Avoid Doing Too Good a Job: Is the Deal Fair to Both Sides?

Not so long ago, vendors such as Indian IT suppliers did not push back if confronted with demanding customers. Today, however, savvy customers are not necessarily happy when vendors "roll over" on "hard" clauses. Experienced vendors today actually know the consequences of harsh contract clauses.

Whether you are in India, China, Pakistan, or Peru, the simple reality is that while you understandably want the best deal you can get, the people across the table also have to make a reasonable profit for a deal to succeed. Risk avoidance must be factored into the transaction, or, as has been observed elsewhere, inadequate profit margins may lead your vendor or partner to "opportunistic behavior."[7]

Mark Hollands reports that a widely held view of consultants he interviewed was that "in the most extreme cases, user organisations set their service providers up for failure, believing they have legal recourse if service levels are not reached."[8] As we will see in the next chapter, if that's the game a client company is playing, they may be sadly disappointed with the actual legal recourse available to them.

Vendors can also be slow to know when to end a transaction. They may hope to use your client's transaction as a sort of a "loss leader" to obtain more volume or more profitable business. If that does not pay off, it is not surprising that they start putting resources toward other clients' work that will make them money—and service to your client significantly drops in quality.[9] As Hollands points out,

> everything comes back to the way the commercial relationship is established at the start of the negotiation. If you do not get that right, if each party does not understand each other's needs and motivations, then there will be issues down the track.[10]

At the same time, it is also fair to ask just how willing or able this vendor or partner is to be flexible and accommodate your needs. It is reasonable to assume that if they cannot or will not listen and work cooperatively with you in the course of negotiations, you are likely to see more of the same as the relationship develops.[11]

---

7. Dr. Leslie P. Wilcocks, *Myth Understanding*, 3 THE OUTSOURCING INSTITUTE (Winter 2005), http://www.outsourcing.com/content.asp?page=01b/other/oe/q405/mythunderst.html&nonav=false.
8. Hollands, *supra* note 5.
9. *Id.*
10. *Id.*
11. Reid, *supra* note 3, at 7.

Getting More Specific: Some Current Key Issues

Depending on your industry and the nature of the subject transaction, you may have many more specific items to address during negotiations. Again, the following issues are hardly meant to be all-encompassing, but they highlight some of the more recognized issues that may or may not have application to your deal.

Benchmarking

Naturally, benchmarking primarily has arisen out of IT transactions. Nevertheless, in the metrics-mad business climate of today, extrapolated application to other industries is not hard to imagine. "Don't underestimate the need to ensure the quality of the product," Samir Gandhi, of Sidley Austin, warns.

> You will need to think about how you can adjust the scope of the agreement to accomplish the necessary oversight to accomplish this. You will need to develop benchmarks. You will need to demand practical audit rights. This will include the right to conduct on-site inspections, receipt of regular productivity reports, and quality audits. Communication is important in this context. How easy is it to communicate with the vendor? Does the difference in time zone or language create barriers to interaction? Do they listen and are they responsive to you? How well do they respond to criticism? What happens if the vendor can't deliver adequate quality?

Chocko Valliappa, CEO of Bangalore-based business process outsourcing (BPO) provider Vee Technologies, does not quarrel about having benchmarks for service or quality levels; he just advises against setting those benchmarks at an unrealistic level (i.e., overengineering) in light of the overall deal being negotiated. "You can set up operations to be 100 percent fool proof," Valliappa explains, "but then the cost becomes high." On the other hand, if a service-level agreement (SLA) requires 98 percent accuracy levels and his firm hits the target, the remaining 2 percent sometimes "gets magnified to a great extent." Keeping a realistic set of expectations based on the level of service or product you are actually paying for will make for a smoother relationship as time goes on. As John McCormick, of Accenture, says, "there is no Porsche for $5000."

Benchmarking can be good for vendors, too, if, for instance, it is found that, based on the metrics, the vendor has exceeded required service levels. They can then ask for more on the succeeding contract to adjust for this.[12] Common sense dictates that benchmarks of some kind are needed in a modern business environment. They simply need to be used in such a way as to create a win-win proposition for both parties, not as a sledgehammer to beat further concessions out of a vendor or partner.[13]

Service-Level Agreements—Terms and Penalties

Service-level agreements (also known as master service agreements or MSAs) are defined by the Financial Services Roundtable as

> contractual arrangements that give U.S. firms a mechanism to specify detailed performance requirements and metrics for their vendors. Individual SLAs within a contract often cover required performance levels, monitoring arrangements, frequency of audits, privacy and security practices, and, in some cases, remedies or procedures for handling any failure to meet contractual requirements.[14]

The general scope of this book does not allow for any kind of exhaustive listing of basic provisions, which will obviously vary depending on the industry involved and other unique circumstances of the parties. As just one example, Bhalla, of EXL, notes that most high-level BPO agreements cover such issues as IP, confidentiality, security, performance, scope, and termination.

One general issue worth considering in negotiating your agreement is the extent to which the SLA should dictate means and methods of producing

---

12. Hollands, *supra* note 5.
13. *Id.*
14. INFORMATION POLICY INSTITUTE, HOW SAFE AND SECURE IS IT? AN ASSESSMENT OF DATA PRIVACY AND SECURITY IN BUSINESS PROCESS OUTSOURCING FIRMS IN INDIA, FINANCIAL SERVICES ROUNDTABLE 16 (2005).

the subject product or service. Some clients have a very particular need for specific processes or methods. However, if you are open to exploring the innovative capabilities or fresh thinking of your new vendor or partner, you may wish to let them control more of the production methods while you focus oversight on the end result. As Exervio Management Consulting notes, whether to do this is a function of the client's risk tolerance.[15]

If innovation from the provider or partner is desired, it is only reasonable that compensation for that value-add is accounted for in the agreement between the parties. In a traditional gain sharing arrangement,

> the vendor gains if it controls costs, but the client does not provide an incentive for it to add value. Both parties agree to the cost-of-service, and the vendor updates the customer on an ongoing basis of those costs. If the cost turns out to be higher than anticipated, the customer pays the provider the difference. If costs are lower than expected, the provider and customer share the difference according to some agreed-upon percentage split.[16]

A fixed-price agreement, by contrast, "rewards the vendor for improving the process, which is usually measured in reduced costs, greater productivity or improved efficiency."[17]

Where a client concludes that a macromanagement, as opposed to micromanagement, approach is desirable, one way to achieve this is to appoint a business manager to oversee the vendor, not a technical person who thinks he or she has a better way of doing things.[18]

Exit Strategy

Given the distances involved and the peculiarities of foreign legal systems, you may find that disengaging from a faraway vendor or business partner may be more difficult than it would appear at first blush. One way

---

15. Exervio Management Consulting, *Do You Really Want to Outsource that Process?*, 4 (May 2004), http://www.exervio.com/docs/Do%20You%20Really%20Want%20To%20Outsource%20That%20Process.
16. *Id.* at 5.
17. *Id.*
18. Hollands, *supra* note 5.

to minimize this is to use a nearshoring alternative.[19] In any event, you should negotiate protocols for what materials, equipment, and data are to be returned at the end of the pact, regardless of whether it ends by mutual or unilateral agreement.[20] Timetables, assignment of costs associated with the handover of various items, and terms of confidentiality are among the issues that should be discussed at the time of contracting,[21] rather than leaving these issues unresolved until such time as the parties are actually separated and may be less than amicable or cooperative with each other.

Indemnification for Compliance with New or Changed Regulations

Given the amorphous nature of regulatory affairs in many developing countries, a great deal of attention is being paid to the division between the parties of the responsibility for compliance with new or changed regulations affecting the subject transaction. Chenevert gives an example of a situation where the Chinese government was rolling out new construction equipment regulations. It required manufacturers to make adjustments to products sold there in order to comply with changes in emissions, warranties, and so on. Before that, there had been no rules on these things. Now it is an ongoing part of doing business there. Who pays for such adjustments? This again is an issue that would be best considered and discussed among the parties before the transaction goes forward, rather than at a point where costs suddenly manifest themselves and decisions then need to be made quickly.

Structuring a Joint Venture

With regard to many of the issues discussed in this book, I found very little disagreement among the experts. That was not true when it came to how to structure a joint venture—and more particularly, how to divide up control of the new entity.

Cohen insists that his clients either maintain a 51-percent ownership share or at least determine what items they can retain veto power over. In his view, this allows his clients to maintain control over at least those

---

19. Dominic Conlon, *Nearshore/Offshore Outsourcing, Part II: Implementation*, A&L GOOD-BODY (April 12, 2005), http://www.hg.org/articles/article_1171.html.
20. *Id.*
21. *Id.*

issues that matter to them as the transaction moves forward. Hallab agrees, noting that a large percentage of JVs are set up on a 50/50 control basis. Hallab does not mince words, calling such arrangements "a lawyer's biggest nightmare." He adds, "people commit without thinking about control, terms and conditions."

Perhaps because of his entrepreneurial bent, Knoblauch takes the opposite approach:

> 50/50 JVs are the only ones that work. You could set up 80/20 in your favor, but you don't really have control. If you can't get true cooperation, then you have nothing. Even a 51/49 arrangement sows the seeds of discontent. It gives you the delusion that you have the power. It doesn't matter how hard the issue is. We did a JV in India with Tata Industries; it was one of the first high tech JVs with an Indian company. Tata would not do anything other than a 50/50 JV. Later, they sold 20 percent of the JV to the market, but made a point of maintaining ownership at 40/40/20. On the surface, it's not efficient; but you have to remember something: you're doing business in *their* country. They have a million ways to get around your control if they want to. The Tatas were superb partners, people of unquestioned moral compass, and people who really and truly understood partnership. Finding a partner of this quality is far, far more important than the specifics of any deal you might choose to make.

Each of these men have many years of experience to back up their views. A middle position that suggests itself is a 50/50 JV distribution with limited veto rights over a discrete set of issues determined to be most critical to protecting your client company's ownership interests. Keep in mind that, depending on the industry and locale involved, the amount of your ownership interest and control over a foreign JV may be determined for you by local regulatory bodies.

Intellectual Property Issues

As noted in Chapter 8, review of local law is essential here. Some countries will not allow their nationals to waive their "moral rights" to such property;

in other places appropriate waivers must be drafted and executed with careful attention to governmental requirements.[22]

Some experienced Indian businesspeople suggest that foreign suppliers do not always take process as seriously as they should. "Indian court processes," one observes, "can be difficult." Kumkum Dalal, president of Global Reach Consulting, Inc. of Naperville, Illinois, agrees. One of her manufacturing vendors told her that from their perspective, it would not be in the interest of a high-caliber, successful vendor to steal a client's IP, particularly if one understands how the injunction process in India works:

> Having an injunction granted against the Indian business by an Indian court can be a death knell for the business. As injunctions are not hard to obtain, and with the Indian courts' slow-moving nature, it might take years to get the injunction removed.

The moral of the story is not to suggest management of a cross-border relationship through the Indian (or any other) legal system, but to reemphasize the importance of careful vendor selection and development of a relationship. Dalal points out that once a business relationship enters any court system, it becomes a lose-lose proposition for both sides.

Sarbanes-Oxley/U.S. Regulatory Issues

The Sarbanes-Oxley Act of 2002, or "SOX," as it is often called, has stricken fear into the heart of more than one public corporate officer. One of the legislation's many requirements, Section 404, imposes a duty "to evaluate the effectiveness of the company's internal controls and procedures over financial reporting and the related requirement for auditors to attest to management's evaluation."[23]

---

22. Caroline Horton Rockafellow, *Outsourcing Puts More Than Jobs at Risk: Firms' IP Rights Are Also Put on the Line*, TECHWIRE (March 31, 2004), http://www.wral.com/business/local_tech_wire/opinion/story/1155805/.
23. Robert Gareis & Michael S. Mensik, *Business Process Outsourcing Under Sarbanes-Oxley: Challenges and Complexities*, OUTSOURCING CENTER (April 2004), http://www.outsourcing-center.com/2004-04-business-process-outsourcing-under-sarbanes-oxley-challenges-and-complexities-article-37782.html.

The Securities and Exchange Commission's rules have set out a wide range of activities that fall within this requirement, including

> controls over initiating, recording, processing, and reconciling account balances; classes of transactions and disclosure and related assertions included in the financial statements; controls related to the initiation and processing of non-routine and non-systematic transactions; controls related to the selection and application of appropriate accounting policies; controls related to the prevention, identification, and detection of fraud.[24]

Regardless of whether you turn over complete operation control of a given company function to a third party, your management's SOX obligations are nondelegable and subject to criminal penalties including up to a $10 million personal fine or 20 years in prison.[25] Having processes in place to allow you to satisfy your SOX obligations is naturally of critical importance.

Where a vendor is considered part of the company's internal control over financial reporting, the U.S. client company's managers and auditors must evaluate the vendor's activities to "support its opinion on internal control."[26] One approach that gets inserted into negotiations requires the vendor to hire an independent auditor

> to review and report on the systems it uses to process the company's transactions or engage an auditor to test the effectiveness of the controls applied to the company's transaction to enable the auditor to evaluate controls of the supplier.[27]

The reason for this is simple: auditors are expensive, and customers do not want to have to pay for them.

---

24. Id.
25. Id.
26. Id.
27. Id.

That being said, as noted above, SOX duties are nondelegable, and there are some sensitive areas in which using a vendor's audit results should be avoided, including:

- Controls that are part of the control environment, including controls specifically established to prevent and detect fraud that are reasonably likely to result in material misstatement of the financial statements.
- Controls over the period-end financial reporting process, including controls over procedures used to enter transaction totals into the general ledger; to initiate, record, and process journal entries in the general ledger; and to record recurring and non-recurring adjustments to the financial statements (for example, consolidating adjustment, report combinations, and reclassifications).
- Controls that have a pervasive effect on the financial statements, such as certain information technology general controls on which the operating effectiveness of other controls depend.[28]

As Mike Mensik, of Baker & McKenzie, reminds us, all these issues require a basic understanding of what the compliance issues are and what the law requires. If some of these issues fall into uncertain, grey areas, Mensik relates, "you still need to agree who is going to do what." In terms of SOX, though, Mensik notes that there is often a complete disconnect between vendor and customer, as when customers concern themselves over a vendor's controls over its own processes. Mensik points out that the client customer should only concern itself with the vendor's controls that impact the activities the vendor is doing for the customer.

No set of negotiations will ever anticipate every possible problem that can arise in the real world, "so hit the obvious ones," Mensik advises. What negotiations can and really must do is generate agreement as to all foreseeable issues in a way that reflects the trust and goodwill that hopefully have by this point developed between the partners. Additionally, if done correctly, the proper groundwork will have been laid to help resolve

---

28. *Id.*

even unforeseeable issues as they arise—taking the interests of both parties into account in a spirit of fair dealing and compromise. Just like any good marriage.

Jeffrey Paulsen adds one final, important point:

> U.S. lawyers have to keep an open mind. We are trained in United States. That legal training doesn't always work well elsewhere. Some of the best U.S. lawyers won't be culturally attuned for handling a transaction in another country. To be effective internationally, yes, a lawyer must be competent of course but . . . the key to success is a strong sense of emotional and cultural intelligence. Getting a deal completed requires different skill sets from country to country and deal to deal.

This brings us full circle: always make sure you have the right people on your ark that possess the skills you need.

At this point then, you are ready to take the verbal terms of a hard-won deal and translate them into a written contract. That is the subject of the next chapter.

Chapter 11

Reducing the Agreement to Writing

In many respects, getting through the negotiations to the point where you are simply trying to memorialize an agreement means the battle has largely already been won—well, almost. As Don Chenevert, of Caterpillar, notes, "if the parties are both represented by competent counsel, both sides will continue to negotiate issues to the benefit of their client right to the end." There are cultural and, occasionally, language issues to overcome, as well. The purpose of this chapter is to help you navigate through the final obstacles and reach the agreement that will allow you to start conducting your overseas business.[1]

Start with Clarity

Perhaps the most important thing any written agreement should strive to accomplish is a clear description of all the "material aspects" of the contractual relationship, "including the rights, responsibilities and expectations of all parties."[2] It has rightly been observed that "a written contract is an important management tool and appropriate contractual provisions can

---

1. Note: This book provides what is hoped to be a helpful set of checklists and forms to compare against your final agreements in Appendixes A–I, reproduced by permission of their author, Harvey Cohen, of the Dinsmore & Shohl law firm.
2. Basel Committee on Banking Supervision, *Outsourcing in Financial Services*, THE JOINT FORUM, 2 (Feb. 2005), https://www.bis.org/publ/joint12.pdf.

reduce the risk of nonperformance or disagreements regarding the scope, nature and quality of the service to be provided."[3]

Contracts drafted in the United States, however, often have wording that attempts to address a particular state court's decision or otherwise relate to circumstances that have nothing to do with the transaction at hand in the subject jurisdiction. Lawyers may mindlessly copy this verbiage, or businesspeople may insist on familiar provisions. This, however, leads to draft agreements that are difficult to understand for lawyers speaking English as their first language, let alone businesspeople for whom English is a second, third, or fourth language. As Charles Hallab, of Baker & McKenzie, points out, there can be sensitivity on the part of foreign lawyers to such "overdrafting."

Therefore, in preparing your international agreement, examine all "boilerplate" provisions carefully and ask: Why is this here? Can we do without this language? Is there a better way to clearly express the parties' intentions without losing precision? Of course, this assumes that you are not dealing with a case in which ambiguity is placed in an agreement intentionally, either to the advantage of your client or to get around loggerheads. Moreover, Jeffrey Paulsen, formerly of Brunswick Bowling and Billiards Corp., reminds us that language in the document doesn't always translate exactly from one language to another. "Sometimes," he states, "you have to give up on producing a perfectly written document in order to get a business deal completed."

Hallab recounts the sale of company in the Philippines in which the local counsel drafted a purchase agreement that was "amusingly short," perhaps six or seven pages. That was not going to be acceptable to the sophisticated companies and counsel involved, Hallab says. Still, in his experience, more and more agreements appear similar, as foreign lawyers gain more international experience. For instance, a deal between two countries in the Persian Gulf used language that Hallab recognized as applicable in the state of Delaware.

---

3. *Id.* at 15.

Cultural and Language Issues: Ensuring a Meeting of the Minds

It is perhaps fortunate for Americans that we live in an age in which English is deemed to be the language of business across much of the world. As such, it is standard practice that contracts are written in English, although that fact does not eliminate all issues of language and culture in the drafting process.

"In drafting," reflects Harvey Cohen, of Dinsmore & Shohl, "people do use cultural differences to their advantage." When they do, he says, it is usually a provocation by one side or the other:

> If you hear the opposite party saying, "We use a simpler agreement," it probably allows them to avoid having to take responsibility in some area. Perhaps for example it has to do with who is responsible for servicing something. You need to make sure that you delineate who is responsible for that regardless.

Not all instances of misunderstandings are intentional, of course. If an agreement is written in English, the language skills of the vendor or partner's negotiating team may be relatively strong or weak.

Moreover, certain phrases that Americans commonly use, such as "as soon as possible," could have different cultural meanings elsewhere in the world. Good communication flow during the drafting process will help to identify potential language and cultural misunderstandings.

Hallab notes that in the Middle East, documents often have to be notarized in Arabic—a critical and sometimes overlooked point in this subject area. Generally, Hallab agrees that when dealing with non-Romance languages, making sure that contracts reflect a common understanding is quite important.

Use of Local Counsel

Should you call on local counsel to assist in drafting the final agreement? As with many other issues in the context of cross-border transactions, the answer likely depends on the issues involved and the nature and complexity of the subject transaction.[4] The coordinating counsel, or "quarterback," needs to "issue spot" for the client company and, when appropriate, locate and supervise the work of experienced local counsel. They should be able to provide in-depth knowledge of local law and procedure[5] to avoid potential problems arising from the effect of obscure or new legal authority on the subject transaction.

How much to rely on local counsel depends on cost, suggests Samir Gandhi, of Sidley Austin. Gandhi normally recommends that where having local counsel is advisable, they should be brought in early to let them do most of the work and talk through strategy with the rest of the negotiating team.

Overview of Key Provisions

As Hallab advises, counsel should anticipate where disputes will arise and prepare to draft accordingly. "A minor inconvenience today may save a major inconvenience tomorrow," he warns. Clearly, a client becoming embroiled in a multimillion-dollar dispute because they were unwilling to incur one day's attorney's fees in drafting is not a sensible choice.

The author recognizes the futility of trying to provide a definitive or all-inclusive listing of "must have" provisions that would apply to all transactions generally, regardless of circumstance. That being said, there are some basic terms and conditions that are appropriate and necessary in many, if not most, contexts involving cross-border transactions:

---

4. John Brockland, *Legal Briefs*, 3 THE OUTSOURCING INSTITUTE (2005), http://www.outsourcing.com/content.asp?page=01b/other/oe/q405/lawyers.html&nonav=false.
5. *Id.*

1. Clear definitions of all activities involved, including appropriate service and performance benchmarks in both quantitative and qualitative terms
2. Provisions for access to all books, records, and other data of the vendor or partner relevant to those activities
3. Clauses mandating continuing monitoring and assessment by the client entity of the vendor or partner's service or production to allow implementation of immediate corrective measures
4. Exit provisions (discussed further below)
5. Choice-of-law provisions and dispute resolution mechanisms (also discussed further below)
6. Conditions and limitations concerning (or prohibitions against) subcontracting of subject activities to third parties
7. Mechanisms for protection of the client entity's confidential or proprietary information (and that of customers or other protected third parties) from unauthorized disclosure
8. Clear integration of procedures needed for the client entity to satisfy its regulatory obligations to all appropriate agencies[6]

Which provisions prove to be most important may depend on what type of transaction you are trying to close. Patricia Gill, formerly of Motorola, says unequivocally that "the most important thing if you are selling overseas is that your contract terms should assure that you get paid!" She explains:

> Say the buyer contracts to make an initial payment, a second payment and then a final payment under the terms of an agreement. The buyer might balk on making the final payment, stating that he has received delivery of the equipment but it has not yet been installed.

Clearly, any ambiguity in timing of payment, or the conditions under which payments are due, can and likely will be used against you as a function of human nature.

---

6. Basel Committee on Banking Supervisions, *supra* note 2, at 15–17.

Choice of Law Issues

Experienced lawyers are generally familiar with conflict of law issues and recognize that it is of critical importance to clearly express what state or nation's law applies to disputes under a given contractual relationship. It should not be surprising, then, when companies doing business in a country whose laws have a reputation for weak or inconsistent legal enforcement of contracts would seek application of the law of another jurisdiction—usually their own.

In addition to specifying a given jurisdiction, reference to compliance with specific laws is a common practice. The Financial Roundtable reports that

> the U.S. financial services firms that we surveyed require contracts that provide both for U.S. jurisdiction over disputes as well as compliance with relevant U.S. laws, including The Gramm-Leach-Bliley Act (GLBA), the Fair Credit Reporting Act (FCRA), the Right to Financial Privacy Act (RFPA), the Sarbanes-Oxley Act (SOX), the Federal Debt Collections Practices Act (FDCPA), and the Health Insurance Portability and Accountability Act (HIPAA). U.S. regulators often have access to these vendor firms in principle; contracts and regulatory obligations transferred through contracts give U.S. agencies such as the Office of the Comptroller of the Currency (OCC) the power to audit vendors.[7]

Simply including a provision that the agreement will be interpreted under U.S. law does not solve all problems involving the intersection of multiple jurisdictions' laws, however. Local law may apply to the agreement notwithstanding the choice of law provisions it contains, such as data protection or liability limitation statutes.[8] The law of a given locality may also affect enforcement of rights under the contract,[9] as with the example of transferring intellectual property (IP) rights, which may impose formal requirements to be valid in China, for example, or with regards to tax or technology

---

7. INFORMATION POLICY INSTITUTE, HOW SAFE AND SECURE IS IT? AN ASSESSMENT OF DATA PRIVACY AND SECURITY IN BUSINESS PROCESS OUTSOURCING FIRMS IN INDIA, FINANCIAL SERVICES ROUNDTABLE 6 (2005).
8. *Id.* at 15.
9. Kevin C. Taylor, *Legal Briefs*, 3 THE OUTSOURCING INSTITUTE (2005), http://www.outsourcing.com/content.asp?page=01b/other/oe/q405/lawyers.html&nonav=false.

transfer.[10] As a German colleague of Baker & McKenzie's Michael Mensik once quipped, "choosing New York law doesn't get rid of British VAT laws."

Scope of Services

Especially where a client company is new, or relatively new, to outsourcing or otherwise operating overseas, the long-term success of a deal often depends on a clearly defined scope of services. Failure to reach a common understanding of which products and services fall within the boundaries of the agreed-upon terms—and which do not—causes friction and often ultimately the failure of relationships.

Even if the principal or "master" agreement has a clearly defined scope, many complex transactions have multiple additional agreements relating to various aspects of the arrangement. It is important that each of these supplemental or side agreements are carefully drafted to ensure that they do not create confusion—or that they do not contradict the scope of services in the master agreement.[11]

At the same time, at least some flexibility in terms can be helpful, if only because it is impossible in any given deal to anticipate every contingency that will occur. While this may seem like a contradiction, it is fairer to say that these qualities are on a continuum, and a good agreement allows for flexibility without causing undue confusion or ambiguity. In the outsourcing context, surveys suggest that one major reason for the failure of relationships is that a contract is either too rigid or too flexibly written.[12]

Lawyers Stuart Pergament and Linda L. Rhodes, of Mayer, Brown, Rowe & Maw, note that vendors generally seek to define scope of services with one of three things:

- A description that describes each category and each major subcategory of the services. This will generally be augmented by a matrix that covers

---

10. Brockland, *supra* note 4.
11. Mark Hollands, *Deal or No Deal*, 3 THE OUTSOURCING INSTITUTE (2005), http://www.outsourcing.com/content.asp?page=01b/other/oe/q405/dornod.html&nonav=false.
12. *8th Annual Outsourcing Index: Money Matters*, 3 THE OUTSOURCING INSTITUTE (2005), http://outsourcing.com/content.asp?page=01b/other/oe/q405/moneymatters.html&nonav=false.

the tasks for such categories and subcategories and allocates the related responsibilities to supplier, customer or both.
- A provision that acknowledges that all subtasks necessary to perform the services are included in the services.
- A provision that acknowledges responsibility for those services within such categories and subcategories that were performed in the last 12 months, to the extent that such services were confirmed during due diligence, the supplier is hiring the customer employees that were performing such services and the supplier has built in a reasonable risk premium to cover any potential gaps in the foregoing."[13]

According to Pergament and Rhodes, vendors also generally insist on "contract change language" that requires the parties to discuss scheduling and fees in light of a change in the client's requirements under certain circumstances.[14] These circumstances include

(a) the customer's request for new services or changes in services that are different from prior services, (b) certain performance failures by the customer (e.g., the failure to provide adequate or accurate information, the failure to perform timely any of its responsibilities) and/or its other service providers, (c) certain events that are not within the control of the parties (e.g., *force majeure* events experienced by the customer) or (d) a failure of assumptions in a statement of work not being realized in any material respect.[15]

Many vendors seek exclusivity provisions, sometimes extending to services beyond the terms of the contract. While this may provide the vendor with a source of stable revenue,[16] you should carefully consider the scope and terms of such provisions, as more than one company has found that

---

13. Stuart Pergament & Linda L. Rhodes, *Key Issues in Outsourcing: A Supplier's Perspective*, MONDAQ, http://www.mondaq.com/unitedstates/x/35446/Outsourcing/Key+Issues+In+Outsourcing+A+Suppliers+Perspective.
14. *Id.*
15. *Id.*
16. *Id.*

separating themselves from an unsatisfactory but exclusive distributor or supplier can be a costly and frustrating exercise.

Monitoring and Audits

Given the significant duties created by modern regulatory authorities, the Financial Services Roundtable recommends that contracts explicitly state that services performed be "subject to U.S. regulatory requirements and examination," and that English-language copies of contracts, diligence-related materials, and audit reports, among other materials, be maintained for inspection.[17]

Although client companies in the United States have nondelegable duties under regulatory schemes such as SOX, including the monitoring of information technology IT security measures, according to some experts, few companies—some say as low as 10 percent to 20 percent—bother to actively audit vendor security measures.[18] Ken Wheatley, vice president, corporate security, at Sony Electronics, says that client companies "assume that people in different countries have the same mind-set and safeguards and sense of due diligence, and that's just not the case."[19] Bottom line: given the serious legal consequences of failing to meet regulatory obligations, a contractual right to audit, coupled with specific procedures written into the contract, is a must—and should be followed up with continuing diligence.

Terms that mandate appropriate, audited security measures and any required registrations and compliance with import/export technology transfer should be included.[20] Where there is a breach of security, liability can be fixed within the contract's terms. For instance, Indian business process outsourcing firms surveyed by the Financial Roundtable "reported they assume at least one-year's revenue as a minimum liability requirement."[21]

---

17. Basel Committee on Banking Supervision, *supra* note 2, at 15.
18. Christopher Koch, *Don't Export Security*, CSO MAG. ONLINE (May 2005), http://www.csoonline.com/read/050105/offshore.html.'
19. *Id.*
20. Brockland, *supra* note 4.
21. INFORMATION POLICY INSTITUTE, *supra* note 7, at 6.

Criteria for Selection and Training of Workforce

Many companies operating overseas, particularly in the outsourcing context, are also too willing to shift responsibility for hiring and training to the outsourcing vendor. The better practice, as laid out by the Financial Services Roundtable, is to "specify the criteria for the selection, training and monitoring of personnel, including qualifications, background checks, training, and sanctions for breaches of standard operating practice."[22]

Operating on a proverbial autopilot in terms of a vendor's employees can prove devastating. Ramesh K. V., formerly of the Indian law firm of Kochhar and Co., reminds us that in certain locales, such as India, if workers are employees of the vendor, there is no privity of contract, and the client company will not be able to enforce injunctive relief against the individual for any breach of the contract between client and vendor. That fact argues for individual agreements with each vendor employee to establish the predicate privity of contract in those jurisdictions.

Process Management

Gandhi encourages clients to review whether specifications for development are adequately reflected in the final agreement. Moreover the specifications as agreed upon must be properly aligned with business goals. Milestones and acceptance criteria need to be reflected in the agreement, and Gandhi further notes that you must define consequences if the vendor does not meet them. A practical change order procedure must also be developed to provide for circumstances not considered in the original agreement.

Other operational issues that have been identified in diligence and negotiations should also be addressed. For instance, Kenneth Shiu advises that provisions may need to be crafted to address staff attrition or turnover issues, as well as "business continuity and disaster recovery processes."[23]

---

22. *Id.* at 16.
23. Ken Shiu, *Outsourcing: Are You Sure or Offshore? Identifying Legal Risks in Offshoring*, NSW Soc'y for Computers & L. (June 2004), https://www.nswscl.org.au/index.php?option=com_content&view=article&id=130:outsourcing-are-you-sure-or-offshore-identifying-legal-risks-in-offshoring&catid=28:june-2004-issue&Itemid=31.

Labor and Tax Law

As noted in detail in Chapter 9, many nations have much more complex labor laws than the United States does. Although in India, for example, supervisors and wage earners beyond a specified amount might be exempt from some regulations, employment agreements must be reviewed for their notice, termination, and noncompete provisions to ensure these are enforceable within the parameters of local law.[24]

Assuming that diligence has been done correctly, tax consequences should be carefully analyzed as well and minimized to the extent practicable. What is important in this phase is to ensure that the agreement follows through on the tax planning that has been done and avoids creating circumstances that result in unnecessary tax liability. An example would be a nonresident entity conducting business in India through an agent, branch, or sales office that "habitually exercises an authority to conclude contracts or regularly delivers goods or merchandise or habitually secures orders on behalf of the foreign/non-resident company."[25] In that case, the client company may be deemed to have a "permanent establishment" in India, and profits will be taxable under Indian law.[26]

Dispute Resolution

As will be discussed in more depth in the next chapter, in a few unfortunate cases, a cross-border business relationship will deteriorate to the point that some sort of dispute resolution mechanism will be necessary to sort out conflicts that develop. The time to make decisions about the nature of the resolution process and the rules under which it will be conducted is not when the relationship has already deteriorated, but at the time that the contract is initially drafted.

Gandhi notes that there are many different types of processes that can be used. The parties may wish to have some sort of nonadversarial procedure, such as mediation, before entering into a more contentious process such as arbitration. In any event, Gandhi notes that the parties need to consider in

---

24. Shalini Agarwal & Sakate Khaitan, *The Case for Offshore Outsourcing in the Legal Sector* 3 (Chatham House 2004).
25. *Id.* at 5.
26. *Id.*

relation to the process fundamental "rules of the road," such as what law will be deemed controlling in the proceedings and which parties will bear the associated costs involved. Hallab recommends an "escalation clause" that raises a dispute from the floor to managers to senior executives before arbitration is invoked.

Many cross-border transactional agreements seek to substitute arbitration for traditional litigation, often in the interest of avoiding the substantial costs that proceedings in open court entail. Still, the parties should contemplate at the contract drafting stage what type of arbitration they can agree to have, advises Ramesh. Will they have one arbitrator? Three? Some other number? Will the arbitration be held in the vendor's jurisdiction, or somewhere else? Ramesh reminds us that it may be impractical for smaller vendors to arbitrate outside their home country. Moreover, Jeffrey Paulsen sees another benefit to putting the seat of arbitration in a neutral spot: potential goodwill. "The U.S. court system might be pretty intimidating to [foreign partners]," Paulsen observes, and using a third-party venue "imparts a feeling of mutual respect and opportunity for a fair resolution to a dispute for all involved."

International arbitrator Jeff Dasteel warns against using nonstandard dispute resolution clauses—you risk that courts won't enforce them. Standard form clauses, on the other hand, have been tested.

As you draft the dispute resolution provision, special consideration should be given where a governmental entity is involved in the transaction.[27] Establishing a clear waiver of sovereign immunity and "act of state" doctrine defenses is recommended.[28] Take note of special requirements that exist in certain jurisdictions regarding governmental entities participating in arbitrations. Saudi law forbids sovereign entities from participating in arbitration in a foreign country, while engaging in depositions and written discovery would be illegal in other states.[29]

In trying to protect IP rights, be aware that many countries disfavor or otherwise limit IP arbitrations, including Brazil, Korea, India, South Africa,

---

27. *International Enforcement of Arbitral Awards against Sovereign Entities*, Arbitration Association of the R.O.C., 2 CAA Arb. J. 58 (2003).
28. *Id.* at 59–64.
29. *Id.* at 64–65.

Israel, Spain, Japan, Finland, Ireland, and France.[30] Carving IP disputes out of the dispute resolution clause may be necessary where these nations' laws might apply.[31] These examples illustrate the importance of involving local counsel in drafting agreements, as they are more likely to be aware of idiosyncrasies in local law than lawyers from outside the jurisdictions.[32]

Exit Provisions

Creativity in drafting should extend even to the termination of the contract. There is wisdom in providing the parties with multiple exit options, which allow the parties to end any portion of the relationship that is not working as expected, while saving an overall relationship that is still beneficial.[33] The contract could include terms that set up financial penalties for missing benchmarks or providing for credits to be applied to other aspects of the transaction.[34]

Minimum time periods to execute termination allow production or provision of services to be moved to another vendor or entity, or else returned to the control of the client company.[35] Recommended terms related to exit provisions include

> provisions relating to insolvency or other material changes in the corporate form, and clear delineation of ownership of intellectual property following termination, including transfers of information back to the regulated entity and other duties that continue to have an effect after the termination of the contract.[36]

Gandhi recommends that you consider, given the jurisdiction you are in, how much faith you can put into any termination clause. He advises that,

---

30. *Id.* at 65.
31. *Id.*
32. *Id.* at 67.
33. Thomas Hoffman, *"Prenuptials" for Offshoring*, COMPUTERWORLD (Jan. 23, 2006), http://www.computerworld.com/s/article/107882/_Prenuptials_for_Offshoring?taxonomyId=060.
34. *Id.*
35. Basel Committee on Banking Supervision, *supra* note 2, at 15.
36. *Id.*

from a risk-management standpoint, you should determine whether business interruption insurance will cover you, and if so, to what extent.

Dealing with Last-Minute Changes or Attempts to Renegotiate

In many developing countries, after reaching what you think is a final agreement, you may get an unpleasant surprise, warns Chenevert—finding out that a certain governmental official must also approve the deal. Chenevert adds that you may find that, indeed, several officials must bless the deal before it can proceed:

> You must get all the various levels of governmental officials on the same page. Sometimes doing so requires you to renegotiate the deal several times. Each time someone else has to approve, it generally increases the price of the sale. It's not really different from the U.S.—"you mean now I have to deal with the zoning board?"

To cope with this, Chenevert concludes, the seller *must* be your ally when it comes to dealing with government officials. It is crucial to build into your agreement that the sale terms are conditional on obtaining all necessary approvals. Otherwise one official's decision in your favor might be overruled by another, with all the attendant delays and costs involved while trying to get the determination reversed.

You may find yourself renegotiating terms for business reasons, as well. Loring Knoblauch, former chief executive officer of Underwriters' Laboratories, was working for a Detroit-based equity firm, building a portfolio of international businesses as he was attempting to close a deal in Amsterdam. The parties had negotiated all but the last few pieces of an agreement. A large meeting was called with all the primary players, but rather than having the effect of wrapping things up, everything fell apart instead.

What had happened was that business had gotten much better since negotiations had started, to the point where the Dutch felt that the Americans should pay more for the acquisition. "The financial guru for the Americans,"

Knoblauch recalls, "proceeded to piss off everyone. It was politely suggested to him that the negotiations might proceed better without him, and to his credit, even though he was 'the boss,' he went home, and the deal was made."

So, what happened then? The parties started the negotiations from scratch. "The Dutch," Knoblauch observes, "are tremendous negotiators." When the deal changed, it changed the terms of all of the mezzanine financing covenants. It gave both sides a good excuse to reopen negotiations. This was necessary, Knoblauch explains, because either the Dutch needed a better deal, or else they had lost faith in the people they were dealing with. The parties spent another three to four months in order to finally close the deal. It proved to be worth the extra time invested.

You now have a written agreement that, after perhaps months of negotiations and careful attention to avoid cross-cultural confusion, expresses the intentions and agreement of the parties. Some lawyers would believe that their job is done. It is time for the businesspeople to take over from this point, they might think. Yet, there is a role for counseling in avoiding or managing conflict in the implementation of the agreement, and in attempting to resolve disputes that may arise to preserve the relationship between the parties. That is the subject matter of the next chapter.

Chapter 12

Implementation and Dispute Resolution

With the master service agreement, joint venture (JV) agreement, or other contracts that define the relationship of your client company to its foreign counterpart complete, there is a natural tendency for the lawyers involved to turn the process over to the businesspeople, and rightly so, for the most part. It is the business experts who should be counted on to do what they do best. Besides, for cost-conscious small to medium-sized enterprises (SMEs), the idea of spending fees in addition to those incurred in planning and completing the agreement may be a hard sell. Still, as Michael Mensik, of Baker & McKenzie, cautions, "signing the agreement is only the beginning."

Indeed, the special complications that can arise with cross-border transactions make an excellent case for retaining legal counsel for the implementation phase. If the implementation process goes awry, you can be sure that lawyers will become involved in the arbitration or other litigation that will almost certainly result. Far better to spend a little at the implementation stage to avoid not only wasting the money and time invested in the relationship thus far but also the disruption to operations and even potential liability that might flow from a bitter end to the business relationship.

This chapter offers suggestions to businesspeople and lawyers alike to help anticipate problems during the set-up and execution of international transactions generally, so that they can be defused before exploding into a full crisis. For those ill-fated relationships that cannot be saved despite the hard work and best intentions of all involved, there are also a few thoughts for navigating the dispute resolution process.

Converting Paper Oversight into Practical Oversight

As with all the other major milestones in putting together a cross-border operation, implementation requires a focused team of individuals with both a stake in the outcome and sufficient responsibility to get all necessary agenda items through to completion. The team should have representatives from all areas crucial to success, including financial, human resources, and operational experts.[1]

"When you're implementing," muses Howard Mills, of Deloitte, "sometimes you can put together a nice plan, but it still doesn't end up working with the joint venture partner for whatever reason." On the tax end of things, for example, perhaps there is a problem with withholding or with qualifying for a treaty. Whatever the issue, Mills warns, you will be forced to rethink and reshape it on the fly to get to the best possible answer under the circumstances. It may not be the best possible answer metaphysically, but, says Mills, "it's the best possible answer given the parameters that exist at the time."

Mensik agrees. At some point, your vendor or business partner will need to take control of key functions—"this is when details will actually be established and put in operation." It is only once a vendor gets its proverbial "hands dirty" that you create a framework for further discussion, says Mensik. "In the transition, you tell the vendor, 'this is what I need you to actually implement.' If you reach outside this set of parameters, the result will likely be a change order."

Some relationships with vendors are endangered by the tendency of management on conclusion of the agreement to consider the process, service, or other relationship to be "out of sight, out of mind."[2] There are a variety of

---

1. Dominic Conlon, *Nearshore/Offshore Outsourcing, Part II: Implementation*, A&L GOODBODY (April 12, 2005), http://www.hg.org/articles/article_1171.html.
2. Kristin Robertson, *How to Maintain Quality and Control with an Outsourcer*, KR CONSULTING (May 2004), http://www.krconsulting.com/how-to-maintain-quality-and-control

ways to keep the relationship within the line of sight of the appropriate parties within the client company. Assigning responsibility for the upkeep of the relationship through formal organizational structure is one way. A "vendor manager" (or managers) can be chosen to oversee day-to-day operational issues. That manager in turn could report to an "executive sponsor" within senior management to provide big-picture vision for the relationship and bring critical issues to the attention of the highest reaches of the company.[3]

Whether through creation of formal positions within the client company or otherwise, appropriate personnel have the same task: to consistently "monitor, manage, modify, and steer" both vendor or partner and contract over time.[4] That is accomplished by regular reporting, of the daily, weekly, monthly,[5] and quarterly varieties.[6] Remember the concept "verify, then trust," or as one author puts it, "trust that they're doing a good job, but skeptically monitor everything."[7]

However, you should not take the concept of "skeptical monitoring" as a license to withhold well-earned trust or to micromanage the outsourcing relationship, advises John McCormick, of Accenture. According to McCormick, this is a second way that client-vendor relationships get ruined. When he hears clients ask for something that technically does not exist, he asks, "When do you want the train wreck to occur? Before or after signing?"

That being said, Lalit Arora, formerly of IBM Consulting, says that Indian information technology (IT) vendors "need constant monitoring and constant management." In his experience, what is needed is at least a weekly meeting in which you can ask why dates were not met or discuss any potential issues. When you reach the time when you are close to going live, he recommends increasing the frequency of meetings to every morning. In this way you avoid the "end surprise."

Chocko Valliappa, chief executive officer (CEO) of Bangalore-based Vee Technologies, offers another vendor's perspective on implementation:

-with-an-outsourcer/.
3. Id.
4. Warren S. Reid, *Outsourcing: The 20 Steps to Success* 5 (1996), http://www.wsrcg.com/Articles/OutSourcing.pdf.
5. Robertson, *supra* note 2.
6. Reid, *supra* note 4, at 5.
7. Robertson, *supra* note 2.

What happens is everyone gets to the [negotiating] table and we only look at the positive, then start moving ahead. We don't look at the drawbacks, and the drawbacks can actually pull us down. A better way is to look at the drawbacks which you can build a foundation on. Then you can look at the upside which is what everyone wants. To look at things and why they won't work, and mitigate it. That is a bottom up approach as opposed to a top down approach, which I strongly recommend.

If there is a single key to proper implementation of cross-border business arrangements, it is training. It should come as little surprise that Indian vendors, many of whom are judged to be operating at world-class levels, emphasize training and testing of their employees.[8] Training as to process, protocols, and preferred methods of communication is even more important where the vendor is lacking experience or specific expertise.[9] As the Financial Services Roundtable aptly notes, "given that liability is passed down through contracts, BPO [business process outsourcing] firms have a strong incentive to regularly train and monitor employees."[10] This may include general courses on data privacy and security, and project-specific training as well.[11] Testing and retesting of training subjects and utilizing intranets and screensavers with updated information helps to reinforce key concepts.[12]

As noted above, though, the client company cannot expect the vendor to do all this without guidance and supervision. A better practice is to partner with the vendor to create a comprehensive training program, complete with client-led "train the trainers" involvement.[13] A client company trainer should monitor the vendor's first in-house training session to ensure that

---

8. INFORMATION POLICY INSTITUTE, HOW SAFE AND SECURE IS IT? AN ASSESSMENT OF DATA PRIVACY AND SECURITY IN BUSINESS PROCESS OUTSOURCING FIRMS IN INDIA, FINANCIAL SERVICES ROUNDTABLE 25 (2005).
9. Exervio Management Consulting, *Do You Really Want to Outsource that Process?*, 5 (May 2004), http://www.exervio.com/docs/Do%20You%20Really%20Want%20To%20Outsource%20That%20Process.
10. INFORMATION POLICY INSTITUTE, *supra* note 8, at 25.
11. *Id.*
12. *Id.*
13. Robertson, *supra* note 2.

concepts are conveyed as expected.[14] Failure to properly train employees, particularly in industry-specific knowledge, can lead to a significant increase in operational risks, where vendor employees make inappropriate decisions.[15]

Valliappa has run into these situations first-hand. He told one client that "this is not going to work where the head of training doesn't focus on making the program work." So the client chose to send a trainer to India, empowered to make the Indian training succeed. Valliappa lives by the old phrase "if you plan to succeed, you will fail, but if you plan to fail, you will succeed."

Even advanced degree holders need process- and project-specific training.[16] Reportedly, knowledge process outsourcing workers are receiving up to 90 days of training at entry level.[17] While management-level employees may be hired with experience in project management or research and development, they are still given appropriate subject-specific training.[18] As Arora notes, in the pharmaceutical sector, vendors can be assessed penalties by the Food and Drug Administration (FDA) for failing to properly validate their work—and the FDA mandates "tons of documentation." No matter what their education level or credentials though, Indians will not understand or implement regulations they have never seen. Training must close the gap.

A United Nations Conference on Trade and Development survey suggests that SMEs "usually transfer incomplete packages of technical and organizational information" and insufficient "codified information through blueprints and other documents."[19] Perhaps this is because smaller companies often rely on institutional knowledge in the minds of their people rather than documentation. The same survey also identifies a lack of "financial and managerial resources" as a common problem in technology transfer.[20] The upshot of this survey suggests that smaller companies need to step up

---

14. *Id.*
15. N. Raja Venkateswar, *Mitigating Operational Risk in Outsourcing*, INFO. MGMT. (May 2005), http://www.dmreview.com/specialreports/20050524/1028024-1.html.
16. Kusum Makhija, *The Knowledge Processors*, THE FINANCIAL EXPRESS (Aug. 2, 2005), http://www.financialexpress.com/news/the-knowledge-processors/138916/0.
17. *Id.*
18. *Id.*
19. Claude Marcotte & Jorge Liosi, *Small and Medium-Sized Enterprises Involved in Technology Transfer to China: What Do Their Partners Learn*, 23 INT'L SMALL BUS. J. 28 (Feb. 2005).
20. *Id.*

their investment in training where necessary to ensure adequate knowledge transfer.[21]

Research suggests that the first phase of training in vendor and partner firms is adaptation to locally available materials or adaptation of production scale through "learning-by-doing."[22] At that stage, client companies focus on transferring information on how to solve immediate problems with the new technology.[23] Typically it is after this that vendors or partners learn how to modify and improve the transferred technology.[24]

The monitoring of vendor employees provided for in the contract must be fleshed out and properly administered in order to satisfy the client's regulatory responsibilities. Background checks, physical security including closed-circuit television monitoring, separate work areas per client, and any other mandated security requirements should be periodically audited.[25]

A quality program is yet another vehicle by which you can limit problems in implementation. These programs generally involve collection of end customer and employee feedback, monitoring data, and agreed-upon operational metrics.[26] Setting up joint meetings in which the client and vendor review audit results together is commonly recommended to harmonize expectations.

Of course, cultural issues in the implementation phase are often not given the attention they deserve. They are more likely to be given higher priority if senior management is involved actively in operations, rather than just in a traditional review and oversight role.[27] Moreover, client management can assist in aligning the vendor's work with the strategic goals of the client company and avoid long-term mismatch in direction, which naturally would lead to various operational difficulties.[28]

---

21. *Id.*
22. *Id.* at 32.
23. *Id.* at 36.
24. *Id.*
25. INFORMATION POLICY INSTITUTE, *supra* note 8, at 31.
26. Joe Caliro, *Secrets to Building a Customer-Driven Service Platform*, QUALITY DIGEST (December 2, 2008), http://www.qualitydigest.com/inside/quality-insider-article/secrets-building-customer-driven-service-platform.
27. Venkateswar, *supra* note 15.
28. *Id.*

Managing from a Distance versus Expatriate Placement

In smaller firms that rely on institutional or "tacit" knowledge in the conduct of their daily operations, employees of the client firm are more likely going to be required to personally teach unwritten knowledge and skills to the vendor or partner's employees, which is both costly and possibly disruptive to normal domestic operations.[29] It has been suggested that in the realm of technology transfer, though, there may not be a choice but to make this investment:

> In some cases the transfer of a formula or a chemical compound, the blueprints for a special device, or a special mathematical algorithm may be all that is needed to effect the transfer. However, more is frequently needed ... Know-how cannot always be codified, since it often has a tacit dimension. ... In short, the transfer of knowledge may be impossible in the absence of the transfer of people.[30]

In part this may be because in addition to providing technical assistance, the client company employees may have to adapt the technology to conditions on the ground in the foreign location.[31] For this reason, it has been suggested the implementation team should be prepared to physically move to the vendor or partner's location "for a potentially significant period of time immediately prior to and following commencement of provision of the services."[32]

C. Allen Bargfrede, formerly of Orbitz, notes that if you create an alliance with an Indian firm, you do have the option of sending vendor employees to the United States for training. The practical problem with this, as many companies trying to do business in a post-September 11, 2001, world know well, is that you may run into a visa issue. As one businessman now based

---

29. Marcotte & Liosi, *supra* note 19, at 30.
30. *Id.*, citing David J. Teece, *The Market for Know-how and the Efficient International Transfer of Technology*, THE ANNALS OF THE ACADEMY OF POLITICAL AND SOCIAL SCIENCE (November 1981), 81, 86.
31. *Id.* at 30.
32. Conlon, *supra* note 1.

in China observed, "the one thing that is not global yet is human capital." So every few months you may end up sending someone else for training.

Mills observes that often his clients underestimate the amount of effort that needs to go into a foreign location:

> You can have a good team up and going in the foreign location. You have a trusted right-hand person over there but it needs a lot more attention and there is a lot more of a learning curve on the foreign location than there is domestically. It's much more difficult to stay abreast of changes [in that foreign location] even if you have people there, and to understand these slight changes from an American's perspective and what they mean to your business operations abroad. Even though your business might be 80 percent U.S. and 20 percent foreign, executives need to divide their time about 50/50 in order to make that foreign venture effective.

In deciding how much attention to pay to foreign operations, C-level executives should consider the observation that even where client companies staff operations with their own people, the distances involved may cause the link to headquarters to be strained.[33]

Often, smaller businesses in the United States operate with a minimum of processes and with methods that do not translate readily to managing overseas business relationships such as IT or BPO, Global Reach Consulting's Kumkum Dalal notes. A CEO may think, with misguided confidence, that he or she can manage the project during some of his or her "free time." Without sufficient directives from upper management, however, even competent project managers can become embroiled in negative personnel and communication issues. Dalal says that when this happens it does not lead to success:

> Outsourcing does not work without teamwork, and considerable time and energy have to be invested in that effort to guarantee a successful

---

33. Mike Ricciuti & Mike Yamamoto, *Companies Determined to Retain "Secret Sauce,"* CNET (May 5, 2004), http://news.cnet.com/2009-1022_3-5198605.html.

project outcome. Setting up an overseas outsourcing operation is not a "no-brainer." Too often inadequate planning and impatience leads to a failed experience.

Maurice Zarmati, past President and CEO for North America at Costa Crociere Cruise Lines, argues that in his experience, sometimes it is better to hire local managers than to rely on expatriates. When Costa chose to expand to Asia, the decision was made to hire Asians and teach them Italian hospitality. They learned how to say hello in Italian and also to speak English. For the tourism industry, brand continuity was important, and Costa sought to "import the brand's culture into the best of the local culture." More on that in a minute.

Former Brunswick Bowling and Billiards Corp. General Counsel Jeffrey Paulsen drafted and negotiated JV's for bowling centers in Brazil and Asia. Paulsen recounts that the company moved expatriates from the United States into Brazil to run the JV there. The rationale behind that choice was a feeling that the company needed someone who understood Brunswick's operations to be on the ground in Brazil. In Asia, however, they hired new Asian employees to manage those operations. Why? In Brazil, the U.S. expatriates knew what they didn't know and they had a better understanding and ability to learn the local culture. Whereas in Asia, it was most important to understand the culture of the local consumers and customers first.

On the other hand, when you think about managing work from a distance, Dalal advises you ask one fundamental question: How do you get people to work together who have never seen each other? On that point, Bargfrede also agrees. "Despite the marvels of videoconferencing," he concludes, "there will always be a place for face-to-face meetings." His rationale is that "it's much harder to sit across the table from someone and be a complete jerk." Mills, of Deloitte, has a different take. He observes that new hires coming out of college "are so comfortable with technology, e-enabled and remote accessed" that having face-to-face meetings is more of a surprise to them than setting up a videoconference with somebody halfway around the world. So perhaps as this new generation assumes managerial responsibility, face-to-face meetings will go the way of typewriters and telex machines.

Transition

After all the time and money invested in setting up cross-border arrangements, there will undoubtedly be pressure to get the operation up and running "as soon as possible." However, there is wisdom in staggering the phase-in of a new venture to give you an opportunity to work out "bugs" in new procedures and address vendor/partner deficits before you rely on them for full execution of their perhaps critical role in your business.[34] A realistic time frame that includes the ability for both parties to move certain benchmarks back if they are not ready is optimal, says McCormick.

One observer, Virginia Graville, of Alcatel Australia, puts the transition issue in the starkest of terms: "How the first few months are handled will set up the deal for success or failure."[35] Each party assigning executives with a background in change management is recommended; at all costs mistakes felt by the client's end customer must be avoided.[36] "It is reasonable to expect vendors will make honest mistakes," reflects McCormick, and the client should make sure that the vendor clearly understands the client's needs. "Don't assume we have crystal balls," he concludes.

Management of Issues Based in Culture

As one representative of a U.S. company doing business in China put it, "culture is both the glue that holds society together and the lubricant that allows the workforce to run together smoothly." There are many similarities across cultures but there is also the potential for misunderstandings.

It is absolutely necessary for both parties to adapt to a cross-cultural agreement.[37] U.S.-based management must be able to recognize and work with business cultures in developing countries that incorporate largely

---

34. Conlon, *supra* note 1.
35. Mark Hollands, *Deal or No Deal*, 3 THE OUTSOURCING INSTITUTE (2005), http://www.outsourcing.com/content.asp?page=01b/other/oe/q405/dornod.html&nonav=false.
36. *Id.*
37. Marcotte & Liosi, *supra* note 19, at 32.

unfamiliar values, such as collectivism and high-power distance.[38] In China and other Asian countries, the concept of "face" must be reckoned with in all interactions with employees from those cultures.[39] It is counterproductive—to say the least—to conduct business in such a way as to cause people in these countries to lose face by direct criticism.[40] As such, supervisors need to be trained to convey expectations, but in culturally sensitive ways.

Former Costa Crociere Cruise Lines CEO Maurice Zarmati warns that Americans lose sight of simple yet profound cultural differences. For example, the prototypical "ugly American" who travels to France needs to realize that when he is there, he must ask for permission to get in a taxi. "After all," Zarmati explains, "that cab may not be going your way—it may be cocktail hour, or there may be a girl at the bar for the cab driver to meet." While an American cabbie would likely let the girl wait to get the fare, the French cab driver might not. The key, Zarmati concludes, is to realize how such seemingly small differences in how people in different places view similar situations actually impacts how they react—and therefore how you should act in order to get to the result you want.

In the case of employees in India, Lalit Arora, formerly of IBM Consulting, bluntly states that "if they are not managed properly, the work product will be wasted." In Arora's view, many Indians do not have enough understanding of how business is done in the West. He explains that in Indian business culture, they are used to dealing with a lot of red tape and bureaucracy. Kids fresh from college are eager and hardworking; you just need to focus them in the right direction. You must reemphasize what you want, then they will try to do it. When working with Indian employees, Arora advises that it is important to look for someone with strong managerial capabilities. He adds that the situation is improving as Indian vendors master more skill sets. Eventually, he concludes, business cultural differences will largely disappear.

Local holidays and customs must also be taken into account when considering overseas operations. Valliappa notes that a problem he has had to face is how to handle Indian holidays in the context of working for

---

38. *Id.*, citing Geert Hofstede, CULTURE'S CONSEQUENCES: INTERNATIONAL DIFFERENCES IN WORK-RELATED VALUES. Sage Publications, 1980.
39. *Id.* at 41.
40. *Id.*

Western clients. A major holiday in India is the festival of lights, called Diwali, which is celebrated in October or November. He explains that in the first year he was working for a client, he did not have that much staff in during Diwali because it is a major holiday, like Christmas in the West. If you had a 500-person operation in the United States and wanted everyone to show up on Christmas, it would present a great problem in the United States, Valliappa notes.

Unfortunately, the client took it all very badly, so the second year Valliappa's company was able to orchestrate cash incentives and parties to encourage attendance over the holiday. This evolved into a scheme in which raffle tickets are given to every employee that comes in and works during those days.

Strategies for Addressing Vendor Knowledge Deficits

The first step in addressing knowledge deficits in a foreign culture is communicating adequately. As Dalal points out, "in India, one size does not fit all." Language skills and familiarity with Western terminology vary from company to company. Dalal's recommendation to the U.S.-based company doing business in India is

> be clear in your communication, rigorously practice teamwork, and above all, *be patient*. Practice collaboration. If your overseas colleagues believe that you are all working to achieve the same goals, they will bend over backwards to accommodate your needs.

Dalal points out that as an American, you have to appreciate that there are some words, slang, and abbreviations that may not make sense to someone from another culture. Some examples include "ASAP," "FYI," and "BTW." U.S.-based employees must learn to write and speak with a minimum of slang expressions that are bound to confuse foreign employees.

"Understanding another's perspective works wonders," states Valliappa. As he puts it, a common problem is trying to implement "third-generation strategies operated by second-generation operators with first-generation managers." So both sides "need to grow up and understand what we are servicing," Valliappa states. He offers the example of a client project manager in India who took the time to buy a book on the Kannada dialect and used the word *namaskara* (which means "hello") in e-mails. This project manager also got up in the middle of the night to watch cricket matches. Valliappa acknowledges that these are subtle things, but he holds that they got a lot of his team excited and brought a feeling of oneness.

Understanding does not mean giving vendors or partners a "free pass." Instead it means recognizing the gaps in knowledge and politics within the client organization. In the case of the project manager mentioned above, Valliappa notes,

> if anything goes wrong he gives us the stick. And we appreciate it. And if it goes right [and the client is critical anyway] he actually goes and fights with the management in the U.S. If we were wrong, we were wrong; but if we were right we were right. Many times it hurts in the process of learning that a person [in the client company] who thinks or perceives their job is getting undermined is the person controlling the relationship.

While it may be understandable that the client firm wants to safeguard its valuable intellectual property, research suggests that failing to share sophisticated knowledge with partners may create "serious obstacles to learning":

> Although resource constraint in smaller organizations was an important element in some of the cases, it did not appear to be the main factor associated with learning. The factors that we identified as predominant are the capacity of recipient firms to take some initiative in organizational change and technological improvement, the capacity of transferors to adapt to the Chinese cultural context, and their willingness to share their knowledge as well as their capacity to do so even when disagreements occur with their partners.[41]

---

41. *Id.* at 42.

Use of Inspections and Audits

The more physical distance between you and vendors or business partners, the more you need to have clear, enforceable rights to obtain information and monitor performance.[42] The extra expense involved in external audits may cause the foreign business partner to object; at the very least, audit procedures should be mapped out during the negotiation phase.[43] Otherwise, the vendor may have to accept unanticipated costs that rob them of profits and threaten the relationship.[44]

Audits and inspections include not just financial records and IT security, but physical operations, as well.[45] Work should be conducted in facilities that have adequate power backup and up-to-date fire suppression and safety features, and backup facilities should be available to avoid workflow interruption in case of manmade or natural disaster.[46]

"Scope Creep": Relationship versus the Deal

Dean Davison argues that "there is no such thing as a fixed-price contract."[47] That is, in a project of any complexity, the work will necessarily deviate from the assumptions made at the outset; no one has a crystal ball that can anticipate every obstacle or change in imagined circumstance.[48] And vendors, not surprisingly, do not want to work for free. Davison reckons that most projects change by a factor of 10 percent to 15 percent during development.[49]

Still, Arora warns that you must be extremely careful in evaluating what the vendors have agreed to up front as you implement. If they agree to

---

42. Conlon, *supra* note 1.
43. Christopher Koch, *Don't Export Security*, CSO MAG. ONLINE (May 2005), http://www.csoonline.com/read/050105/offshore.html.'
44. *Id.*
45. *Id.*
46. *Id.*
47. Dean Davison, *Top 10 Risks of Offshore Outsourcing*, META GROUP (Feb. 16, 2004), http://searchcio.techtarget.com/originalContent/0,289142,sid19_gci950602,00.html.
48. *Id.*
49. *Id.*

more than they can handle, it leads to "scope creep," especially for bigger projects, where the problem has greater impact. On projects ranging from $80 to $100 million, Arora says, every day that completion is pushed back incurs serious financial loss.

The most successful companies are constantly re-evaluating their plan even after they get the transaction done, observes Mills. They realize that they're in a fluid, dynamic environment and that they need to stay on top of the changes in facts, circumstances, or law. Mills points out, "the one sure thing is change. You're not going to have a static environment; you don't have it if you're operating just domestically, and you multiply that level of change exponentially when you go abroad."

This suggests that at the heart of the "scope creep" issue often is the tension between the desire to squeeze continuing improvements out of the vendor or partner and the equal but opposite desire for the client company to tightly control processes.[50] So in some sense, the issue is about how to design proper incentives for vendors or partners to creatively address changes in circumstances or to provide improvements in operations or processes without allowing a surreptitious renegotiation of price and terms by the vendor or partner.

Zarmati, formerly of Costa Crociere, suggests putting together a team early in the life of an operation and getting them talking to the CEO and senior vice presidents. If, for instance, an idea for design doesn't work, the principal department heads need to speak to each other. What are the main goals? What are the challenges to those goals? Zarmati cautions against managers operating in silos and leaving it up to the CEO to be peacemaker between them. "You create peace by encouraging dialogue," Zarmati explains.

---

50. Daniel Trefler, *Offshoring: Threats and Opportunities* 25 (July 22, 2005) (prepared for the Brookings Trade Forum 2005, *The Offshoring of Services: Issues and Implications*, May 12–13, 2005, Washington, D.C.).

Working the Relationship: Resolving Everyday Disputes

Loring Knoblauch, of Underwriters Laboratories (UL), notes in regard to dealing with the everyday conflicts in international transactions,

> "I have done 10 international deals, and we never once went back to the contract. It sits in a drawer somewhere. It only becomes relevant if the relationship breaks down. Once this happens, all is lost and the lawyers are left to sift through the ashes and pick up what pieces they can. But if it gets to this, the business is forever done and the chances of a follow-on deal are nonexistent".

Or as Virginia Graville, of Alcatel Australia, put it, "if you pull out a contract, then I promise you that the conversation ends in argument."[51]

Some clients (and perhaps even some counsel) might ask: "Why spend weeks or months negotiating the terms of a contract and then not actively use it to resolve the disputes that inevitably arise from the transaction it was designed to govern?" This is a reasonable question to ask, but the answer is simple: the relationship you are trying to build is more important than determining who is "right" and who is "wrong" per the terms of the written document. The contract exists partly as a memorialization of the agreement between the parties *at the time the agreement was entered into*, and partly as a mechanism for sorting out the aftermath of a relationship that has failed ("the last line of decision," as Dr. David Liu puts it). Routine disputes should be resolved not with legalistic accusations linked to contract provisions, but with cooperative give and take that places the good of the relationship first.

Again, the comparison to a marriage is apt: in any given couple's argument, each party is probably a little right and a little wrong. If spouses focus on their need to be right, rather than on the health of their relationship, trouble awaits. Instead of pointing to the contract, which is the static understanding of the parties prior to encountering unanticipated challenges, consider periodically updating the contract over time as needed to ensure

---

51. Hollands, *supra* note 35.

that under the circumstances you currently face, both parties' needs and expectations are adequately met.[52] As consultant Dalal observes, "people will bend over backwards to work things out if you have built up a good working relationship."

Mark Probyn, of Gartner, believes that there is an "art and craft" to contract negotiations designed to ensure the longevity of a deal rather than set parameters that either party may not be able to meet.[53] As an example of this, Harvey Cohen, of Dinsmore & Shohl, relates that he has drafted agreements "with executive escalation going up two or three levels before an arbitration can be filed, except for emergency injunctive relief." Occasionally, Cohen has taken this strategy as far as drafting agreements with a very lopsided consent to jurisdiction clause, an inconvenient venue, or even no arbitration clause at all. Counterintuitive as this may be, it is done to force the parties to negotiate, if at all possible. If there is going to be arbitration, Cohen suggests a neutral third venue.

Often, relying on the contract documents—and the lawyers that seek to enforce them—can be a tricky business. Rawdon Simon, managing director of the independent consultancy Compass, serves as an arbitrator when deals go awry. He points out that some deals involve several different contracts, some of which contradict each other in some sense. As such, Simon says, "it is no wonder that so many outsourcing deals dissolve into argument."[54] To save a relationship in trouble, you need to talk personally, says Shrikar Dole, formerly of EEPC and now JD Director General of the Federation of Indian Export Organisations. Dole puts it memorably:

> In India, lawyers are kept not at arm's length, but at *pole's* length. If they show up, you are on the brink of the relationship being dead. Don't ask the lawyers to talk—at most you want the lawyers to confirm the agreement reached between the business managers of both sides.

---

52. Reid, *supra* note 4, at 5.
53. Hollands, *supra* note 35.
54. Id.

Clearly, since the CEOs of both entities are often the parties who breathed life into a business relationship in the first instance, they might well need to be called in to discuss the dispute one on one and use the personal good will they have developed to find a mutually agreeable solution.

If a relationship becomes increasingly unworkable for the client company or unprofitable for the vendor or partner, Probyn holds that one of three scenarios results: "They can recast the deal, go their separate ways or the client can go legal, which is becoming an increasingly familiar outcome."[55] When you start to consider legal redress with your vendor or partner, "does it make sense going nuclear?" as one practitioner I interviewed managed to sum it up. Probyn concludes, "I would never recommend termination unless the marriage cannot be retrieved after every avenue has been explored ... changing suppliers is very expensive and can cause a lot of trouble for staff on both sides of the fence."[56]

When considering whether to take one last stab at negotiating your way out of a dispute, keep in mind the cautions of Samir Gandhi, of Sidley Austin, who simply warns that you should not "put excessive faith in termination and dispute resolution provisions to sort out matters in the contract." Why not? Because in many developing countries, enforcement of contracts in a court of law is not as straightforward a matter as you might be used to in your home jurisdiction. As Charles Hallab, of Baker & McKenzie, puts it,

> the reality is that you can draft the heck out an agreement—make it most robust—but at the end of the day, you are in Saudi Arabia or China or Cambodia or Algeria. You have to reconcile that you may not be able to force a going forward [of the deal]. You will need to do a cost-benefit analysis: do you try to force something onward to extract value from something—or is it a situation that is best left alone?

Overall, it seems fair to say that your client company would be best served by your taking the time to carefully consider whether there is a compromise or creative solution to the dispute before proceeding to legal action.

---

55. Id.
56. Id.

International Arbitration: Using the Contractual Dispute Mechanism

Despite best efforts, a relationship may deteriorate to the point that some form of legal recourse is the only reasonable alternative for both parties. As Mensik, of Baker & McKenzie, says, "when a deal gets to this point, there's never just one thing wrong." In many instances, the contract documents will set out a dispute resolution mechanism that mandates arbitration of the dispute, rather than traditional litigation in the court system. This is because contract enforcement in the subject venue may be unrealistic, and judgments issued by foreign courts may not be enforceable there.[57]

Arbitration can be pursued where the subject jurisdiction has adopted the United Nations Convention on the Recognition and Enforcement of Foreign Arbitral Awards,[58] a 1958 agreement in which signatories agreed to honor arbitration decisions reached in the United States.[59] More than 70 countries enforce foreign awards as parties to the Convention.[60] There are still exceptions, however. In India, for instance, the award must not be against public policy or be otherwise contrary to fundamental policies of Indian law.[61]

Oftentimes, arbitration is thought of as a less time consuming and, perhaps more importantly, less expensive alternative to traditional litigation. While this may be generally true, it has been noted that the time and cost associated with arbitrations can vary widely.[62] Michael Bolton, senior counsel at Baxter, notes that if the arbitration clause in your underlying agreement is well structured, arbitration can be cheaper than litigation. But not always. Andrew Miller QC, of 2 Temple Gardens, advises that arbitrations subject

---

57. John Brockland, *Legal Briefs*, 3 THE OUTSOURCING INSTITUTE (2005), http://www.outsourcing.com/content.asp?page=01b/other/oe/q405/lawyers.html&nonav=false.
58. *Id.*
59. Kevin Parekh, *Best Practices in Contract Development*, GLOBAL SERVICES (Aug. 15, 2004), http://www.globalservicesmedia.com/Content/general200705211184.asp.
60. INFORMATION POLICY INSTITUTE, *supra* note 8, at 17.
61. Shalini Agarwal & Sakate Khaitan, *The Case for Offshore Outsourcing in the Legal Sector* 3 (Chatham House 2004).
62. Thomas Hoffman, *"Prenuptials" for Offshoring*, COMPUTERWORLD (Jan. 23, 2006), http://www.computerworld.com/s/article/107882/_Prenuptials_for_Offshoring?taxonomyId=060.

to U.K. law are dealt with in much the same way as a court case. Solicitors and barristers involved are going through the same process, and the parties have to reckon with the additional expenditure of arbitration itself.

Jeff Dasteel, a former partner at Skadden Arps who later moved on to an independent international arbitration practice, emphasizes the importance of the rules set used in cost management. Will you be subject to administered rules or ad hoc? The International Chamber of Commerce (ICC), International Centre for Dispute Resolution (ICDR), and London Court of International Arbitration (LCIA) are examples of organizations utilizing administered rules. They make sure an arbitration proceeds, handling administrative tasks and distributing fees. By contrast, UNCITRAL is an example of an organization that uses ad hoc rules. That is, the parties have to appoint and hire arbitrators themselves. Because administrative functions cost money, administrative rules may be somewhat more expensive than ad hoc rule sets, Dasteel points out.

If the parties can work well together, you can use ad hoc, Dasteel notes. If you are not certain about that, however, you could be spending a lot of time in court. For instance, say there is a dispute over the selection of arbitrators. If you have administered rules, the ICC will make the decision, and its choice will generally be upheld by courts. In Dasteel's opinion, the ICRD, ICC, and LCIA have a leg up on bodies promulgating newer rules sets because courts generally trust that these more established organizations afford appropriate due process.

As it happens, arbitrator selection has become an emerging issue. When should an arbitrator be disqualified? Should a body disclose the reasons for an arbitrator's disqualification? Also in recent years, a heightened examination of arbitrator conflict of interest has emerged. Of concern is not only stock ownership and personal and professional relationships but even whether an arbitrator has heard a case with the same parties or counsel previously—things that would not be considered a conflict for a judge could be for an arbitrator, Dasteel advises.

Most of the major international arbitration organizations allow the parties to choose resolution by submissions of briefs and documents only, but the American Arbitration Association (AAA) requires an oral hearing.[63] Otherwise though, it has been noted that the AAA and the Arbitration Institute of the Stockholm Chamber of Commerce (SCC Institute) allow the parties flexibility in procedural matters compared to the ICC or LCIA rules.[64] Arbitration fees vary widely between organizations, as well.[65]

Parties have drafted arbitration and dispute resolution clauses that specify the number of depositions that can be taken; limit or even ban written discovery; and even specify the amount of time that the arbitration can be heard and decided in an attempt to rein in costs and avoid unreasonable delay in the process. On the other hand, might having more discovery and arbitrators who take fact finding seriously be of benefit to you?

Another reason that arbitration is often preferred over traditional litigation is the fact that, unlike in the courtroom, the proceedings before the arbitrators—and the decision resulting from them—can remain confidential.[66] Where there is no mandate for arbitration and the parties have the decision about whether to arbitrate or litigate, Bolton advises that you consider how important the public nature of the dispute is. Some companies may have distribution agreements with literally thousands of distributors. In that instance, you might choose to litigate in open court, Bolton says, because you can use the public forum to demonstrate to others your willingness to fight on a certain point. If, on the other hand, the dispute is not something you want made public, arbitration is the way to go.

Cynthia Photos Abbott, senior litigation counsel at Motorola, advises that when trying to decide whether to litigate, you should analyze the enforceability of any potential judgment. Look at where the defendant's assets are located—can you get at them? If the defendant's operations are outside the United States, she points out, you might not have jurisdiction over them in a U.S. court. Also, she notes, keep in mind that some nations' courts will

---

63. Michael L. Morkin & H. Henry Chang, *A Comparison of the Major International Arbitration Rules*, 1 CAA ARB. J. 243 (2002).
64. *Id.* at 243–44.
65. *Id.* at 241–42.
66. Ken Shiu, *Outsourcing: Are You Sure or Offshore? Identifying Legal Risks in Offshoring*, NSW SOC'Y FOR COMPUTERS & L. (June 2004), https://www.nswscl.org.au/index.php?option=com_content&view=article&id=130:outsourcing-are-you-sure-or-offshore-identifying-legal-risks-in-offshoring&catid=28:june-2004-issue&Itemid=31.

not recognize a U.S. judgment. In instances like those, Photos Abbott suggests arbitration may be advisable. Dasteel raises China as an example. In China, courts are still relatively new to enforcement of arbitration awards where the arbitration took place outside of China. But they are beginning to enforce international arbitration awards.

Still another factor raised by in-house attorneys is: what kind of dispute exactly are you dealing with? If it's construction, arbitration may be the way to go because arbitrators likely will understand the dispute better than a court would. Andrew Miller agrees. If, for example, you have a technical issue with a power plant, you can contract for a three-person panel consisting of a lawyer, engineer, and architect and build in a timetable for the length of the proceeding. "The element of control powers arbitration," Miller concludes, adding, "An additional benefit is that by choosing arbitration and choosing both the applicable law and procedural rules is that you can avoid unfamiliar law and procedural rules in foreign jurisdictions."

Another point Bolton makes is that arbitration most often cuts off the time and expense of the appellate process, which in some venues could add several years to the resolution of a dispute. Generally the only exception would be in the case of an award that was obtained by fraud. Of course, this assumes that you are confident enough in the arbitration process and arbitrators selected that you are willing to forego the protection of the appellate process. This requires you to have the prescience to look ahead and have some notion of whether you are likely to be a plaintiff or a defendant (or an appellee or an appellant) in the disputes that are likely to arise under the contract. Bolton warns that some parties make the mistake of using their last dispute experience to disadvantage one side or the other—and then find themselves disadvantaged by that very process later on.

Dasteel raises some other interesting considerations that in some ways represent the other side of the coin. In arbitration, the arbitrator or panel has the exclusive right to render a decision—they can be wrong and yet still be upheld. Small holes that allow you to attack the merits of a decision are closing. "A decision can be as crazy as arbitrators want it to be," Dasteel relates, "but as long as they followed procedures, they are not likely to be reversed." A losing party in arbitration is often stuck with only procedural challenges to the award in court. This is particularly troubling if you happen to have a billion-dollar dispute. In litigation, you generally have the protection of an appeal.

Also keep in mind that unlike in the United States, in an international arbitration context, mediation is rarely used. International mediation is a new field, and this merely reflects cultural differences between the United States and much of rest of world, where lawyers are simply secondary to businesspeople. So if a given arbitration looks as if it is going badly for you, what to do? Generally, Dasteel observes, the lawyers will suggest that the opposing businesspeople meet to negotiate among themselves informally.

Finally, if your case involves an interplay between common law and civil law, Dasteel advises choosing arbitration and making clear in the arbitration agreement which substantive law the arbitrators must apply to settle the parties' rights. Otherwise, "You risk that a contract drawn up under one system of jurisprudence might be reviewed very differently under another system of jurisprudence," Dasteel concludes, creating unnecessary uncertainty. Again, Andrew Miller QC, of 2 Temple Gardens, agrees. The fact that participants from civil law countries are uncomfortable with common law environment—and vice versa—can actually drive settlement. Miller gives an example of a reinsurance case involving an earthquake in Mexico, which was ultimately dealt with in the courts. At issue were requirements that roads were built to internationally accepted standards. Mexico's inquisitorial system wasn't designed to consider that there could be conflicting evidence from opposing experts.

Preparing for Arbitration: Clear Identification of Desired Results

It is beyond the scope of this book to offer detailed suggestions for the mechanics of preparation for an arbitration, and indeed, it is assumed that many if not most readers of this text have significant technical experience and expertise in litigation. From this author's perspective, the important point to address as outside counsel prepares for arbitration is the counseling function. That is, outside counsel and the client company's businesspeople need to analyze what the best-case, likely case, and worst-case outcomes of the arbitration will be, and to continually refine them as the process goes on. This is a critical function because, as discussed further below, a negotiated settlement that once was deemed impossible or undesirable may indeed become preferable if the tenor of the proceedings foretells a worst-case outcome for either party.

Choosing the Arbitration Forum and Arbitrators

In many instances, the arbitration clause will specify the forum to be used. Generally, when the forum is specified, Western companies tend to insist on one of six internationally recognized arbitration organizations: AAA, ICC, LCIA, the United Nations Commission on International Trade Law (UNCITRAL), SCC Institute, and the Singapore International Arbitration Center (SIAC).[67]

In a few instances, Karen Klein, formerly of Kayak.com, relates, you have to agree to a local arbitration forum for business reasons. There are centers for arbitration in many developing countries. Dole notes that in India, for instance, you can use the Arbitration Council of India, which is part of the International Arbitration Council. In China, Dr. Liu states, there is a system for hearing grievances, the Chinese Council for the Promotion of International Trade (CCPIT), which is arbitration based. If the CCPIT fails to resolve a dispute, then the parties go to court.

Bolton says that although he has had good experiences with the International Institute of Conflict Prevention and Resolution—citing their roster of sophisticated arbitrators—he feels that if you have a role in selecting the arbitrators, you can use any of the major systems. Bolton adds one caution: the subject matter of the dispute may influence your decision. For example, the AAA has built an excellent reputation resolving personal injury matters, but one would have to consider whether their panels could decide a matter that hinged on a complex niche subject such as microbiology, for instance. Photos Abbott, of Motorola, adds that, much as in the same way you would choose an arbitrator for a domestic dispute, you should look for personal recommendations from colleagues you trust, and from as broad a network as possible.

Beware the possibility that your choice of arbitrators may be limited in certain locales. For example, Saudi law requires arbitrators to be Muslim,

---

67. Morkin & Chang, *supra* note 63, at 228.

and Venezuelan arbitrations applying Venezuelan law must be presided over by arbitrators who are Venezuelan lawyers.[68]

If you are going to arbitrate in a foreign forum, Bolton adds, you would be well advised to involve lawyers familiar with the local law. Even if they apply U.S. law, they are likely to do so with a local spin or viewpoint.

Venue

All six of the major international arbitration organizations listed previously allow the parties to choose the place of arbitration.[69] New York and London are common venues for international arbitrations. Other centers that are often recommended include Geneva, Hong Kong, and Singapore. Bolton argues that although the rules chosen by forum and the identity of the individual arbitrators are perhaps the two most important factors to consider, it is the place of the arbitration that determines which language will be used during the proceedings. Bolton warns that counsel should not underestimate the cost and delay that can result from having to translate the proceedings from beginning to end.

If the parties fail to agree as to place of arbitration, the organizations each have their own method for selecting one. Not surprisingly, the LCIA and SIAC rules specify London and Singapore, respectively, unless the tribunal designates a more appropriate place.[70] AAA chooses the venue absent party agreement unless the tribunal chooses one within 60 days of its formation.[71] UNCITRAL rules leave the decision to the tribunal, while the ICC and SCC Institute articles hold that the decision is made by the institutions themselves.[72]

Choice of Law

Not surprisingly, most U.S. transactional lawyers seek to have the law of the state their client is domiciled in as controlling law over the international agreements into which their clients bind themselves. The reason is

---

68. Michael L. Morkin & H. Henry Chang, *International Enforcement of Arbitration Awards against Sovereign Entities*, 2 CAA ARB. J. 65 (2003).
69. *Id.* at 235.
70. *Id.*
71. *Id.*
72. *Id.*

simple: these lawyers are typically familiar with that state's law and can generally predict with reasonable accuracy how disputes will be resolved under that precedent.

Still, Bolton reveals that in his experience, choice of law is perhaps the issue that is most often compromised in business negotiations. Bolton indicates that if a client company has retained a local counsel in the foreign jurisdiction that can with assurance indicate a comfort level with how disputes would be resolved under that precedent, the application of the foreign law to the contract can be compromised.

Photos Abbott relates that her contracts will not always require application of U.S. law. Her office is generally happier with the application of the law from common law, rather than civil law, jurisdictions, however. She points out that your judgment as a lawyer is based on the experience you have with the system you know—and it is quite difficult to adjust to a new system. U.S. lawyers are often quite creative in coming to legal solutions, but this trait does not always mix well with civil law systems in her experience. She feels you are well served when you have excellent local counsel but also a "quarterback" or coordinating firm that understands how you think.

In arbitration, if the parties have not agreed on applicable law, the AAA, ICC, and SCC Institute give the tribunal the right to apply the law it deems appropriate, while the UNCITRAL rules allow the tribunal to apply conflict of law rules to reach the applicable law.[73] SIAC rules apply Singapore's International Arbitration Act, while the LCIA applies the arbitration law of the place where the arbitration is held.[74]

In any event, your insistence on a particular choice of law provision may not in the end guarantee that it will be followed, particularly if the case ends up getting litigated in a foreign court. It has been observed that the courts in some countries will apply their own law in some circumstances, despite the previous agreement of the parties.[75]

---

73. Morkin & Chang, *supra* note 63, at 239.
74. *Id.*
75. Conlon, *supra* note 1.

Negotiating Through the Dead Spaces

As noted above and as with most litigation, the likely outcome of international arbitrations may change for the better or the worse as evidence is considered and by virtue of signals sent by the arbitrator or panel. As such, the parties need to be willing to continue negotiations even while the arbitration proceeds. Bolton warns that unlike in the United States, foreign arbitrators may not always encourage a negotiated settlement. Therefore the parties need to be more proactive and actively request a third-party mediator be brought in at such times as fresh negotiations are indicated.

Traditional Litigation and Enforcement of Judgments

As discussed above, some parties may have various reasons to prefer litigation over arbitration of disputes. If the U.S.-based company is initiating litigation, it will be faced with the dilemma of whether to litigate in U.S. courts and try to enforce the judgment obtained there in a foreign jurisdiction, or to simply go straight to the foreign courts themselves and try the dispute there.

Clearly, for U.S. lawyers and their U.S. clients, U.S. courts are cheaper, more convenient, generally quicker, and more predictable than foreign courts.[76] For instance, one source estimates that Indian contract cases can take up to 15 years to settle.[77] If the foreign party has assets in the United States that can be attached, it would generally be preferable to litigate in the United States. If not, however, all the U.S. court can do is issue a judgment that your client must take to a foreign court and hope to have enforced there. As the Financial Services Roundtable notes,

> the lack of reciprocity in judgments potentially suggests that judgments obtained in U.S. courts over contractual disputes would have to be resubmitted to Indian courts and reconsidered with reference

---

76. Hoffman, *supra* note 62.
77. Brendan B. Read, *Tailoring Outsourcing to Foreign Customers*, CALL CTR. (Aug. 5, 2003), http://business.highbeam.com/1913/article-1G1-106227794/tailoring-outsourcing-foreign-customers-outsourcing.

to Indian law. This could be problematic since Indian law has different limits than the United States on damages obtained in civil cases.[78]

The Indian government has reciprocation with some jurisdictions, including the United Kingdom, and judgments issued by courts in those countries can be enforced directly by filing execution proceedings under the Indian Code of Civil Procedure, as if they were decrees of an Indian Court.[79]

Dr. Liu sounds a cautionary note about the courts in China:

> Very few cases actually go to court in China. There is a system, and you should follow it—but don't rely on it. In China, when it comes to the maturity of the legal system, there can be a big difference between appearance and reality. Don't expect the same effectiveness of enforcement in China. If your opponent is a government official, or has stronger connections than you, you are going to lose, regardless of the merits.

To win disputes, Liu advises, you must cultivate local relationships:

> In the U.S. who you know might decide a dispute 10 percent of the time; in China, it's more like 50 percent of the time. You must stay on good terms with all levels of government. Remember that government officials in China are like one family.

Knoblauch, of UL, gives a final cautionary example on cross-border litigation from his experience at Honeywell. One of the Honeywell companies, Visitronics, sold a complex, integrated circuit to the camera industry, which, for the first time, allowed companies to offer "auto focus" in their cameras. While very detailed contractual arrangements were worked out, what made the business work were the personal relationships between the key people at Honeywell and the key people in the Japanese companies. For five years everything worked perfectly, but when management changed (as

---

78. INFORMATION POLICY INSTITUTE, *supra* note 8, at 17.
79. Agarwal & Khaitan, *supra* note 61, at 5.

it often does in the United States as good managers get promoted), new people took over, and slowly, imperceptibly, the relationship was lost. One of the Japanese customers (Minolta) got frustrated with the lack of cooperation from Honeywell and decided (patent or no patent) to start making their own chips, assuming that any disputes could be quietly worked out as they normally were in Japan, by after-the-fact cross-licensing agreements between the parties. Honeywell filed patent infringement litigation in the United States and ultimately recovered a total of nearly $400 million from Minolta and others in the Japanese camera industry.

Honeywell may have won the battle, but there were no winners here, as the relationship with the camera industry was forever destroyed. The moral of the story: international business is about people, critical people who build cross-cultural relationships that help companies survive all the choppy seas that come along. Legal contracts and lawyers only come into play once the relationship has died. International businesspeople know that no contract can ever anticipate all the eventualities. Good partners find mutually agreeable solutions when times get tough and keep their eyes on the long-term relationship, not short-term profit.

Epilogue: A Look Ahead

Predicting the future rarely ends well for the would-be oracle. I lay no claim to prophetic gifts or any means of time travel that would allow me some sort of special insight into what the world will look like in 2015 and beyond. One only has to cast back to September 10, 2001, and think about how many futurists at that time could have accurately imagined the events of the following 13-plus years. The truth is that, as I type this text sitting in the exit row of a Southwest flight from Buffalo to Chicago, totally unexpected events halfway around the world may once again be coalescing in such a way as to fundamentally transform the global economy and our individual places in it. And as history has shown us repeatedly, those events can change everything in a New York minute.

With that very significant caveat set forth, it occurs to me that one of the principle messages of this book is the need to project forward what we know about the world now in order to game out future events and thereby better understand both the risks and opportunities that a business faces in the future. In reality, that is a lot more easily accomplished for an individual business than for the world writ large. Still, I would argue that as we progress through 2014 and beyond, there are a number of trends that we can project out at least a few years into the future that should provide some guidance to you about risk and opportunity, at least in the short term. So with that, I give you some musings on what a few current trends *might* mean for global business in the coming years.

Increased Overseas Political Risk for U.S.-Based Businesses

Christine Lagarde, the Managing Director of International Monetary Fund (IMF), gave a speech on the future of the Global Economy and her organization in Washington, D.C., on October 11, 2013. In that speech, she highlighted projections that over next decade, the share of emerging and developing economies in global gross domestic product (GDP) will increase from about one-half to nearly two-thirds; this will set the stage for a future in which "economic power will be far less concentrated in the advanced economies—and more vastly dispersed across all regions."[1] Explicitly, Ms. Lagarde spoke in terms of this economic shift leading to a "more multipolar world."[2]

Americans who haven't already gotten their minds around the practical consequences of these megatrends would be well disposed to start now. To put it simply, the rise of emerging economies, and the relative economic weakness of the United States and European Union (EU) member nations suggest a world in which traditionally less empowered trading partners of the West feel more and more at liberty to take political action against western businesses within their territorial ambit. Anti-American feelings that in some quarters had been muted have of late increasingly been seen and heard out in the open. For example, during the October 2013 Washington dispute over funding the federal government and raising the U.S. debt ceiling, the Chinese news agency Xinhua garnered significant international attention by openly calling for a "de-Americanized world":

> Under what is known as the Pax-Americana, we fail to see a world where the United States is helping to defuse violence and conflicts, reduce poor and displaced population, and bring about real, lasting peace.
>
> Moreover, instead of honoring its duties as a responsible leading power, a self-serving Washington has abused its superpower status and introduced even more chaos into the world by shifting financial risks overseas, instigating regional tensions amid territorial disputes, and fighting unwarranted wars under the cover of outright lies.
>
> As a result, the world is still crawling its way out of an economic disaster thanks to the voracious Wall Street elites, while bombings

---

1. Christine Lagarde, *The Future Global Economy and the Future Fund*, INT'L MONETARY FUND (Oct. 11, 2013), http://www.imf.org/external/np/speeches/2013/101113.htm.
2. *Id.*

and killings have become virtually daily routines in Iraq years after Washington claimed it has liberated its people from tyrannical rule.

Most recently, the cyclical stagnation in Washington for a viable bipartisan solution over a federal budget and an approval for raising debt ceiling has again left many nations' tremendous dollar assets in jeopardy and the international community highly agonized.

Such alarming days when the destinies of others are in the hands of a hypocritical nation have to be terminated, and a new world order should be put in place, according to which all nations, big or small, poor or rich, can have their key interests respected and protected on an equal footing.[3]

Whether such feelings are broadly held throughout China, Asia, and the rest of the world, and moreover whether they will be increasingly acted upon in coming years, history will judge. In terms of China however, there are growing warning signs of antiforeign enforcement activities. A recent *Wall Street Journal* article, while acknowledging China's overall openness to foreign investment, also noted the following:

> What concerns many Western business executives is not just that price-fixing investigations have concentrated on foreign companies—often accompanied by shrill denunciations of their corporate targets in state media. Individuals within companies and their networks are also being singled out. And, say lawyers and others, there are disturbing Mao-era echoes in the tactics employed.
>
> One Western lawyer describes what he calls "inquisitions" of several of his multinational dairy and pharmaceutical clients by regulators . . . as the economy has slowed, the risk of domestic protectionism has grown. China is shifting its export and investment-led growth model toward consumption, a process that will produce both winners and losers. Foreign consumer companies with strong brands and a reputation for quality ought to be the winners. But expect

---

3. Liu Chang, *Commentary: U.S. fiscal failure warrants a de-Americanized world*, XINHUA (Oct. 13, 2013), http://news.xinhuanet.com/english/indepth/2013-10/13/c_132794246.htm.

state-supported "national champions" to push back aggressively, enlisting the support of their allies in the bureaucracy.

Western executives who have sat through a grilling by regulators "are terrified," says the Western lawyer.[4]

Not everyone is sitting still for this treatment however. The *Wall Street Journal* reports that after having been fined $9.8M over the past three years for alleged misleading pricing and selling poor quality products, Wal-Mart executives have met in recent months with China's Food and Drug Administration, urging officials to step up their inspections of all food purveyors, including locally based ones.[5]

China is hardly the only place where such political risk is of increasing concern. Another recent *Wall Street Journal* piece focused on the growth and evolution of regional political entities in Indonesia through the lens of small U.K.-based Churchill Mining, and their claims that revocation of their license to extract billions of dollars of coal was a blatant attempt by a local regent to appropriate the rights for himself and his allies.[6] The article suggests that efforts to decentralize political power have led to the creation of more than 200 new administrative regions, which in turn has created confusion for businesses caused by the resulting overlapping authority and rules.[7] Perhaps not coincidentally, more than 30 percent of acting governors, mayors, and district heads in the country are under investigation for corruption according to Regional Autonomy Watch, and more than 40 have already been sent to prison since 2004.[8] The challenge of the local regent's action resulted in a victory for Churchill in the first round of arbitration in the World Bank's arbitration court in February 2014; the Indonesian government indicated it would object to the ruling, after the International

---

4. Andrew Browne, *A New Challenge for Multinationals in China: Mao-era Politics*, WALL ST. J. (Sept. 30, 2013), http://online.wsj.com/article/SB10001424052702303643304579106694013203808.html.
5. Laurie Burkitt and Shelly Banjo, *Wal-Mart Cries Foul on China Fines*, WALL STREET JOURNAL (April 13, 2014), http://online.wsj.com/news/articles/SB10001424052702304157204579473272856969150?mg=reno64-wsj.
6. Eric Bellman, *Regional Powers Sting Firms in Indonesia*, WALL ST. J. (Oct. 8, 2013), http://online.wsj.com/article/SB10001424052702303442004579120711962482266.html.
7. Id.
8. Id.

Center for Settlement of Investment Disputes ruled it had jurisdiction over the matter.[9] The loss of the license had previously led to Churchill's share price plunging more than 85 percent from its highs in 2010.[10]

Such news should not unduly unsettle the prospective cross-border dealmaker, however. A regional general counsel with years of experience in Latin America reminds us:

> There will *always* be surprises in international operations. If political risk does develop into an actual crisis or controversy . . . DON'T PANIC. Shareholders and the home office may read the news and think that everything is coming terminally unglued. Not necessarily. Remember: generally political risk isn't focused on you—it just feels that way if a host government sees foreign investment as a convenient scapegoat.

Jed Hepworth says: "At its heart, surviving political risk is a function not only of the external environment (will the situation permit you to do business sustainably and profitably, even if not comfortably and predictably?) but of the patience and agility and optimism and determination of the enterprise to endure and operate in that environment."

Cultural differences play themselves out in international negotiations and in the context of political risk. A regional general counsel observes that in Latin America, although things are changing, the lawyer as lead negotiator is still uncommon. National government officials expect to negotiate with the President of the company, not its lawyers. In business negotiations as well, the prevailing culture is still that of talking principal to principal, with the lawyers expected to be implementors and scriveners.

To manage political risk, Jed Hepworth offers the following advice: use ALL the resources available to you. That means seeking out the advice or involvement of the local American Chamber of Commerce, U.S. Embassy, local business organizations, and other foreign investors. They will provide

---

9. Fidel Ali, *Indonesia to File Objection to Arbitration Ruling in Favor of Churchill Mining*, JAKARTA GLOBE (February 28, 2014) http://www.thejakartaglobe.com/business/indonesia-to-file-objection-to-arbitration-ruling-in-favor-of-churchill-mining/.
10. Bellman, *supra* note 6.

perspective and insights and experience, even if they don't directly advocate for you. Political risk is cyclical as well as challenging and intimidating, so you can find people and companies who have survived political risk and who can help you avoid giving up in despair.

Sometimes understanding the big picture can be of great assistance in defusing political situations. Paul Wright, formerly a member of Exxon Mobil's law department, relates a case involving a huge pipeline project being built across a poor West African nation. Unfortunately, the country had a change of government virtually every six months. To deal with the political risk more so than any real need for financing, a credit application was filed with the IMF. It worked like a charm. The reason? The government didn't want to lose their credit standing with the IMF.

In dealing with political risk, Wright asks you to examine what kind of presence you have in the country, who your local counsel is, and what kind of rapport they and you have with the government in question.

Wright suggests that to deal with potential political risk, it may be advisable to insert stability clauses into your agreement. The purpose of the clauses is to protect you against changes in future legislation. The stability clause causes the parties to be subject to international arbitration in a different country. Venezuela, where the oil companies have been state-run entities, was one location where Wright would encourage the use of such clauses.

Another possible mechanism to deal with potential political risk involves invocation of bilateral investment treaties. Some 140 countries are signatories. This tool can put you into a special forum, the International Centre for Settlement of Investment Disputes, based out of Washington.

All kinds of disputes pull governments in one direction or the other. That's where politics and diplomacy (through special negotiators) come in. "It takes a lot of choreographing," says Paula Stern of The Stern Group, Inc. She ought to know: her 16 years in government service included a stint as Chair of the U.S. International Trade Commission (ITC), which hears complaints from domestic companies on issues such as dumping, patent and copyright infringements, and so on. One of her specialties today is in resolving commercial disputes. She has also done political risk assessments for corporations in South Africa and Korea.

"When a government gets involved in private commercial disputes, domicile makes a huge difference," Stern advises. One example she cites involved her work, over more than a decade, on behalf of several U.S. multinational corporations caught in a business dispute with a Pakistani company. Although her clients received a favorable ruling from an International Chamber of Commerce (ICC) Arbitral Panel in 2000, and a Lahore civil court upheld the ICC decision in 2005, local parties continued litigating the matter in Pakistani courts for many years. In short, the arbitration clauses in contracts signed in Pakistan were not being upheld, and Stern asserted that a weak judicial system and lack of respect for the rule of law were major impediments to foreign investment there.

The appropriate response required finding all the levers in Washington and international multilateral institutions that affect, influence, permit, or constrain a local company in Pakistan running roughshod over its own court system. Stern persuaded the U.S. government to list her clients' case as a priority issue for U.S. negotiators in the congressionally mandated National Trade Estimate Report on Foreign Trade Barriers for 2004, as well as each year after until the local disputant agreed to resolve the dispute in 2009. In the end, Stern had convinced the Government of the Islamic Republic of Pakistan to respect international arbitral awards and to enforce the International Chamber of Commerce arbitral decision.

That experience—having someone as a guide who can harness the various avenues of redress—can be most helpful in navigating political risk situations. Many companies have limited resources and must decide when to turn to a trade advisor or other expert. As Stern herself acknowledges, each dispute is different. That said, getting expert advice early on may allow a company an opportunity to head off a potentially very disruptive dispute. If, in fact, countries in emerging economies choose in the coming years to assert themselves against western-based companies, identifying a trusted expert like Stern would be well worth considering.

Chinese and Asian Companies: Coming to a Location Near You?

For the past 20 years and more, China has been largely seen as a cheap place to manufacture goods and the world's largest untapped market. What is already taking place, and is likely to become more and more prominent, says Michel Feldman of Seyfarth Shaw, is the arrival of more Chinese and Indian brands in the U.S. marketplace. What this means for businesses that supply global companies in the United States today, Feldman explains, is that they need to follow their customers around the world. "Otherwise," Feldman warns, "their customers may find other overseas vendors who then decide to come over here to take away the U.S. business of those (suppliers)."

Chinese brands that are already actively seeking global reach include Li-Ning sportswear, Chery automobiles, and Haier appliances. Feldman also observes that there are Chinese groups who want to find U.S. manufacturing companies with an existing sales and marketing presence in America. The Chinese group would purchase the company, take the manufacturing back to China, and keep the marketing face in the United States. Ironically, however, U.S. manufacturing may end up being their low-cost manufacturing centers, as American facilities are mostly automated. These Chinese groups have been looking to buy everything in areas where they don't already have expertise, Feldman says. It only makes sense given the need the Chinese have to reinvest their growing foreign reserves.

But you don't have to take Feldman's word for it: evidence of Chinese investment in the United States is all over the financial pages. Research firm Rhodium Group estimates that Chinese Foreign Direct Investment in the United States could create between 200,000 and 400,000 jobs in the United States by 2020.[11] Chinese tech firms are hiring Silicon Vallet executives, executing aggressive marketing campaigns, and reaching a "critical mass" of expertise, talent, and financial firepower.[12] Chinese developers

---

11. Thilo Hanemann & Adam Lysenko, *The Employment Impacts of Chinese Investment in the United States*, Rhodium Group (September 27, 2012), http://rhg.com/articles/the-employment-impacts-of-chinese-investment-in-the-united-states.
12. Juro Osawa & Paul Mozor, *The Rise of China's Innovation Engine*, WALL ST. J. (January 17, 2014) at B1.

and investment firms, having already purchased properties in New York and San Francisco, are now investing in cities such as Houston, Atlanta, Portland, Boston, and Seattle "as they seek geographic diversity as well as bigger lot sizes."[13]

Chinese e-commerce leader Alibaba recently invested over $200 million in San Mateo, California-based ShopRunner Inc. ahead of an anticipated multi-billion dollar U.S. initial public offering.[14] Joe Tsai, Alibaba's executive vice chairman and co-founder, is quoted as saying "coming into this market is about learning about American consumers and how the market operates."[15] Meanwhile, Shuanghui International Holdings Ltd. paid $4.7 billion to acquire Smithfield Foods Inc. in what at the time was the largest Chinese takeover of a U.S. company in order to ramp up pork exports to China and other Asian markets.[16] "The integration of the two companies will be closely watched amid speculation the merger could spark other major food and agriculture deals between the U.S. and China," the *Wall Street Journal* noted.[17]

As often happens, the bright light focused on China means less attention is paid to other Asian nations' investments and moves within the U.S. economy. Rest assured, however, that it is not just the Chinese or established European and Japanese coming to do business in America. South Korean tire manufacturer Hankook recently announced plans to build its first production plant in the United States at a cost of $800 million, while Indian-based Apollo Tyres is working on a $2.5 billion purchase of Cooper Tire and Rubber Inc.[18]

So what do U.S.-based companies and their counsel make of such trends? Like everything else we have discussed, the global economy poses both risks

---

13. Esther Fung, *Chinese Property Investors Widen Footprint in U.S.*, WALL ST. J. (Sept. 24, 2013), http://online.wsj.com/article/SB10001424052702303983904579094723756080610.html.
14. Greg Bensinger, *Alibaba Storming to America*, WALL ST. J. (Oct. 11, 2013), http://online.wsj.com/news/articles/SB20001424052702304500404579127750508042392
15. *Id.*
16. David Kesmodel, *Shuanghui to Boost Smithfield Exports as First Priority*, WALL ST. J. (Sept. 26, 2013), http://online.wsj.com/news/articles/SB10001424052702304795804579099421443260970.
17. *Id.*
18. Jeff Bennett, *Hankook Lands in U.S.*, WALL ST. J. (Oct. 15, 2013), http://online.wsj.com/news/articles/SB20001424052702304106704579135391061515588?mod=itp_wsj.

and opportunities. Clients and their counsel who prepare for the integration of more offshore businesses into the U.S. economy can likely profit and prosper from the investment, rather than be left behind. As we said in Chapter 1, there are fewer and fewer truly local and regional businesses today, and there will likely be even fewer in the future. Learning the skills necessary to understand a global marketplace for your (or your client's) company is simply crucial looking forward.

China and Greater Southeast Asia's Place in the World of the Future

Talk of China continues to dominate much of global business's attention, as it has for some time now. Moreover, it seems to be conventional wisdom that China will be (or is already) the biggest winner and dominant economic player of the twenty-first-century world. There is no doubt that China's growth over the past 30 years has been meteoric and an unabashed success in many ways. But ruler of the world? Lyric Hughes Hale, former CEO of China Online and a widely renowned international affairs expert, begs to differ.

The world's second-biggest economy faces a complex web of serious challenges in the coming decades that Hale suggests will create significant headwinds against its future dominance. Just some of the problems China's leadership is facing or soon will be forced to address include (1) a health care system which in 2006 saw 80 percent of expenditures spent on just 8.5 million government officials; (2) one-child policy aftermath that by 2040 will (assuming currents trends) cause the current ratio of 6:1 working adults to elders to drop to a 1.6:1 ratio; (3) income inequality already greater than that of the United States; (4) an asymmetric information gap with the rest of the world as the Central government limits Internet access to its citizens; (5) lack of access by small to medium-sized enterprises (SMEs) to domestic capital; and (6) Chinese consumption that cannot approach current U.S.

standards (absent massive technological leaps), as it would currently take the resources of four Earths to do so.[19]

Presciently, Hale warned in a speech before the Federal Reserve Bank in January 2013 that a flare-up of regional disputes might also distract China—a prediction manifestly borne out in subsequent news headlines. Recent issues between China and some of her neighbors regarding disputed islands are a cause of concern. The small amount of territory involved isn't the point, Hale explains—the islands are mere symbols for decades' if not centuries' worth of unresolved problems. As she points out, China had anti-Japanese boycotts in place in 1907. Hale estimates that there is as much as a 20–25 percent chance of military conflict between China and Japan going forward. The exit question from Hale's standpoint is: Will China's rise really be harmonious?[20]

This question is set against a backdrop in early 2014 of an economic slowdown that has spread across broad swaths of the Chinese economy, including retail, manufacturing, housing, and investment,[21] coupled with rising borrowing costs that could weaken profits and even bring about corporate defaults on the mainland.[22]

As this book went to press, China's commercial and residential property sectors were reportedly not doing well, especially in the city of Hangzhou, where "Grade A office buildings at the end of 2013 had an average occupancy rate of 30 percent, according to real estate broker Jones Lang LaSalle." In Hangzhou's residential sector, occupancy was deemed weak and prices were declining due to massive overbuilding. Data from the National Bureau of Statistics showed that while new home prices across the country were still

---

19. Lyric Hughes Hale, *China's 99%—Why China Will Not Surpass the U.S.* HUFFINGTON POST (Nov. 3, 2011), http://www.huffingtonpost.com/lyric-hughes-hale/why-china-will-not-surpas_b_1069623.html?ref=fb&src=sp&comm_ref=false.
20. Lyric Hughes Hale and David Hale, Independent International Affairs Professional and Board Director, Japan American Society of Chicago, Speech before the Federal Reserve Bank of San Francisco: *What's Next in Asia? Ten Things You Might Not Be Expecting in 2013*, 1 (Jan. 9, 2013), http://www.frbsf.org/banking-supervision/programs/asia-program/events/2013/january/us-asia-relationship-implications-american-economy/.
21. Bob Davis and Richard Silk, *China Reports Broad Economic Slowdown*, WALL ST. J. (March 14, 2014) at A5.
22. Shen Hong, *Perils Mount as Debt Costs Swell in China*, WALL ST. J. (February 11, 2014) at C.

going up, percentage increases had declined for three consecutive months, leading some to conclude the numbers were signaling a possible peaking.[23]

Projections into the mid-twenty-first century suggest Asia will indeed dominate global output, but more as a result of the collective growth of China, India, and Indonesia together, says David Hale, Chicago-based global economist and Lyric Hughes Hale's husband.[24] He notes that in 1700, Asia was deemed to have generated 58 percent of global output, compared to Europe at 25 percent. After World War II, the United States became dominant. By 2050 however, Asia is expected to once again produce over 50 percent of global output, with the United States and Europe at 21 percent. As David Hale rightly states, such a massive shift in global economics presents nothing less than a structural challenge over the next 30–40 years.[25] Clearly, such a tectonic shift in the order of global economics will require Asian nations to encourage and develop much more domestic consumption over the long term. How successfully the region can convert from export-driven growth will be one of the primary factors in determining how smooth a transition toward an Asian-driven global marketplace will actually be going forward.

Looking across greater Asia, David Hale notes that falling birth rates, which had primarily been Japan's concern, may also affect China in coming years as well as other established economies such as South Korea, Taiwan, and even Singapore.[26] By contrast, nations expected to have labor force growth—including Malaysia, India, Indonesia, the Philippines, and Myanmar—are poised to benefit. In particular he highlights the recent growth of the Philippines, which features a growing business outsourcing market employing more than 600,000 workers, and Myanmar, which just received its first U.S. Presidential visit (by Barack Obama) and which in addition to industrial growth may see as many as three million tourists annually by 2015.[27]

---

23. Jerin Mathew, *China Housing Market Bubble Start to Pop as Economy Faces Hard-Landing*, INTERNATIONAL BUSINESS TIMES (April 14, 2014), http://www.ibtimes.co.uk/china-housing-market-bubble-start-pop-economy-faces-hard-landing-1444648.
24. Hale, *supra* note 18.
25. *Id.*
26. *Id.*
27. *Id.*

Whither India?

Over the past several years, there has been a growing concern with India's performance in the global economic scene—and some unfavorable comparisons with China in particular. India's economic growth rate has scaled back significantly, from 9.3 percent in the first quarter of 2010 to only about 5 percent in 2013.[28] While it is fair to say that this slowing is at least in part due to the overall "global malaise" that continues to affect growth rates across a wide swathe of emerging economies, rosy projections of the Indian economy perhaps eclipsing that of the United States by 2040 have been revised to the point that emerging market analyst Ruchir Sharma refers to the Bharat as no more than a "50/50 bet."[29]

Why? As it happens, there are as many economic, societal, and public policy challenges facing India as a nation today as those facing China—arguably even more. From an economic standpoint, public borrowing has quadrupled in the past five years, the national deficit is growing, inflation is high, and a number of major Indian-based companies such as Tata Steel, Hindalco Industries, Tata Power, Larsen & Toubro, and others face dollar debts amounting to as much as double their market capitalization.[30]

Beyond these formidable issues, a host of public policy challenges arguably hobble Indian aspirations. These include a lack of privatization of publicly owned businesses, haphazard modernization of the financial system, stalled efforts at land reform needed to stimulate industrialization, woefully inadequate infrastructure, and a rampant "black economy" evading taxes estimated to have grown to 50 percent of national GDP by 2006.[31] Meanwhile, India has been suffering from a lack of investment in manufacturing,[32]

---

28. William Dalrymple, *What Happened to India's Economic Miracle? The Elephant Untethered*, NEW STATESMAN (July 5, 2013), http://www.newstatesman.com/2013/07/elephant-untethered.
29. Id.
30. Jason Overdorf, *India's Economy Is Collapsing. How Bad Will It Get?*, GLOBAL POST (Aug. 30, 2013), http://www.globalpost.com/dispatch/news/regions/asia-pacific/india/130829/india-economy-collapse-how-bad-future-consequences.
31. Paul Beckett, *In India, Doubts Gather Over Rising Giant's Course*, WALL ST. J. (March 30, 2011), http://online.wsj.com/news/articles/SB10001424052748703313304576131792120382006.
32. Natasha Brereton-Fukui & Tom Wright, *Asian Manufacturing Indexes Show Strong Export Orders*, WALL ST. J. (Oct. 1, 2013), http://online.wsj.com/article/SB10001424052702

whose share of the economy in 2009 stood at 16 percent, the same as it was in 1991, according to the World Bank.[33] The entire software and technology-services sector, including call centers and outsourcing, directly employs only 2.5 million workers, in a country of 1.2 billion, in which dependence on agriculture remains high.[34]

India's rules on foreign investment continue to be a concern as well. Wal-Mart recently announced an end to its six years of efforts to open retail stores in India with joint venture partner Bharti Enterprises Ltd., apparently driven away by continued government requirements such as a mandate that foreign retailers get 30 percent of their products and services from local small businesses.[35] In September 2012, India allowed foreign retailers to own stakes of as much as 51 percent in supermarkets, but with restrictions in place on how foreign firms build and supply their stores.[36] On the other hand, India'a Foreign Investment Protection Board did approve $1.5 billion in investments from U.K.-based Vodafone Group and Tesco in December 2013.[37]

Beyond all these high-concept issues, however, India faces some that might be considered more existential. Widespread societal inequality raises concerns about long-term social stability. Microsoft's former India chairman is quoted as saying "about 400 million people have seen benefits, and 800 million haven't."[38] Figures compiled by economists Amartya Sen and Jean Drèze tell a shocking story: one-quarter of the Indian population remains effectively illiterate, one-third of Indians do not have electricity, and fully half of Indian homes remain without toilets, forcing their residents to practice open defecation.[39] Child malnutrition in India is higher than in Eritrea; and the country only spends 1.2 percent of its GDP on health care, with

---

3043731045791088920277790238.html.
33. Beckett, *supra* note 31.
34. *Id.*
35. Shelly Banjo & R. Jai Krishna, *Wal-Mart Curbs Ambitions in India*, WALL ST. J. (Oct. 10, 2013), http://online.wsj.com/news/articles/SB20001424052702303382004579124703326968442.
36. *Id.*
37. Mukesh Jagota & R. Jai Krishna, *India Clears Big British Investments*, WALL ST. J. (December 31, 2013) B3.
38. Beckett, *supra* note 27.
39. Dalrymple, *supra* note 28.

only 8 out of 25 sub-Saharan African countries having immunization figures as bad as India's.[40]

While India's path out of deprivation might be seen as running through its world-famous services sector, continued growth may begin to be handicapped by deficiencies in the education system there. Call-center company 24/7 Customer Pvt. Ltd. has been seeking workers in the Philippines and Nicaragua, since it finds that the vast majority of Indian high school and college graduates cannot communicate effectively in English and have inadequate reading comprehension skills.[41] Schools are hampered by bureaucracy and a focus on rote learning that causes some 75 percent of technical graduates and more than 85 percent of general graduates to be unemployable by India's high-growth global industries.[42] Given that more than half of India's population is under the age of 25, and one million people a month are expected to seek to join the Indian labor force over the next decade, finding a way to address these grim statistics may likely be necessary to ensure basic social order.[43] Doing so in the near term may be even more problematic, considering that the IMF warns that India's standing among developing countries is unusual both in terms of the severity of growth slowdown and the fact that it is also battling elevated inflation at the same time.[44]

Samir Gandhi, a partner at Sidley Austin, agrees that in comparing India to China, it is easy to sense some disappointment with India. While some regions such as Gujarat have completed projects with accelerated time frames, he notes that there is "not a large amount of confidence that large projects will be completed timely or at all."

Still, Gandhi finds lots of excitement and opportunities in India today. He is seeing more SME's in India today in manufacturing, building products, and medical equipment. Issues he sees are time frames and continued

---

40. *Id.*
41. Geeta Anand, *India Graduates Millions, but Too Few Are Fit to Hire*, Wall St. J. (April 5, 2011), http://online.wsj.com/news/articles/SB10001424052748703515504576142092863219826.
42. *Id.*
43. *Id.*
44. Victor Mallet, *IMF Warns India over Taper Risks to Growth*, Financial Times (February 21, 2014) at 4.

concern about government action. "India is still moving forward," Gandhi says, "it's just moving slower than might have been expected a few years ago."

India has done very well because it is tech savvy, but Gandhi admits there is no longer a tremendous cost savings in India. As a result, companies are looking at other countries such as Vietnam, the Philippines, Eastern European countries, and Brazil.

That said, India has a few things going for it, Gandhi concludes. It has been a player in global services for a number of years now. Also, China is likely to see wages go up more rapidly as a result of its one-child policy. Conversely, India's large population under age 35 will serve to drive down wages there. For India to branch out beyond services to areas such as manufacturing and shipping, however, will take a lot of infrastructure, he reasons.

Legal process outsourcing (LPO) companies have rightly been pushing more outsourcing of the legal profession, especially on the litigation and discovery side, Gandhi notes. The extent to which this industry can experience breakout growth will be determined by how much companies in India are going to be able to replicate the quality that clients expect in the West. How much oversight is needed by U.S. law firms—will they find themselves paying twice for the same work? What are the LPO's' capacity to do large amounts of document processing? What kind of back-up facilities do they have? One must also consider issues of continuity, such as the mobility of key people. All in all, Gandhi concludes, there is definitely a place for LPO's; the question is, will companies get the same quality for the price? The jury is still out on that. Still, Indians will continue to get better. With more experience with western clients, he believes they will probably meet the challenge.

In bigger picture terms, Gandhi predicts there will be a big place for India in pharmaceuticals, with health costs the way they are likely to be in the future. But, Gandhi foresees a huge weakness in Indian information technology going forward. He expects we will see more restrictions in investment there because India wants to remain owned by Indians. Additionally, there are potential issues in India surrounding intellectual property protection and bankruptcy. India has instituted new IP laws, but people don't necessarily believe that they have a lot of teeth, Gandhi observes.

In thinking about the challenges we have laid out for India in the coming years, Gandhi draws a comparison not to China but to Egypt. He notes that Egypt experienced a doubling of its population in the past 30 years and exponential growth in educated people, but not the same growth in its economy. The result for Egypt was unrest. The same challenge exists in India, Gandhi concludes.

Despite all the challenges—and sometimes because of them—India offers opportunities in the coming years. Wal-Mart's recent experience aside, the Indian retail market is expected to expand from $400 million today to more than $1.3 trillion by 2020, according to estimates by Rachna Nath, a retail analyst for PricewaterhouseCoopers Inc.[45]

Recognizing the gap between available graduates' skills and job requirements, leading companies such as Tata and Wipro have stepped up internal training programs.[46] This begs the question for multinational service providers: What opportunities in connection with Indian-based firms does this portend? Will the sweeping 2014 election victory of the ostensibly pro-business Narendra Modi mark a turning point for Indian growth? Only time will tell.

Africa Rising

For all the attention that Asia gets from the dispensers of conventional wisdom, truly forward-thinking businesses are increasingly looking at Africa as the next big thing in globalization. Surprised? Well, then you haven't really been paying attention. Africa's economy is growing faster than that of any other continent, according to the African Development Bank, with the share of the population within the continent living below the poverty line falling from 51 percent in 2005 to 39 percent in 2012.[47] Africa's collective GDP is now roughly equal to Brazil's or Russia's, with more middle-class households than India,[48] and according to the IMF's World Economic Outlook released

---

45. Banjo & Krishna, *supra* note 35.
46. *Id.*
47. *Africa's Economy Seeing Fastest Growth*, BBC (July 11, 2013), http://www.bbc.co.uk/news/business-23267647.
48. Acha Leke, Susan Lund, Charles Roxburgh & Arend van Wamelen, *What's Driving Africa's Growth*, McKinsey & Company, June 2010, http://www.mckinsey.com/insights/economic_studies/whats_driving_africas_growth.

in October 2012, 11 of the world's 20 fastest-growing economies were in Africa.[49] Despite an April 2014 terrorist bombing that killed 71 people in the nation's capital and continued attacks by Boko Haram in Borno state, Nigeria found that explosive growth in mobile telecoms, manufacturing, and the entertainment sector had in part driven its GDP up 12 places in the global rankings, leaving it just out of the G-20.[50] So-called "Frontier markets" such as Zimbabwe are attracting some mutual fund managers to invest there as they are deemed "what emerging market countries like Brazil, Russia, India, and China were 20 to 25 years ago."[51]

Many point to Africa's riches in resources to explain this development. International affairs commentator Lyric Hughes Hale observes that while the United States is increasingly becoming energy independent, the same cannot be said for Asia, and the big winner as a result has been Africa. It is true of course that the price of oil increased seven-fold from 1999 to 2008, and prices for minerals, grain, and other raw materials also soared on rising global demand.[52] And it is equally true that Africa possesses 10 percent of proven world oil reserves, 40 percent of global gold production, and 80–90 percent of the world's chromium, as just a few examples.[53]

What might surprise many readers though is that only 32 percent of Africa's recent growth comes from natural resources and the related government spending they financed.[54] All the rest came from other sectors, including wholesale and retail, transportation, banking, telecommunications, and manufacturing, and notably, countries without significant resource exports had similar GDP growth rates to those who did.[55] An African Development Bank Annual Development Effectiveness Report said the growth was largely driven by the private sector, thanks to improved economic governance and

---

49. Francis Njubi Nesbitt, *Five Countries to Watch*, T. Row Price (Dec. 2012), http://individual.troweprice.com/public/Retail/Planning-&-Research/Connections/Africa/Global-Economy-African-Countries-Growth.
50. Ian Birrell, *Africa Is Refuting the Usual Economic Pessimism*, Wall Street Journal (April 16, 2014), http://online.wsj.com/news/articles/SB10001424052702303603904579492100427297122?KEYWORDS=nigeri[A[a&mg=reno64-wsj.
51. Javier Espinoza, *Next Stop: Frontier Markets*, Wall St. J. (March 4, 2014) at R2.
52. Leke, Lund, Roxburgh & van Wamelen, *supra* note 46.
53. Id.
54. Id.
55. Id.

a better business climate on the continent.[56] Several African countries have halted their deadly hostilities, reduced inflation rates, trimmed foreign debt, shrunk their budget deficits, privatized state-owned enterprises, opened trade, lowered corporate tax rates, and strengthened regulatory and legal systems.[57] With investment-friendly policies like that, it should not be that surprising that foreign direct investment into Africa skyrocketed from $9 billion in 2000 to $62 billion in 2008.[58]

China has led the way into this brave new world, with an estimated one million Chinese currently resident in Africa, leading to trade of $200 billion with Africa in 2013.[59] Former Chinese Vice-Minister of Commerce Wei Jianguo famously told *China Daily* that Africa will ultimately surpass the United States and the European Union to become China's largest trading partner.[60] Investment in Africa today is hardly limited to China, however. Western multinationals such as IBM, Nokia, and Nestlé are investing heavily.[61] In September 2013, Wal-Mart's South African arm Massmart Holdings Ltd. set plans to open 90 stores across sub-Saharan Africa over three years.[62]

Most recently, General Electric announced plans to double sales in sub-Saharan Africa during the next few years, and Glaxo Smith Kline revealed plans to invest $216 million over five years in several new factories. The same rapid evolution is visible in Ethiopia, Ghana, Kenya, Mozambique, and Tanzania.[63]

All of these developments would be exciting enough on their own, but when cross-border business casts its eyes on the future of Africa in the decades to come, well, that's where this story gets *really* interesting. According to United Nations projections, in the next 90 years Africa as a whole will see its population quadruple.[64] By that time, if these projections hold

---

56. *Africa's Economy Seeing Fastest Growth*, *supra* note 47.
57. Leke, Lund, Roxburgh & van Wamelen, *supra* note 61.
58. *Id.*
59. Adam Gordon, *What to Expect from the African Economy in 2063*, Forbes (May 15, 2013), http://www.forbes.com/sites/adamgordon/2013/05/15/goodbye-black-power-hello-black-scholes/.
60. Nesbitt, *supra* note 52.
61. *Id.*
62. Banjo & Krishna, *supra* note 35.
63. Birell, *supra* note 50.
64. Max Fisher, *The Amazing, Surprising, Africa-driven Demographic Future of the Earth, in 9 Charts*, Wash. Post (July 16, 2013), http://www.washingtonpost.com/blogs/worldviews/wp

up, Nigeria alone—a country with a current population of around 167 million in a landmass the size of the state of Texas—will grow to a nation of 1 billion people.[65] As strange as the concept may be, one has to wonder if Nigeria will be the next China.

Of course, such massive population growth will be superimposed on countries already straining to cope with high levels of destitution, disease, and infant mortality rates,[66] as well as political corruption, religious conflict,[67] and terrorism, among many other issues. Good governance and resource management will be crucial in preventing what could be a great opportunity for Africa from descending into chaos,[68] as will access to finance and continued improvements in infrastructure—given that the African Development Bank reports investment in that area currently at only 4 percent of collective GDP.[69] And finally, from a social stability standpoint, the issue is can Africa grow its economy faster than its inequalities?[70]

Some interesting insights into how Africa "can get there from here" come from an important current political player in the continent, Kingsley Moghalu, the deputy governor of the Central Bank of Nigeria. As he sees it, "Africa has no automatic future. The continent will have a future that it shapes by itself."[71] From Moghalu's vantage point, that needs to be a future that no longer seeks out foreign aid:

> From the nature of today's global political economy we can conclude that foreign aid, one of the major reasons why Africa fell behind because it robbed many African countries of the incentive to strive for an endogenous development path, is in decline. But it did enough damage that its consequences are still felt in the continent, with many

---

/2013/07/16/the-amazing-surprising-africa-driven-demographic-future-of-the-earth-in-9-charts/.
65. Id.
66. Leke, Lund, Roxburgh & van Wamelen, *supra* note 48.
67. Fisher, *supra* note 65.
68. Id.
69. *Africa's Economy "Seeing Fastest Growth," supra* note 47.
70. Gordon, *supra* note 59.
71. Kingsley Moghalu, Emerging Africa: How the Global Economy's "Last Frontier" Can Prosper and Matter (Bookcraft 2013), *excerpt retrieved from* http://www.howwemadeitinafrica.com/emerging-africa-how-the-global-economys-last-frontier-can-prosper-and-matter/27677/.

Africans still seeking and relying on foreign assistance and no exit strategy from the vice-grip of the aid mentality. All development begins, first, in the mind. And to develop, minds must be free to determine their collective destiny. With few exceptions, to juxtapose "aid" and "development," as in the phrase "development aid," is an oxymoron.[72]

Finally, Moghalu cites the rise of China outside of the conventional western economic consensus as proof that the African nations "can write our own rules for ourselves"—that is, that African cultures can develop variants of capitalism that serve them best, provided that "property rights, capital formation and innovation are developed."[73]

So, should a business give serious consideration to jumping into Africa now, rather than waiting until the year 2100? As soon as 2030, it is estimated that increasingly urban Africa's top 18 cities will have a combined spending power of $1.3 trillion.[74] It is true enough as Stephen Hayes, the President and chief executive officer of the Corporate Counsel on Africa, says that "the storms of Africa have not passed entirely, and there will be challenges enough for future generations to confront."[75] But that said, I agree with McKinsey & Company, a global management consulting firm, which says the following:

Companies already operating in Africa should consider expanding. For others still on the sidelines, early entry into emerging economies provides opportunities to create markets, establish brands, shape industry structures, influence customer preferences, and establish long-term relationships. Business can help build the Africa of the future. And working together, business, governments, and civil society can confront the continent's many challenges and lift the living standards of its people.[76]

---

72. *Id.*
73. *Id.*
74. Leke, Lund, Roxburgh & van Wamelen, *supra* note 48.
75. Stephen Hays, *Cautious Optimism for Africa's Future*, U.S. News & World Report (April 5, 2013), http://www.usnews.com/opinion/blogs/world-report/2013/04/05/us-must-help-develop-african-private-sector.
76. Leke, Lund, Roxburgh & van Wamelen, *supra* note 48.

That is with the straightforward caveat that all the planning in areas of diligence, compliance, IP, and others has to be carefully engaged in—no matter the opportunity.

A Few Thoughts on the Middle East

It is far beyond the scope of this book to try to explain the long and tumultuous history of the Middle East and its many conflicts back to their source. It is fair to say that many observers see something of a paradigm shift in the demonstrations and upheaval that began in 2011 and became known in common parlance as "the "Arab Spring," in reference to the ill-fated "Prague Spring" of 1968. Clearly, it is not feasible to do business in this area without reckoning with the political risk endemic to the region.

In terms of getting a handle on the state of affairs there since the Arab Spring, this author highly recommends an article by Cambridge University fellow George Joffe titled "The Future of the Middle East and North Africa," which in a concise and methodical way surveys the region's conflicts and aspires to foresee the likely outcomes over the succeeding five years. Given its troubled present, it should be of little surprise that Joffe sees few easy answers ahead for the region. Some of the more interesting observations Joffe makes include: (1) the dominant purpose of policy in the region—stability—has in itself been a primary progenitor of the crises that have erupted; (2) the actual trigger for the Arab Spring was a sudden rise in food and energy prices, which provoked riots throughout the region because of widespread poverty and inequality, although this was related to both the economic downturn of 2008 and structurally high unemployment that had been a microeconomic consequence of economic liberalization; (3) most Gulf governments have bought social peace at the price of massive consumer subsidies, which now mean that the average minimum price at which they can profitably sell their oil has risen dramatically in the past two years; (4) because of the region's continuing importance as an energy producer and trade route, it continues to maintain a geopolitical focus of much of the world, even as U.S. global supremacy gives way to a multipolar world; (5) the external geopolitics have replicated a sort of second cold war in the region with western powers on one side and Russia and to some extent China on the other; (6) Middle Eastern powers following this shift have aligned themselves into the Shi'a "arc of extremism" (Iran, Syria, Hizbullah in Lebanon, and, increasingly, Shi'a-led Iraq) and the so-called Sunni "arc of moderation" (Gulf Cooperation Council states and Jordan); and (7) of the two key conflicts in the region currently—Iran's nuclear ambitions and the Syrian Civil War—it is Syria that Joffe sees as "set to become a political vacuum of stupendous proportions . . . with incalculable consequences for regional stability."[77] Overall, Joffe sees little chance of progress on conflicts in the region until the West reexamines what he sees as its "normative assumptions about the way in which the problems of the . . . region should be addressed."[78]

Another interesting insight into the near-term future of the Middle East comes from the observations of Jed Chaaban, an Assistant Professor at the American University of Beirut. Chaaban notes that much of the Middle East is suffering from water shortages, and that as a result,

> the Gulf countries can solve the water issue and they have started. For instance, a couple of years ago Saudi Arabia dropped wheat production because it was draining their resources, and instead they decided to invest abroad in buying farmland to produce wheat abroad. . . . This decision was made because they could afford, obviously, to buy land outside and produce wheat in other places.
>
> The problem is that other countries . . . do not have the same endowments and do not have the same resources. We are talking about countries like Yemen, some parts of Egypt, and some parts of Morocco, where water shortages are often linked with poverty and dry areas where there are no job opportunities. There is environmental stress, which compounds demographic and social stresses, and one ends up having political tensions and conflict. I think one of the features of the recent Yemeni conflict is also that it is a conflict [over]

---

77. George Joffé, *The Future of the Middle East and North Africa*, NOREF (Aug. 20, 2013), http://www.peacebuilding.no/Regions/Middle-East-and-North-Africa/Publications/The-future-of-the-Middle-East-and-North-Africa.
78. *Id.*

fertile land and water access. It is not openly said so, but if you were to put a map of the Middle East and [its] water endowments over another map showing the places of conflict, you would have a strikingly complementary picture.[79]

Surprising in connection with this phenomenon and underscoring the importance of this issue is the fact that the Gulf States have gone well beyond their own region to obtain arable land, going as far afield as the Philippines, Vietnam, and Laos.[80]

Recognizing the political and religious turmoil that has roiled and continues to roil this region of the world makes predictions especially difficult, I nonetheless reached out to a true legal and global business expert in Charles Hallab, who chairs the Middle Eastern Practice Group at Baker McKenzie, for his insight. Not entirely surprisingly, he begins with an observation not unlike what we have heard in other contexts: "Generally, we make a collective mistake in North America of viewing the Middle East as homogenous." It is just as true in the Middle East as it is in Asia, Latin America, Europe, and elsewhere that one must resist the urge to overgeneralize:

> Factors in Tunisia that cause unrest may not be the same as in Bahrain or in the rest of the Gulf. In order to realistically assess a given locale, you need to reference the specific history of a given area, and its particular demographic. If you want to do something in Saudi Arabia or Egypt, you need to look at each individually.

While resisting the urge to make too many specific predictions ("It's not my job to offer political advice," he modestly states), Hallab will say that for the most part, he does not believe that the Gulf Cooperation Council (GCC) countries (i.e., Bahrain, Saudi Arabia, Kuwait, Oman, United Arab Emirates, and Qatar) will have many uprisings.

---

79. *The Middle East and the New Global Economy: The Drive for Competitiveness, Skills and Innovation*, Brookings Institute Middle East Youth Initiative (2009), http://www.shababinclusion.org/userfiles/file/MEYI%20Series%204%20-%20Region%20-%20Yousef-Chaaban.pdf.
80. *Id.*

Bahrain, however, has a quite different system from the rest of the GCC, Hallab notes. Bahrain features a Shiite populace with Sunni leadership, and "the Shiites there don't feel that they are getting their share of the rewards." That situation doesn't exist in other Gulf countries, which don't have "have nots" as exist in Egypt for example, Hallab observes.

Saudi Arabia has a population of 20–30 million, and unlike in the heyday of the Organization of the Petroleum Exporting Countries in the 1970s, 1980s, and 1990s, the vast majority of this population today is very young and very poor, Hallab notes. Struggling with a poor and very disenchanted population drives economic and employment policies fixated on employing those young people. The Saudis lack a culture of employment, since the current generation's parents and grandparents didn't have to work, Hallab explains. What this adds up to is the possibility for unrest in the future, but that being said, not all the necessary factors are in place at this time, says Hallab:

> Personal and tribal factors here offset a significant uprising. They will win the day for the time being—perhaps for the next few years. The Saudis don't yet have maturity with social media there.
>
> There is anxiety about royal succession. All these things make people anxious but I am not dissuading clients from investing in the Gulf.

One game changer that Hallab identifies has been development of indigenous media:

> Al Jeezera has been very important, as it gives the people in the Middle East a lens on the rest of the world and a lens on themselves. It's a game changer when you add in the internet and social media. Dictators didn't see it coming and didn't know what to do with it if they did.

As to security, individual circumstances must guide you, Hallab advises. So far, none of the uprisings of the Arab Spring have taken on an extremist, fundamentalist tone. While unrest can be dangerous", "it is not as insidious as when extreme anti-Western sentiment comes veiled in Islamic ideals," Hallab states. Overall, he is cautiously optimistic about everything going on in the Middle East. "It would have happened eventually in any event," Hallab concludes.

Significantly, Hallab believes that there are opportunities now in the Middle East that didn't exist before the uprisings began. "Lots of people have been spooked and [are] pulling back," he notes, this at a time when the Gulf States are still fixated on improving their countries, such as by upgrading technology. For some companies that can afford to be more risk tolerant, this provides an opportunity. Where before a request for proposals there might have drawn 12 competitors, now perhaps it draws only three, reflects Hallab. Indeed, there does not seem to be a lack of opportunity in the region, as is evinced by the planned construction of Kingdom Tower in Jeddah, Saudi Arabia—which at 3,281 feet would be almost twice the height of the 1,729-foot-tall Willis Tower in Chicago (formerly known as Sears Tower).[81] One anonymous in-house attorney sees what would have previously been deemed unusual countries such as Uzbekistan and Kazakhstan getting into the global mix, not just for supply of workforce but also as customers. To sum it up, as in any region where political risk is high, the diligence laid out in this book is crucial, but Middle Eastern transactions that are properly investigated and implemented continue to offer growth opportunities for cross-border operations.

Latin America: Growing Pains from Emerging Market to Strategic Market

Beneficiary of a decades-long boom, and a world-class commodities powerhouse, Brazil came to represent the twenty-first-century face of an expanding Latin America. However, a very large component of the rapid GDP growth, which reached 7.5 percent in 2010, was the spending of Brazil's emerging middle class, which led to a doubling of consumer loans (to around

---

81. Ted Thornhill, *Onwards and Upwards: The Incredible Skyscrapers That Are Set to Cecome the Tallest in the World Including One That'll Be 1,000 Metres High*, DAILY MAIL (Nov. 1, 2013), http://www.dailymail.co.uk/news/article-2475154/The-incredible-skyscrapers-built-East-including-tower-1-000-metres-high.html.

$600 million) in a five-year span.[82] With credit card defaults on the rise, banks in 2013 grew warier of lending, which caused consumption to expand at its lowest rate since 2004.[83] The consumption surge of the previous several years coupled with weaker exports to China and a manufacturing slump caused by a strong currency drove up inflation, which it turn required Brazil's central bank to raise its benchmark rate to 9.5 percent.[84]

Given that 2012 GDP growth had already slowed to a rate of just 0.9 percent,[85] higher interest rates have naturally led to concerns of even slower growth going forward. Worse, the Brazilian economy is also coping with a host of other issues, including a high cost of living, poor public services, political corruption, a lack of infrastructure, and what *The Economist* magazine refers to as "the world's most burdensome tax code."[86]

As with all the other regions we have examined, the picture is not entirely negative, of course. Brazil remains the world's third-largest food exporter, is poised to become a major oil exporter by 2020, is developing a world-class research base, and hosts a number of world-class consumer brands that are poised to go abroad in the near future.[87]

Clearly, political risk in certain parts of this region remains. In November 2013, the Associated Press reported that Venezuela seized control of two oil rigs owned by a unit of Houston-based Superior Energy Services for which state-owned oil company PDVSA was months behind on payments.[88]

Ed Bathelt, General Counsel at ⊠Komatsu America Corp, has the experience that allows him to recognize the many issues facing businesses new to Latin America:

---

82. Loretta Chao and John Lyons, *Bill Comes Due for Brazil's Middle Class*, WALL ST. J. (Oct. 8, 2013), http://online.wsj.com/news/articles/SB10001424052702304795804579097412611960306.
83. *Id.*
84. *Id.*
85. *Has Brazil Blown It?*, ECONOMIST (Sept. 28, 2013), http://www.economist.com/news/leaders/21586833-stagnant-economy-bloated-state-and-mass-protests-mean-dilma-rousseff-must-change-course-has.
86. *Id.*
87. *Id.*
88. *Venezuela Seizes U.S.-Owned Oil Rigs in Dispute over Unpaid Bills*, ASSOCIATED PRESS (Nov. 1, 2013), http://www.foxnews.com/world/2013/11/01/venezuela-seizes-us-owned-oil-rigs-in-dispute-over-unpaid-bills/.

If you are in a country you have not done work in before, such as Peru—How do you know whom to hire? You hire them and then they give advice. How do you vet that the first time you are there? You have to establish infrastructure and support—it takes time.

For those entering a new market in Latin America, Bathelt's advice comes down to three words: "explore the market." He recommends that in-house legal staff turn to U.S. outside counsel to set up the legal aspects of the distribution network. If after finding a lawyer there, you sit waiting for an answer to a critical question because "we haven't heard back from lawyer X," Bathelt simply advises his in-house counterparts to let retained U.S.-based attorneys coordinate finding someone else who can respond.

All that in-house counsel can do is plan out the infrastructure before the company jumps. This is often a luxury, Bathelt observes, "because so often you are chasing a train that is already leaving the station." This then underscores the need to partner with businesspeople on a strategic level, as Bathelt explains. If there is a strategic plan for Argentina, in-house counsel needs to get a lawyer there and set up the latticework. Tax issues? Establish an entity there. Labor issues? Well, business people already want to sell. Ideally, in-house counsel that are prepared can say, "other people went to Argentina and here's what they dealt with." But, Bathelt concludes, "to do that, you need to do your homework first."

One further difference Bathelt sees in Latin America is exposure to criminal liability. For instance, injured employees there have different rights; an injury may lead to a criminal action brought by the victim's family. Also, collection actions may be a criminal action in a debtor suit.

U.S. Backlash: Always Looming

If this survey of the emerging economies has done anything, it should underscore that while they have a lot of potential to assume leadership in the global economy of the future, they also face tremendous roadblocks in getting there. This realization should give some perspective to American leaders as they survey the challenges this country faces going forward.

Indeed, it was somewhat surprising that following the recession of 2008, the amount of protest and resistance from protectionist forces to the spread of globalization in the United States was so muted, compared to that in the comparatively prosperous circa 2004 time frame. Perhaps sufficient groundwork has been laid by years of multinational corporate endeavors that the bulk of the U.S. public accepted international operations as a given in today's business landscape. After all, since 2008, it would have seemed likely that, given the severity and depth of the economic downturn, a great deal of protest and backlash against American companies should have been expected. Yet, backlash against outsourcing did not rise much into the *zeitgeist*, such that cautions about the need to prepare for backlash from politicians and various interest groups seemed unnecessary.

As soon as the election cycle of 2012 took hold, however, protectionism emerged once again on the national political scene. After a *Washington Post* story accused Republican Presidential nominee Mitt Romney's former company, Bain Capital, of investing in companies that specialized in shipping jobs to low-cost labor nations, President Obama's campaign began to refer to Romney as "Outsourcer in Chief."[89]

Meanwhile, a bill known as the "Save New Jersey Call Center Jobs Act" was introduced in that state's legislature, seeking to strip state loans, grants, and other incentives from companies who transferred more than 30 percent of their workforce overseas.[90]

After the election, the anti-outsourcing meme seemed to fade once again. But this experience exemplifies that a new cycle of backlash may erupt again, and it is still likely worthwhile to consider how to handle it before a public relations crisis engulfs your client.

Historically, the antiglobalization case breaks down into four basic lines of argument: (1) the negative effect of globalization on certain parts of the U.S. workforce; (2) the negative effects of globalization on the U.S. economy in general; (3) the negative effects on global social justice and human rights;

---

89. Sabrina Siddiqui, *Mitt Romney "'Outsourcer-in-Chief,'" Obama Campaign Ads Say*, HUFFINGTON POST (June 26, 2012), http://www.huffingtonpost.com/2012/06/26/romney-outsourcer-obama-campaign-ads_n_1626247.html.
90. Jared Kaltwasser, *Unions Push Bill to End Incentives for Companies that Send Jobs Overseas*, NJBIZ.COM (June 13, 2012), http://www.njbiz.com/article/20120613/NJBIZ01/120619933/Unions-push-bill-to-end-incentives-for-companies-that-send-jobs-overseas.

and (4) notwithstanding all of the above, that globalization has failed to provide the benefits it was supposed to deliver.

As the client company formulates its responses to various critics, it is important to recognize that many arguments that are couched in terms of social issues or human rights are still in reality proffered for the purpose of keeping jobs from moving elsewhere, often whether or not there is a logical business reason to do so. Determining the actual motivation for the criticism of your client company is essential in formulating a proper response.

In dealing with the press, media consultant Cheryl McPhilimy advises trying to identify the question behind the question—that is, determining what the reporter is really asking, and why:

> It is wise to consider the audience of a media outlet. Who watches this station? Who reads this paper? Journalists are responsible to their audiences. In a layoff situation, for instance, keep in mind that the readers of the local newspaper may be the people losing their jobs. Are you sensitive to that?

In addition, McPhilimy encourages executives to try not to take a reporter's questions personally:

> Media will ask sometimes deeply probing questions. It is their job to do so. A wise spokesperson is prepared to answer. "Why are you taking jobs overseas?" "Does this make you a 'less American company'?" "What are you offering the workers here?" etc. . . . It is important to remember that such questions are appropriate. Our media operate in a culture of free speech, which is ultimately for the greater good of society. Many injustices and issues are brought to light and important topics are raised because media are doing their jobs and asking questions. Keeping that in mind can help a spokesperson buffer feelings of being attacked when questions come flying. Respect the questions, stay calm, and deliver thoughtful answers. A spokesperson's role is to help illuminate the issues as he or she sees them for the media.

Simply compiling facts and figures and preparing press releases will not necessarily create an effective backlash management strategy. It is important for client companies and the industry associations to which they belong to monitor legislative and regulatory changes being proposed, particularly when their primary aim is to destroy cost savings and otherwise simply impede overseas operations for the benefit of a particular constituency. Once you have determined the motivations of the critics involved and compiled the facts, then it is possible to create and deliver a defense, based on both rational explanation and emotional intelligence.

Takeaways

SMEs *can* in fact take advantage of cost savings, access to new markets, and the possibilities for growth that are presented in today's global marketplace. But big or small, your client company will only get the competitive advantage promised by the global economy if it engages in it—smartly. Just keep in mind Michel Feldman's sage advice: "Be very open minded and be globally minded." And remember these key points:

- Select a "quarterback" attorney who matches well with the capacities of your in-house legal and technical staff and to the task at hand—someone who is willing to question the bases of internal decision making and offer alternatives.
- Create a network that incorporates U.S. and foreign knowledge bases, including consultants who "see the big picture."
- Engage in thorough strategic planning through the use of a management steering committee and scenario building, and by focusing on the end business goal.
- "The more you invest, the more sophisticated your diligence should be"—always weigh one-time set-up costs against potential long-term benefits.
- Create a defined business scope and objectives by which to craft due diligence criteria.

- Invest the time and money necessary to visit the offshore location. Save money by seeing the situation on the ground for yourself and learning from others' mistakes.
- Build a relationship with your vendor or overseas partner—start by communicating clearly what you want and need.
- As you contemplate risk, focus on the top three to six issues and anticipate what else to look for as business grows.
- For successful negotiations, make sure the key decision makers are engaged on both sides, and do not seek a deal that robs the other side of its ability to make a profit.
- No matter how carefully you draft them, do not put too much faith in termination and dispute resolution clauses of your contract.

I close with words taken from the January 1989 Farewell Address of U.S. President Ronald Reagan who, although he was talking about our interaction with the Soviets, could just as easily have been talking about doing business in a globalized world: "It's still trust but verify. It's still play, but cut the cards. It's still watch closely. And don't be afraid to see what you see."

Appendix A

U.S. Purchase Order Terms and Conditions

Appendices A through I were provided by Harvey Cohen of Dinsmore & Shohl.

Overview and Checklist
- I. Basic Premises and Concepts
    - A. Create terms that favor purchaser within limits
    - B. Anticipate content of sellers' forms
    - C. Tailor forms to purchaser's history and specific problems
    - D. Train those people using forms
- II. Front of Form
    - A. Call attention to existence of terms and conditions on reverse side
    - B. Provide place for vendor to sign and return an acknowledgment copy of form accepting buyer's order
    - C. Include "battle of the forms" language on front or reverse side?
    - D. Include payment terms, discounts, and freight terms?
- III. Specific Provisions
    - A. Battle of the forms language—Purchase order is limited to purchaser's terms and conditions; all conflicting or additional terms communicated by vendor are objected to by purchaser
    - B. Buyer's property
        1. Form should address two types of property

a. Buyer's property transported to vendor
b. Property paid for by purchaser but made and held by vendor
   2. Issues
      a. Insurance
      b. Labeling and location
      c. Maintenance
      d. Accounting
      e. Return to purchaser
      f. Indemnification for loss or damage
      g. UCC filings
      h. Inspection by purchaser on vendor's premises
C. Buyer's remedies
   1. Form remedies and UCC remedies are accumulative
   2. Incidental and consequential damages
   3. Reject nonconforming shipments
   4. Full indemnification
   5. Cancel order and obtain item elsewhere
D. Termination for convenience (limit vendor's damages)
   1. Issues
      a. Notice and mechanics for stopping work
      b. Vendors' compensation
         - purchased material?
         - labor expended?
         - overhead?
         - profit?
      c. Limit vendor's anticipation of contract material needs
E. Changes or modifications
   1. Types of changes
      a. Drawings, designs, or specifications
      b. Packaging, delivery, and destination (or place of performance)
      c. Schedule
      d. Quantities
      e. Buyer—furnished property or assistance

2. Additional costs
   a. Vendor obligation to notify buyer of additional costs or delays resulting from change
   b. Vendor obligation to proceed with changed contract while claims for additional costs are resolved
F. Choice of law and forum selection
   1. State of purchaser's home office or where goods will be delivered
G. Compliance with laws—Vendor's representations
   1. Purchased items have been manufactured and provided in accordance with all relevant laws
   2. Purchased items comply with applicable OSHA standards
   3. Purchased items comply with Section 12 of Fair Labor Standards Act
   4. If purchased items will be used to fill any federal government contracts, then include compliance with federal procurement or defense acquisition regulations
   5. Require vendor to provide Material Safety Data Sheet for any chemical
H. Delivery
   1. FOB "origin" or "destination"—who pays freight?
   2. Risk of loss—does not have to be assumed by party who pays freight
   3. Time is of the essence
   4. Purchaser cancellation for late delivery
   5. Vendor's obligation to notify purchaser of any delay
   6. Items delivered in advance are subject to return
I. Entire agreement/integration clause
   1. Standard boilerplate clause that prohibits verbal modification and requires all amendments to be executed by purchaser
   2. Can be very important in the event of litigation
J. Force majeure clause
   1. More important for vendor but include to limit clause in vendor's form and UCC provision

2. Provide purchaser with right to terminate without liability if any event beyond purchaser's control makes contract uneconomic
3. Require notice from vendor of any event of force majeure preventing vendor performance
4. Provide purchaser with right to terminate without liability if force majeure prevents vendor performance beyond specified period

K. Inconsistent terms
1. Terms on front govern over terms on reverse side
2. Typed terms govern over printed terms
3. Handwritten terms govern over typed or printed terms
4. Specifications govern over samples or drawings

L. Indemnification
1. Cover potential situations where vendor's employees are present on purchasers' property
2. Extend indemnification to purchaser's officers and directors
3. Cover all possible claims, costs, and expenses
4. Cover acts and omissions of vendor's employees, representatives, agents, and independent contractors

M. Insurance
1. Required vendor coverages
   a. Contractual liability
   b. Comprehensive/general liability
   c. Automotive
   d. Worker's compensation
2. Vendor must provide certificate of insurance
3. Require purchaser be named as additional insured
4. Require prior notice to buyer of termination of insurance

N. Insolvency/bankruptcy
1. Right to terminate by buyer upon bankruptcy filing by or against vendor (unenforceable under bankruptcy code)
2. Right to terminate by buyer without liability if vendor
   a. Is insolvent
   b. Fails to pay obligations when due

    c. Makes an assignment for benefit of creditors
    d. Ceases production
    e. Ceases to function as a going concern or goes out of business
O. Inspection/testing/rejection
    1. Payment does not constitute acceptance by buyer
    2. Buyer has right to inspect items, including work in progress, at vendor's facility
    3. Inspection by buyer does not relieve vendor of any contractual obligations
    4. Buyer has right to reject nonconforming deliveries
    5. Buyer can charge vendor for expense of inspection of nonconforming items
    6. Acceptance does not relieve vendor of liability for latent defects
    7. Risk of loss for nonconforming goods remains with vendor while items are in purchaser's possession
    8. Purchaser may revoke acceptance of defective items within a reasonable time after defect or nonconformity is discovered
    9. If acceptance is revoked, title reverts to vendor and vendor assumes all liabilities related to rejected items including disposal obligation and other environmental liabilities
P. Mechanics liens
    1. Prohibit
    2. Vendor indemnifies purchaser
Q. Notice of harmful ingredients or defects
    1. Require notice from vendor to purchaser
    2. Usefulness depends on what particular products purchaser is buying and selling
    3. Intended to help to assist purchaser in complying with Consumer Product Safety Act and OSHA hazard communication requirements
R. Patents/patent indemnification

1. If purchased item infringes third-party rights, vendor is obligated to provide replacement noninfringing product or procure license
2. Vendor indemnifies purchaser against damages and cost of defense in any infringement action
3. At purchaser's option, vendor must assume buyer's defense
4. Buyer has right to be involved in defense of the action through its own lawyers

S. Price warranty ("most favored buyer" clause)
1. Same product or substantially similar products?
2. Sold to any customer or just competitors?
3. Similar transaction?
4. Buyer to receive benefit of any price reductions? During what period?
5. Potential antitrust issues

T. Progress reports—Appropriate for long-term contracts for big ticket items

U. Proprietary information
1. Vendor will treat purchaser's property information as confidential
2. Purchaser will or will not keep vendor's proprietary information in confidence

V. Rights of set off—Include right of buyer to set off any amounts that vendor owes buyer against purchase price

W. Substitutions—Prohibit substitution of materials without buyer's consent

X. Suspension of work—Purchaser may want right to suspend work for a certain period (90 days may be typical); should include price adjustment provisions

Y. Taxes—Seller's prices include all taxes, including sales and use taxes

Z. Warranties
1. Types of warranties
   a. Purchased items should meet agreed-upon specifications

b. Vendor warrants all statements made in product literature to buyer?
   c. Vendor warrants all statements made to purchaser?
   d. Purchased items conform to any samples provided to purchaser
   e. Warranty against defects in material and workmanship
   f. Warranty of merchantability
   g. Warranty of fitness for particular purpose
   h. Warranties on packaging or labeling
   i. Warranty of title
2. Warranty period
   a. Period of time from delivery
   b. Period of time from initial use
   c. Period of performance
3. Extend warranties to purchaser's customers

Appendix B

Checklist for Preparation of International Distributor and Sales Representative Agreements

1. Introduction—Preliminary Concerns
   a. In a few countries, it may be required to use a form of contract required by local law (e.g., Saudi Arabia).
   b. Laws of certain countries may prohibit the parties from waiving local law governing legal relations between foreign company and local residents or citizens; determine requirements of any such laws (e.g., restrictions on choice of law or forum selection clauses, required termination payments, required notice periods, etc.).
   c. Certain countries do not permit use of independent distributors (e.g., Algeria); in those cases any local third-party "agent" must be a sales representative.
   d. Determine whether registration with, or the approval of, any local government agency is required for distributor or commissioned rep agreement.
   e. Avoid violations of any antitrust restrictions imposed by local law.
   f. Check relevant tax treaties and tax laws to be sure that U.S. exporter will not create a "permanent establishment" in the

local country by appointing distributor or commissioned rep, thereby subjecting exporter to foreign taxation.
- g. Consider using a subsidiary or an affiliate for international operations. Also consider a tax-advantaged foreign sales corporation.
- h. To obtain answers to these issues and questions, as well as to be forewarned on any other pitfalls of local law, a lawyer practicing in the country should review the agreement before it is signed.

2. Parties
   a. Establish the legal identity and domicile of the party to be appointed.
   b. Include in the agreement the exact name, address, and legal status under local law of distributor or rep.
   c. Determine as soon as possible who will sign on behalf of distributor or rep.
   d. Restrict ability to assign agreement to unrelated third parties.
   e. If at all possible, appoint a legal entity recognized under local law, not an individual, in order to minimize the possible application of local labor laws to the agreement.
      However, if an individual is appointed, then:
      i. Make sure compensation is through a commission or profit on the resale of product, not a flat fee or salary.
      ii. Do not dictate in the agreement the details of how the business should be run.
      iii. The individual should not service supplier exclusively.
      iv. U.S. supplier should not provide start-up capital.
      v. Do not allow the individual to operate under U.S. supplier's name.
      vi. Goods should not be sent on consignment.
   f. Request copies of organizational documents and certificates from local government regarding legal status, references, and financial statements.

3. Products
   a. Identify by individual product or product line what is covered under the agreement.
   b. Spare parts?

c. Specify trademarks and trade names under which products shall be sold (important in international agreements).
   d. Is there supplier discretion to add or subtract products or trademarks?
4. Territory[1]
   a. Identify with specificity.
   b. Does it prohibit locations outside of territory?
   c. Does it prohibit solicitation of sales outside of territory?
   d. Does it prohibit sales outside of territory?
   e. Does it prohibit shipments outside of territory?
   f. Does it prohibit sales or shipments to a customer that distributor has reason to know will resell or remove the product to another territory?
   g. Does supplier have complete discretion to add or subtract geographic markets to the agreement? Only in the case of breach? None?
5. Customers or Markets[2]
   a. Identify any customer markets (house accounts) from which distributor or rep is restricted.
   b. Can solicitation of sales be restricted?
   c. Can actual sales be restricted?
   d. Does supplier have complete discretion to add or subtract customer markets to the agreement? Only in the case of breach? None?
6. Exclusivity of Rights
   a. Are rights exclusive or nonexclusive? These are vague terms.
   b. Does supplier reserve the right to sell directly in the territory? With or without a commission to distributor? Limited to certain products? Limited to "house" accounts? Limit to certain portions of the territory? Who will service direct sales?

---

1. Legality of territorial restrictions must be considered under applicable competition and antitrust laws, especially in distributor agreements.
2. Legality of territorial restrictions must be considered under applicable competition and antitrust laws, especially in distributor agreements.

c. Does supplier reserve the right to appoint other distributors in the area?
   d. Does supplier reserve the right to appoint other sales reps in the territory?
   e. Short of termination, are there any circumstances under which supplier may modify or take back any exclusive rights?
7. Duration
   a. How long should the agreement last?[3]
   b. Renewal provisions.[4]
8. Obligations of Distributor or Representative
   a. Sales quotas are highly recommended.
      i. How are quotas measured? Product units? U.S. dollars? Local currency?
      ii. Are there separate quotas for individual products or one aggregate quota for all products?
      iii. Are there separate quotas for different parts of the territory?
      iv. How are quotas established? Unilaterally by supplier? By supplier after consultation with distributor or rep? Only upon agreement by both parties? If parties cannot agree, does the agreement terminate?
      v. Will quotas change from period to period? If so, how? At supplier's discretion? After consultation? By mutual

---

3. From a legal standpoint it is preferable if the agreement is for a fixed, definite, and relatively short term, ideally no longer than two years. In some countries a contract for an indefinite duration may only be terminated upon payment of compensation by the terminating party. Moreover, these agreements can become stale and outmoded from a legal and business standpoint with the passage of time and need to be updated from time to time, preferably without going through the administrative burden and legal risk of terminating each one so that an updated agreement can be put in its place.

4. Automatic renewal provisions, successive deliberate nonautomatic renewals, or continued relations beyond the stated expiration date can create an expectancy in the minds of distributors and reps that they will continue indefinitely, which can create legal problems when the manufacturer wishes to terminate, especially in certain countries where automatic renewal provisions, successive renewals, or continued relations beyond the expiration date can cause the agreement to be regarded as having an indefinite term, entitling the distributor or rep to compensation upon termination.

agreement? In accordance with an index, a percentage escalator, or specific quantity increases?
    vi. If rep fails to attain one quota, can party aggregate over two periods?
    vii. On failure to obtain the quota, does the agreement terminate or become nonexclusive?
  b. Inventory quotas for distributors (not applicable to reps).
    i. Products.
    ii. Parts.
    iii. Must address same issues as under sales quotas (see above).
    iv. Restocking rights and charges.
  c. If no quotas, then consider other performance requirements.
    i. Advertising and promotion? Expenditure? Frequency? Specified publications?
    ii. Attendance at trade shows? Number? Location? Frequency? Who pays?
    iii. Best efforts in soliciting sales of the products in the territory.
  d. Training and sales meeting attendance requirements.
    i. Where? Mandatory? Frequency? Alternate locations?
    ii. How often?
    iii. At whose expense? Travel? Lodging? Meals? Costs of providing training?
  e. Design, engineering, or other consulting services required from distributor or rep prior to customer ordering product.
  f. Requirement or right to, or prohibition on, further manufacture or modification of any product or packaging.
  g. Requirement to repair or service products.
    i. Installation and start-up service.
    ii. Complaints and troubleshooting.
    iii. Warranty repairs.
    iv. Out-of-warranty repairs.
    v. Sale of repair parts.
    vi. Inventory of repair parts.

- vii. Apply to all products located in territory or only those sold by distributor or rep?
- viii. Apply to products sold by distributor or rep and located outside of territory?
- ix. Subcontract repair work.
- x. Insurance requirements.
- xi. Compensation for warranty work.
- xii. Requirement to return parts replaced under warranty. At whose cost?
- xiii. Any special equipment, tools, machinery, etc. required to perform service and repair functions.
- xiv. Inspect and verify proper use, operation, and maintenance of products by customer.
- xv. Service or maintenance contracts.

h. Consignment of parts to reps.
  - i. Storage and security arrangements.
  - ii. Shipping costs and duties.
  - iii. Insurance.
  - iv. Risk of loss.
  - v. Tax issues.

i. Staff requirement.
  - i. Sales.
  - ii. Service.

j. Facilities requirements.
  - i. Sales.
  - ii. Service.
  - iii. Location of inventory and sales offices.
  - iv. Condition.
  - v. Prohibition on expansion to perform obligations under the agreement without supplier consent.
  - vi. Temperature, security, and security interest requiring segregation of goods and signage. Priority of security interest and methods depend on local law.

k. Distributor or rep required to bear all costs and expenses of performing obligations under the agreement?

i. Costs of complying with testing and other regulations in the territory? Certification organizations? Registration in supplier's name suggested.
ii. Permit costs?
iii. Costs of translating product literature and brochures.

l. Reports and records required from distributor or rep.
   i. Content: Sales? Orders? Sales calls? Inventory levels? Customer complaints and suggestions? Warranty and nonwarranty service? Changes in applicable laws and regulations? Competitive activities? Rolling sales forecasts?
   ii. Frequency.
   iii. Language.

m. Inspection rights given to supplier.
   i. Facilities.
   ii. Records.

n. Appointment of subdistributors or subrepresentatives or otherwise subcontracting or assigning responsibilities.
   i. Permitted or not?
   ii. If permitted, then hold harmless or indemnification clause?
   iii. Distributor or rep remains responsible for performance under the agreement.

o. Insurance obligations (more prevalent where distributor takes title to or possession of any product or performs installation or service obligations).
   i. Coverages—general liability, contractual obligations, automobile, casualty (on building).
   ii. Name manufacturer as additional insured.

p. Confidentiality obligations.
   i. Restrict use.
   ii. No disclosure to third parties.
   iii. Separate agreements with key employees and subparties.
   iv. Return of information.
   v. Survival of obligations.
   vi. Truly enforceable under local law?

q. Financial obligations including minimum working capital (more applicable to distributor or rep who services product or purchases parts on credit).
r. Compliance with legal requirements (particularly in international agreements).
   i. Customs requirements and duties.
   ii. Taxes.
   iii. Registration of the agreement.
   iv. Governmental approval for using product in the territory.
   v. Governmental approval for making payment.
   vi. Foreign Corrupt Practices Act. Export controls laws. Anti-boycott legislation.
s. Must reps effect, or assist in effecting, collection of amounts owed by customers to supplier?
t. Reps may only offer product under prices, terms, and conditions of sale, including methods of payment and product warranties, promulgated by supplier.
u. May distributor offer any warranty beyond that provided by supplier? If permitted, distributor should indemnify supplier against all costs and expenses relating to any such broader warranties?
v. Translation of advertising materials and product literature into local language.
w. Standard trademark protection provisions.
   i. Prior approval of advertising, promotional, and product literature and copy.
   ii. Notify supplier of any infringement of any of supplier's marks or claims of infringement against distributor or rep by any third party and assist supplier in any related litigation.
   iii. Use by unapproved locations or locations outside of territory.
   iv. Prohibit registration by distributor and assist supplier's registration.
   v. Prohibit use of supplier's name as part of distributor or rep's name.

        vi. Right to sell product under distributor's trademark?
    x. Distributor or rep indemnification of supplier.
        i. All claims, liabilities, costs, expenses, etc. arising out of any act or omission of distributor or rep.
        ii. Insure indemnity obligation.
9. Obligations of Supplier
    a. Referral of inquiries from customers located in the territory? Mandatory for all orders? For certain kinds of orders? Discretionary on the part of supplier?
    b. Provide quantities of advertising materials, product manuals, catalogues, price lists, and other product literature.
        i. Language.
        ii. Quantities.
        iii. Who pays costs?
    c. Obligation to keep distributor or rep apprised of changes in prices, terms, models, and specifications of products.
    d. Obligation to provide distributor or rep with marketing and sales assistance or consultation.
        i. Mandatory or discretionary?
        ii. Include face-to-face customer presentations in the territory? At the customer location?
        iii. Whose cost?
    e. Provide training [see 8(d)].
    f. Shipping obligations.
        i. To distributor or rep's facility.
        ii. Drop ship direct to customer's location in the territory? Outside the territory? Does drop shipment outside territory depend on whether the order originated from a purchasing office inside or outside the territory?
    g. Extension of credit to distributors (more likely for domestic than international distributors). Details, interest, currency risk. Letter of Credit? Cannot ship product until all invoices are paid? Security interest?
    h. National or institutional promotion or advertising.
    i. Free samples for testing or sales demonstrations?

10. Products orders, sales, and payment
    a. Procedure for ordering products.
        i. Oral or in writing? Electronic data interchange?
        ii. If oral, confirmed in writing?
        iii. Telex or telecopy if international? With written order to follow?
        iv. Rep may only solicit orders upon prices and terms as established by supplier.
        v. Must report to U.S. government all violations of antiboycott laws.
    b. Supplier has sole discretion to reject any orders for any reason.
    c. Commissioned reps have no authority to accept orders on behalf of supplier.
    d. Incorporate and attach copy of exporter's standard terms and conditions of sale governing orders from, and sales to, distributors and customers of reps.
        i. Agreement governs over terms in case of conflict.
        ii. Covers risk of loss, delivery, transfer of title, insurance, returns, and other logistics.
        iii. Product warranties.
        iv. Incorporate International Commercial Terms?
        v. All these details can be placed in the agreement.
    e. Payment provisions.
        i. Credit?
        ii. Confirmed irrevocable letter of credit payable at U.S. bank?
        iii. Other security?
11. Commission arrangements (applicable only to commissioned representatives).
    a. Calculate and pay only on amounts *actually collected* (especially in international transactions).
    b. Rates.
    c. Amounts collected upon which commissions shall not be paid (may depend on whether supplier earns a profit on the charge).
        i. Taxes.
        ii. Freight.

  iii. Insurance.
  iv. Customs fees and duties.
  v. Engineering, installation, repair, and training charges.
  vi. Lease of equipment.
  vii. Discounts and uncollected amounts (if initially calculated on sales rather than amounts collected).
 d. Sales upon which commissions shall be paid.
  i. All sales in the territory or merely those obtained by rep?
  ii. Sales to any affiliate of supplier?
  iii. Sales outside of territory?
  iv. Sales to restricted classes of customers?
 e. Timing of payment.
 f. Currency.
 g. Place of payment (preferably a location in the territory).
 h. Commission splitting arrangements.
  i. Extraterritorial sales.
  ii. Dependent on which distributor or rep performs certain specific functions for sale in question.
 i. Will supplier provide a statement of sales and commissions earned simultaneous with payment? With limitation on period during which rep may object?
 j. Obligation to pay further commissions upon termination or expiration of the agreement.

12. Any other restrictions on distributor or rep[5]
 a. Sales of competitive products?
 b. Manufacture of competitive products?
 c. Restrictions only applicable inside territory?
 d. Sales of competitive parts or accessories?
 e. Approved source provision covering competitive parts.
13. Termination provisions[6]

---

5. Legality of restrictions must be reviewed under applicable antitrust and competition laws. Generally speaking, there is more discretion allowed in restricting representatives as opposed to distributors.
6. For international agreements, must be reviewed under laws of distributor or rep's resident country.

a. Without cause upon notice by supplier? By distributor or rep?
   i. How much notice?
b. With cause upon notice by supplier? By distributor or rep?
   i. How much notice?
   ii. Any breach of the agreement?
   iii. Cure provisions?
   iv. Repetition of a breach of the agreement of the same kind previously cured?
   v. Dispute among the principals of distributor or rep? Change in ownership?
   vi. Material inaccuracy of any information provided by distributor or rep?
c. Causes for immediate termination.
   i. Death or incapacity of owner or any key personnel.
   ii. Change in ownership or transfer of substantially all of distributor or rep's assets.
   iii. Violation of any statute such as U.S. Foreign Corrupt Practices Act.
   iv. Insolvency, failure to function as a going concern, or other similar events. Credit insurance may only cover insolvency.
   v. Promulgation of any applicable laws, rules, or regulations inconsistent with the agreement.
   vi. Any assignment or attempted assignment of any rights or obligations without manufacturer's consent.
   vii. Breach of confidentiality, intellectual property, or noncompetition clauses.
   viii. Provide that list of causes in not exhaustive.

14. Post-Termination Obligations.
    a. Cessation of use of trademarks.
    b. Return of all manuals, price and customer lists, marketing and advertising information, and engineering and technical data.
    c. Supplier's right or obligation to repurchase inventory.
       i. Price.
       ii. Terms.
       iii. Products and parts covered.

                iv. Supplier's option: repurchase or permit sales for 90 days?
        d. Waiver by distributor or rep of all rights to any compensation.
                i. If terminated in accordance with its terms.
                ii. Waive consequential.
                iii. Sometimes unenforceable.
        e. Provisions for filling orders from distributor or rep submitted during phase-out (recommend sales to terminated distributors only on cash on delivery, letter of credit, or payment in advance).
        f. Continued rights or obligations of distributor or rep to service product.
        g. Acceleration of distributor or rep indebtedness.
        h. Noncompete. Period? Geographical scope?
        i. No effect on accrued rights.
        j. Right to set off.
15. Dispute Resolution.
        a. Arbitration (more common in international agreements), rules (ICC, AAA, UNCITRAL, etc.), and site (home or neutral location such as London, Stockholm, or Toronto).
        b. Choice of law, forum selection, and submission to jurisdiction (help avoid local protective laws).
        c. Waiver of United Nations Convention on International Sale of Goods.
        d. In English, English-speaking arbitrators.
        e. Who pays costs? Loser? Party loses but refused settlement? Party wins but less than settlement offer?
16. Boilerplate Provisions.
        a. Relationship of parties—independent contractor.
        b. Force majeure. Not for payment of money. Over 60 days, other party may terminate agreement?
        c. Notice—should be clear especially for termination.
        d. Governing language—English text should govern if English-speaking forum.
        e. Others.
                i. Internal Statute of Limitations for actions versus supplier.
                ii. Limit damages versus supplier.

iii. Limit causes of action such as consequential damages versus supplier.
iv. Warranty exclusions and exceptions.
v. Exclusive remedy is more conforming product.
vi. Prohibition on hiring supplier employees.

Appendix C

Motivating the Distributor, Sales Rep, or Licensee; Performance Levels; and Other Standards and Termination for Nonperformance

I. Local law and law specified in the contract.
   A. Licensor should investigate local law for similar concerns.
II. Term—critical.
   A. Definite or indefinite duration.
   B. Defines expectations and intentions. Less investment.
   C. Critical effect on termination damages.
   D. Avoid going over two years.
   E. Trial period.
III. Renewals are pitfalls.
   A. Avoid automatic renewals if no action taken—"evergreen" clauses. Better if take action to effect renewal.
   B. Repeated renewals can equal indefinite terms—need new agreements.
   C. Once expired, avoid continuing. Equals an implied renewal. Monitor the expiration date.
IV. Termination.
   A. Type of intermediary often key.
   B. Reason for termination—cause or without cause.

C. Determine rights to terminate with or without cause.
  1. With cause.
     a. List events that make party less desirable, such as death, bankruptcy, loss of license, etc.
     b. Change in market conditions, failure to fulfill duties or reach quotas. Be specific.
     c. Breach (i.e., confidentiality, licensure, laws, change in ownership, loss of key personnel, immoral activity, damage to reputation, or competition).
     d. Right to cure.
     e. Some countries specify causes.
  2. Without cause.
     a. Good faith.
     b. Reasonable notice—some countries specify. Usually three months is enough.
     c. Inventory repurchase, sale for limited period.
     d. Reimbursement for certain expenditures.
V. Consequences of termination.
  A. Supplier fear of damages or a form of indemnification.
     1. Actual damages—lost commissions and profits on pending sales.
     2. Consequential damages—future commissions and profits.
     3. Expenditures on facilities and equipment.
     4. Promotional and advertising expenditures.
     5. Training and personnel costs.
     6. Injury to reputation for being terminated.
     7. Inventory.
  B. Limit damages in contract.
  C. Intermediary can indemnify supplier, waive beneficial laws (enforceable?).
     1. Some jurisdictions permit a waiver of these laws by a party.
     2. E.g., Dominican Republic
        a. Direct expenses and losses.
        b. Value of investment.
        c. Promotional expenditures and inventory value.

                d. Gross profit five years and 10 percent of average annual profit for each additional year agreement in force.
         D. Parties can always negotiate. Strict host country laws will enhance bargaining position of the intermediary.
         E. Supplier assets or receivables in host country at risk. If not, good reason to block enforcement in United States? One reason may be U.S. state law specified in contract but host country court uses its law.
  VI. Post-termination provisions
         A. Depends on local law.
         B. Return of inventory, tools, tangible assets.
         C. Deliver copy of customer list.
         D. Return confidential information.
         E. Nondisclosure and nonuse provisions to continue.
         F. Commissions post-termination.
         G. Continuing competition restrictions.
         H. Cease use of trademarks and intellectual property—from signs to literature, business cards.
         I. Cease all promotions.
         J. Return manuals.
         K. Regulate existing orders.
         L. Disclaim damages, indemnify supplier, waive beneficial laws.
  VII. Duties of agent or distributor.
         A. Motivate party by reward for achievement and penalty for failure.
         B. Set out parties' intentions and expectations.
         C. Basis for termination for cause; be specific.
         D. Some jurisdictions specify which failure, if any, terminates agreement or only gives rise to damages.
         E. Penalties: agreement nonexclusive, reduce territory, lower commission, decrease discount, or terminate.
         F. General duties.
                1. Promotion—is agreement exclusive? Devote all its time and best efforts. Competing goods.

a. Efforts—marketing plans, annual reports, advertising and promotional budgets, number of employees, competent personnel, training.
   b. Specify customers or numbers of customers.
   c. Frequency.
   d. Response, following supplier leads.
   e. Supplies of literature.
2. Market research and reports.
   a. Periodic forecasts; market analyses; projected sales; customer profiles; market conditions; relevant technological, economic, legal, and political developments.
   b. Can tie payments to these.
3. Minimum performance.
   a. Minimum quotas—net sales. Net of expenses, packing, insurance, transportation. Exclude sales to affiliates, sales at irregular discounts, sales to replace defective goods.
   b. Unit sales.
   c. Increases in sales over specified periods.
   d. Sales to new or specified customers.
   e. Market share.
   f. Annual, quarterly, etc.
   g. Credit one year to next? Average?
   h. Must be capable of precise calculation.
   i. Agree in advance year by year or termination.
4. Service and support.
   a. Inspection, maintenance, repair, provision of warranty service, other aftermarket support.
   b. Maintain facilities suitable for receipt, repair, and return.
   c. Skilled personnel.
   d. Inventory of spare parts.
   e. Tools.
   f. Offer support.
5. Consequences.

a. Termination.
b. Loss of exclusivity.
c. Reduction in territory.
d. Decrease in commission rate, decrease discount.
e. Positive reinforcement—higher commissions or bonuses or discounts.

Appendix D

Checklist for International Expansion

- Determine Structure of New Operation
    - Parent/subsidiary/worldwide structure
        - Agreements maintain operations between arm's-length parties
    - Joint venture with foreign entity
    - Agency relationship with foreign entity
    - Structure should allow "spin off" of subsidiary or joint venture
        - Without need to rewrite or renegotiate company agreements
    - Structure of board, officers, ability to bind entity, formal limits on local signature authority, local powers of attorney
    - Expose assets of other entities in only the most limited circumstances
    - Capitalization—equity, debt, equipment, solvency over time
    - Keep the corporate formalities of the parent and subsidiary separate
        - Each entity should keep its own books and records
        - Loan payments and other intercompany debts should be repaid within terms
    - Requirements under credit facilities
    - Use of worldwide and local counsel, accountants
- Keys to Successful International Expansion
    - Proactive strategy and business plan
    - Management
    - Country and competitor research
    - Due diligence on potential partners

- Trademarks to protect brands
- Sales and distribution, warehouse
- Tax and Accounting Issues
  - Choice of entity: Permanent establishment triggered? Avoidance? Corporation, LLC, branch or representative office-type presence?
  - Consider management or services agreement with fees to parent
  - Consider trademark or other IP royalty payments to parent
  - Availability, use, and timing of tax credits strategies; timing of repatriation of income
  - Tax laws' local registrations; VAT, GST, PST, etc. Any VAT not creditable?
  - Incentive tax credits and tax free zones
  - Research requirements for favorable tax treatment
    - Revenue-specific requirements
    - In-country employee requirements (personal tax issues)
    - Length of stay in the country
  - Make sure other tax requirements do not offset the favorable treatment
    - Employment related taxes
    - Import taxes
  - Need a good local accountant. Audited statements? Differences in accounting systems? Consolidation?
  - Duties, free trade agreements, country of origin issues and marking
  - Cash/currency management and exchange
- Intellectual Property Concerns
  - Registrations needed? Protection of patents, copyrights, trademarks, and confidential information
  - Do laws and culture of the country respect intellectual property?
  - Existence of multilateral treaties, clear-cut registration policies, and statutory protection
  - Existence of registration system
    - Is it well defined?
    - If no registration system, is it a member of a regional system?
  - License agreements for all technology, software, etc.
- Possible Necessary Documentation

- Create services agreements if helpful
  - Terms under which the parent will provide certain professional services
- Distribution and sales representative form agreements
- Supplier and customer form contracts
- Form employment/independent contractor agreements
- Real Estate
  - Lease versus buy
  - Environmental
  - Necessary agreements
- Employment/Immigration Issues
  - Ensure labor laws do not transcend employment agreements. Understand mandatory bonus, vacation, and termination payment laws
  - Does "at-will" employment exist?
    - If not, employer responsible for payment after employee termination
  - Must a training program be created and registered?
  - Native hiring
    - Does the country have this requirement?
    - How many citizens must be hired?
  - Are "noncompete" agreements recognized?
  - Employee inventions
    - Level of employee right to ownership
  - Visa requirements for U.S. workers (personal tax ramifications)
  - Employment agreements, policies, handbooks
  - Expatriate package, tax and estate planning, tax equalization
  - Mandatory profit sharing requiring the consideration of alternate structures?
- Regulatory Issues
  - Permits, licenses, and certifications
    - Are they required?
- Cost
  - Industry standard for products
- Developed in Country
- Imported into Country

- Cross-border transaction restrictions
  - Restrictions that affect information sharing between parent/subsidiary
  - Security, privacy, data protection restrictions
- Privacy policies and the EU Directive
  - Limitations of information sharing regarding citizens
  - What information may a company use or share?
- Analysis of Areas of Potential Legal Liability
  - Identify legal issues related to the project
    - Negotiating, drafting, and implementing agreements
    - Project specific
    - On-going
  - Identify a country with a stable legal system
    - Existence of formal legal norms
    - Enforcement infrastructure
    - Informal and cultural norms of contract adherence
  - Periodically review legal climate of the country
    - Ensure the laws remain favorable
- Foreign Corrupt Practices Act, RICO, and Unfair Trade Practices
  - Do U.S. laws conflict with the foreign country's business community?
    - Payments to government officials for permits, grants, release of cargo
  - Contract-specific issues
    - Are traditional limitation-of-liability clauses in contracts valid?
- Must the Liability Limitations Be Freely Negotiated?
- Are Boilerplate Limitations Valid?
- What Damages Are Excludable?
  - Status of arbitration system
  - Are choice of law provisions accepted?
- Will Outside Judgments Receive Comity/Recognition?
  - Validity of merger clauses
- Written Terms of Contract Only?
- Are Oral Representations Valid?
- Insurance
  - Determine availability of insurance, worldwide policies

- What are the requirements for insurance?
- Formulate an Exit Strategy
  - Repatriation
  - Redemptions
  - Restrictions on transfer
- Implementation Plan
  - Create document checklist of legal documents required
    - Formation documents
    - Specific licenses
    - Permits
    - Visa applications
    - Government registrations
    - Insurance applications
    - Bank account applications
  - Create due diligence process
- Creditors' Rights
  - Solvency
    - Level of minimum capitalization required
    - Level required to be located in the country
  - Bankruptcy
    - Bankruptcy rules
    - Extent to which creditors control the timing of bankruptcy filing
    - Back-up plan to repatriate the foreign operations

Appendix E

Letter of Intent for a Joint Venture

_____, 20__

Mr. Leo Smith
Foreign Group
38–40 Foreign Rd.
Foreign, Victoria 3081
Australia

Dear Leo:

Thank you for all of your efforts to this point in working with U.S. Co. ("U.S. Co.") to create an equity joint venture ("JV") between our companies. As you know, it is our goal to create a manufacturing JV in Australia through which our companies can provide products to the Australia and New Zealand markets, and perhaps others as well.

The following items are suggested to serve as a nonbinding outline of terms and conditions to be contained in a definitive equity JV contract and related agreements (the "JV Contract") by and between U.S. Co. and Foreign Group ("FG"). Unless and until such a JV Contract has been executed, neither U.S. Co. nor FG shall be under an obligation to complete the transaction contemplated by this letter; however, U.S. Co. and FG do agree to be bound by the terms and conditions contained in paragraphs 13 and 14 below and to negotiate in good faith to bring this transaction to a close.

1. Joint Venture Entity

The parties shall form an equity JV (the "Company") with the objective of selling and distributing products (the "Products") to customers. Each party will agree on the type of Australian entity to be used and any related tax elections. FG will hold a 58 percent ownership interest in the Company while U.S. Co., or a wholly owned subsidiary of U.S. Co., will hold the remaining 42 percent ownership interest. The JV will have a perpetual term.

2. Capitalization

The parties hereto agree to make the following contributions to the capital of the Company and to provide other described services at no charge:

As its sole formal capital contribution, FG shall contribute a press for manufacturing (at its expense, FG shall obtain and deliver to the Company a lien search to ensure the press is contributed free and clear of all liens or other encumbrances). The contribution of such equipment shall constitute a [$_____] (USD) contribution to the capital of the Company.

In addition, upon formation of the Company and for the first twelve (12) months thereafter, FG agrees to provide all working capital (i.e., cash) needed by the Company to commence and continue operations.

As its sole formal capital contribution, U.S. Co. shall contribute two machines to be used in the manufacturing of the Products (at its expense, U.S. Co. shall obtain and deliver to the Company a lien search, or otherwise warrant the equipment unencumbered, to assure FG that the machines are contributed free and clear of all liens or other encumbrances). The contribution of such machines shall constitute a [$_____] (USD) contribution to the capital of the Company.

3. Board of Directors

The Board of Directors of the Company shall be comprised of four (4) members: two (2) of whom shall be appointed by FG and two (2) of whom shall be appointed by U.S. Co. One (1) of the directors appointed by FG shall be named the Chairman of the Board. For the purpose of breaking deadlocks of the Board, the Chairman shall have both a deliberative and a casting vote in all matters that do not require the unanimous consent of the Board. The

Board of Directors shall hold semi-annual meetings, alternating between Oz, Australia and Hometown, Ohio.

4. Officers and Employees

By unanimous action, the Board will choose all the officers and other members of management of the Company for year-to-year terms. The Company's staff will be chosen by the General Manager. The staff and officers will sign customary employment agreements (compensation and other terms to be agreed). FG agrees to provide all necessary administrative and accounting staff and services to the JV without remuneration therefor for a period of five (5) years.

5. Minority Protections

The JV Contract shall provide numerous customary protections for U.S. Co. as a minority equity holder of the Company. For example, the JV Contract shall provide that numerous actions may not be taken by the Board of Directors without the unanimous approval of all of the members of the Board of Directors (e.g., incurring any expenses or obligations greater than $25,000 USD; borrowing money or guaranteeing debt other than that detailed in the applicable agreed Business Plan; creating, acquiring, or disposing of any subsidiary of the Company, and the like).

6. Audit and Reporting

The Company will have an annual audit and a quarterly compilation by a mutually agreeable, non Big 4 accounting firm. In addition, as the parties shall agree in the JV Contract, the Board of Directors of the Company shall deliver monthly, quarterly, and annual financial statements to the equity holders of the Company.

7. Sales

Sales will be made in Australia in accordance with the terms of an exclusive distribution agreement between the Company and FG (which shall have a right to appoint sub-distributors and sub-sales agents). [**Terms, minimum sales, commission rate, or resale?**] In addition, the Company shall appoint a distributor(s) who shall sell the Products in New Zealand. By unanimous action of the Board, the Company may appoint the New Zealand or any other Distributor for any other territory. During the term of the JV Contract and for a period of three (3) years thereafter, both U.S. Co. and FG, and each of their affiliates, shall be bound by noncompete provisions or agreements that prohibit them from selling products that compete with the Products. Neither FG nor the Company may sell Products in the following U.S. Co. market area, Austrasia.

8. Facility

The factory and offices of the Company shall be located within an existing facility owned by FG and will be provided to the Company pursuant to a five- (5) year, rent-free lease. Protections for the lease shall be obtained from the building owner and any lien holder. Prior to entering into such lease or the joint venture, FG will send a copy of the applicable Environmental report for consideration by U.S. Co. Improvements to the facility must be agreed upon by the parties, provided, however, that all expenses related to such improvements shall be paid by FG.

9. Intellectual Property

U.S. Co. shall enter into a nonroyalty bearing license agreement with the Company that shall permit the Company to use certain U.S. Co. trademarks and patents in the manufacture, distribution, and sale of the Products. All intellectual property developed by the Company, whether through alteration, improvement, or modification, shall be owned by the Company, provided, however, the Company shall license such developed intellectual property royalty free to the equity holders for use in the manufacture, distribution, and sale of the Products.

10. Transfer of Ownership

Neither U.S. Co. nor FG shall be permitted to transfer or otherwise alienate its respective ownership interest in the Company without the prior written consent of the other party, rights of first refusal, etc. Certainly, allowances shall be included in the JV Contract that permit either of the parties to transfer their respective ownership interest to an affiliate entity (subject to certain conditions).

11. Buy-Sell

The JV Contract may be terminated due to a breach by either U.S. Co. or FG, impasse after two (2) years, or in general after ten (10) years. As to breaches, the nonbreaching (or otherwise ending the joint venture) party shall have the option to purchase the other party's ownership interest for the greater of (i) two times the Company's Earnings Before Interest, Taxes, Depreciation, and Amoritization (EBITDA) based on the Company's previous year's audited financial statements or (ii) an amount equal to the net book value of the assets of the Company as determined in accordance with Australian GAAP (or such other value as the parties may agree). [**Discuss process for impasse or after ten (10) years**]

12. Mandatory Tax Distribution

In order to allow the parties to pay all taxes incurred as a result of their ownership interest in the Company, at a minimum, prior to April 15 of each year, the Company shall distribute 40 percent of all of the prior year's taxable income to the parties.

13. Confidentiality

U.S. Co. and FG agree that all information provided by each party to the other party during the process of forming the JV and thereafter is confidential and proprietary to the party providing the information, and no party shall use any information provided by the other party for any purpose other than as permitted or required for formation of the JV. Each party agrees not to disclose or provide any information provided by the other party to any third party. It is expressly agreed that this paragraph 13 shall survive termination of this letter.

14. Exclusivity

You will not initiate, engage in, or continue discussions with any individual, corporation, or other entity (except U.S. Co.) concerning any Australian joint venture or any other similar transaction involving FG. You also agree to prohibit any affiliates, agents, or representatives from engaging in such discussions and to make us aware of any proposal that FG may receive after the date of this letter. In the event we mutually agree to terminate our efforts and negotiations toward completing this transaction, we shall, at your request, release you in writing from the obligations contained in this paragraph 14.

No affiliate of the Company or FG may compete with U.S. Co. or the Company, as applicable, during the term of this letter or the Company's existence and for three (3) years thereafter. The parties hereby expressly agree that this paragraph 14 shall survive the termination or expiration of this letter for any reason.

15. Timeline

U.S. Co. and FG agree to develop a Business Plan that sets forth in detail the first two (2) years of operation of the Company within thirty (30) days of the execution of this letter. It is the desire of U.S. Co. and FG to finalize the joint venture (including receipt of all regulatory approvals) within six (6) months from the date of acceptance of this letter.

16. Termination

This letter of intent may be terminated, and the transactions contemplated hereby may be abandoned or terminated, at any time by the mutual agreement of U.S. Co. and FG. Each party hereto shall pay its own costs and expenses incurred or to be incurred in connection with the transactions contemplated hereby.

This letter of intent shall expire and be of no further force and effect in the event the JV Contract is not executed by October ___, 20__, provided, however, that it may be extended by the written mutual agreement of the parties. Both parties agree to use their commercially reasonable best efforts to complete the transaction by such date.

17. Disputes

U.S. Co. and FG shall make every effort to settle amicably and in good faith all disputes between the parties regarding the JV before utilizing any type of dispute resolution mechanism. In the event a dispute is unable to be amicably resolved by the parties alone, each party agrees to submit to mediation proceedings in order to facilitate a resolution. Finally, if mediation does not result in a resolution of the dispute, the parties agree to submit to binding arbitration proceedings in the United Kingdom.

18. Additional Terms

The JV Contract also will contain such additional terms, conditions, representations, and warranties as are customary in transactions such as this and such provisions and protections as you and we shall respectively consider necessary.

If the terms of this letter are acceptable to you, we propose that our respective representatives immediately begin the preparation of a definitive JV Contract (including all related agreements). We plan for our counsel to draft documents for your review. We will pay for our counsel's fees, and you will incur fees for any counsel you may select.

This letter of intent may be executed in one or more counterparts.

We trust that you will conclude that the terms outlined in this letter of intent are attractive and fair to you and that we can move expeditiously to sign a JV Contract and later consummate the transactions contemplated in this letter. Should you have any questions, please do not hesitate to contact me.

Please indicate your acceptance of this letter by signing the enclosed copy of this letter and returning it to us.

Very truly yours,
Bill Jones

To U.S. Co.:

The undersigned hereby accepts this letter upon the terms and conditions set forth in the foregoing letter.

FOREIGN GROUP

By: Leo Smith, President

Appendix F

Basic Outline of Initial Terms and Conditions to Be Addressed for the Proposed Joint Venture

Joint Venture Structure
- Form of entity and identity of joint venture partners
- Formal legal name and owners of each joint venture party
- Will a party use a wholly owned subsidiary? If so, describe
- Location of JV

Capital Structure
- Percentage ownership of common stock/ultimate control at JV party and board levels
- Preferred stock (or nonvoting common) and its terms
- Dividend policy

Capitalization
- Source and amount of funds. Debt?
- Valuation of noncash contributions
- Land, building contributed? Building improvements by the JV? Land and/or building leased to JV by a party? Term, terms of lease
- Equipment contributed or leased?
- Technology transfer (with indemnification)—joint venture company owner or a licensee of technology

- Terms of license/know-how agreement. Royalty?

Method of Payment and Schedule of Capital Contributions, Expansion, and/or Additional Capital
- Business plan/projections feasibility study. Which products are in the JV? Which ones remain to be sold by each party? Preemptive rights?

Control at Board Level, Management Voting, Changes in Structure
- Equal representation on the board or does one party control? Alternate chairman annually to break deadlocks? Cumulative voting?

Unanimity at Shareholder Level to Protect Minority Interest, if Minority Venturer so Requires
- Debt
- Calls for capital
- Guarantees, loans
- Sales of assets
- Material compensation issues
- Material change in business purpose
- Litigation
- Annual budget and/or business plan
- Amendment to articles or bylaws
- Appointment and change in auditors
- Selection and change in insurance
- Issuance of additional shares, redemption, etc.
- Dividends
- Material contracts or capital expenditures
- Dissolutions, mergers, etc.

Management Appointments and Functions of Officers
- Selection of general manager and his/her duties
- Incentive plan for general manager
- From which party? Salary? Bonuses? Criteria for bonus/firing?

Impasse or Planned Buy Out
- Buy-Sell (formula, arbitration, CPA's valuation or roulette, etc.)

- Triggers for buy out and terms
- No buy out for first 2–3 years?

Restrictions on Transfer of Ownership
- Right of first refusal
- Right to buy out other venturer and terms of buy-out.
- Triggers, i.e., death of joint venturer (if applicable), change in control, sale to a competitor

Noncompete/Confidentiality
- Territory? What restricted? During JV's term and for how long after? Affiliates bound? Personal signatures?

Warranty for Products Sold by JV to Customers, Products Sold to JV by a Partner
- Terms of sale of any inputs to JV by a party

Insurance
- Carrier? What type?

Default [needed to prepare documents]

Terms and Conditions of Employees and Loaned Employees
- Other employment agreements? Union?

Term
- Locked in for a long time or can one party go off on its own after a short time?

Transfer of Technology and Know-How
- Indemnity for infringement
- See above issues on economic terms, royalties

Protection of Technology and Know-how
- Licensing party to register its intellectual property—not the JV or other party
- Name of JV? Register name? Register JV trademarks?

Document Preparation/Government Approvals
- Which filings? Time for approvals. Filing fee?
- Which counsel to prepare which agreement and filings?
- Does either party have a local office to close?

Production, Distribution, Marketing, and Sales
- Will sales be through a party? Commissions? Reseller profiting by a discount to list? Other terms on exclusive territory, products.

Taxation
- Tax treatment to JV and parties. Dividends worse than royalties to a licensing party, real or personal property lease payments to a party, commissions/profit on sales of JV products through a party or profit on sales of inputs to the JV by a party?

Currency Exposure Policies
- Repatriation? Better through above contractual means instead of dividends? Local limitations/regulations?

Finance, Accounting, and Auditing
- Who are the independent auditors? Each party to have an employee reviewing the JV's books? Financial controls? Expenditure signature authority? Which bank for the JV?

Dispute Resolution/Place and Rules of Arbitration, if Any
Language
Termination or Exit Provision
Visas for Employees
Other Provisions Required by Statute or Regulation
Investment/Tax Incentives
Agreements and Documents
- Letter of intent, stand-still evaluation, and confidentiality agreement
- Business plan/feasibility study
- Joint venture agreement/shareholders' agreement

- Organizational documents, i.e., articles of incorporation, by-laws, and minutes
- Marketing/sales/consulting/warranty service agreements
- General services agreement
- Will one party provide accounting, bookkeeping, or other services for a fee?
- Employment/noncompetition agreements with general manager, other key employees. Terms.
- Incentive Agreement for general manager
- Consulting agreement between key employee and joint venture to board approval
- License agreement, if any
- Technical assistance agreement, if any
- Supply agreements, if any
- Leases (real and personal property)
- Government filings

Appendix G

Detailed Outline of Initial Terms and Conditions to Be Addressed for the Proposed Joint Venture

Joint Venture Structure
- Form of entity and identity of joint venture partners [will need this information to prepare the documentation and provide advice]
- Formal legal name and owners/shareholders of each joint venture party
- Incorporation and/or set-up details of each joint venture party [i.e., jurisdiction, board members, location, share structure, officers/management staff/management structure] [very often we need this information during the drafting approval process; therefore it is good to have it provided at the beginning of the process]
- Will a party use a wholly owned subsidiary? If so, describe structure and jurisdiction of subsidiary
- Location of JV: economic zone, free trade zone
- Summary of business plan including product description, special product considerations, and location of where raw materials are produced [having the business plan for us to review gives us information we will need when completing the feasibility study and also the other documents; it ensures we have the opportunity to consider all aspects of the proposed structure/plan before we finalize the enterprise structure]

- Intellectual property that JV partners will be licensing/transferring to the JV [important because of technology transfer issues, licensing issues, IP protection issues, and licensing fee issues]
- Type of JV parties want/need—equity or cooperative JV? [we want to make sure we have the clients' instructions clearly set out subject to legal/accounting advice]
- Offshore management contract? [to determine if we are looking at cutting down profit of FIE or some other plan to "strip" the FIE (Foreign Invested Enterprise) of profit to an offshore company]
- Preliminary legal/taxation opinion concerning the structure of the proposed JV? [some clients want this before they make a final decision on the matter, as it factors into the cost]

Capital Structure
- Percentage ownership of the JV/ultimate control at JV party and board levels
- Will the percentage of ownership change at some future time? What conditions? [with the WTO market access schedule, we need to be sure if the client wants to take over the FIE at some future time when that may be legally possible]
- Repayment of loans policy [if the client will be lending the FIE additional funds, we need to know the repayment terms]
- Dividend policy
- Investment conditions/terms [to determine the type of JV needed for the project]

Capitalization
- Source and amount of investment: registered capital amounts and total investment amounts [investment includes capital contribution and funds from other sources such as loans to the JV]
- Security for investment by way of loans? [would relate only to funds loaned to the JV; if so, there will be security issues/approvals for the loan from the offshore partner]
- Valuation of noncash contributions

- Land, building contributed? Ownership details? [lease/land use right details] Building improvements by the JV? Land and/or building leased to JV by a party? Term, terms of lease
- Equipment contributed or leased?
- Materials/inventory contributed [details required]
- Technology transfer (with indemnification)—joint venture company owner or a licensee of technology
- Terms of license/know-how agreement. Royalty?
- Return of capital: priority between the JV parties? [will affect the type of JV recommended]

Method of Payment and Schedule of Capital Contributions, Expansion, and/or Additional Capital
- Business plan/projections feasibility study [see Joint Venture Structure section]—which products are in the JV? Which ones remain to be sold by each party?
- Obligation on parties to contribute additional capital and consequences if JV party does not/cannot make contribution [needed for preparation of documentation]
- Loans from a JV partner to the JV—terms/security [same comments as noted above related to loans from the client]

Control at Board Level, Management Voting, Changes in Structure
- Equal representation on the board or does one party control? Alternate chairperson annually to break deadlocks? Number of directors on the board?
- Management structure: general manager/deputy general manager—who appoints whom? [needed for the JV documents]
- Auditor—who appoints and qualifications? [needed for the JV documents]

Unanimity at Shareholder Level to Protect Minority Interest, if Minority Venturer so Requires [information requested will assist with documentation preparation and also to ensure that we have considered all relevant matters before finalizing the JV structure]

- Debt
- Calls for capital
- Guarantees, loans
- Sales of assets
- Material compensation issues
- Material change in business purpose
- Litigation
- Annual budget and/or business plan
- Amendment to articles or bylaws
- Appointment and change in auditors
- Selection and change in insurance
- Issuance of additional shares, redemption, etc.
- Dividends
- Material contracts or capital expenditures
- Dissolutions, mergers, etc.

Management Appointments and Functions of Officers
- Selection of general manager and his/her duties
- Incentive plan for general manager
- From which party? Salary? Bonuses? Criteria for bonus/firing?

Impasse or Planned Buy Out
- Triggers for buy out and terms
- No buy out for first 2–3 years?
- Buy-sell (formula, arbitration, CPA's valuation, or roulette, etc.)

Restrictions on Transfer of Ownership
- Right of first refusal
- Right to buy out other venturer and terms of buy out.
- Triggers, i.e., death of principal of joint venture (if applicable), change in control, sale to a competitor
- Restrictions on sale of equity in offshore holding company? [relevant terms that may come up in negotiations]

- If sale, how is intellectual property licenced/transferred to JV handled? Renegotiated? Returned? [need this information to protect IP owner's rights]

Noncompete/Confidentiality
- Territory? What restricted? During JV's term and for how long after? Affiliates bound? Personal signatures?
- Terms of confidentiality [required for document preparation]

Warranty for Products Sold by JV to Customers, Products Sold to JV by a Partner
- Terms of sale of any inputs to JV by a party

Insurance
- Carrier? Amount? What type?

Default [needed to prepare documents]
- Notice provisions
- Default consequences
- Buy/sell provisions?

Terms and Conditions of Employees and Loaned Employees
- Other employment agreements? union?
- Pension plan—private/government?

Term
- Locked in for a long time or can one party go off on its own after a short period of time?
- Length
- Termination of term options/conditions [so that we clearly understand the JV terms to facilitate document preparation/recommendations]

Transfer of Technology and Know-How
- Indemnity for infringement
- See above issues on economic terms, royalties

Protection of Technology and Know-how
- Licensing party to register its intellectual property—not the JV or other party
- Name of JV? Register name? Register JV trademarks?
- Licensing terms
- Termination of IP use rights/conditions?

Documentation Preparation/Government Approvals
- Letter of intent/memorandum of understanding? [sometimes used as part of the negotiation process]
- Which filings? Time for approvals? Filing fee?
- Which counsel to prepare which agreement and filings? [e.g., Chinese government deals only with Chinese partner for filings]
- For Chinese ventures, procedure to be followed for prior approval of all documents submitted by Chinese partner to regulatory agencies in China [again a procedure sometimes used by parties to ensure no surprises several months into the registration process]
- Does either party have a local office to close?

Production, Distribution, Marketing, and Sales
- Will sales be through a party? Commissions? Reseller profiting by a discount to list? Other terms on exclusive territory, products?
- Obligations of each party in the distribution of products [sometimes an issue]
- Goods to be distributed outside of China? [could affect recommendation concerning tax issues, etc.]
- Import of raw materials? If acquired from a JV partner, terms [supply agreement issues]

Taxation
- Tax treatment to JV and parties—dividends worse than royalties to a licensing party, real or personal property lease payments to a party, commissions/profit on sales of JV products through a party, or profit on sales of inputs to the JV by a party?

- Withhold tax obligations on JV [want to know how each party is expecting the JV administration of tax payments to be carried out]
- Advance tax opinion obtained?

Currency Exposure Policies
- Repatriation? Better through above contractual means instead of dividends? Local limitations/regulations?
- Management payments offshore?

Finance, Accounting, and Auditing
- Who are the independent auditors? Each party to have an employee reviewing the JV's books? Financial controls? Expenditure signature authority? Which bank for the JV?
- Access to financial records [important when it comes to future sale of company, due diligence, etc.]
- Cooperation of the JV partners concerning due diligence on sale of interest [same comment as noted above]

Dispute Resolution/Place and Rules of Arbitration, if Any
- What arbitration institute to handle
- Option to arbitrate or litigate?

Language
- Governing language, interpretation

Termination or Exit Provision
Visas for Employees
Other Provisions Required by Statute or Regulation
Investment/Tax Incentives Agreements and Documents
- Letter of intent/stand-still evaluation and confidentiality agreement
- Project proposal for submission to government agency
- Business plan/feasibility study
- Joint venture agreement
- Organizational documents, i.e., articles of association and post set-up resolutions

- Bank reference letters [will be required at some stage of the process]
- Powers of attorney for registering party [may be needed]
- Marketing/sales/consulting/warranty service agreements
- General services agreement
- Will one party provide accounting, bookkeeping, or other services for a fee?
- Employment/noncompetition agreements with general manager, other key employees; terms
- Incentive agreement for general manager
- Consulting agreement between key employee and joint venture to board approval.
- License agreement, if any
- Technical assistance management agreement, if any
- Supply agreements, if any
- Land use right assignments and/or leases (real and personal property)
- Government filings
- Business license application
- Representative/office winding up?

Appendix H

FCPA Illustrative Red Flags List

- A government official recommends that the company hire a specific person or company to act as a contractor, supplier, or partner. The official may be seeking to enrich himself or herself through kickbacks received from a favored third party.
- A third party requests, without reasonable explanation, fees, commissions, or discounts that are much greater than what is typical. A request for unusually high compensation may indicate that part of the fee will be used for improper payments.
- A third party proposes to be paid a large contingency fee if, for example, a government contract is awarded or a favorable regulatory change is achieved. This type of compensation structure can create an incentive for the third party to make an improper payment in order to achieve a favorable result.
- A third party requests that payments be made to another party, or to a third country or offshore bank account, or other unusual financial arrangements.
- There are unusual payment patterns or financial arrangements.
- A third party requests to be paid in cash for services that are typically paid by bank transfer or other noncash means.
- A third party (including a JV partner) refuses to certify that it will not take any action in furtherance of an improper payment. All third parties that do business with the company should be prepared to give this standard commercial assurance.
- A third party has a reputation for paying bribes.

- A third party is not listed in industry directories or is not known in the industry.
- A third party is to provide services different than it typically provides.
- A contractor or third party lacks qualifications to perform the services offered.
- The third party is related to or closely associated with the foreign official.
- A third party requests that his or her agreement be kept secret from his or her employer.
- A background check of the principals of a third-party company uncovers unusually close links to, some degree of ownership by, or a blood relationship with a government official.
- There has been a one-time payment to a contractor.
- Payments are made in large round numbers.
- There are sequential duplicative invoice numbers from a contractor.
- There is a lack of transparency in expenses and accounting records.
- Duplicate invoices have been paid twice.
- A contractor has the same address or bank account as an employee.
- There is a payment to a country in which the company does not do business.
- There is a payment to a politician's family or associate.
- There is a payment to an invalid address or PO box.
- A third-party services agreement only has vaguely described services.
- A third party is a shell company and possibly organized in an offshore jurisdiction.

Appendix I

FCPA Compliance Program Checklist

1. Goals
   - Prevention and detection
   - Demonstration of commitment to legal business practices
2. Risk Assessment of Foreign Operations
   - High-risk countries
   - Interaction with foreign governmental officials
   - Foreign governmental approvals or regulation
   - Business dealings with foreign governments
   - Business partners
   - Foreign tax issues
   - Customs and import/export
   - Third-party consultants, agents, and advisors
     - sales agents
     - customs brokers
     - government relations consultants
     - tax advisors
     - customers
     - consultants assisting with permitting or licensing
     - outside lawyers interacting with government officials
   - Foreign acquisitions and joint ventures
   - Existing compliance functions
   - Past instances of noncompliance

- Applicable local laws
3. Responsibility
   - Compliance officer
   - Senior management
   - Audit committee
4. Written Policy
5. Training
   - Summaries of the law
   - PowerPoint presentations
   - FAQ's/hypotheticals
   - Online training modules
   - Targeted groups—e.g., sales force, internal auditors, third-party consultants
6. Specific Guidance
   - Permissible payments
     - facilitating payments
     - promotional or marketing expenses
   - Political contributions
   - Foreign charities
   - Meals, entertainment, gifts
   - Travel, lodging
   - Vendors
   - Hiring
   - Red flags
   - Books and records (back-door enforcement)
7. Periodic Certification
8. Due Diligence Procedures for Existing/Future Third-Party Relationships
   - Contractual representations
   - Structure of compensation
   - Checklists/questionnaires
   - Background checks
9. Monitoring and Auditing
10. Periodic Evaluation
11. Procedures for Reporting and Investigating Violations
12. Hotline or Helpline

13. Disciplinary Procedures
14. Documentation of Compliance

Index

A

AAA. *See* American Arbitration Association (AAA)
ACFTU. *See* All-China Federation of Trade Unions (ACFTU)
ACTA. *See* Anti-Counterfeiting Trade Agreement (ACTA)
ADA. *See* Americans with Disabilities Act (ADA)
ADEA. *See* Age Discrimination in Employment Act (ADEA)
Africa, 7, 399–401
African Development Bank, 399, 400
African Regional Intellectual Property Organization (ARIPO), 222
Age Discrimination in Employment Act (ADEA), 269
Agreement on Trade-Related Aspects of Intellectual Property Rights (TRIPS), 74, 197–198, 231
Agreements
   choice of law issues, 342–343
   cultural and language issues, 339
   dispute resolution, 347–348
   labor and tax law, 347–348
   last-minute changes, 350
   monitoring and audits, 345–346
   overview of key provisions, 340–341
   process management, 346–347
   renegotiation, 350
   role of clarity in, 337–339
   scope of services, 343–344
   selection/training of workforce criteria, 346
   use of local counsel, 340–341
   writing, 337
Alien Tort Claims Act (ATCA), 287–289
All-China Federation of Trade Unions (ACFTU), 279
Alternative Fines Act, 153
American Arbitration Association (AAA), 372, 376, 378
Americans with Disabilities Act (ADA), 269
Antarctic Field Research, 12
Anti-American feelings, 384–385
Antibribery violations, affirmative defenses to, 152–153
Anticorruption laws, 166–167

Anti-Counterfeiting Trade
    Agreement (ACTA),
    230–231
Antiglobalization, 411
Anti-money laundering provisions,
    187
Anton Piller order, 218
Arab Spring, 404
Arbitration
    choosing forum and arbitrators,
        376–377
    contractual dispute mechanism,
        371–372
    negotiating through dead
        spaces, 379
    preparing for, 375–376
    venue, 86, 377–378
Arbitration Council of India, 376
Arbitrators, 376–377
Argentina, 285
ARIPO. *See* African Regional
    Intellectual Property
    Organization (ARIPO)
Asian Development Bank, 81, 117
Association of Certified Fraud
    Examiners, 130
Association of Corporate Counsel,
    127
Attorney-client relationship
    cross-border issues and, 20–21
Audits, 119, 345–346, 366
Australia, 248, 285

B
Backlash, 410–411

Bahrain, 406, 407
Baker Hughes case, 138
Bangkok Film Festival, 143
Bank Secrecy Act, 187
Belgium, 285
Benchmarking, 328–329
Berne Convention of 1886, 227
BF Goodrich v. Wohlegmuth,
    117 Ohio App. 493, 192
    N.E.2d 99 (Ohio Ct. App.
    1963), 217
Blocked persons, 187–188
Botswana, 246
Bowoto v. Chevron Corp., 621
    F.3d 1116 (9th Cir. 2010),
    289
Bowoto v. ChevronTexaco, 312 F.
    Supp. 2d 1229 (N.D. Cal.
    2004), 289
BPO. *See* Business process
    outsourcing (BPO)
Brazil, 160, 167, 216, 218, 247,
    248, 300, 348, 361,
    408–410
Bribery, 129–131
Build, own, operate, and transfer
    (BOOT), 48
Bullying, 284–286
Business environment, 89–91
Business process outsourcing
    (BPO), 3–5, 105, 119–120
Business transfer, 248

C
Call center workers, 52

Canada, 68, 160, 301
Capital repatriation, 66
Carter, Jimmy, 129
CFAA. *See* Computer Fraud and Abuse Act (CFAA)
Check-the-box entity, 67–69
Chevron Corp., 289
Chief Legal Officer (CLO), 127
Chile, 285
China
    anticorruption enforcement, 166–168
    brands in U.S. marketplace, 390–391
    business transfers, 248
    challenges in, 392–394
    corresponding punishment provisions, 276
    courts in, 380–381
    cultural issues, 313–314, 315–316
    defined business scope in, 75
    dispute avoidance, 279
    due diligence, 116
    employee labor disputes, 276
    employment agreements, 278
    employment contracts, 270
    financial considerations, 108–109
    foreign counsel in, 37–38
    generic drug manufacturing, 16
    global economy and, 6–7
    Google in, 87
    governmental and regulatory issues, 118–119
    immigration issues, 300
    indemnification for compliance, 331
    intellectual property issues, 215–216
    intersection with vendors/vendors' counsel, 37–38
    investments in U.S., 390
    IT multinationals in, 11
    labor law, 242, 243
    legal system in, 82
    management of issues based in culture, 362–364
    market access, 89
    McDonald's Corporation in, 84
    negotiations, 322
    political risk, 384–385
    property management approvals, 118
    residents in Africa, 401
    small and medium enterprises, 14
    trade secrets, 218–220
    use of service providers in, 12
    use of wholly foreign-owned entities, 14
    whistleblowers, 180
Choice of law issues, 342–343, 377–379
CI. *See* Competitive intelligence (CI)
Civil Rights Act, Title VII, 475
Clients
    attorney-client relationship, 17–18, 20–21

Clients (*continued*)
  global vision of, 55–56
CLO. *See* Chief Legal Officer (CLO)
Codes of conduct, 171, 172, 282–284
Collaboration, 14
Collective bargaining agreements, 266, 267
Colombia, 248
Communications, 91–92
Competencies
  core versus noncore, 50–52
  prevalence of distinctive, 95–96
  technical, 111–112
Competitive intelligence (CI), 120
Compliance issues
  indemnification, 331–332
  labor, 269–270
  Office of Foreign Assets Control and, 185–187
  payroll and benefits, 276–278
Compliance programs, 168–169
Compliance risk, 106, 174–176
Computer Fraud and Abuse Act (CFAA), 207–209
Computer Sciences Corporation, 24
Confidentiality agreements, 208, 211–213, 212
Consultants, 70–71, 103, 120–121
Contingency plans, 63, 86
Contract breaches, 210–212
Contractual terms, 182–183
Cooper Tire and Rubber Inc., 391

Cooption, 121–122
Coordinators, 29–30
Core competency, 50–52
Corporate Counsel on Africa, 403
Corporate subsidiaries, 67
Cost-benefit analysis, 52–54
Costs, 58–59
Counsel
  capabilities of in-house, 23–24
  foreign, 36–37
  intersection with regulators, 39–40
  intersection with vendors/vendors', 37–38
  key issues to consider for cross-border transaction, 50–52
  outside, 25–26
  quasi-general, 23
  use of local, 340–341
Cox Report, 234
Credit risk, 106
Cross-licensing agreements, 73
Cuba, 85
Cultural experts, 33–34
Cultural issues, 311–312, 315–316, 339, 358
Culture, 91–92, 198, 214
Currency, 67, 85

D
Data privacy, 270–272
Deferred Prosecution Agreements (DPAs), 165–167

Democratic National Committee, 129
Digital Millennium Copyright Act (DMCA), 229
Disputes
  avoidance, 279–281
  resolution, 347–348
  resolving everyday, 368
Distributor, sales rep, or licensee motivators, 437
DMCA. *See* Digital Millennium Copyright Act (DMCA)
Dodd-Frank Wall Street Reform and Consumer Protection Act of 2010, 147–149, 179
Doe v. Unocal, 963 F. Supp. 880 (C.D. Cal 1997), 287–289
DOJ. *See* U.S. Department of Justice (DOJ)
DPAs. *See* Deferred Prosecution Agreements (DPAs)
Drafters, 211
Driving forces, 63
Due diligence, examining vendor partners, 99
Due diligence issues
  defined scope and objectives, 75–76
  legal structure, 66–67
  managing investigation, 61–62
  operational considerations, 64–66
  protecting intellectual property, 73–74
  regulatory concerns, 74–75
  retaining and managing consultants, 70–71
  strategic considerations, 61–63
Due diligence, labor context, 253–255
Due diligence process, 30–31

E
EC Acquired Rights Directive 2001/23/EC, 247, 248, 253
Economic espionage, 234–235
Economic Espionage Act (EEA), 207
Ecosystem and trade options, 89–90
EEPC India. *See* Engineering Export Promotion Council (EEPC India)
Electronic Communications Privacy Act, 270
Embraer S.A., 167
Employee handbooks, 276
Employee monitoring, 270–272
Employment agreements, 277–279
Employment diligence topics, 255
Employment discrimination laws, 283
Engineering Export Promotion Council (EEPC India), 111
Entity structure, consideration in choosing, 251
Ethics, 115–116
Ethiopia, 401

EU. *See* European Union (EU)
European Trade Commission, 231
European Union (EU), 160, 216, 247, 248, 270–272
Evaluation criteria, 47
Exervio Management Consulting, 330
Exit provisions, 43, 349–350
Exit strategies, 86, 330–331
Exogenous factors
  business environment, 89–91
  ecosystem and trade options, 89–90
  physical and time zone displacement, 87–88
  prevailing labor costs, 78–79
  socio- and geopolitical risks, 79–80
  types of, 78
Expatriate placement, 359–360
Expatriate policy, 292–293
Export control clause, 182
External forces, 44–45

F
Facilities, 58–59
FactRight LLC, 169
Fair Credit Reporting Act (FCRA), 342
Fair deals, 326–327
FBI. *See* Federal Bureau of Investigation (FBI)
FCPA. *See* Foreign Corrupt Practices Act (FCPA)
FCPA Professor, 163
FCRA. *See* Fair Credit Reporting Act (FCRA)
FDCPA. *See* Federal Debt Collections Practices Act (FDCPA)
FDIC. *See* Federal Deposit Insurance Corporation (FDIC)
Federal Bureau of Investigation (FBI), 128, 141, 234
Federal Debt Collections Practices Act (FDCPA), 342
Federal Deposit Insurance Corporation (FDIC), 342
Federal Financial Institutions Examination Council, 106
Filártiga v. Peña-Irala, 630 F.2d 876 (2d Cir. 1980), 287
Financial issues, 85
Financial Services Roundtable, 4, 99, 116, 119, 122, 342, 345, 356–358, 379
Fines, 153–155
Finland, 348
Foreign Corrupt Practices Act (FCPA)
  criticism and potential reform of, 158–159
  defenses, 149–151
  enforcement of, 139–141
  finders and, 116–117
  opinion procedure, 155–157
  overview and history of, 128–129
  presentation, 40

process, 131
red flags, 136
red flags list, 471
resource guide, 160–161
Foreign counsel, 36–37
Foreign governments, 234–235
Foreign taxes, 66
France, 243, 278, 285, 348
Fraud triangle, 169

G
Gabon, 141
Garden Leave, 218
Gates, Robert, 234
GCC. *See* Gulf Cooperation Council (GCC)
GE. *See* General Electric Company (GE)
General Agreement on Tariff and Trade, 197
General Electric Company (GE), 12, 401
Geopolitical risks, 79–80
Germany, 243, 265, 285
Ghana, 401
Giant Bicycle Corporation, 51
Gifford, Kathie Lee, 283
Gifts, 172–173
Give and take, 323–324
GlaxoSmithKline plc, 401
GLBA. *See* Gramm-Leach-Bliley Act (GLBA)
global competition and, 17–18
Globalization, 2, 8–10, 15–17
Global mobility

expatriate policy, 292–293
general considerations, 291–293
immigration issues, 297–299
Global mobility issues, 85
Gold Key Matching Service, 104
Google, 87, 228
Governmental issues, 118–119
Gramm-Leach-Bliley Act (GLBA), 342
Great Recession, 5
Guam, 82
Gulf Cooperation Council (GCC), 406–407

H
Halliburton Company, 155, 181
Hand gestures, 322
Health Insurance Portability and Accountability Act (HIPAA), 342
Hindalco Industries, 395
HIPAA. *See* Health Insurance Portability and Accountability Act (HIPAA)
Holidays, 363–364
Holland, 267
Honey trap, 235
Hong Kong, 248, 260
HR. *See* Human resources (HR)
Human Genome Project, 12
Human resources (HR), 48–49, 240, 275–276
Human rights issues, 282–284

I

IBM. *See* International Business Machines Corporation (IBM)
IBM Consulting Services, 100, 103, 363
ICC. *See* International Chamber of Commerce (ICC)
ICDR. *See* International Centre for Dispute Resolution (ICDR)
ILO. *See* International Labor Organization (ILO)
IMF. *See* International Monetary Fund (IMF)
Immigration issues, 297–299
Implementation
   addressing knowledge deficits, 364–365
   managing from distance versus expatriate placement, 359–360
   oversight, 354–355
   scope creep, 366–367
   transition, 362–363
   use of inspections and audits, 366
India
   arbitration, 376
   business environment, 89
   call center workers in, 52
   communications, 91
   cultural issues, 91
   employee/labor friendly policies, 260
   employment agreements, 347
   General Electric Company in, 12
   generic drug manufacturing, 16
   global economy and, 6–7
   immigration issues, 300
   intersection with vendors/vendorsí counsel, 38
   IP arbitrations, 348
   knowledge deficits, 364
   local laws in, 83
   management of issues based in culture, 363–364
   merger and acquisition transactions and, 248–250
   negotiations, 322
   small and medium enterprises, 15–16
   tax incentives, 66
   tax issues in, 83
   trade secrets, 218
   turnover of key personnel, 121
Indian Code of Civil Procedure, 380
Indonesia, 243, 250, 394
Industrial espionage, 198
Information exchange, 321–322
Information Policy Institute, 4
Information technology (IT), 2, 3
Infosys Limited, 300
Infrastructure, 58–59, 94–95, 117–118
Infringement, 213–215

In-house counsel, capabilities of, 23–24
In-house training, 95, 176, 356–358
Innovation, 13
Inspections, 366
Intellectual property (IP)
 confidentiality agreements, 211–213
 contract breaches, 210–212
 contracting for ownership of, 204–205
 contractual provisions regarding, 205–206
 copyrights, 195, 227–230
 dispute resolution, 348
 enforcement, 198–199
 forming security steering committee, 199–200
 formulation/implementation of security plan, 202–204
 infringement by third parties, 213–215
 issues, 193
 litigation, 194
 mapping out inventory, 200–201
 negotiations, 332–333
 patents, 195, 221–222
 protecting, 73–74, 199–200
 rights conflicts, 211–213
 staffing, 212–214
 trademarks, 195, 224–226
 trade secrets, 196, 217–218
 types of, 195–196
 unfair competition, 233–235
Internal drivers, 44–45
Internal Revenue Service, 212
International arbitration clause, 86
International Business Machines Corporation (IBM), 55
International Centre for Dispute Resolution (ICDR), 372–373
International Centre for Settlement of Investment Disputes, 388
International Chamber of Commerce (ICC), 372–373, 376, 378, 389
International distributor and sales representative agreements checklist, 423
International Finance Corporation, 81
International Institute of Conflict Prevention and Resolution, 376
International Labour Organization (ILO), 240, 241, 268
International Monetary Fund (IMF), 5, 81, 160, 383, 388, 399
International Space Station, 12
International Trade Association, 5
International Trade Commission (ITC), 220, 230, 388
Intuition, 123–124
IP. *See* Intellectual property (IP)
Ireland, 348

Islamic Republic of Pakistan, 389
ISO 27002 standards, 273
Israel, 348
Issue agreement, 325–326
Issue specialists, 28–29, 33–34
IT. *See* Information technology (IT)
Italy, 218
ITC. *See* International Trade Commission (ITC)

J

January 2014 World Economic Outlook Update, 5
Japan, 5
Joint ownership, 205–206
Joint venture agreements, 353
Joint ventures
    basic outline of initial terms and conditions for proposed, 457
Joint ventures letter of intent, 449
Joint ventures proprietary information and, 220
Joint ventures structuring, 331–332
Judgments, enforcement of, 379–380

K

Kadic v. Karadzic, 70 F.3d 232 (2d. Cir. 1995), 287
Karadzic, Radovan, 287
Kazakhstan, 141
Kenya, 401

Kiobel v. Royal Dutch Petroleum, 621 F.3d 111 (2d Cir. 2010), 289–291
Know-how, 196
Knowledge deficits, 364–365
Knowledge process outsourcing (KPO), 4–6
Knowledge transfer, 121–122
Korea, 243, 348
KPO. *See* Knowledge process outsourcing (KPO)
Kuwait, 406

L

Labor compliance issues, 269–270
Labor law issues
    agreements, 347–348
    challenges of international, 240–242
    compliance issues, 269–270
    dispute avoidance, 279–281
    due diligence, 253–255
    employment agreements, 277–279
    general considerations, 258–259
    human rights, 282–284
    labor organizations, 265–267
    merger and acquisition transactions and, 243–245
    payroll and benefits compliance, 276–278
Labor organization issues, 265–267
Larsen & Toubro Limited, 395

Last-minute changes, 350
Latin America, 7, 216, 236, 243, 387, 408–409
LCIA. *See* London Court of International Arbitration (LCIA)
Leadership, 109–110
Legal structure, 66–67
Legwork, 95–97
Lenovo Group Ltd., 55
Liability standards, 91
Licensure, 189–190
Lieberman, Joseph, 3, 40
Lindsey Manufacturing Co., 135
Liquidity risks, 106
Lithuanian Labor Code, 253
Local environment, 258–259
London Court of International Arbitration (LCIA), 372–373, 376, 377, 378

M
Malawi, 246
Maliquadoros, 10–11
Massachusetts Bankers Association, 106
Master service agreements (MSAs), 329, 353
Materiality scrape, 262
Mauritius, 83
McDonald's Corporation, 84
McKinsey & Company, 403–404
Mergers and acquisitions (M&A), 157, 180–181, 243–245, 262–264, 277

Mexico, 89, 310–311
Middle East, 404–405
MNCs. *See* Multinational corporations (MNCs)
Monitoring, 184, 345–346
Mozambique, 401
MSAs. *See* Master service agreements (MSAs)
Multinational corporations (MNCs), 52
Myanmar, 394

N
Nanjing Auto Corporation, 55
NASSCOM. *See* National Association of Software and Services Companies (NASSCOM)
NATCO Group, Inc., 141
National Association of Software and Services Companies (NASSCOM), 141
Nazarbayev, Nursultan Äbishuly, 149
Negotiations
  assembling negotiating team, 305–306
  cultural issues, 315–316
  cultural team, 311–312
  current key issues, 328
  financial team, 310–311
  in-house team, 308–309
  outside legal team, 309–310
  pre-negotiation preparation, 313–315

Negotiations (*continued*)
   tips for cross-border deal, 321
Negotiators, 32
NeoGroup Inc., 78, 89, 95
NeoIT, 110
Nestlé S.A., 81
New Zealand, 285
Nike Inc., 283
Nixon Administration, 129
Noncore competency, 50–52
Nonpredictive risks, 65
Notorious Markets list, 215

O

Obama, Barack, 394, 411
Objectives, 75–76
OCC. *See* Office of the Comptroller of the Currency (OCC)
OECD. *See* Organization for Economic Cooperation and Development (OECD)
Office of Foreign Assets Control (OFAC)
   application of, 132
   basics, 185–187
   current sanctions programs, 188–189
   designing and monitoring compliance, 189–191
   licensure, 189–190
   penalties, 189–190
   regulations on blocked persons, 187–188
   regulations on specially designated nationals, 187–188
   travel arrangements, 85
Office of the Comptroller of the Currency (OCC), 342
Office of the United States Trade Representative, 230
Oman, 406
Online Protection and Enforcement of Digital Trade Act, 230
Open source licenses, 208
Operational considerations, 64–66
Operations/transactional risk, 106
Opportunity, 15–17
Organisation for Economic Cooperation and Development (OECD), 13, 135, 142, 160
Organization of American States, 160
Outside counsel
   as coordinator of other disciplines, 29–30
   as drafter and negotiator, 32
   as due diligence nexus, 30–31
   as issue specialist, 28–29
   as risk manager, 31–32
   as strategic consultant, 25–26
   cultural experts and, 33–34
   intersection with other disciplines, 32–33

intersection with U.S. and foreign regulators, 39–40
intersection with vendors/vendors' counsel, 37–38
qualities for, 27–28
Outsourcing Institute, 101, 115
Oversight, 57–58, 354–355
Ownership, 204–205

P
Paraguay, 287
Parameters, 56
Patent Cooperation Treaty, 222
Patent pools, 194
Patents, 195, 211, 221–222
Patent trolls, 223
Payroll and benefits compliance, 276–278
Penalties, 153–155, 189–190
Pepsico v. Redmond, 54 F.3d 1262 (7th Cir. 1995), 217
Performance levels, 437
Performance management, 275
Permanent establishment, 263–264
Personal relationships, 123–124
Philippines, 94, 260, 338
Phonograms Convention of 1971, 227
Physical/time zone displacement, 87–88
PIPA. *See* PROTECT IP Act (PIPA)
Political risk, 81, 384–385
Population growth, 401–403
Post-closing anticorruption compliance needs, 180–181
Pre-negotiation preparation
ability to commit, 318
agenda, 319–320
choosing location, timing, and language, 318–319
cultural issues, 315–316
Pricing, 122–124
Privacy laws, 74
Process management, 346–347
Procter & Gamble Co., 81
Product technicians, 35–36
Professional employer organization (PEO), 9
Project on Government Oversight, 159
Property management approvals, 118
Proprietary information, 220
Protectionism, 411
PROTECT IP Act (PIPA), 229–231
Purchase agreement drafting, employment issues and, 261–263
Purchase order terms and conditions, 415

Q
Qatar, 406
Quality control, 111–112
Quasi-general counsel, 23

R

Racketeer Influenced and Corrupt Organizations Act (RICO), 143
Reagan, Ronald, 99, 414
Red flags, 136, 176
Red flags list, 471
Reebok International Limited, 283
Regulators, 39–40
Relationships, 121–122
Renegotiation, 350
Reputation risk, 350
Request for proposal (RFP), 350
RFP. *See* Request for proposal (RFP)
RFPA. *See* Right to Financial Privacy Act (RFPA)
RICO. *See* Racketeer Influenced and Corrupt Organizations Act (RICO)
Right to Financial Privacy Act (RFPA), 342
Risk assessment, 168–169
Risk managers, 31–32
Risks
    compliance, 106, 174–176
    evaluating, 50–52
    of working with offshore vendors, 106
    operational, 64–66
    political, 81, 384–385
    socio- and geopolitical, 79–80
Rome Convention of 1961, 227
Romero v. Drummond Company, 552 F.3d 1303 (11th Cir. 2008), 289
Romney, Mitt, 411

S

Safe Harbor Privacy Agreement, 303
Sanctions, 85, 185–187
Sanctions programs, 186, 188–189
Sarbanes-Oxley Act of 2002 (SOX), 2, 139, 333–334, 342, 345
Saudi Arabia, 345
Scenario planning, 27–28
Schwinn Bicycle Company, 51
Scope creep, 366–367
SEC. *See* U.S. Securities and Exchange Commission (SEC)
Security consultants, 120–121
Security plans, 202–204
SEC v. IBM Corporation,,00-Civ-3040 (D.D.C. Dec. 21, 2000), 134
Semi-exogenous factors
    communications, 91–92
    culture, 91–92
    infrastructure, 94–95
    prevalence of distinctive competencies, 95–96
    types of, 78
Sensenbrenner, Jim, 158
Sentencing guidelines, 139, 147, 152, 171, 176

Service-level agreements, 329–330
Services, scope of, 343–344
Service technicians, 35–36
Sexual harassment, 169, 283, 285, 286
SFO. *See* U.K. Serious Fraud Office (SFO)
Shanghai Automotive Industrial Corporation, 55
ShopRunner Inc., 391
Shuanghui International Holdings Ltd., 391
SIAC. *See* Singapore International Arbitration Center (SIAC)
Singapore, 214, 248, 260, 394
Small and medium enterprises (SME's)
  additional fees, 353
  advantages of, 13
  cost-benefit analysis and, 52–55
  formulation/implementation of IP security plan, 202
  globalization and, 8
  importance of training for, 357
  key points for, 413
  knowledge process outsourcing, 5
  protecting intellectual property, 73, 194
  retaining and managing consultants, 70–71
  strategic support plan for, 47
  technical competence and quality control, 113–114

Smithfield Foods Inc., 391
Society of Corporate Compliance and Ethics, Health Care Compliance Association, 170
Sociopolitical risks, 79–80
Software, 208–210, 216
SOPA. *See* Stop Online Piracy Act (SOPA)
Sosa v. Alvarez-Machain, 542 U.S. 692 (2004), 289
Sourcing, 46, 48
South Africa, 348
South America, 215–217
South Korea, 214, 248, 394
SOX. *See* Sarbanes-Oxley Act of 2002 (SOX)
Spain, 285, 348
Specially designated nationals, 187–188
Staffing, 212–214
Steering committees, 61–63
Stop Online Piracy Act (SOPA), 229–231
Strategic consultants, 25–26
Strategic risk, 106
Strategic sourcing plan, 46
Strategic support plan, 46
Supply chain vendors, 169
Sustainable AgroEnergy, 163
Sweden, 285

T
Tacit knowledge, 13–14, 54, 359
Taiwan, 394

Tanzania, 401
Target Corporation, 106
Tata Group, 10
Tata Power, 395
Tata Steel, 395
Taxes, 66, 68, 83
Tax laws, 347–348
Tax specialists, 33–34
TCC. *See* Trade Compliance Center (TCC)
Technical competence, 111–112
Technology, 52–53
Termination for nonperformance, 437
Tesco PLC, 396
Thai Tourism Authority, 143
Third-party vendor outsourcing arrangement, 69
Tier I companies, 9, 119
Tier II companies, 9, 44, 119
Time frame, 57–58
Time out, 324
Title VII, Civil Rights Act, 269, 270
T.J.Maxx, 106
TJX Companies, Inc., 106
Trade Compliance Center (TCC), 40
Trademarks, 195, 224–226
Trade options, 89–90
Trade secrets, 121–122, 196, 207, 217–218
Training, 95, 176, 346, 356–358, 357
Transition, 362–363

Translators, 322
Transparency International 2013 Global Corruption Barometer, 151
Travel Act, 142, 161
TRIPS. *See* Agreement on Trade-Related Aspects of Intellectual Property Rights (TRIPS),
Turnover, 121–122

U
Uganda, 223
U.K. Bribery Act, 160–162
U.K. Serious Fraud Office (SFO), 163, 163–164
Unanticipated factors, 324–325
UNCITRAL. *See* United Nations Commission on International Trade Law (UNCITRAL)
Unfair competition, 233–235
United Arab Emirates, 406
United Kingdom, 218, 248, 284, 285, 301, 371
United Nations, 160, 401
United Nations Commission on International Trade Law (UNCITRAL), 372, 376, 377, 378
United Nations Convention on the Recognition and Enforcement of Foreign Arbitral Awards, 371

United States v. Kay, No. 05–20604, 2007 WL3088140 (5th Cir. Oct. 24, 2007), 150
United States v. Noriega et al., 10-1031 (C.D. Ca. 2010), 135
Uruguay Round, 197
USA PATRIOT Act, 187
U.S. Census Bureau, 6
U.S. Chamber Institute for Legal Reform, 158
U.S. Chamber of Commerce, 81
U.S. Commercial Service, 104, 137
U.S. Congress, 129, 229
U.S. Copyright Office, 227
U.S. Department of Commerce, 40, 104
U.S. Department of Justice (DOJ), 133, 137–139, 139, 142, 143–144, 144, 155–157, 158
U.S. Department of Labor, 212
U.S. Department of State, 236
U.S. Department of the Treasury, 85, 185, 188
U.S. Department of Transportation, 74
U.S. Embassy Commercial Services Division, 81
U.S. Food and Drug Administration, 16
U.S. Securities and Exchange Commission (SEC), 129, 134, 139, 141, 142, 144, 153, 158, 179–180, 202, 212, 334
U.S. Supreme Court, 150, 290

V

Vannoy v. Celanese, ALJ Case No. 2008-SOX-00064, ARB Case No. 09 -118 (ALJ July 24, 2013), 212
Vendor partners, due diligence in examining
  capacity for growth, 113–115
  comparable business ethics, 115–116
  comparable strategic direction, 114–115
  competitive selection, 104–106
  danger of cooption, 121–122
  decision, 124–125
  establishing criteria, 101–102
  financial considerations, 108–109
  Gold Key Matching Service, 104
  governmental and regulatory issues, 118–119
  history and reputation, 110–111
  infrastructure, 117–118
  leadership, 109–110
  overview, 99–100
  personal relationships and intuition, 123–124
  pricing, 122–124
  strength and capabilities of key suppliers, 116–117

Vendor partners (*continued*)
  technical competence and quality control, 111–112
  turnover of key personnel, 121–122
  use of consultants, 103
Vendors' counsel, 37–38
Venezuela, 249
Venue, 377–378
Visa issues, 359
Vodafone Group, 396

W
Wage arbitrage, 52–53
Wal-Mart, 395
Watergate hotel, 129
Water shortages, 405–406

Whistleblowers, 179–180, 212
Wholly foreign-owned entities (WFOEís), 14
Workforce criteria, 346
Workplace bullying, 284–286
World Bank, 81, 130, 160
World Intellectual Property Organization, 222
World Trade Organization (WTO), 40, 74, 197
WTO. *See* World Trade Organization (WTO)

Y
Yahoo, 228

Z
Zimbabwe, 399